❧ History and Community

INCIPIT EPISTOLA WILLELMI COENOBITE AD WILL
ELMVM ORTHODOXVM ANGLORVM REGEM
IN HONOREM NORMAN DVCVM GESTIS.

GLORIOSISSIMO ATQVE ORTHO-
DOXO SVMMI regis nutu
anglorum regi VVillelmo.
Gemeticensis cenobica omniu
cenobearum indignissimus
Wuillelmi ad concerendos ho-
stes saxonum fortem cladissi[m]e-
addicer[n]endu iudiciu salomonis
abyssu. Opus hoc prudentissime
Rex & serenissime in normanno[rum]
ducu gestis de diuersis excerptu.
codicib[us] iuxta mea exiguitatem
industrie contextu usq[ue] dicam idem
costruxerim ob recolenda pceo[rum] patru[m] me[orum] pcipuas lautarum
dignitacu administrationes pissimo[rum]q[ue] Aceu[m] exempla-
cronico[rum] bibliotbece delegandu decreui. Qua o[m]n rectoru[m]
ueisulta exornaru[m] qutrace. n polita sermonis uenali lepore
seu uitate. sed inelimato stilo. centu oracione & plana deduc-
tu cuilibet lectori ad liqidu elaboraui. Vix eg[o] maiestatis
lacera ambiunt solari uiri literaru[m] peita admodu cedu[n]t
q[ui] strictis caladis cuiuscu[m]q[ue] circuiu[n]cces eliminau[n]t prauoru[m]
infidis seculis salomonis huius legis pugili munimine
braagine euem uberrissimu[m] a[t]q[ue] ingenii uigore celsi dis-
pensatoru[m] prerogatiua uobis collati & sue in arduaq[ue] regi-
minis sue in cutiori qb[us] incendere.q[ue] ppende pponat mira
ualere efficacia. multis nut[er]modis phauor[um] Munusculen
& uaraslu nu laboris placida maru[m] sumice nobilissima
cesta celebri memoria dignissima ira & antiqua
phas paginas recolere Principu[m] itaq[ue] narrationes usq[ue]
ad Ricardu sedm a dudonis pori uii historia collegi.
q[ui] posteris ppagandu karae co[m]dauit. a dudulo compe-
cipnu Ricardi fre Mulgeni[us] exsuunt. Relq[ui] u[er]o a parte relatu
plurimo[rum] ad corroboranda fide eque idoneos Anuu & rerum
cognitus certissimus Inde pprio usu dona priuau[m] mea dono Sane
genealogia. Rollonis a paganis maioribus nata & multa[m] ctate sua
in paganismo acta. tandem ad scam infancia[m] saluberrimo fonce e-
renatricem somnii et cu plurib[us] id generi ab historica serie
deseru animaduertenter ea pene abulatoria nec spere honestr

History and Community

Norman Historical Writing in the
Eleventh and Twelfth Centuries

Leah Shopkow

The Catholic University of America Press
Washington, D.C.

Frontispiece: Rouen, Bibliothèque municipale, Y. 14, 116r

Library of Congress Cataloging-in-Publication Data
Shopkow, Leah.
  History and community : Norman historical writing in the eleventh
and twelfth centuries / Leah Shokow.
    p. cm.
  Includes bibliographical references and index.
    1. Normandy (France)—History—To 1515—Sources. 2. Normandy
(France)—Historiography. 3. Normandy, Dukes of. 4. His-
torians—France—Normandy—Influence. 5. Great Britain—
Relations—France. 6. France—Relations—Great Britain.
7. Normandy (France)—Genealogy. I. Title.
DC611.N856S56 1997
944'.2—dc20
96-32081
ISBN 0-8132-0882-3 (alk. paper)

To Dirk, a lover of books,
whose love made this one possible

Contents

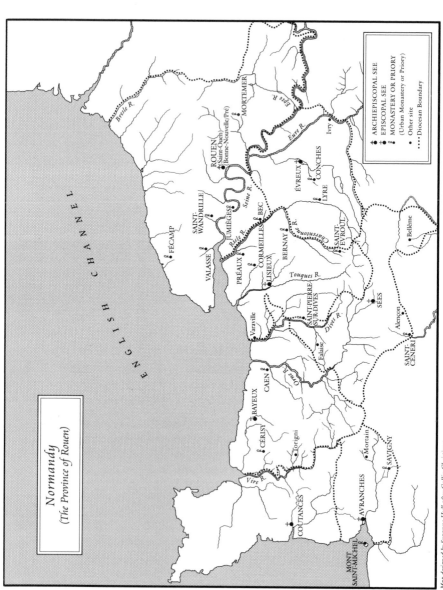

Normandy
(The Province of Rouen)

ENGLISH CHANNEL

Brisle R.

FÉCAMP

SAINT-
WANDRILLE

VALASSE

Seine R.

JUMIÈGES

Risle R.

PRÉAUX

CORMEILLES

LISIEUX

BEC

BERNAY

Touques R.

ROUEN
Saint-Ouen
Bonne-Nouvelle/Pré

MORTEMER

Epte R.

Eure R.

Ivry

ÉVREUX

CONCHES

LYRE

Charentonne R.

SAINT-
ÉVROUL

Bellême

SÉES

Varaville

SAINT-PIERRE-
SUR-DIVES

Dives R.

Falaise

Orne R.

CAEN

BAYEUX

CERISY

Torigni

Vire R.

Alençon

SAINT-
CENERI

Mortain

SAVIGNY

COUTANCES

AVRANCHES

MONT-
SAINT-MICHEL

ARCHIEPISCOPAL SEE
EPISCOPAL SEE
MONASTERY OR PRIORY
(Urban Monastery or Priory)
Other site
Diocesan Boundary

Map designed by Suzanne Hull after Gallia Christiana.

❧ *Preface and Acknowledgments*

Many academics like to imagine themselves as monks, quietly walking the cloisters of knowledge, keeping civilization intact and the barbarians at bay. There is a sense of pride in that shared occupation in Richard Southern's declaration that:

There is something in the writing of history which has called forth at all times the best resources of the Benedictine scholar: it opened a field for the laborious, exacting, patient work of compilation and arrangement which the spirit of the Rule required. At the same time, it was fostered by the very practical and human desire which members of a community feel to preserve and glorify their past, to justify their position in the world, and—more questionably—to defend their privileges and assert their independence. Here was a vast field of research in which practical expediency and literary ambition could both find their place, and where the work to be done ranged from the classification of the monastic archives, the defence of its holy relics, and the history of its landed properties, to the writing of annals, biographies and the major histories of the time.[1]

1. Richard W. Southern, *The Making of the Middle Ages* (New Haven, Conn.: Yale University Press, 1953), 192.

This pride in the role of the historian did not prevent Southern from recognizing that history has, in our own day, slipped from the central position it occupied as a means of identity formation in the nineteenth century into what he described as a "private luxury."[2]

As I have worked on the Norman historians, all of whom were clerics and most of whom were monks, I too have felt a kinship with them. My sense of connection arises partly from the sensation of touching other individuals across the centuries through their works. If one sits in the municipal library in Rouen with a copy before one of the *Deeds of the Dukes* of William of Jumièges written out by Orderic Vitalis, both of those men do seem present. And as a historian I share some of their frustrations. Orderic was aware, as were many of his contemporaries, that the world did not value his labors as he did. He complained that the brothers would not read his work but wanted more emotionally satisfying fare. Meanwhile his abbots wanted him to write a history of the monastery's property for which they had their own practical purposes. None of this deterred Orderic from his self-appointed task of writing a history of the world, but it did leave him slightly defensive.

It seems to me that our case as modern historians is not so very different. Like Orderic, we still put a great deal of energy into telling the story of the past and not necessarily the parts of the past that interest our potential readers or patrons. We similarly occupy a space between the sometimes cloistered environs in which we work and the wide world in which we are also forced to live. Our superiors still expect history to pay its way, by permitting practical applications such as cultural indoctrination. History still fails to serve the pragmatic and practical as well as it meets other needs, the desire for the connection with the past that Southern identified as its main function.

This book began as a dissertation, although in the ten years

2. Richard W. Southern, "Aspects of the European Tradition of Historical Writing: 4. The Sense of the Past," *Transactions of the Royal Historical Society,* 5th ser., 23 (1973), 245.

since I completed that earlier incarnation, it has sloughed off much of its bulk and added much new material; where necessary, I will refer the reader to my dissertation rather than rehearse material which has, in the process of revision, become tangential to my interests. Nonetheless I owe deep debts of gratitude to those who helped me complete the progenitor as well as those who have helped me wrestle the material into this rather different form. Thanks are due to the government of Ontario, the University of Toronto, and the Social Sciences and Humanities Research Council of Canada who supported my research during graduate school through grants and fellowships. Indiana University provided a summer fellowship in 1988 which permitted me to travel to Normandy to examine manuscripts of historical works written and copied there, which proved to be intellectually invaluable, as well as a further fellowship in the summer of 1994.

While financial support has been enormously helpful, the contributions of teachers and colleagues have been crucial. I am conscious of a gratitude to Jocelyn Hillgarth, my dissertation supervisor and now friend, that I am incapable of expressing fully. I found in him an advisor with the learning and generosity to help me be a better scholar, not in his own superlative mold, but in the way that best suited my abilities and inclinations; nor has his benevolence toward me ended with our formal academic tie. Without his good sense, advice, and support I would be much the poorer. Thanks are also due to Brian Stock, whose direction by indirection, after initial perplexity, always led to my amusement and enlightenment. Gabrielle Spiegel has also been generous with her help. Eleanor Searle and Gerda Huisman both permitted me to read some of their work in manuscript, and although it has since been published, I am still grateful. Ann Carmichael and Ellen Dwyer acted as unpaid editors; their help and encouragement was of a price far beyond rubies. Helen Nader also read the manuscript and offered encouragement. Finally, I must thank both Felice Lifschitz and Stephen White who read the manuscript for the press. They offered numerous suggestions, qualifications, and criticisms that have helped me to improve the book. Although I have not agreed with or followed all their conclusions, the debate greatly clarified my thinking.

On a more personal note, I would like also to thank another friend, Gerald Bond of the University of Rochester who, with his enthusiasm and encouragement, set me, when still in academic swaddling clothes, to becoming a medievalist, and who taught me about the active pleasure of the scholar's life with an intellectual magnanimity not often found in the academic world. I tender special thanks to Ken Margerison of Southwest Texas State University whose encouragement came at an hour of great need and to Warren Hollister whose kindness to me has been unstinting. Finally I would like to thank my friends at Indiana University. Jeanne Peterson's friendship and enthusiasm for my work kept me going. Thanks also to the other members of the SRG, whose friendship, intellectual company, and encouragement has made life at Indiana stimulating and challenging.

ℒ Abbreviations

AA SS	*Acta sanctorum quotquot toto orbe coluntur.* Paris, 1863–.
CG	*Catalogue général des manuscrits des bibliothèques publiques de France: Départements.* 43 vols. Paris, 1885–1904.
CHP	*The Carmen de Hastingae proelio of Guy, Bishop of Amiens.* Edited by C. Morton and H. Muntz. Oxford, 1972.
De moribus	Dudo of Saint-Quentin. *De moribus et actis primorum Normanniae ducum.* Edited by J. Lair. Caen, 1865.
DN	Stephen of Rouen. *Draco Normannicus.* In *Chronicles of the Reigns of Stephen, Henry II, and Richard I.* Edited by Richard Howlett. Vol. 2, pp. 589–781. Rolls Series 82. London, 1885.
Dragon	Stephen of Rouen. *Le Dragon Normand.* Edited by Henri Omont. Rouen, 1884.
EH	Orderic Vitalis. *The Ecclesiastical History of Orderic Vitalis.* Edited and translated by Marjorie Chibnall. 6 vols. Oxford, 1969–80.

Gallia Christiana	*Gallia christiana, in provincias ecclesiasticas distributa.* 16 vols. 2d ed. Paris, 1739–1880.
GG	William of Poitiers, *Histoire de Guillaume le Conquérant.* Edited and translated by Raymonde Foreville. Paris, 1952.
GND	William of Jumièges. *Gesta Normannorum ducum.* Edited by Jean Marx. Rouen, 1914.
GRA	William of Malmesbury. *Gesta regum Anglorum atque Historia Novella.* 2 vols. Edited by T. D. Hardy. London, 1840.
HA	Henry of Huntingdon. *Henrici archidiaconi Huntendunensis Historia Anglorum.* Rolls Series, vol. 74. Edited by Thomas Arnold. 1879. Reprint edition: Wiesbaden, 1965.
His. de France	*Recueil des historiens des Gaules et de la France.* Rev. ed. 19 vols. Paris, 1869–80.
Jumièges	*Jumièges: Congrès scientifique du XIIIᵉ centenaire.* 2 vols. Rouen, 1955.
Manuscrits datés	*Catalogue des manuscrits en écriture latine portant de indications de date, de lieu ou de copiste,* vol. 7, *Ouest de la France et pays de Loire.* Edited by Monique-Cécile Garand, Geneviève Grand, and Denis Muzerelle. Paris, 1984.
MGH	*Monumenta Germaniae historica.*
MGH, Auctores Antiquissimi	*MGH, Auctores Antiquissimi.* 15 vols. Berlin, 1881–99.
MGH, Scriptores	*MGH, Scriptores.* 30 vols. Hannover, 1826–1934.
Millénaire Monastique	*Millénaire monastique du Mont Saint-Michel.* 2 vols. Paris, 1967.
PL	*Patrologia cursus completus, Series latina.* 221 vols. Edited by J. Migne. Paris, 1878–90.
Rob. of Tor.	Robert of Torigni. *Chronique de Robert de Torigni, abbé du Mont Saint-Michel.* 2 vols. Edited by L. Delisle. Rouen, 1872–73.
RRAN	*Regesta regum Anglo-Normannorum.* 3 vols. Edited by H. W. C. Davis, C. Johnson, H. A. Cronne, and R. H. C. Davis. Oxford, 1912–68.

van Houts, *GND*

van Houts, E. M. C. *Gesta Normannorum ducum*. Ph.D. Dissertation, University of Gröningen, 1982.

van Houts, *GND* (2)

van Houts, E. M. C., ed. and trans. *The Gesta Normannorum ducum of William of Jumièges, Orderic Vitalis, and Robert of Torigni*. 2 vols. Oxford, 1992–95.

The Dukes of Normandy (911–1204)

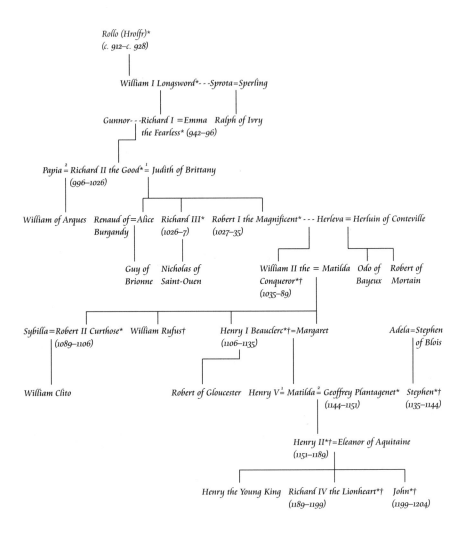

Rollo (Hrolfr)*
(c. 912–c. 928)

William I Longsword*- - -Sprota=Sperling

Gunnor- - -Richard I =Emma Ralph of Ivry
the Fearless* (942–96)

Papia $\overset{2}{=}$ Richard II the Good*$\overset{1}{=}$ Judith of Brittany
(996–1026)

William of Arques Renaud of=Alice Richard III* Robert I the Magnificent* - - - Herleva = Herluin of Conteville
Burgandy (1026–7) (1027–35)

Guy of Nicholas of William II the = Matilda Odo of Robert of
Brionne Saint-Ouen Conqueror*† Bayeux Mortain
(1035–89)

Sybilla=Robert II Curthose* William Rufus† Henry I Beauclerc*†=Margaret Adela=Stephen
(1089–1106) (1106–1135) of Blois

William Clito Robert of Gloucester Henry V$\overset{1}{=}$ Matilda $\overset{2}{=}$ Geoffrey Plantagenet* Stephen*†
(1144–1151) (1135–1144)

Henry II*†=Eleanor of Aquitaine
(1151–1189)

Henry the Young King Richard IV the Lionheart*† John*†
(1189–1199) (1199–1204)

*Dukes of Normandy   †Kings of England
- - -Informal Unions
Dukes of Normandy are assigned their Norman regnal years and regnal numbers

Introduction: Historical Writing and the Norman Community

*H*istorians are themselves caught in the web of history. Paul Veyne ends his consideration of classical historical writing, *Did the Greeks Believe in Their Myths,* by asserting that, like the ancient Greeks, we modern people also believe our myths.[1] His point was not that we believe evident fictions but that our fictions are not evident to us because they are sustained by what he calls "programs of truth," systems which help people distinguish what is true from what is not. These programs of truth, however, also sustain belief in things that, viewed through a different program, would be untrue. Not all programs of truth are historical—some are religious or philosophical or scientific—and not all societies find history useful,[2]

1. Paul Veyne, *Did the Greeks Believe in Their Myths,* trans. Paula Wissing (Chicago: University of Chicago Press, 1988), 129.
2. See Donald E. Brown, *Hierarchy, History, and Human Nature: The Social Origins of Historical Consciousness* (Tucson: University of Arizona Press, 1988), 19–41, for a discussion of the Indian situation; also Y. H. Yerushalmi, *Zakhor: Jewish History and Jewish Memory* (Seattle: University of Washington Press, 1982), 7. Both of these works address

but historical programs of truth govern the assumptions historians and readers share about what constitutes "true" history. These programs of truth belong to the intellectual *longue durée*. Histories are borne along by them like ships carried by prevailing winds, until a shift in the breeze sends them off on another tack.

While speeded forward by these gusts, however, each ship encounters local currents and eddies and each captain trims the sails in an idiosyncratic way. If histories are written within the framework of widely accepted programs of truth, they are also a response to arrays of circumstances unique to particular times and places. Histories have, to use Gabrielle Spiegel's felicitous phrase, a "social logic" and are produced by a "moment of choice, decision, and action that creates the social reality of the text, a reality existing both 'inside' and 'outside' the particular performance incorporated in the work, through the latter's inclusions, exclusions, distortions, and stresses."[3] As Spiegel has shown for French vernacular prose texts of the early thirteenth century, there is nothing "natural" about a work of history.[4] When a sea voyage seems propitious, the captain launches the ship, often at the behest of its owner. Like sailing a great vessel, writing a history requires both training and skill, a marshalling of considerable resources, and a weather eye to the currents and winds of politics.

Historians do not, however, have to negotiate the sea and wind entirely alone. The ships of history sail in fleets. The sailors share with their fellow travellers not only the general lore of the sea but also advice about particular stretches of water. The ships coming later wallow in the wake of those that have come before.

The Normans were in their origins great seafarers, so it is only

---

the question of why some cultures either did not produce history or did not write works we would accept today as "historical."

3. Gabrielle M. Spiegel, "History, Historicism, and the Social Logic of the Text in the Middle Ages," *Speculum* 65 (1990): 84; on "social logic," see also *Romancing the Past: The Rise of Vernacular Prose Historiography in Thirteenth-Century France* (Berkeley and Los Angeles: University of California Press, 1993), 9.

4. Spiegel, *Romancing the Past,* 2, raises this explicitly with respect to the use of vernacular prose, but the understanding that all aspects of a work have ideological implications runs throughout her work.

fitting that their historians comprised a sizeable flotilla consisting of some stately ships that sailed out toward the ocean and a multitude of small craft that hugged the shore. All felt, to a greater or lesser degree, some of the great winds that blew consistently between late antiquity and the fifteenth century, but all were driven by the local tides as well and experienced the wash of the ships that had passed through these waters before. The task of this book is to describe some of the vicissitudes of the Norman voyage in the larger sea of medieval history.

ℭ

Most studies of medieval historical writing have striven either to address the medieval historian's program(s) of truth or the web of circumstances surrounding the production of one or a few individual histories. The former project has produced a number of broad syntheses, covering all aspects of historical writing in the Middle Ages, and some studies of medieval historical genres. Studies of individual historians have also been extremely numerous.[5] Each type of study has its advantages and its flaws. The syntheses shed a light on the commonalties of medieval historical practice, but they tend to rob individual histories of their integrity and to

---

5. See, for example, Herbert Grundmann's *Geschichtsschreibung im Mittelalter,* (reprint; Göttingen: Vandenhoeck & Ruprecht, 1965) which has deeply influenced the discussion of medieval historical genres, although his categories have been criticized. Bernard Guenée, *Histoire et culture historique dans l'occident médiéval* (Paris: Aubier-Montaigne, 1980), and Franz-Joseph Schmale, *Funktion und Formen mittelalterlicher Geschichtsschreibung: Mit einem Beitrag von Hans-Werner Goetz* (Darmstadt: Wissenschaftliche Buchgesellschaft, 1985), have contributed the most recent studies of the methods of historians and the meaning of history. Of the genre studies, most notable are probably Anna-Dorothee van den Brincken's *Studien zur lateinischen Weltchronistik bis in das Zeitalter Ottos von Freising* (Dusseldorf: Michael Triltsch Verlag, 1957) on universal chronicles and Michel Sot, *Gesta episcoporum, gesta abbatum* (Turnhout: Brepols, 1981). Amos Funkenstein's *Heilsplan und natürliche Entwicklung: Formen der Gegenwartsbestimmung im Geschichtsdenken des hohen Mittelalters* (Munich: Nymphenburger Verlagshandlung, 1965), which concerns the shift from apocalyptic to evolutionary thinking among medieval historians, is one the best of the thematic studies. The studies of individual works or historians are too numerous to list without being entirely arbitrary.

reduce them to anecdotes.[6] Studies of particular histories treat individual works in loving detail but sometimes at the cost of failing to situate them within a larger context. The thick description of a history can be highly resonant, but it is in itself not sufficient to show what was common to many historians, what reflected an individual's particular genius or ineptitude, or indeed why the study of medieval histories matters at all.[7] A few studies have treated groups of works, such as Gabrielle Spiegel's *Romancing the Past*, which examines four French prose histories, and Nancy Partner's *Serious Entertainments*, which uses three English twelfth-century historians to examine the writing of history in this period. Partner's interest is in the way historical writing changed with the passage of time in England. Spiegel, in contrast, is more interested in what the writing of history says to and about one specific group who produced and read histories, the Franco-Flemish elite of the early thirteenth century.[8]

As an alternative to these approaches, I offer an intermediate course, a study of a local "historical culture," the historical writing produced by the inhabitants of one community, that of Normandy in the eleventh and twelfth centuries.[9] Although histories are written by and sometimes for individuals, they are products of a community's life and views. This is true in an obvious way, because the

6. See Roger Ray, "Medieval Historiography through the Twelfth Century: Problems and Progress of Research," *Viator* 5 (1974), 58–59.

7. Clifford Geertz, "Thick Description: Toward an Interpretive Theory of Culture," in *The Interpretation of Cultures* (New York: Basic Books, 1973), 21, comments in regard to the microscopic aspect of ethnographic description, "That is not to say that there are no large-scale anthropological interpretations of whole societies, civilizations, world events, and so on. Indeed, it is such extension of our analyses to wider contexts that, along with their theoretical implications, recommends them to general attention and justifies our constructing them." The weakness of some studies in this regard is well illustrated by Peter Edbury and John Rowe's *William of Tyre* (Cambridge: Cambridge University Press, 1988), which is a rich study of William's history but does not show how his work relates to that of his contemporaries.

8. Nancy Partner, *Serious Entertainments: The Writing of History in Twelfth-Century England* (Chicago: University of Chicago Press, 1977).

9. The term "historical culture" comes from Guenée, *Histoire et culture historique.*

individual is shaped through socialization within a community, but it is true in a number of other ways as well. Communities are the repository of memory for their members, and in the Middle Ages, when history was what Paul Veyne calls a "vulgate" or a tradition, a report of what people remembered, history was more directly the expression of a community than it is today.[10] Indeed, the maintenance and creation of traditions and histories is one way in which societies, communities, seek social order.[11]

Medieval communities came in all sorts. Some were extremely local in character such as the community of a monastery and the body of people who interacted with it. Patrick Geary has argued recently that this sort of association, enacted through rituals of donation and participation in monastic life, played a fundamental role in preserving the pasts of the medieval elite, most of whom did not participate in the writing of history until the rise of the

10. On history as a vulgate, see Veyne, *Did the Greeks Believe in Their Myths,* 5–15, esp. 9ff. For a modern view of the social function of memory, see James Fentress and Chris Wickham, *Social Memory* (Oxford: Blackwell, 1992), ix–x, and for comments on the relationship between history and memory, ibid., 144–46. The classical work on the social nature of memory, which Fentress and Wickham correct, is Maurice Halbwachs, *The Collective Memory,* trans. Francis J. Ditter and Vida Yazdi Ditter (New York: Harper, 1980). There is a vast literature on memory and history, some of which tends to see the two forms as oppositional. See, for example, Yerushalmi, *Zakhor,* for a discussion of memory and history in the Jewish tradition and Amos Funkenstein, "Collective Memory and Historical Consciousness," *History and Memory* 1 (1989): 12f., for a response to Yerushalmi. See also, Pierre Nora, "Entre mémoire et histoire: La Problematique des lieux," in *Les lieux de mémoire,* ed. Pierre Nora, vol. 1 (Paris: Éditions Gallimard, 1984), xv–xlii, for an extremely hostile view of history.

11. See S. N. Eisenstadt, "Some Observations on the Dynamics of Traditions," *Comparative Studies in Society and History* 11 (1969): 451. Eisenstadt defines the acceptance of traditions as "the givenness of some actual or symbolic past event, order, or figure as the major focus of . . . collective identity." Michel de Certeau, *The Writing of History,* trans. Tom Conley (New York: Columbia University Press, 1988), 45, makes similar remarks about history: "Historical discourse makes a *social identity* explicit, not so much in the way it is 'given' or held as stable, as in the ways it is *differentiated* from a former period or another society." De Certeau's remarks are explicitly about modern history, which makes the past into an object separate from the present, but his observation about history creating or stabilizing social identities is certainly true of medieval histories as well, as Gabrielle Spiegel's work has shown.

vernacular.[12] Monasteries were the site of much medieval historical writing, and local issues were often played out in histories before the monastic audience. Towns were another kind of local community; they produced both Latin and vernacular historical texts, and they did so in great abundance from the fourteenth century on. At the other extreme were the larger political communities. These were not initially communities at all, in that the inhabitants only gradually came to see themselves as having a shared existence. In the thirteenth century, however, the nation began to be imagined into being as a community. When this happened, chroniclers like Matthew Paris at Westminster and Primat at Saint-Denis were present to chronicle its existence. There were abstract communities as well, such as the community of Christendom (a community which seems to have emerged around the time of the First Crusade) and the community of the learned. These abstract groupings certainly influenced individuals but more subtly than the bodies that allocated resources or provided regulations or laws. For medieval France in the central Middle Ages, however, the community of the county (when the county did in fact constitute a community, which was not invariably the case) often loomed large on the horizon.[13]

12. Patrick Geary, *Phantoms of Remembrance: Memory and Oblivion at the End of the First Millennium* (Princeton: Princeton University Press, 1994), 48–51, argues that the Carolingian elite family, which might have held lands widely spread across the empire, began to fragment into branches during the tenth century. As the family lost contact with the monasteries where their memory was preserved, it lost its recollection of its own past. Geary (79) points to Fulk le Réchin of Anjou's comment in his fragmentary history of the counts of Anjou that he did not know much about his ancestors because he did not know where they were buried. For an illuminating study of the nexus between the elite and monasteries, see Stephen White, *Kinship, Customs and Gifts to the Saints: The* Laudatio Parentum *in Western France* (Chapel Hill: University of North Carolina Press, 1992).

13. For a wonderful discussion of all these types of communities, see Susan Reynolds, *Kingdoms and Communities in Western Europe, 900–1300* (Oxford: Oxford University Press, 1984). For a discussion of French regional and national identities, see Brigitte Bedos-Rezak, "French Medieval Regions: A Concept in History," *Historical Reflections* 19 (1993): 151–66, as well as the other essays in that volume. Bedos-Rezak points out that in proposing a study of the French region, she is not suggesting a particular size or definition of region (153). Indeed, the essays in the volume concern

In recent years scholars have paid considerable attention to the differences between the counties of France, the varying processes by which they formed, and the diverse bases upon which they were built. The process always involved the efforts of one or more important families, most often the descendants of the Carolingian elite (although the families did not always remember this), to enhance its power.[14] However, the strategies used by the families varied, and thus the results varied also. Not all attempts to amass land and authority resulted in the creation of permanent counties or coherent communities. The Herbertian family of Vermandois, for example, amalgamated a large number of holdings in the tenth century, although these were eventually divided among the sons of Herbert II (d. 943). The counts of Blois and Champagne, however, were descended from them.[15] Some counties, like Berry, did not enjoy stable boundaries for a long time, and its development changed direction in the late eleventh century.[16] The authority of the ruler of a county ebbed and flowed over time, and no ruler, whatever he styled himself, whether marquis, consul, count, prince, or duke (all titles used by the Norman rulers), had irresistible authority.[17]

---

pagi and villages, as well as counties, and one essay, by Jeremy duQuesnay Adams, "The *Regnum Francie* of Suger of Saint-Denis: An Expansive Ile-de France," ibid., 167–88, considers the evidence in Suger's writing that "Francia" was beginning to describe more than simply the Ile-de-France.

　14. For a summation of the process, see Jean Dhondt, *Études sur la naissance des principautés territoriales en France (IXᵉ–Xᵉ siècle)* (Bruges: De Tempel, 1948), 1–79. For some qualifications, see Reynolds, *Kingdoms and Communities,* 229–31. The work of Karl Ferdinand Werner has clarified the descent of some of the important tenth-century families. See Karl Ferdinand Werner, "Untersuchungen zur Frühzeit des französichen Fürstentums (9.–10. Jahrhundert), *Die Welt als Geschichte* 18 (1958): 256–89; 19 (1959) 146–93; 20 (1960): 87–119. On the failure of memory of these families, see Geary, *Phantoms of Remembrance,* 50.

　15. On the Herbertians, see Werner, "Untersuchungen zur Frühzeit," pt. 3, 87–115; also Michel Bur, *La Formation du comté de Champagne, v. 950–v. 1150* (Nancy: University of Nancy, 1977), 87–125.

　16. Guy Devailly, *Le Berry du Xᵉ siècle au milieu du XIIIᵉ* (Paris: Mouton & Co, 1973), 61, 233–34.

　17. On these titles, see Karl Ferdinand Werner, "Quelques observations au sujet des débuts du 'duché' de Normandie," reprinted in *Structures politiques du monde franc (VIᵉ–XIIᵉ siècles)* (London: Variorum, 1979), 698–701.

Counties developed their bodies of norms and customs and their bureaucratic institutions at different rates, so that each county became a community in the full sense at a different time. As I will argue in the first chapter, the counties where such institutions were most precocious were the earliest and most copious producers of histories.

℘

The Viking settlement along the Seine in Normandy was officially recognized by the king of France around the second decade of the tenth century. However, Normandy seems to have come into existence as a community somewhat later, around 1000. The features of that community were described around the end of the eleventh century by an anonymous historian writing at Fécamp in his account of the first officially recognized Norman settlement:

> [The Normans] are given the seven farthest maritime provinces by the gift and concession of Charles, the king of France, which they may improve by a settlement of their labor from abroad, and defend and protect against the invasions of assaulting barbarians . . . . When the Normans, renewed by the grace of spiritual sacraments, had accepted their provinces, they called them Normandy, *North* meaning wind in their language. First Rollo, then second William, the son of Rollo, held the dukedom of this land.[18]

The Fécamp Anonymous defined Normandy's community in four ways. It was religious, because Normans were all Christians. It was a geographic unit composed of seven provinces, although the seven provinces the author refers to were the seven dioceses that corresponded only roughly to the political boundaries of the duchy.[19] The community also had an ethnic character, for the converted pagans comprised a foreign settlement. As a token of its ethnic

18. *Libellus de revelatione, edificatione et auctoritate Fiscanensis monasterii,* in *PL* 151:713.
19. The diocese of Rouen included the French Vexin, which the Norman dukes continually desired, and the diocese of Sées contained Perche, neither of which were normally part of political Normandy. See David Bates, *Normandy before 1066* (London: Longman, 1982), xii.

origins, the province took its name from their language. Finally, it was a political entity, the territory ruled by one individual, the duke. This description of Normandy is precious evidence that a Norman community was in ideological existence. The question is whether it also had a physical existence, what kind of existence that was, and when it came into being.

The first officially recognized Viking ruler of Normandy, Rollo (d. c. 928), received a grant of territory consisting of Rouen, its surrounds, and the Pays de Caux (the channel littoral east of the Seine).[20] I shall refer to Rollo and his successors as dukes for the sake of simplicity, although Richard II (996–1026) was the first to be so styled. Later grants theoretically added territories west of the Seine to the original holding but in practice to gain real control over the new lands took the efforts of several dukes. William I Longsword (c. 928–942) did not have much authority in these grants to the west of the Seine, an area where other Vikings seem to have continued to settle in effectively independent colonies through the tenth century.[21]

Succeeding dukes gradually extended Norman authority in what came to be western Normandy. William's son, Richard I (942–96), began the serious process of westward expansion. His concubine, Gunnor, later his wife, was probably the daughter of a Viking chieftain from the Cotentin. It is reasonable to assume that it was a political alliance aimed at increasing Richard's authority in that area.[22] Richard II (996–1026) married Judith, the sister of

---

20. Eleanor Searle, *Predatory Kinship and the Creation of Norman Power, 840–1066*, (Berkeley and Los Angeles: University of California Press, 1988), 71; Bates, *Normandy before 1066*, 13.

21. Searle, *Predatory Kinship*, 53–54; see also Bates, *Normandy before 1066*, 9–10, 13.

22. *De moribus*, 289; Eleanor Searle, "Fact and Pattern in Heroic History: Dudo of Saint-Quentin," *Viator* 15 (1984): 135. Richard also enhanced his western prestige indirectly by sponsoring the reform of Mont Saint-Michel in the 960s. On the reform of Mont Saint-Michel, see *De moribus*, 290. See also Jacques Hourlier, "Le Mont Saint-Michel avant 966" in *Millénaire monastique du Mont Saint-Michel* (Paris: P. Lethielleux, 1966): 26–27. Cassandra Potts, "Normandy or Brittany? A Conflict of Interests at Mont Saint-Michel (966–1035)," *Anglo-Norman Studies* 12 (1989): 135–

the count of Brittany, creating an ally for himself on his western border, while the count married Richard's sister. Judith's dower lands lay in many parts of the duchy, demonstrating the success of the dukes in moving beyond their power base in eastern Normandy.[23] William II the Conqueror (1035–87) was the first duke to make his authority felt relatively equally throughout the province, which he did from a new base he constructed in central Normandy.[24] Scholars are generally in agreement that Normandy was already geographically well defined by 1090. Normandy's ideological birth, however, was earlier, for the first Norman historian, Dudo of Saint-Quentin (c. 1015), already envisioned a Normandy roughly coincident with the later boundaries of the county.[25] The borders of the province were contested in both the eleventh and twelfth centuries, but the core of its territory remained a unit as long as the county existed.

The growth of Normandy as a religious community was roughly contemporary with its geographic formation. Neustria was Christian before the Viking invasions and Christianity survived their incursions, but paganism among the new inhabitants persisted until the early eleventh century. Religious institutions were devastated. Only Rouen had continually resident bishops, and all the monasteries except Mont Saint-Michel were abandoned. Saint-Ouen in Rouen seems only to have been abandoned for a few years, but Jumièges was deserted for something like fifty years. Fécamp, a community of nuns, collapsed sometime in the ninth century, to be restored as a house for men in 990. Other monasteries went underground much longer, like Deux-Jumeaux, which was reconstituted in the 1130s.[26]

56, has demonstrated that for a long time after the reform, Mont Saint-Michel remained as much in the Breton sphere, economically and socially, as in the Norman.

23. Bates, *Normandy before 1066*, 153.

24. Searle, *Predatory Kinship*, 205, 222–25; Bates, *Normandy before 1066*, 152.

25. *De moribus*, 168. The territory Dudo describes runs from the Epte to the sea. He does not mention eastern or western boundaries, but he also says that the Normans were granted Brittany. His statement may represent only what the dukes of his day laid claim to, but see Bates, *Normandy before 1066*, 9–10.

26. On the disappearance and restoration of Norman monasteries, see Lucien

When monasteries were reestablished, they at first took up the threads of their interrupted existence. They recovered some of their earlier holdings; to do so after a half-century of dereliction, as Jumièges did, strongly suggests that the traditions and records of the earlier monasteries were preserved.[27] Many of the important saints of the new Norman monasteries were the Merovingian founders. In fact, founders were given new prominence as they came to be the patrons both of refoundations and new churches.[28] After 1025, however, Norman monasteries moved away from Carolingian traditions and practices. Thereafter, the experiences they shared helped to create a distinctive Norman monasticism. All of the monasteries refounded or reformed before 1030 were recreated either at the dukes' behests or with ducal support and were subject to the religious policy of the dukes. The monasteries mostly lost or got rid of their property outside of Normandy. At the same time, they became linked to the economic life of the province through ducal gifts of revenues and tolls.[29] Norman abbeys shared a reli-

---

Musset, "Monachisme d'époque franque et monachisme d'époque ducale en Normandie: Le problème de la continuité" in *Aspects du monachisme en Normandie (IVe–XVIIIe siècles)* (Paris: J. Vrin, 1982), 55–74. Saint-Ouen was restored perhaps by 912 but more likely in 918. Jumièges disappeared probably in the 880s (although it was burned in 841) and was refounded in 940. Fécamp disappeared after 833 and was restored in 990. Saint-Evroul, an interesting case, survived the initial pressure of the Vikings only to be destroyed around 900. It was restored in 1050, after several earlier attempts.

27. For Jumièges, see Lucien Musset, "Les Destins de la propriété monastique durant les invasions Normandes (IXe–XIe s.): L'Example de Jumièges" in *Jumièges: Congrès scientifique du XIIIe centenaire* (Rouen: Lecerf, 1955), 1: 52; see also Lucien Musset, "Ce qu'enseigne l'histoire d'un patrimoine monastique: Saint-Ouen de Rouen du IXe au XIe siècle," in *Aspects de la Société et de l'économie dans la Normandie médiévale (X^e–XIIIe siècles)*, ed. Lucien Musset, Jean-Michel Bouvris, and Véronique Gazeau (Caen: Centre d'Études Normandes, 1988), 123f., for Saint-Ouen's property; and Lucien Musset, "Les Abbayes normandes au moyen-age: Position de quelques problèmes," in *Les Abbayes de Normandie* (Rouen: Société d'emulation de la Seine-Maritime, 979), 22–23.

28. For example, Fontenelle was refounded as Saint-Wandrille. On this process see Jean Fournée, "Le Culte populaire des saints fondateurs d'abbayes pré-normandes," in *Abbayes de Normandie* (Rouen: Société libre d'emulation de la Seine-Maritime, 1979), 60–61.

29. On these trends, see Musset, "Les Abbayes normandes," 16–17, 22–23. See

gious culture through the Cluniac-style reforms of William of Volpiano (d. 1031), who became abbot of Fécamp around 1001, but whose influence radiated out to encompass all of the Norman monasteries.[30] The bonds between Norman monasteries created by a common experience of reform was reinforced by periodic exchanges of personnel. Jumièges in the period of this study provided abbots to Saint-Wandrille, Saint-Evroul, Saint-Sever in Calvados, Montebourge, Saint-Pierre-sur-Dives, and Mont Saint-Michel.[31] Proximity also created ties. When monasteries were linked by a river system, as were Bec and Lyre, frequent contacts might ensue and monasteries might come to see themselves as particularly allied.[32]

Starting in the mid-eleventh century, the Norman church was also drawn together by the centralizing efforts of the archbishops of Rouen.[33] There were no fewer than nine provincial synods held

also Musset, "Problème de la continuité," 73; "Destins de la propriété monastique," 55, on the changes of the eleventh century.

30. William was succeeded at Fécamp by one of his Italian followers, John of Fécamp (d. 1079), while another, Suppo of Frutturia, ruled Mont Saint-Michel (1033–48). (See Musset, "Les Abbayes normandes," 17.) The role of foreigners and those educated outside of Normandy in Norman religious life was marked until the second part of the eleventh century. See Leah Shopkow, "Norman Historical Writing in the Eleventh and Twelfth Centuries" (Ph.D. diss., University of Toronto, 1984), 12–14; and Bernard LeBlond, *L'Accession des Normands de Neustrie à la culture occidentale* (Paris: A. G. Nizet, 1966), 40–71.

31. Emile Bertaud, "Moines de Jumièges, évêques et abbés," in *Jumièges: Congrès scientifique du XIIIᵉ centenaire* (Rouen: Lecerf, 1955) 1:317–26.

32. For example, the annals of Lyre (Evreux, *Bibliothèque municipale,* ms. 60, 2v–3r) are clearly dependent on the annals of Bec. The Lyre annals list the obits of the abbots of Bec and the building of the new church at Bec in 1074 (1073 in the Bec annals). Apart from references to Lyre itself, a marginal note for the year 1147 about the third crusade next to the entry for 1104, and a few omissions, the annals of Lyre follow the short annals of Bec until 1135, whereafter the two texts diverge. See Léopold Delisle, "Les Courtes annales du Bec," in *Notices et documents publiés pour la Société de l'Histoire de France a l'occasion du cinquantième anniversaire de sa fondation* (Paris: Renouard, 1884): 93–99. On ties between other monasteries, see Jean Laporte, "Jumièges et Saint-Wandrille" in *Jumièges: Congrès scientifique du XIIIᵉ centenaire,* 1:91–98 (Rouen: Lecerf, 1955); Paul Grammont, "Jumièges et le Bec" in ibid., 1:209–16; and Hans Wolter, "Jumièges et Saint-Evoul" in ibid., 1: 223–32.

33. Although all dioceses had bishops again as of 990, these bishops were not

between 1050 and 1080 in Normandy, and councils were held at
Rouen in 1108, 1118, and 1128. In addition to these formal and com-
pulsory gatherings, there were other assemblies at church conse-
crations, ducal baptisms, and the like.[34] The archbishops of Rouen
made their authority felt in less comfortable ways as well, as they
challenged the quasi-episcopal authority of some of the Norman
monasteries, including Fécamp.[35] Norman bishops attempted in
the late eleventh century to require the abbots of their monasteries
to give written professions of obedience, an innovation that abbots
stoutly resisted.[36] The Anonymous of Fécamp was a partisan in the

---

all resident until mid-century. The bishops of Coutances, for example, reigned from
Rouen until Geoffrey Mowbray (1048–93) took up residence in his See (Bates, *Normandy before 1066,* 30). On the bishops more generally, see David C. Douglas, "The
Norman Episcopate before the Norman Conquest," *Cambridge Historical Journal*
13 (1957): 101–15; Bates, *Normandy before 1066,* 101ff.

34. See Bates, *Normandy before 1066,* 199. John of Avranches held councils at
Rouen in 1072 and 1074; the archbishop and his suffragans also met in 1091 to elect
bishop Serlo of Sées, and William Bonne-Ame held a council at Rouen in 1108. The
clergy met with the duke at Lillebonne in 1080, where some ecclesiastical matters
were treated, but the duke presided. On Norman councils, see Giovanni Mansi,
Sacrorum conciliorum nova et amplissima collectio (reprint, Graz: Akademische Druck-
u. Verlagsanstalt, 1960), 20:33–40, 397–400, 575–78, 739–40, 1231–34, 21:185f., 275f.
David Bates, "The Rise and Fall of Normandy, c. 911–1204," in *England and Normandy in the Middle Ages,* ed. David Bates and Anne Curry (London: Hambledon,
1994), 30 and n. 47, makes reference to Raymonde Foreville's argument that the
infrequency of these synods in the later twelfth century is a symptom of a more
general decline of Norman cohesion in the later twelfth century.

35. Fécamp, Jumièges, and Saint-Ouen had more than monastic privileges. Fécamp was exempt entirely from episcopal and secular jurisdiction and had the power
to ordain priests as well as authority over rural churches, some as far west as Caen.
Jumièges and Saint-Ouen also received responsibility for rural churches, although
neither was as completely exempted from episcopal control as Fécamp. See Bates,
Normandy before 1066, 193–94, and map 10.

36. On the challenges to Norman monasteries, see *Gallia Christiana,* 11:208 and
Instrumenta, 18–19 for William Bonne-Ame's challenge to Fécamp. The monks refused to comply with an archiepiscopal interdict pronounced against the possessions of Robert Curthose in 1089, on the grounds that their abbot was absent in
England and that they were exempt from archiepiscopal authority. The matter
found its way to the papal court; similar challenges were made against the authority
of Saint-Wandrille (*Gallia Christiana,* 11:169) and the version of the *Acts of the Archbishops of Rouen,* written at Saint-Ouen, details how Archbishop John attempted to
demonstrate his authority over the monastery (Rouen, *Bibliothèque municipale,* Y.

battles between the archbishop and his monastery, which is probably why he referred to Normandy as comprising seven provinces rather than one ecclesiastical province, a tacit snub for the archbishop. However, in his day, the Christian community he referred to had a strong basis in physical reality.

It is a more vexed question whether Normandy was a community in a political or ethnic sense. Ethnicity is a slippery concept today, and it was in the Middle Ages as well. Norman historians consistently argued for a distinctive Norman identity which derived from the Scandinavian origins of the Norman elite.[37] The degree to which the Normans really were different because of these origins is currently hotly debated. Eleanor Searle, on one side of the issue, has argued that the ducal family operated through a distinctly Germanic system of kinship alliances. Place names of Scandinavian origin replaced many earlier names, complicating the process of tracing landholdings through the Viking period. Some Scandinavian customs survived as well.[38]

41, 9v, l. 25ff.). On John and Maurilius, see Bates, *Normandy before 1066,* 210; on the shift in the role of monasteries, ibid., 225. See *Gallia Christiana,* 11:39 for William's controversies with Saint-Wandrille; on the battle with Fécamp, see also Mathieu Arnoux, "La Fortune du *Libellus de revelatione, edificatione et auctoritate Fiscannensis monasterii:* Note sur la production historiographique d'une abbaye Bénédictine normande," *Revue d'histoire des textes* 21 (1991): 137. Saint-Evroul too was threatened by episcopal attempts to exert their authority over monasteries. Orderic Vitalis mentions that Abbot Serlo (1089–91) was never consecrated because he refused to make a written profession of obedience to the bishop of Lisieux and that Roger of Le Sap (1091–1126) also refused to make a written profession. The bishop of Lisieux, Gilbert Maminot, was eventually forced to back down (*EH,* 5:260–64).

37. See, for example, G. A. Loud, "The *Gens Normannorum*—Myth or Reality?" *Anglo-Norman Studies* 4 (1982): 104–16. R. H. C. Davis, *The Normans and their Myth* (London: Thames and Hudson, 1976), argues that the Normans who settled in different parts of Europe did not see themselves as belonging to one people, but that the historians writing in Normandy, although not greatly interested in Normans abroad, continued to stress the Viking heritage of their dukes.

38. Searle addresses these points throughout *Predatory Kinship,* but see especially pp. 1–11 and ch. 14. In her account, the main traits of Norman marriage were the significance of cognatic ties and the selection of successors from among a large pool of heirs born from multiple and simultaneous relationships. These unions varied in formaility. On names, see Musset, "Patrimonie de Saint-Ouen," 125, and Bates, *Normandy before 1066,* 16–18; and Jean Adigard des Gautries, "Les Noms de

On the other hand, David Bates has argued for a conscious policy on the part of the dukes to imitate Carolingian forms. Bates argues that the Normans did things differently from inhabitants of other counties, but no more than Poitevins, for instance, did things differently from Angevins.[39] As a minority, albeit a fairly substantial one, the Norman Vikings did not undermine most local customs. They were dependent on the local population to continue to farm in the sparsely populated area, to help them learn how best to use the land, and to provide women. Under these circumstances, rapid linguistic assimilation to French occurred.[40]

The Normans were not the only people to recognize problems and opportunities presented by kin. For instance, the eleventh-century counts of Anjou used their kin cooperatively, appointed their heirs as their co-rulers while they were still alive, and sometimes fought fratricidally with them.[41] Counties other than Normandy developed as strong regional identities, which were felt to manifest themselves in shared regional characteristics. At the beginning of the Black Book of Saint-Ouen, there is a list of the vices and virtues of different peoples ("De vitiis gentium" and "De virtutibus earum"). Some of the *gentes* are members of distinct lin-

---

personnes d'origine scandinave dans les obituaires de Jumièges," in *Jumièges: Congrès scientifique du XIII⁰ centenaire,* 1:57–67 (Rouen: Lecerf, 1955). Scandinavian names were more common in the areas in which Viking settlement was heaviest. On customs, see Elisabeth van Houts, "Scandinavian Influence in Norman Literature of the Eleventh Century," *Anglo-Norman Studies* 6 (1984): 107–21.

39. See David Bates, *Normandy before 1066,* 237 and passim.

40. Ibid., 21.

41. Olivier Guillot, *Le Comte d'Anjou et son entourage au XI⁰ siècle* (Paris: Picard, 1972), 102–3 on designation; 108–111 for an account of the war between Geoffrey le Barbu and Fulk le Réchin. Jane Martindale, "Succession and Politics in the Romance-Speaking World, c. 1000–1140," in *England and Her Neighbours, 1066–1453,* ed. Michael Jones and Malcolm Vale (London: Hambledon, 1989), suggests that the family strategies of the Normans should be considered in the larger European context; see 28–30 for a discussion of the Norman and Angevin cases. Many scholars have argued for the importance of kinship outside of Normandy during this period. For example, White, *Kinship, Custom and Gifts to the Saints,* ch. 4, in discussing kinship among the donors of five French monasteries outside of Normandy, shows a similar complexity of behavior, comprising both cooperation and conflict, both the recognition of kinship and its denial.

guistic groups, such as the Egyptians, Greeks, Romans, Spaniards, Scots, and Franks. Some, however, are regional groups, like the Poitevins, Gascons, and Normans. Categories of ethnicity and geography, therefore, blur together in this list. However, Normans felt that their Viking origins were important in creating their unique identity. In this list the Norman vice is rapacity and the virtue *communio,* the ability to act together. These characteristics clearly point to a recollection of the Viking origins of the Normans.[42]

I have left politics and culture (the latter something which the Anonymous did not mention) until last because these are the most difficult issues and the ones about which there has been the most scholarly controversy. In what sense could the Normans be considered a political or cultural community? Before 1066, Normandy was a territorial principality. However, from 1066 to 1087, 1106 to 1144, and 1154–1204, the duke was the king of England as well. For at least part of this period, members of the Norman elite held lands on both sides of the Channel, and for the entire period, institutions did. One of the first things the Conqueror did was to award lands to Norman monasteries and to his followers and to fill the English church with Norman clerics.[43] French became the vernacular of the elite of England and remained so until the end of the twelfth century.

On the other hand, although Normandy and England were linked and shared a ruler, many scholars currently argue that there was only a relatively brief period during which the two enjoyed a

42. The Black Book (Rouen, Bibliothèque municipale, Y. 46) is a collection of hagiographic readings which also contains one version of the history of the archbishops of Rouen. The folio on which the "De vitiis gentium" and "De virtutibus earum" appears is one of two singletons (fol. A verso) that was not part of the original manuscript. On the manuscript, see CG, 1:404 and *Manuscrits datés,* 329. The manuscript as a whole was executed for Nicholas, Abbot of Saint-Ouen (1042–92), and the inserted pages may date from approximately the same time or from the twelfth century. On the ideological importance of the Viking origins of the Normans, see Bates, *Normandy before 1066,* xv–xvi. On the medieval meaning of *"gentes,"* see Reynolds, *Kingdoms and Communities,* 254–55.

43. David C. Douglas, *William the Conqueror* (Los Angeles and Berkeley: University of California Press, 1964), 324f.

strong cultural rapprochement and that the two remained politically separate. Despite its links with England, and later Anjou and
the Angevin holdings south of the Loire, Normandy continued to
have its own courts, treasury, and officials and its own customs,
which came into being by the end of the eleventh century and were
codified in the late twelfth.[44] David Bates, Judith Green, and David
Crouch have all shown that there were many members of the elite
in Normandy who had no significant holdings in England. Most
of those who did belonged to the wealthiest and most important
class. Those beneath them were local in their loyalties and accordingly in their politics. Even among those who did have cross-
channel estates, both inheritance patterns and the Anarchy con-
trived to split families into English and Norman branches. Rather
than a steady congress between England and Normandy, the influx
of Normans into England was over more or less by 1100, although
there are some signs of a reverse migration in the later twelfth
century.[45]

    Culturally the contact with England did influence Normandy
somewhat, although this influence was felt even before the two
territories shared a ruler. For example, English book production
influenced Norman books before the Conquest, even if after the

44. On political institutions, see John Le Patourel, "Normandy and England,
1066–1144" in *Feudal Empires Norman and Plantagenet* (London: Hambledon Press,
1984), article VII. Le Patourel saw Norman institutions as influencing English ones,
and vice versa, but he argued that the complexities of ruling an empire on both
sides of the channel meant that each territory was forced to create separate courts,
treasuries, and the like. On the law, see Emily Zack Tabuteau, *Transfers of Property
in Eleventh-Century Norman Law* (Chapel Hill: University of North Carolina Press,
1988), 223–24; Le Patourel, "Normandy and England," 21–22. The Norman cus-
tumal, one of the earliest to be written, is printed in *Coutumiers de Normandie, textes
critiques,* 3 vols. (Rouen: E. Cagniard, 1881–1903).

45. On these issues, see Bates, "Rise and Fall of Normandy"; and David Crouch,
"Normans and Anglo-Normans: A Divided Aristocracy?"; and K. Thompson,
"William Talvas, Count of Ponthieu and the Politics of the Anglo-Norman Realm,"
in *England and Normandy in the Middle Ages,* ed. David Bates and Anne Curry
(London: Hambledon Press, 1994), 19–35; 51–67; 169–84. See also Judith Green,
"King Henry I and the Aristocracy of Normandy," in *La "France anglaise" au moyen
age* (Actes du IIIᵉ congrès national des sociétés savantes, vol. 1) (Paris: CTHS, 1988),
161–73.

Conquest the flow of scribes, like that of colonists, went from Normandy to England. Anne Lawrence has argued that it is possible to speak of an Anglo-Norman style of book production for the first half of the twelfth century but not before or after.[46] Architecture shows the same pattern as book production. English buildings influenced a few Norman buildings during the reign of Henry I, but influences were considerably weaker at other times.[47] Historical writing shows an identical pattern. Works of history written in Normandy circulated in England, but the number of works that flowed back across the channel were few. Most of those works, which included Eadmer's life of Anselm, Henry of Huntingdon's *History of the English [Historia Anglorum]*, and Geoffrey of Monmouth's *History of the Kings of Britain [Historia regum Britanniae]* arrived in Norman libraries during the first half of the twelfth century.

If communities have to be hermetically sealed at the edges to exist, Normandy was not a political or cultural community, but then it would be impossible ever to talk about medieval communities at all. Instead, I would suggest we think about communities as being populations organized around a center, rather like electron clouds around a nucleus. As one progressed away from the center, the strength of the attraction was lessened and if another nucleus existed, the pull might be quite strong. The Norman aristocrats whose lands lay along the borders with France, for instance, were continually troublesome subjects, as Judith Green and Kathleen Thompson have pointed out.[48] Lands on the geographic periphery were also likely to be contested and even to change hands, as happened commonly along the border between the dukes of Normandy and their rivals, the kings of France and counts of Anjou. There was a continual flow of people, materials, and ideas across the Norman border. During the eleventh century, Nor-

46. See Anne Lawrence, "Anglo-Norman Book Production," in *Normandy and England in the Middle Ages,* 79–93.

47. Lindy Grant, "Architectural Relations between England and Normandy, 1100–1204," in *Normandy and England in the Middle Ages,* 117–29.

48. See above, n. 45.

mandy experienced a great influx of outsiders whose contributions to "Norman" intellectual life are undeniable. Many Norman monasteries belonged to communities of prayers with other monasteries; Saint-Evroul had links to Cluny, for instance. But the common foci—the dukes, the archbishops—and the frequency of local contacts kept members of the Norman community oriented more toward each other than toward the outside, and thus they formed an identifiable community.

There is some evidence that the Normandy community was not in an entirely healthy state in the second half of the twelfth century, but throughout this period, it still retained the features that had shaped it as a community.[49] When Normandy was conquered in 1204, however, it joined the French royal demesne and no longer had its own duke. While Philip II permitted the Normans to keep their customs, because the Norman dukes had been the leaders of the Norman church, important patrons of art and literature, and political leaders, their disappearance disrupted Norman traditions. One manifestation of this break was that Normandy ceased to write its own history for a century. The kings of France took their historical patronage not to a Norman house but to Saint-Denis in Paris where their royal status was celebrated. Normandy was still a geographic, religious, and ethno-regional community, but its political heart had been torn out.

If Normandy was a community, what were its histories? Medieval historians almost never defined history; the names they gave to works we call history suggest that history was a fairly amorphous field. The term *historia* occupies a broader semantic field than its English cognate, designating the portion of a saint's life used in the liturgy, the literal sense of the Bible, a pictorial narrative cycle, or simply a story, as well as writing about the past.[50] *Narratio*

---

49. For a summary of these factors, see Bates, "Rise and Fall of Normandy," 33.

50. *Dictionary of Medieval Latin from British Sources,* fasc. 4, ed. D. R. Howlett

was a similarly broad term. It could mean histories, stories of any type, the portion of a charter containing the description of the circumstances under which it came to be granted, and testimony in court.[51] The terms *annales, chronica, series temporum,* and *gesta* were not used consistently to refer to specific historical forms, as one might expect. To complicate matters, historians might use several different terms to describe the same text.[52] That does not mean that writers confused these various uses, although Karl Morrison, in arguing that history was akin to the visual or dramatic arts conflates all of the various uses of the term *historia.*[53] When medieval writers made distinctions between one sort of writing about the past and another, it might be in terms of style rather than format.[54]

The only discussion of history available to medieval writers was that of Isidore of Seville. For Isidore, the writing of history belonged to the study of grammar, and so most of that discussion occurs in the first book of the *Etymologies.* History was "the narration of deeds, through which things that were done in the past

---

(Oxford: Oxford University Press, 1989), 1160–61 for *historia, historialis, historiographia* and other variants; Charles Du Cange, *Glossarium mediae et infimae latinitatis,* vol. 4 (New edition. Paris: Librairie des sciences et des arts, 1938), 209–10. Dudo of Saint-Quentin uses the term *historialiter* to refer to a cycle of frescos (*De moribus,* 291).

51. *Novum glossarium mediae latinitatis,* fasc. L-N, ed. Franz Blatt (Hafniae: Ejnar Munksgaard, 1967), 1058–60; Du Cange, Glossarium mediae et infimae latinitatis, vol. 5, 569.

52. Orderic Vitalis, for instance, used a number of different terms for histories: *historia, chronographia, chronica, annales, annalem historiam,* and *narratio,* and he refers to his own history as an *annalem historiam* (*EH,* 6:154, 436), a *chronographia* (*EH,* 1:138, 150; 3:214; 4:312), and simply as an *historia* (*EH,* 1:162; 4:228), although most of the text is narrative history. The history of John of Worcester, which we would tend to call a chronicle, Orderic calls an *annalem historiam* (*EH,* 2:186), a *chronica* (*EH,* 2:186, 188), a *chronographia* (*EH,* 2:186), an *historia* (*EH,* 2:186) and *annales* (perhaps) (*EH,* 2: 246).

53. See Karl Morrison, *History as a Visual Art* (Princeton: Princeton University Press, 1990).

54. On the question of genre, see Guenée, *Histoire et culture historique,* 203–7. For example, chronicle and history might be distinguished one from another by the relative amplitude of the narratives or the language used by the historian (ibid., 205).

are known."[55] Isidore had his own synonyms for history, such as *monumenta* (because histories preserve the memory of things done), and *series* (from garlands of flowers gathered together—a term that may have inspired Bernard Guy to call his history, *Flowers from the Chronicles [Flores chronicorum]*). Isidore also discussed several genres of history, which he distinguished from one another by the units of time into which entries were divided and by whether the historian was an eyewitness to the events or merely a reporter of material from the remote past.[56] Isidore concluded by differentiating history from arguments and fables through its factuality:

> There is this difference between history, argument, and fable: histories are things that have happened; arguments are things that, even if they have not happened, could happen; fables, however, are things that neither have happened nor could happen because they are against nature.[57]

Isidore's comments, like those of the writers who came after, show how much semantic play there was in the terms used to describe history. For example, he used *historia* to describe the whole enterprise of writing about the past, but an *historia* could be either a work that was not subdivided into temporal units or a work written by an eyewitness. The fluidity of the nomenclature does not mean that medieval writers were completely unclear about what they were doing but that there was no commonly agreed upon system for labeling different kinds of historical works. When writers commented on history, they tended to refer to content (things that have been done), form (annalistic arrangement or narrative), and style (high style or middle style). No commentator discussed

---

55. For Isidore's comments on history, see Isidore of Seville, *Isidori Hispalensis episcopi Etymologiarum sive originum libri xx,* ed. W. M. Lindsay (Oxford: Oxford University Press, 1911), vol. 1, 1:xl (hereafter cited as Isidore, *Etymologies*).

56. *Etymologies,* 1:43, 44. For example, Isidore mentions the diary (in which the time unit is the day), the calendar (the month), the annal (the year), and the history (many years).

57. Ibid., 1:41–44. For a discussion of Isidore's views of history, see Arno Borst, "Das Bild der Geschichte in der Enzyklopädie Isidors von Sevilla," *Deutsches Archiv für Erforschung des Mittelalters* 22 (1966): 1–62.

methods which are the primary way modern historians differentiate history from other sorts of works.

So, what is a history? The answer to this question is not so clear, even to modern scholars. De Certeau, for instance, calls history a region of "rich fuzziness." However, de Certeau also offers a useful way to think about history that is consonant with Isidore's comments. History is a written discourse about the past.[58] History must be written because for medieval writers it belonged in grammar, the discipline of the written. I would add to this something that neither Isidore nor de Certeau argued directly: that histories must also be systematic treatments of the past. This qualification arises from de Certeau's reflection that histories concern origins.[59]

These qualifications separate histories from the many other ways in which medieval people encountered the past. They might do so in collections of exempla, which might contain stories about the past but which were chosen for their moral lessons rather than for their chronology. In the monastic culture from which nearly all eleventh- and twelfth-century historians came, the past was present in the liturgical round that formed the monastic day, in the inscriptions and epitaphs in the monastic precinct, in the monastic obituary where dead monks and patrons mixed, in buildings the monks knew to have been constructed by this or that abbot, in the celebration of the saints, in Christianity itself. Some of these recollections of the past were written, but many were inscribed in the body as it moved through a particular space.[60] The noble adoption of toponyms in the eleventh and twelfth century is a lay counterpart of this kind of connection to the past.

58. de Certeau, *Writing of History,* 21; for discourse, see ibid., 20ff.; on truth, see ibid., 12 and 16, n. 25.

59. Ibid., 12.

60. On this issue, see Michel Sot, "Organisation de l'espace et historiographie épiscopale dans quelques cités de la Gaule carolingienne," in *Le Métier d'historien au moyen age: Études sur l'historiographie médiévale,* ed. Bernard Guenée (Paris: University of Paris, 1977), 40. On the power of the body to evoke recollection, see Pierre Bordieu, *The Logic of Practice,* trans. Richard Nice (Stanford, Calif.: Stanford University Press, 1990), 69.

By any definition of history, medieval or modern, certain medieval texts are history. Annals and chronicles, with their unrolling sequences of dates are as unambiguously historical as any text ever gets. They are systematic, concerned only with the unfolding of the past, and they show all the markers of being factual (one kind of truth). Other texts, however, are more difficult to classify. For example, there does not seem to be a dividing line between cartularies and serial biographies such as the *Liber pontificalis* (sometimes referred to as *gesta*), except, perhaps, a functional one, the distinction between a work written for administrative purposes and one written to evoke the past.[61] The discourse of hagiography similarly overlaps the discourse of history, although in ways that scholars are still debating.[62] A work like Christine de Pisan's *Book of the City of Ladies* is extremely difficult to categorize. Although it contains a large number of narratives about the past, these are organized according to a moral scheme—women who demonstrated reason, rectitude, and justice—rather than a chronological scheme. Christine is concerned with the origins of anti-feminism but not of female virtue which is innate.

A different sort of problem is presented by the text which to the modern reader is fiction but which medieval readers might accept as history. Jean Bodel famously paraphrased Isidore of Seville's distinction between history, argument, and fiction by averring that:

There are only three subjects heard by every man, that of France and of Britain and of Rome the great, nor do these three subjects have any resemblance to each other. The tales of Britain are light and pleasing; those of France are evidently true every day; those of Rome are wise and teach wisdom.[63]

61. As Geary has recently and very convincingly argued in *Phantoms of Remembrance*, esp. 90–93. Folcuin himself called his cartulary of Saint-Bertin the *gesta abbatum* (102), while a similar compilation at Cluny was called a *narratio* (105), both terms commonly used for histories.

62. The literature on the relationship between hagiography and historiography is huge; on this subject and some of the issues it raises, see Appendix 1.

63. Jean Bodel, *Les Saisnes*, cited in Suzanne Fleischmann, "On the Rep-

To modern scholars, however, all three sorts of works are fiction. Similar problems arise with other kinds of texts. Would medieval readers have considered *Fulk Fitzwarren* as historical as, for example, a roughly contemporary biography, the *Life of William the Marshal*? While modern scholars confidently label the former a family romance and the latter a history, it is harder to say what medieval readers thought about the two. Modern historians themselves have been stumped about how to characterize Geoffrey of Monmouth's *History of the Kings of Britain,* a text that divided medieval writers as well.[64]

When works lie along a continuum, a "horizon of expectations," it is always a problem to draw a boundary between what is included and excluded.[65] That does not mean, however, that contemporaries made no distinctions between texts and that we ought not to either. Medieval people did distinguish between things that had really happened and things that had not, even if they sometimes disagreed among themselves, did not come to the same conclusions that we might about what had happened, and used different criteria for judging.[66] This study will, no doubt, not include some works

resentation of History and Fiction in the Middle Ages," *History and Theory* 22 (1983): 299 and n. 57. On *Les Saisnes,* see also Spiegel, *Romancing the Past,* 62.

64. Robert of Torigni and Henry of Huntingdon, for instance, accepted Geoffrey of Monmouth at face value, while Gerald of Wales and William of Newburgh thought him a liar. Such decisions, however, were sometimes made as much for personal reasons as for historical ones. See Partner, *Serious Entertainments,* 62–65, especially 64. R. W. Southern, "Aspects of the European Tradition of Historical Writing: 1. The Classical Tradition from Einhard to Geoffrey of Monmouth," *Transactions of the Royal Historical Society,* 5th ser., 20 (1970): 193–94, accepts Geoffrey as a historian by medieval standards, while John Ward, "Gothic Architecture, Universities and the Decline of the Humanities in Twelfth-Century Europe," in *Principalities Powers and Estates: Studies in Medieval and Early Modern Government and Society,* ed. L. O. Frappel, (Adelaide: Adelaide University Union Press, 1979), 68–69, places Geoffrey within the sphere of court satire, along with Walter Map and Walter of Chatillon.

65. The term "horizon of expectations" is borrowed from Hans Robert Jauss, *Toward an Aesthetic of Reception,* trans. Timothy Bahti (Minneapolis: University of Minnesota Press, 1982), 22–24.

66. See Fleischmann, "On the Representation of History and Fiction," esp.

other scholars might argue, with justice, are history, and it will probably include works that some would see as not properly historical.

One omission from this study requires some further comment: I have chosen not to discuss vernacular texts. The vernacular began to come into its own as a language of composition in the twelfth century. The earliest history in Anglo-Norman, Geoffrey Gaimar's *History of the English* (c. 1135), was written in England for an English patron and draws on oral traditions circulating in England, such as stories about Havelok the Dane, and on the written tradition of the *Anglo-Saxon Chronicle*. It also brought English history down to 1100 and thus told some Norman history as well. Wace began his never-completed *Romance of Rollo [Roman de Rou]* some twenty years later. Gaimar was a contemporary of Robert of Torigni, Wace of Stephen of Rouen. Thus vernacular works do overlap with the Latin histories that are the subject of this book.[67]

However, while vernacular and Latin histories both belonged to the discourse of history, they were linguistically separate. Sociolinguistic theorists argue that language is not transparent or purely communicative. Some see language as reflecting the norms of the culture that produced it, while others see language as structuring cognition. Different sorts of language are certainly used to convey social meaning. The Humanists had available to them both Latin and the vernacular, and they used the different registers of each language as well as the languages themselves to structure their social relationships.[68] Medieval writers were aware of different registers within Latin. Historians, for example, began to avoid the high style in the eleventh century.[69] The gulf between Latin and

---

305–6. Fleischmann addresses directly the issue as to whether we can assume that the Middle Ages made any such distinction (278–80).

67. For a lengthy discussion of the riches of Anglo-Norman writing, see Brian Merilees, "Anglo-Norman Literature," *Dictionary of the Middle Ages,* vol. 1 (New York: Charles Scribners' Sons, 1982), 259–72.

68. See Nancy Steuver, "The Study of Language and the Study of History," *Journal of Interdisciplinary History* 4 (1974): 402–3, 405.

69. On the rhetoric appropriate to history, see Guenée, *Histoire et culture historique,* 214ff. William of Jumièges was already making the claim to write simply

the vernacular was so marked that literacy was only thought of in terms of Latin until well beyond the twelfth century, and Latin literacy implied clerical status. Thus medieval bilingualism was a form of *diglossia*.[70] Vernacular historians, such as Wace and Benoît of Sainte-Maure (the author of the *Chronicle of the Dukes of Normandy [Chronique des ducs de Normandie]*) occupied the divide between the two languages. They had read the Latin histories of Dudo of Saint-Quentin and his successors, when to read Latin well enough to translate the kinds of texts Wace and Benoît used as sources was to have the kind of linguistic competence most people in the Middle Ages did not have.[71] They then transferred the material from the conventions of Latin prose narrative to those of vernacular epic and romance.[72]

The function of the vernacular historian, at least at this initial stage, was to mediate between cultures in one direction, generally from Latin to the vernacular.[73] This was less true in the later Mid-

---

around the middle of the eleventh century (GND, 2), although that claim was much more commonly expressed in the twelfth. Spiegel argues that a similar shift of register, from verse to prose, in the vernacular during the thirteenth century was occasioned by the same mistrust of rhetoric (Spiegel, *Romancing the Past*, 57–64).

70. On literacy, see Herbert Grundmann, "Literatus—illiteratus: Der Wandel einer Bildungsnorm vom Altertum zum Mittelalter," in *Ausgewälte Aufsätze*, vol. 3 (Stuttgart: Anton Hiersemann, 1978): 1–66. The ideological terms in which literacy was seen did not necessarily fully reflect reality. Grundmann argues that women were probably more commonly literate than men. See also Michael Richter, "A Socio-Linguistic Approach to the Latin Middle Ages," in *The Materials Sources and Methods of Ecclesiastical History,* ed. Derek Baker (Oxford: Blackwell for the Ecclesiastical History Society, 1975): 69–82. Franz Bäuml, "Varieties and Consequences of Medieval Literacy and Illiteracy," *Speculum* 55 (1980): 237–65, has refined some of Grundmann's arguments, showing that the laity could use Latin letters by having clerics read for them and thus in practice were not illiterate. For *diglossia*, see Streuver.

71. See Michael Richter, "Kommunikationsprobleme im Lateinischen Mittelalter," *Historische Zeitschrift* 222 (1976): 45.

72. See Spiegel, *Romancing the Past*, 5–6. This process of translation is the reason Spiegel chooses not to talk much about the Latin originals of the texts she analyzes.

73. On the difference between vernacular and Latin historiography, see Spiegel, "Social Change and Literary Language: The Textualization of the Past in Thirteenth-Century Old French Historiography," *Journal of Medieval and Renaissance Studies* 17 (1987); 135–36; *Romancing the Past*, 6–7.

dle Ages when the vernacular was successfully established as a language of learning. Once this had happened, it was possible, for example, for Francesco Pippino to translate the *Livre d'Eracles* into Latin for use in his Latin chronicle. However, for the earlier period, movement from the vernacular to Latin was exceptional. Stephen of Fougères, in his life of Vitalis of Savigny, several times makes reference to his use of a written vernacular source as well as stories told him by monks at Savigny and others. In the first case, Stephen treats the vernacular text as though it were in some senses not a text at all, for he remarks just after mentioning its existence that "it is truly unworthy if [the life] of such a man were to be passed over in fruitless silence, and not be transmitted for the notice of those who come after through the use of letters."[74] Orderic Vitalis copied the Latin version of the *moniage* of William of Gellona into his history, because he felt that a Latin text was more appropriate for monks to listen to than a song spread by jongleurs.[75] Initially, then, most of the movement from the vernacular into Latin seems to be within the category of hagiography, one of the most popular literary forms. Of course, Latin texts frequently incorporated materials drawn from oral vernacular sources, particularly from epic, the outstanding example being the *Book of St. James (Codex Calixtinus),* which incorporated material from the *Song of Roland.* However, the authors who did this often did not make reference to these vernacular sources, which seem to have been no different than the other kinds of oral reports historians normally used.

Access to texts and control over their production was also asymmetric. When a patron who could not read Latin commissioned a history, he or she depended upon the historian to frame the work in ways that resonated appropriately. The patron necessarily could have had only the most general influence on the final shape of the work. The patron of history was not unlike an architectural patron,

74. Stephen of Fougères, *Vita sancti Vitalis,* ed. E. P. Sauvage, *Analecta Bollandiana* I (1882): 357. He comments later on that he has translated the material into "more manifest letters," ibid., 364.

75. *EH,* 3:218f.

who might have a list of desiderata. Only the builder, however, would have had the expertise to decide what was technologically feasible.[76] In the case of a patron like Henry II of Normandy and England who was fluent in Latin, the influence might be greater. Still, Henry's family was unusually literate and he included among his ancestors a thorough anomaly, the lay historian Fulk le Réchin of Anjou.[77] Patrons of vernacular works were not similarly hampered. They often chose a writer whose work they knew. Wace, for instance, was a denizen of the English court long before he wrote the *Romance of Rollo*.[78] The patron was in a position to be much more specific about the contents of the work and to judge the product of the commission. The resulting work, therefore, although arising from the artistry of the historian, more directly reflected the patron's own sense of his needs and desires.[79]

Until the composition of the *Grandes chroniques de France* began in 1274, the venues of vernacular and Latin composition were also different. While Latin histories might be composed anywhere, in practice, most were composed in a clerical, usually monastic, context and read in clerical circles, even when the work had been commissioned by a powerful lay person. There were, of course, exceptions, such as Gerald of Wales who wrote at the court of Henry II

76. On patrons and builders, see Charles M. Radding and William W. Clark, *Medieval Architecture, Medieval Learning: Buildings and Masters in the Age of Romanesque and Gothic* (New Haven, Conn.: Yale University Press, 1992), 34–35.

77. For Fulk's history, see Louis Halphen, ed. *Chroniques des comtes d'Anjou et des seigneurs d'Amboise* (Paris: Picard, 1913), lxxxix-xc, 232–38.

78. On Wace, see René Reto Bezzola, *Les Origines et la formation de la littérature courtoise en occident 500-122,* 3 pts. in 4 vols. (Paris: Honoré Champion, 1944–63), pt. 3, vol. 1, 150ff.

79. Spiegel, *Romancing the Past,* 6. Spiegel here makes more of a dichotomy than I would between the way patrons influenced vernacular and Latin works. She suggests that vernacular works were more partisan and less collective than Latin works. However, I suspect there was no difference in the degree to which historians, whether writing in Latin or the vernacular, wrote to please patrons. Latin works were just as partisan, just as much a product of a "social logic," as vernacular ones; it was simply that the patron had less choice and less control with Latin works. As Spiegel argues, the lay patron was unacquainted with the conventions of Latin texts but might be prepared to argue aesthetics with an author commissioned to write a vernacular work.

where there was a group of mostly clerical advisors and bureaucrats who composed a literature for their own circle.[80] In contrast, vernacular histories, although generally written by clerics (because they required access to Latin sources), were more commonly written for the court, although the court was not necessarily the only audience. Some of these authors are known, like the Ménéstral of Alphonse of Poitiers and the Anonymous of Béthune, only by the names of the lords they served.

Therefore, while vernacular histories are clearly history in both a medieval and modern sense, they need to be considered as a separate conversation within the discourse of medieval history.

📖

Individual histories are statements or messages within the conversation of history. A message requires a sender, in this case, a historian. The historian is situated in a web of education, social position, and ambition. A message also requires an addressee, sometimes an explicitly-named patron and sometimes only the readers implied by the text. The recipient also resides in a nexus of expectations, both literary and social. A history, like any other message, conveys its meaning in several ways simultaneously. The existence of the history itself implies a relationship between the sender (the historian) and the recipient (the reader or patron) and, because it is written, testifies to the importance of the contents. The language in which the information is conveyed is also richly significant and affects the meaning. The message itself has a referential function, that is, a burden of information that it attempts to convey. That information is conveyed not only by its words but by its very existence, which attests to a relationship between the addressee and addresser and by its code, in this case not only the language of composition but also by the form of the work, which conveys a portion of the meaning of the text.[81] Thus the message

80. On this circle, see the comments of Ward, "Gothic Architecture, Universities and Decline of the Humanities," 67ff.

81. See Roman Jakobson, "Closing Statement: Linguistics and Poetics," in *Style*

takes on a charged aspect. It would be impossible to enumerate all the ways in which this relationship with its written bond plays itself out, but it is possible to explore some aspects of it.

Because I look at histories from a number of different angles, some of which have not been previously explored, I have found no one theoretical model to guide my work. I have, instead, drawn on a number of different models from different disciplines, which I have tended to use to illuminate the Norman histories rather than to explain them comprehensively. Casting a long shadow across my work is the figure of Hayden White, whose ideas about tropes, plots, and ideology are unavoidable for those seriously interested in history's meaning and value. I have made use of theory of history, reception theory and reader-response criticism, memory theory and discussions of medieval memory, literacy theory, and some anthropological work, particularly that of Victor Turner. Although I have worked primarily from printed texts, I have been able to examine some of the manuscripts of Norman histories in the municipal libraries of Rouen and Evreux, and I have used that evidence where it sheds light on historical practice and reading.

The reader may find that my using so many different theoretical approaches results in a wavering, fragmented, and sometimes distorted image, as though one were a fish looking at the historical flotilla from underwater. I suspect this is inevitable. My aim in this book is not to offer a totalizing explanation of historical writing for Normandy or to suggest that one aspect of an historian's experience is more important than any other. Everything matters all together, but each aspect of a history matters in a different way and to different degrees in the work of different historians. The relatively smooth surface of many histories masks their internal turbulence and the negotiation of different agendas within them.[82]

---

in Language, ed. Thomas A. Sebeok (Cambridge: M.I.T. Press, 1960), 353ff. Although Jakobson is mostly concerned with how poetic language may be distinguished from other kinds of language, I have found his schematization a useful way to break down the way texts function.

82. For example, Spiegel, *Romancing the Past,* 99–151 (but esp. 144–51), shows how in the thirteenth-century vernacular classical history, the *Faits des Romains,* the

However, as I turned these histories from side to side peering at them, I found that a generally consistent picture of what it meant to write history in eleventh- and twelfth-century Normandy emerged. In some ways writing history in Normandy was different from writing it anywhere else, if only because Normandy's community was so coherent. In other ways, Norman historians struggled with the same questions and arrived at similar solutions as their contemporaries in other parts of Europe. Their efforts shed light on the whole project of historical writing. The questions I have asked about these particular histories can be asked about other histories, just as the lessons we can draw from Spiegel's notion of "social logic" can be applied to more than the thirteenth-century vernacular prose texts she analyzes.

Finally, although I conclude that medieval historians approached history from a different standpoint than modern historians do, that they used different models of authentication, and that their works performed some different tasks than modern histories and performed differently some of the same tasks as modern histories, this does not mean that I wish to privilege our way of doing things over the medieval way. I have invoked modern practice in many places in this book because it is useful to have something to compare medieval practice to and because changes in the way people wrote history in the Middle Ages and in the early modern period underlie the modern discipline of history. But the reader should not assume along with some crude Darwinians that evolution from one thing to another means evolution from a lower form to a higher. Writing history in the modern way is better at advancing certain ends and worse at bringing about others. The past is foreign country: they do things differently there.

My first chapter is a map of historical writing in Normandy: who the historians were, what their backgrounds were, and where and

---

tension between the ideological desire to show the Franks (who stand in for the French nobility here) as fighting nobly for their autonomy, and the plot of the history, which required Caesar to succeed in subduing the Franks, led the author to an impasse that echoed the experience of the noble audience of loss and irresolution.

when they wrote. I show that Norman histories were not randomly written but appeared at particular temporal nodes and in the institutions most connected with the Norman dukes. I close by comparing the Norman picture with historical writing outside of Normandy.

In the second chapter, I turn to the shape given to Norman history by eleventh-century Norman historians. While they presented Norman history as essentially comedic, they read and wrote history through different interpretive modes. The first Norman historian, Dudo of Saint-Quentin, presented the Norman past as an allegory in which the Normans reproduced the trajectory of other chosen peoples. William of Jumièges, in contrast, demanded that history be read literally and politically, while William of Poitiers gave his history a moral meaning.

The twelfth-century historians who are the subject of chapter three retained these three modes of interpretation, but they no longer saw Norman history as a comedy. Orderic Vitalis imitated William of Poitiers the moralist but painted Norman experience as one of decline into anarchy. Stephen of Rouen read Norman history allegorically but saw the larger picture of history as one of rise and inevitable fall. He thus took an elegiac and nostalgic tone. Robert of Torigni, after revising and extending the history of William of Jumièges, turned away from Norman history entirely to concentrate instead on universal history. However, like William, Robert wrote history to be read from a literal perspective.

The fourth and fifth chapters explore the varying assumptions of the Norman historians that helped them produce histories much different from each other. The fourth chapter considers the divergent notions of truth under which medieval historians in general, and Norman historians in particular, operated and how they authenticated their work. While histories were by definition to be true, Norman historians were not equally concerned about ensuring the truth of their work. The prime means that modern historians use to guarantee history's truth, their adherence to a commonly accepted set of historical methods, was not employed in the Middle Ages. The fifth chapter details the many models Norman historians used to shape their own histories and the varying methods they employed to bring their histories into being.

The sixth and seventh chapters explore responses to historical texts. The sixth chapter looks at the performative aspect of historical writing, what people thought history could or should do. The power of histories did not come merely from their contents but also from their existence as physical objects, books. Books and contents both relayed a consistent message about the importance of the ducal family, mediated in social conflict, provided evidence for legal cases, and created monuments. Only Orderic Vitalis considered the possibility that history might be an abstract sort of knowledge, rather than a useful body of information. For history to be important even in this more concrete sense, however, it required readers. In the seventh chapter, I have asked who read these Norman histories and how they read them. A few Norman histories were widely read, both in Normandy and in England. Some clearly had local significance. Other works, in contrast, failed to secure a significant audience and thus could not perform the actions that historians expected them to.

The pattern of composition and dissemination of historical writing, the "social logic," of these Norman texts, all suggest that there was a sense of the ways—particularly the socio-political ways—that history might be used. History's potential lay in the ways in which it might structure social experience in the world outside of the monastery. Development of that potential, however, was frustrated by the privileging of Latin for the writing of history before the twelfth century, with a consequent failure of history to find a large audience. History was not institutionally controlled, nor was it a discipline in the senses that law, theology, and philosophy were becoming disciplines, and in the sense that history is a discipline today. My concluding chapter sketches out how, in the later Middle Ages, history came to occupy more nearly the space it occupies today.

The water murmurs through the rough places under the puny prow,
The tempest is foaming with the waves of the sea.

The hostile waters now play at will upon the ship,
Which is about to be harmed by this pestiferous embrace,
    by the dreadful winds.
I am like the prey of the furious forces of the sea,
And the wave, violently arisen, beats upon the curved shores.
I now cling, a fearful arbiter, upon the shuddering waves.[83]

83. *De moribus,* 175, epilogue to bk. 2.

1 ❧ History in the County of Normandy

$\mathcal{B}$etween 1000, when Normandy coalesced as a county and a community, and the late twelfth century, when Normandy's autonomy was eroding somewhat, Normandy produced six Latin historians who chronicled Normandy's history. Five wrote or continued histories of Normandy's rulers, while two placed the story of Normandy's past against the backdrop of universal history. In addition to these writers, whose work encompassed the county, Normandy also produced many historians whose labors reflected more local communities. The result was a burst of historical writing spread over nearly two centuries.

The first history to be written in Normandy appeared just after the millennium. Its author, Dudo of Saint-Quentin, was sent, as he tells us himself, as part of an embassy from Albert of Vermandois to Richard I. It is possible to date this journey relatively exactly. Albert's emissaries were to secure Richard's assistance in restoring Albert to the favor of the newly crowned Hugh Capet.

Since Albert died in 988 and Hugh Capet was crowned in May 987, Dudo's mission must have taken place late in 987 or early in 988.[1] Dudo, as a canon at Saint-Quentin in Vermandois of which Albert was the lay abbot, was a natural choice as an emissary. Although he was most likely in his early twenties at the time of the mission, he was a formidably educated man for his day.[2] He was probably educated at one of the cathedral schools of Northern Europe, most likely Liège.[3]

Dudo seems to have pleased Richard, for he returned to Normandy intermittently until 1015, particularly frequently between 994 and 996 when Richard died. He is recorded in one charter as a *fidelis idoneus* of the duke and as the duke's chaplain and chancellor, although what duties were attached to the latter office is not known.[4] The duke's rapid exploitation of the adventitious arrival

1. For Dudo's arrival in Normandy and its circumstances, see *De moribus*, 294; for Albert's death, see *Gallia christiana*, 9:1043.

2. In the closing poem, Dudo comments that he was five decades old (*De moribus*, 301, l.43). Most of the text of this poem copies the closing lines of the *Life of St. Germanus [Vita Sancti Germani]* of Heiric of Auxerre, as does this line. Heiric announced he was three decades and two years old, (*Vita Sancti Germani, MGH Poetae latini aevi Carolini*, vol. 3 [Hannover: Hahn, 1886], 513, l.638), so probably Dudo was being more or less accurate. That would place him in his early twenties in 989.

3. Barbara Vopelius, *Studien zu Dudo von Saint-Quentin, dem ersten Geschichtsschreiber der Normandie (987–1015)*. (Ph.D. diss., University of Göttingen, 1967), 25–82, argues for Reims based on Dudo's knowledge of Boethius's *De musica*, which she believes only to have been available at Reims, Toul, and Fleury. However, the *De musica* was also available at Liège (it was quoted by Egbert of Liège, *Egberts von Lüttich Fecunda ratis*, ed. E. Voigt. [Halle am Saale: Verlag von Max Niemeyer, 1889], 206, l.3 and note), and it was widely known in the late ninth century in northern France (see Susan Rankin, "Carolingian Music," in *Carolingian Culture: Emulation and Innovation*, ed. Rosamund McKitterick [Cambridge: Cambridge University Press, 1994], 291). Because of Dudo's familiarity with the *Vita sancti Lamberti* of Stephen of Liège, it seems slightly more likely that he was educated at Liège than elsewhere. The school was flourishing during the 980s under Bishop Notker, when Dudo would have studied there. It seems likely that Dudo would not have hesitated to allude to the place of his education in his letter to Adalbero (*De moribus*, 115–20) if they had been fellow students. For a further argument that Dudo was educated at Liège, see Leah Shopkow, "The Carolingian World of Dudo of Saint-Quentin," *Journal of Medieval History* 15 (1989): 24–27.

4. See Marie Fauroux, *Recueil des actes des ducs de Normandie de 911 à 1066*

of a learned foreigner makes sense, for Normandy could not provide large numbers of educated clerics in the late tenth and early eleventh centuries and the dukes relied on outsiders.[5] As for Dudo's willingness to stay, Albert's death may have provided him an incentive to seek patronage away from home.

Dudo was rewarded for his literary and other contributions with two small benefices, which he kept after his service in Normandy ended. After 1015, Dudo was recorded as Dean of Saint-

---

(Caen: Société d'impressions Caron et Cie, 1961), 102 (charter 18) and 89 (charter 13). The word *cancellarius* in charter 18 may be in error, as the charter exists only in a fourteenth-century copy. The need for a chancellor, or someone to write documents for the court, was indicative of the gradually increasing dependence on the written word. Charles Homer Haskins, *Norman Institutions* (Cambridge: Harvard University Press, 1918), 52, suggests that the chancery was an organ of the chapel until the Conquest. However, Bates, *Normandy before 1066*, 154, points out that documents tended to be drawn up by the recipients, which suggests that the chancery, despite the existence of a chancellor, may not have existed as any sort of formal body. Four documents survive from the reign of Richard I; see Fauroux, *Recueil*, 70–77 (nos. 3–6).

5. For example, the first abbot of the refounded Jumièges, Martin, came from Saint-Cyprien in Poitiers, while the next abbot came from Micy (LeBlond, *Accession*, 20–21). The *Book on the Authority of Fécamp [Libellus de revelatione, edificatione, et auctoritate Fiscanensis monasterii], PL* 151–720f., mentions that Richard I invited Maiolus of Cluny to reform the Norman monasteries. In inviting William of Volpiano to do the same, Richard II was simply following in his father's footsteps. For Norman ties to institutions outside of Normandy in the late tenth century, see LeBlond, *Accession*, 25–38.

The earliest evidence for the refoundation of Norman schools comes from about 1000. At the beginning of the eleventh century, a collection of verse dialogues, most of which were written in Normandy, was put together. Two are the work of Warner of Rouen, written either at the cathedral school or Saint-Ouen. For these texts, see Jan Ziolkowski, *Jezebel: A Norman Latin Poem of the Early Eleventh Century* (New York: Peter Lang, 1989), 28–33. The satires were not necessarily originally part of the same manuscript—the Warner satires and the *Jezebel* and *Semiramis* are written in different hands. The first satire of Warner concerns an Irish teacher named Moriuht, and the second is a debate with a monk who has come to Saint-Ouen from Mont Saint-Michel to study music. The poem makes clear that both places had functioning schools. See Jean Laporte, "L'Abbaye du Mont Saint-Michel aux Xe et XIe siècles," *Millénaire monastique de Mont Saint-Michel* (Paris: Bibliothèque d'histoire et d'archéologie chrétiennes, 1967), 1:69; see also Lucien Musset, "Le Satiriste Garnier de Rouen et son milieu," *Revue du moyen age latin* 10 (1954): 237–66, which includes the text of this satire.

Quentin and probably no longer spent time in Normandy.[6] But before Dudo left Normandy for good, he rewarded his Norman benefactors with a history that any nascent dynasty might be proud of, *On the Customs and Acts of the First Norman dukes [De moribus et actis primorum Normanniae ducum]* (hereafter cited as *Customs*).[7]

The dukes of Normandy were fortunate in their choice of historians. Although Dudo's highly ornamented style, composed in alternating passages of poetry in assorted meters with sections of rhyming and rhythmic prose, has not found favor with modern readers or indeed with medieval readers of the twelfth century (one family of manuscripts contains little of the poetry), it was a tour de force for its day. The story it told, four books in all, covering Hasting, a Viking predecessor of Rollo, and the first three Norman dukes, cast the Normans in the role of a chosen people destined to occupy the holy land of Normandy. It echoed other such narratives: Jewish scripture, Bede's *Ecclesiastical History,* the *Aeneid,* and the story of Constantine. Dudo stopped frequently, in the way Latin epic and poetic hagiography made popular, to sermonize and comment. The sixteen manuscripts of the *Customs* do not make it a historical best-seller, by any means, but it was in important libraries in Normandy and England.[8]

6. In 1015, Dudo donated two benefices he had received from Richard I to Saint-Quentin, retaining the usufruct for his lifetime. See Fauroux, *Recueil,* no. 18, 100–102. This marks the last time Dudo is known for certain to have been in Normandy. Dudo's return to Saint-Quentin was probably the occasion of the donation. It is assumed that in the interim he went back to Saint-Quentin from time to time, but he does not say and we have no way of knowing. Other hypotheses are that he taught at the cathedral school of Rouen, but this seems unlikely. For his deanship, see *Gallia christiana,* 9:1045.

7. This title was chosen by Jules Lair for his 1865 edition. Gerda Huisman has recently suggested that the text should be renamed the *Gesta Normannorum,* (Gerda Huisman, "Notes on the Manuscript Tradition of Dudo of Saint-Quentin's *Gesta Normannorum,*" *Anglo-Norman Studies* 6 (1984): 122), and while her argument for this change is sensible in that the history was actually referred to by that name in some library catalogues, it seems confusing to shift nomenclature now.

8. On the manuscripts, see Huisman, "Notes on the Manuscript Tradition," 122–35. One manuscript, Alençon, Bibliothèque municipale 20, existed until the nineteenth century when it was lost in a fire while on loan to Jules Lair, Dudo's editor.

Dudo's work, the work of an outsider and foreign servant, sufficed for almost half a century to satisfy the desire for the history of Normandy. It was not until some time in the 1050s that William of Jumièges began writing the *Deeds of the Norman Dukes [Gesta Normannorum ducum]* (hereafter cited as *Deeds of the Dukes*), although the extant versions we have date from 1071 at the earliest.[9] Nothing is known about William, not his family, and not his position within the monastery. William is entirely absent from the charter records, which suggests he was of relatively humble status.[10] It seems reasonable to assume that he was Norman, although he shows no particular interest in any individuals outside the ducal family in his history, nor do his descriptions of battles and the like show any particular intimacy with any one part of Normandy. He mentions Maurilius of Rouen and John of Avranches, the archbishops of Rouen who reigned while he wrote, with warmth, but he shows no special attachment to these men as individuals. It is likely that he knew more about them because Jumièges was in the diocese of Rouen and not very far away from the city. It is probable that William had been an oblate at Jumièges. For someone to be sufficiently accomplished in Latin to write a lengthy history required extensive education in Latin, more usually acquired by those who were destined at an early age by their families for the church. Monastic teachers, the directors of the scriptorium, and the writers of history were, until the disappearance of child obla-

9. The argument that William began writing in the later 1050s has been convincingly advanced by van Houts, *GND* (2) I:xxxii. However, the extant versions date from about 1071 (see Raymonde Foreville, "Guillaume de Jumièges et Guillaume de Poitiers," in *Jumièges: Congrès scientifique du XIIIᵉ centenaire* (Rouen: Librairie Lecerf, 1955), 2:643–54, esp. 645). One further point makes it seem most likely that the first extant version was written before 1073. In the epilogue, Robert is spoken of as Normandy's duke and advocate (*GND*, 143.) William the Conqueror was out of the province but not after 1072 when he returned to Normandy. This epilogue is probably from the original version of the text. On these points, see R. H. C. Davis, "William of Jumièges, Robert Curthose and the Norman Succession," *English Historical Review* 95 (1980), 597–606; also van Houts, *GND*, 83.

10. *GND*, xiv. The William mentioned with his father in a charter of 1097 cannot be our historian (see p. xiv, n. 2). The charters of Jumièges are printed in J. Vernier, *Les Chartes de l'abbaye de Jumièges* (Rouen: A. Lestringant, 1916).

tion, likely to have been oblates, not *conversi*.[11] William was probably in his forties in the 1050s, and perhaps he was chosen to write
the history because he had already demonstrated his competence.[12]

William began where Dudo of Saint-Quentin had left off and
added the biographies of the dukes through William the Conqueror, three books in all (Richard III's reign of less than a year
did not merit a book of its own). William also rewrote all of Dudo's material, reshaping and abbreviating it, transferring it from
rhymed rhythmic prose and poetry into, well, more prosaic language. The story was more down-to-earth as well. William's dukes
were not fulfilling a divine destiny but ruling a turbulent province.

William's sponsors were as fortunate in their choice as Richard I and Richard II had been in choosing Dudo of Saint-Quentin.
William's work was immediately popular, surviving even an unfortunate dedication to the soon-to-be-disgraced Robert Curthose.[13] It did not replace Dudo's work; indeed, in some versions
of the *Deeds*, Dudo's work replaces the first four books, although
in two of the manuscripts, a full but later version of the *Deeds* is
appended.[14] Generally, however, it satisfied different tastes and
succeeded instead in carving out a niche of its own. Because of its
relative brevity and neat division into short chapters, it was much
more readily continued than the *Customs* was, and it was continued

11. Monique-Cécile Garand, "Auteurs latins et autographes des XIᵉ et XIIᵉ siècles," *Scrittura e civiltà* 5 (1981): 94 suggests that this group was primarily responsible for much of the writing of the eleventh and twelfth century.

12. William comments at the beginning of the sixth book of the *Deeds of the
Dukes*, the reigns of Richard III (1026–27) and Robert I the Magnificent (1027–35),
that he is about to begin the history of the dukes of his own time (*GND*, 97), so
we may gather that he reached maturity in the late 1020s or early 1030s, which would
have put him in his forties in the 1050s.

13. The first extant version of the *GND* was probably written with Robert Curthose in mind. It is the first source to call him duke of Normandy, and it originally
ended with his regency. William of Jumièges went back and tacked on another
ending to his history when Robert fell into disgrace. See Davis, "William of Jumièges," 597–98.

14. See Elisabeth M. C. van Houts, "The *Gesta Normannorum ducum*: A History
without an End," *Anglo-Norman Studies* 3 (1981): 109. On these manuscripts, see
van Houts, *GND*, 195–98.

by at least three more historians.[15] All in all, there are forty-five extant manuscripts of the text, which makes the *Deeds* in its various versions the most widely circulated Norman history.[16]

In the meantime, William of Poitiers, a contemporary of William of Jumièges, trained his sights on the history of his own times. William came from the minor Norman nobility. His sister became abbess of Préaux, a convent founded by the Beaumont family, so perhaps William's family belonged in the circle of their retainers.[17] Although Orderic Vitalis, who belonged to the next generation of Norman historians, tells us that William had some military training, he must always have been intended for the church, for his superb and classicizing Latin makes it clear that he had studied it extensively.[18] The major intellectual influence on William's work,

15. The remaining redactions are as follows. Van Houts and R. H. C. Davis, "William of Jumièges," 597–606, believe the C redaction to be the original one. The B redaction contains some original material, including an account of the death of William. See van Houts, "History without an End," 109; on the interpolations, see van Houts, *GND,* 94–106. The texts of the D redaction are mostly incomplete; it seems to be related to C. See van Houts, "History without an End," 108. The E redation contains interpolations generally accepted as those of Orderic Vitalis. See *EH,* 1:29–30; also Elisabeth M. C. van Houts, "Quelques remarques sur les interpolations attribuées à Orderic Vital dans les *Gesta Normannorum ducum* de Guillaume de Jumièges," *Revue d'Histoire des Textes* 8 (1978): 213–22 and van Houts, *GND* (2), I:lxviii. The F redaction contains interpolations and the addition of an eighth book by Robert of Torigni.

16. Alençon, Bibliothèque municipale ms. 20 also contained a version of the *Deeds of the Dukes.* For this manuscript, see *CG,* 2:496–97.

17. The details of William of Poitiers's life and career were saved from total oblivion by Orderic Vitalis, who depended heavily on the *Gesta Guillelmi* for his information about the Conquest. See *EH,* 2:xxxii–xxxiv. For William's sister, see *GG,* vii.

18. Military and literary training in someone intended for the clergy were not necessarily exclusive. Orderic speaks of several fighting clerks, among them Ralph "Ill-tonsured" of Giroie, so called because of his love of the secular life (*EH,* 2:28), and Odo of Bayeux and Geoffrey Mowbray engaged in battle. Odo was known to his contemporaries as a fighting bishop (see Frank Stenton, *The Bayeux Tapestry,* 2d ed. (London: Phaidon Press, 1965), pl. 68; *EH,* 2:172, 228, 266). Such dual training and behavior probably did not result because fighting by clerics was encouraged, so much as that families needed to keep their options open. The loss of the heir might mean that a younger son had to be withdrawn from the religious life. The classical example of this is Gerald of Aurillac, as Janet Nelson point out in a paper delivered in Toronto some years ago.

however, is reflected in the name by which he is known, his years of study in Poitiers, beginning probably around 1048.[19] He may have ended up at Poitiers because of links between Poitou and Normandy created by the marriage between William I of Poitou (935–63) and William Longsword's sister Adela-Gerloc and perhaps renewed by a donation on the part of Richard II's sister Emma, the Queen of England, around 1024 to Saint-Hilaire-le-Grand to help rebuild the monastery.[20]

Both the cathedral school of Poitiers and the school of the monastery of Saint-Hilaire were open to outside students, but William probably studied at Saint-Hilaire.[21] The school of Saint-Hilaire was founded by Hildegar, a disciple of Fulbert of Chartres, in the second decade of the eleventh century, and like all the schools based on Chartres, the schoolmasters there taught the "New Curriculum."[22] Classical texts were used to train students in Latin stylistics, while law was also taught there. William was influenced by these two subjects but less by music, mathematics, and medicine. In addition to these new studies, theology, the Bible, and the Fathers were also taught.[23]

The superb education William acquired at Poitiers no doubt assisted him in his clerical advancement. Like Dudo, William be-

19. *GG,* ix.

20. Lucien Musset, "Le Mécénat des princes normands au XIᵉ siècle" in *Artistes, artisans et production artistique au moyen age,* ed. Xavier Barral I Altet (Paris: Picard, 1987), 2:125 and n. 26.

21. *GG,* ix. The description of the schools of Poitiers that follows is based on M. Garaud, "Les Écoles et l'enseignement à Poitiers du IVᵉ à la fin du XIIᵉ siècle," *Bulletin de la Société des antiquaires de l'ouest,* 3d ser., 14 (1946–48) and R. Favreau, "Les Écoles et la culture de Saint-Hilaire-le-Grand de Poitiers des origines au début du XIIᵉ siècle," *Cahiers de civilisation médiévale* 3 (1960): 447.

22. F. Behrends, ed. and trans., *The Letters and Poems of Fulbert of Chartres* (Oxford: Oxford University Press, 1976), xxi.

23. On the position of the classics, see *GG,* x–xi; Behrends, *Fulbert of Chartres,* xxviii–xxxiv. For medicine and music, see Garaud, "Les Écoles à Poitiers," 91. Hildegar was himself a talented dialectician, musician, and doctor. For the traditional elements, see Favreau, "Les Écoles à Saint-Hilaire-le-Grand," 475. On law, see Raymonde Foreville, "Aux Origines de la renaissance juridique: Concepts juridiques et influences romanisantes chez Guillaume de Poitiers, biographe du Conquérant," *Moyen Age* 58 (1952): 43–83.

came a ducal chaplain (not an exclusive position, for ducal chaplains served in a number of different chapels and in different capacities).[24] Chaplains still drafted documents as Dudo had done, although there were other clerks as well, but they no doubt also served as theological advisors to the duke.[25] Such service under the eye of the duke could lead to higher ecclesiastical office, since Baldwin, bishop of Evreux (1066–70), Gilbert Maminot of Lisieux (1077–1102) and Michael of Avranches (1068–94) all served as chaplains.[26] A collateral benefit of this service for William was an acquaintance with the ducal court and politics he was later to write about. William did not become a bishop, but he was promoted to an archdiaconate at Lisieux. William's legal knowledge would have been particularly useful in what was rapidly becoming a judicial office.[27]

It was probably while William was at Lisieux that he wrote wrote his biography of William the Conqueror, the *Deeds of William, Duke of Normandy and King of England [Gesta Guilelmi Normanniae ducum et regis Angliae]* (hereafter cited as *Deeds of William*), most likely in 1077.[28] In the *Deeds of William*, the chapter on Hugh

24. On ducal chaplains, see Lucien Musset, "La Formation d'un milieu social original: Les Chapelains normands du duc-roi au XIᵉ et au début du XIIᵉ siècle," *Aspects de la société et de l'économie dans la Normandie médiévale (Xᵉ–XIIIᵉ siècles)* (Caen: Centre d'études normandes de l'Université de Caen, 1988), 91–114.

25. *GG*, 120 and n. 1. Lucien Musset, "Chapelles et chapelains du duc de Normandie au XIᵉ siècle," *Revue historique de droit français et étranger*, 4th ser., 23 (1975): 171. Chaplains appear in documents primarily as scribes, financial agents, and officials at ordeals (ibid., 172).

26. Bates, *Normandy before 1066*, 155, 211.

27. On the office of archdeacons, see A. Hamilton Thompson, "Diocesan Organization in the Middle Ages: Archdeacons and Rural Deans," *Proceedings of the British Academy* 29 (1943): 153–94, esp. 157–63.

28. Since William mentions that Eustace of Boulogne had returned to favor (*GG*, 268), which occurred possibly as early as 1073, that is the earliest possible date for the text. The work was almost certainly written after the dedication of the church of St. Stephen at Caen, which Chibnall shows has to have been in April 1077, (*EH*, 3:10–12). Davis, "William of Poitiers," 74, draws similar conclusions about the dating of the *GG*, although he suggests it may also have been written later than 1077 (ibid., 75). Since William refers to Hugh of Lisieux in his description of that bishop's life and habits in the present tense, we may infer that the bishop was alive, at

of Lisieux is by far the longest and the most intimate of all of the descriptions of the bishops of Normandy, so it is possible that Hugh commissioned the work and that his death was the reason it remained unfinished.[29]

In addition to having no ending, the *Deeds of William* is missing its original beginning. As best we can reconstruct, the missing part of the text most likely contained a genealogy of the dukes of Normandy and some mention of the circumstances under which young William II received the title. The historian doubtless included a short exposition of the troubles of the duke's minority.[30] The text as we have it begins with the death of Cnut and the end of the minority of the duke. It ends with the death of Copsi, the point at which the *Deeds of the Dukes* ends; however, the original text continued up until the imprisonment of Morcar and the death of Edwin in 1070. A portion of the missing text is preserved in Orderic Vitalis' history, for Orderic admired William's prose and not infrequently used it virtually verbatim.[31]

---

least when this portion of the narrative was composed. Hugh died on July 17, 1077. If William was in mid-stream upon Hugh's death, the death of the bishop may have been the unfortunate circumstances alluded to by Orderic when he mentions that the text was never completed (*EH*, 2:184).

29. *GG*, 136–42. Most other descriptions are only a few lines long. There are other possible reasons why the *GG* was not completed. After 1068, the Conqueror's lands were shaken by periodic uprisings that seemed to have no permanent solutions. Although the king managed to face each difficulty as it arose, the peace and glory that William of Poitiers fervently believed were the king's due failed to materialize. As Orderic put it, after the death of Waltheof, the Conqueror had no more luck (*EH*, 2:350). It would have been difficult for the historian to fit these unhappy events into the generally optimistic portrait of the king given in the *GG*.

30. Probably not in very great detail; when the historian mentions the revolt of William of Arques, he treats the subject of the count's early disloyalty to the duke as a new subject (*GG*, 52).

31. *EH*, 2:xx. For a complete account of Orderic's debt to William of Poitiers, see *EH*, 2:xviii–xxi; 214, n. 5; 218, n. 1; 233, n. 4; 248, nn. 2, 3; 256, n. 2. We may assume that, since Orderic follows the ordering of events in the *GG* so closely in the part of the text we have, William's narrative would have strongly resembled Orderic's, except where Orderic describes the oppression of the English by the Normans; in this case, Orderic probably speaks rather than William. Among the events likely borrowed from the *GG* are Orderic's accounts of William in England in 1067 and his Christmas court at London in that year; the description of the siege

The original text seems not to have been subdivided (the subdivisions into chapters and books being the work of the modern editor).[32] Despite the lack of formal divisions, however, the narrative does fall into three long sections, each part concerned with a single phase of the Conqueror's career. The first part (capitula 1–35 of the first book in Foreville's edition) tells, in somewhat episodic fashion, how William grew from a child beset on all sides by danger to an independent ruler. The narrative passes smoothly through each event, compressing time as need be and leaving out what would detract from the story.[33] The second part of the text treats the period from Duke William's independence until the beginning of the Conquest of England (capitula 36–59 of book one). The third part of the *Deeds of William* is the Conquest and its aftermath (book two).

William remained an archdeacon of Lisieux until at least 1078, but after that he drifted into obscurity. Orderic Vitalis reported that William continued to write, although no other works of his are known. He may be the William of Poitiers who ended his life as a canon at Dover.[34] His work became similarly obscure. Orderic Vitalis knew and admired the *Deeds of William,* and the work travelled to England, perhaps with its author, if he was indeed the canon of Dover. There a few English writers knew of the work, but it was largely otherwise ignored. No manuscripts of the work have survived; the survival of the text is owing to Duchesne's tran-

---

of Exeter; part of Orderic's account of the northern campaign in 1068 but certainly not all of it. Much of the material on Lanfranc also probably derives from William's history.

32. *GG,* lvi.

33. The capture of Brionne, which actually took some three years to accomplish, is told of in a few lines as though it took no time at all, and the battles of Mortemer (1054) and Varaville (1057) are juxtaposed as though they had happened one after the other (*GG,* 19, n. 4). The deaths of King Henry and Geoffrey Martel are mentioned directly after the battle of Varaville, and the historian implies that their deaths were a sign of divine disfavour, although both men died in 1060.

34. *EH,* 2:258; R. H. C. Davis, "William of Poitiers and His History of William the Conqueror," *The Writing of History in the Middle Ages: Essays presented to Richard William Southern,* ed. R. H. C. Davis and J. Wallace-Hadrill (Oxford: Oxford University Press, 1981), 90.

scription of a manuscript he found in the Cotton Library in the seventeenth century and which is presumed lost in the great Cotton Library fire.[35]

From 1077 to the second decade of the twelfth century, no large-scale works of history were written in Normandy, although the existing works of Norman history were copied and the *Deeds of the Dukes* received a number of interpolations in the process. One copyist added an account of William the Conqueror's death to the narrative, while other narrators interpolated stories into earlier parts of the text. One of the interpolated manuscripts was written at Saint-Evroul by Orderic Vitalis, who from around 1114 began work on an original work, the *Ecclesiastical History*.[36]

The life of Orderic Vitalis is entirely known from his own comments in the course of his history and in his conclusion. He was born in England of an English mother. His father Odelerius was from the Orléanais, not Normandy, but he had participated in the Conquest in the entourage of Roger Montgomery. Odelerius helped found Shrewsbury abbey in 1083 and entered it himself with his older sons, but since the monastery was new and could not yet take children, he committed Orderic instead to Saint-Evroul in 1085 when Orderic was ten. Orderic describes himself as coming, like Joseph, as a stranger to a strange land where he did not know the language. Orderic received all but his rudimentary education at Saint-Evroul and spent the rest of his life (he died after 1141) as a monk in the scriptorium, perhaps as one of its directors. He did, however, travel from time to time in the service of his monastery. He was sent to England, to Cluny, to Cambrai, and to Reims, as well as to priories of his monastery in France.[37]

Orderic's work was originally commissioned as an *opusculum,*

---

35. *GG,* l–liii. The manuscript does not appear in any extant catalog of the Cotton Library from either before or after the fire, although the earliest catalog post-dates Duchesne's transcription, upon which all of the later editions of the *Deeds of William* are based. It is also possible that the manuscript was borrowed from the library by Duchesne but never returned, in which case, it may still exist.

36. *EH,* 1:31. On Orderic's copy of the *Deeds of the Dukes,* see above note 15.

37. On Orderic's early life, see ibid., 1:4–6; on his scriptorium work, see ibid., 1:23–24; on his travels, ibid., 1:25–27. For his autobiography, see ibid., 6:550ff.

a short history of the monastery, perhaps a monastic cartulary-history.[38] The impetus for its composition was the return of the properties of the monastery following the arrest of Robert of Bellême in 1113.[39] The text grew by accretions, as Orderic added a history of Normandy, then a universal history, and finally added the history of his own times. The resulting work was an enormous historical reference text in thirteen books which Orderic compiled over a period of twenty-five years. Its subject matter included two chronicles, the lives of Christ and the apostles, an abbreviated *Liber pontificalis,* eight abbreviated saints' lives (almost all epitomes of earlier texts), an epitome of the *Translation of St. Nicholas* by John of Bari, monastic histories of Saint-Evroul and Crowland, a history of the Normans and English after the Conquest, a history of the First Crusade (based on Baudry of Bourgueil), a treatise on the new monastic orders, a few romance stories and moral exempla, more than thirty epitaphs and other sorts of verse, nineteen documents of various kinds, including five sets of canons and eight charters, and assorted accounts of events in Germany, Italy, Ireland, England, Spain, and the Middle East.[40] This lengthy work (more than 950 columns in the *PL* edition) was difficult to copy and even to keep together. The four volumes of the autograph went their separate ways at some point and one was lost, although most of the lost third volume survived in a copy made at Caen.[41] That volume seems to have been the only one copied in the Middle Ages.

Orderic's younger contemporary, Robert of Torigni, was more successful in promulgating his work. Unlike Orderic, Robert of Torigni came to monastic life as an adult and achieved the higher monastic office more common among non-oblates. He was born

---

38. Ibid., 3:6. For monastic cartulary-histories, see Geary, *Phantoms of Remembrance,* 81ff; also Jean-Philippe Genet, "Cartulaires, registres et histoire: L'exemple anglais," in *Le Métier d'historien au moyen age: Études sur l'histoiographie médiévale,* ed. Bernard Guenée (Paris: Publications de la Sorbonne, 1977), 95–129.

39. Ibid., 1:32.

40. See *EH,* 1:48–63 for the literary sources of the history; ibid., 1:63–77 for the documentary sources.

41. See ibid., 1:121.

in Torigni-sur-Vire in the Bessin around 1106 and became a novice at Bec in 1128. He became prior of Bec around 1149, a position from which he could have expected to be elected abbot of Bec; however, in 1154 he was elected by the monks of Mont Saint-Michel as their abbot, a position he held until his death in 1186.[42]

One of Robert's earliest works was a continuation of the *Deeds of the Dukes,* written in the late 1130s or the early 1140s. Robert made extensive interpolations into the first, second, sixth, and seventh books of Orderic's version of the history, continued the seventh book to the death of the Conqueror, and added an eighth book on the reigns of Robert II Curthose and Henry I, which ended with the death of Abbot Boso of Bec in 1136. The additions are largely regnal years, genealogies, successions, and deeds of the elite of Normandy. There is a lengthy excursus on the foundation of Bec and other monasteries established under William II. Robert also carefully interpolated material from the *Customs of the Dukes,* which William of Jumièges had chosen to leave out, into his version of the *Deeds.*[43]

Robert's second project was a chronicle in the tradition established by Eusebius and Jerome and continued by Sigebert of Gembloux. Robert used the Eusebius-Jerome-Sigebert chronicle as a base text, interpolating entries as far as the year 1100 concerning the Normans, Normandy, the English, and England into the work of Sigebert.[44] In the middle of the entry for 1100, Robert introduced what he considered to be the original part of his work. Robert worked Sigebert's entries for 1100 through 1111 and those of

42. For Robert's life see M. Morlais, *De vita et scriptis Roberti de Torinneio abbatis sancti Michaelis* (Paris: E. Thorin, 1881), 10f. That Robert was from the lower nobility seems likely since both Robert and his nephew Durand, who appears as a witness in some documents, held monastic office (Durand was prefect of the Cistercian abbey of Torigni). It is assumed that Robert became prior of Bec, when the previous prior, Roger, became abbot of Bec.

43. *GND,* 235–47; 252–56; 203–18, 220–22.

44. The modern editor, Léopold Delisle, only notes Robert's interpolations for the period before 1100. This gives a misleading sense of what Robert's text looked like. A medieval reader would have confronted a copy of Sigebert's chronicles as interpolated by Robert but circulating under Sigebert's name.

Sigebert's continuator Anselm into his own text. The first redaction of Robert's chronicle ended in 1152. Robert later returned to the chronicle, extending it to 1169 and finally to 1182.[45]

Robert was also the author of a treatise on the new monastic orders, inspired by Orderic Vitalis' treatise on that topic, and he may have been associated with other historical works written at Bec and Mont Saint-Michel. He probably wrote the early part of the chronicle of the abbots of Bec and either wrote himself or commissioned one of his monks to write the annals of Mont Saint-Michel.[46] After he went to Mont Saint-Michel, Robert continued to work on his chronicle and to send updates to his brethren at their request, but the monks of Bec do not seem to have been interested in following in his footsteps themselves.[47]

One more Bec historian, Stephen of Rouen, tackled the history of Normandy before the close of the century. What little is known about Stephen comes mostly from his own works and from conjecture based on his surviving writings, which are contained in two manuscripts.[48] He was a monk at Bec who had been ordained deacon, perhaps the Stephen mentioned in the monastery consecration list of c. 1143.[49] He must have come from a somewhat socially significant family, since one of his uncles was the abbot of Mont Saint-Michel. Stephen also implies he knew Henry II personally.[50]

---

45. For Sigebert's chronicle and its continuations, see *MGH SS* 6:300–374; 385–535. Sigebert's text exists in many versions. One copy was made at Mortemer in Normandy, around 1155, a version that was continued to 1165, then to 1180, and finally to 1234 (463–69). On the different redactions of Robert's chronicle, see Rob. of Tor., 2:xiii.

46. They were certainly written under Robert and were possibly Robert's work. See ibid., 2:xvi .

47. Ibid., 2:340f.

48. The *Norman Dragon* is contained in Vatican Library, Ottobonensis Lat. 3081 (formerly Reg. 11267) (fifteenth century); Stephen's poems are in Paris, BN, Ms. Lat. 14146. On these two manuscripts and their contents, see *DN*, xci–xcix.

49. *Dragon*, 210, (no. 7, ll.37–38); *DN*, xiv. One Stephen was admitted by Abbot Boso (1124–36); it is more likely that the author was the Stephen consecrated under Abbot Letard (1139–49) around 1143.

50. *Dragon*, 202 (no. 6, opening lines); 210 (no. 7, ll.39–44). Stephen mentions no members of his family other than Bernard but his cousin (or perhaps brother),

By training, Stephen seems to have been a rhetorician or grammarian, and quite possibly a teacher at the monastery, which suggests he was a child oblate. His non-historical writings and his Norman history, the *Norman Dragon [Draco Normannicus]*, show great concern with these topics and have a pronounced didactic character. He wrote a preface to and abbreviation of Quintilian's *Institutiones oratoriae,* a mock forensic oration, complete with comments about the rhetoric of the piece at the end, and many poems. Stephen's poems are a sampler of forms and meters (all announced in rubrics), and they are on various edifying topics: the liberal arts, studying and speaking, the letter A, and the alphabet, for example. None of the poems or other works hint at any interest in history on the part of the author.[51]

The *Dragon* can be securely dated to 1169. It was written after Henry II permitted his sons to do homage to Louis VII in 1169 for the lands they would inherit but before Thomas Beckett's return to England and murder in 1170. The *Dragon* was the first Latin history of Normandy to be written entirely in verse, which Stephen clearly chose because he conceived of his work in epic terms.[52] The arrangement of the material, beginning with contemporary events, then a recapitulation of events that preceded it, followed by a continuation of the narrative from the point at which it began, is strongly reminiscent of the beginning in *medias res* favored in epic. The first book opens with the death of Henry II's mother,

---

another nephew of Bernard, William de l'Arche, was also at Bec (*DN*, xiii). In the second of these passages, Stephen mentions a monk who brought the news to Henry II that his mother had died at the Bec priory of Pré, and he seems here to be referring obliquely to himself. Apart from these few notices, almost nothing is known about Stephen's family (ibid., lxxix).

51. For Stephen's non-historical works, see *Dragon*, 171–259; these are not the complete contents of Paris, BN, Ms. Latin 14146 (*DN*, xcviii).

52. See Morrison, *History as a Visual Art*, 230–38, on the relationship between Otto of Freising's *Gesta Frederici* and the verse version of it by Gunther. Twelfth-century writers had an ambivalent view of the role of rhetoric in history. See Nancy Partner's discussion in "The New Cornificius: Medieval History and the Artifice of Words" in *Classical Rhetoric & Medieval History,* ed. Ernst Breisach (Kalamazoo, Mich.: The Medieval Institute, 1985), 15–18, on the absence of rhetoric in the writing of medieval historians.

Matilda, in 1168, then returns to pick up the threads of her life from 1109, continuing with her son's career to 1165. Stephen then offers a précis of French and Norman history down to 1127. The second book begins with Henry I's death in 1135, then continues the story of the Norman succession up to 1167 (with a detour through Carolingian history). It ends with a letter from King Arthur to Henry concerning Henry's designs on Brittany, and a reply from Henry to Arthur. In the course of this epistolary exchange, the death of Matilda is announced. The third book opens with her funeral, is followed by an account of the papal schism of 1159–1177, and ends with a resolution of the conflict between Henry II and Louis VII over whether Henry would permit his sons to do homage for their father's French lands. Stephen was the last Latin historian to treat the history of Normandy before the French conquest.

While these six historians were producing lengthy and complex histories, other writers were composing histories for largely local consumption, Normandy's numerous shorter histories. Many of the Norman religious institutions kept annals of one kind or another. One family of annals derives from the annals of Rouen, composed sometime around the middle of the eleventh century, probably during the episcopate of Maurilius.[53] The annals of Dijon may have provided the base text (which might have been brought to Normandy by William of Volpiano).[54] The Rouen annals were copied in the succeeding half-century and continued at the monasteries of Saint-Wandrille (c. 1066), Mont Saint-Michel (c. 1100), Fécamp (c. 1100), Caen (between 1100 and 1106), and Jumièges (c.

53. For Maurilius's career, see M. de Boüard, "Notes et hypothèses sur Maurille, moine de Fécamp, et son élection au siège metropolitain de Rouen," *L'Abbaye bénédictine de Fécamp: Ouvrage scientifique du XIIIe centenaire* (Fécamp: Durand et Fils, 1959), 1:81–92, particularly 81–85.

54. Jean Laporte, ed., *Les Annales de l'abbaye de Saint-Pierre de Jumièges* (Rouen: Lecerf, 1954), 8 and 24, n. 4. Another possible base text are the annals of Cologne. The Rouen annals are partially edited in *MGH, Scriptores* 26:489–517, where they are presented alongside the annals of Caen, Mont Saint-Michel, and Saint-Evroul which are dependent on them. Laporte (cited above) has edited the Jumièges annals.

1106).[55] The annals of this family tend to have quite brief entries for each year. However, around 1170 a more prolix historian began to keep the Jumièges annals, and they became a lively work of history in their own right.[56]

Bec had a separate annalistic tradition which it shared with Lyre. The author knew the Rouen annals, although he did not base his work on the earlier annals. The first version of the Bec annals was completed around 1136 and then continued to 1154. A second set of short annals copied the first set as far as 1109, after which they are independent of the first annals. About the time the first version of the Bec annals was complete, the annals were copied at Lyre, where various annalists continued them to 1200.[57]

The Norman religious institutions also produced institutional histories. Shortly after the Rouen annals were written, someone at Rouen composed the *Acts of the Archbishops of Rouen,* written between 1067 and 1075, and a short verse list of the Archbishops of Rouen written during the reign of William Bonne-Ame (1070–1110).[58] Most of the entries concerning the archbishops are relatively brief, mentioning only their parentage, their characters, and their contributions to their churches. In other words, the focus of the *Acta* is quite similar to the *Liber Pontificalis* and no doubt deliberately so: liturgical and monumental, rather than concerned with the miraculous. The text is available in two major versions, one from the cathedral and one from Saint-Ouen, which has ad-

55. Laporte, *Annales de Jumièges,* 8–10.

56. Ibid., 11–13.

57. Léopold Delisle, "Les Courtes annales du Bec," in *Notices et documents publiés pour la Société de l'Histoire de France à l'occasion du cinquantième anniversaire de sa fondation* (Paris: Renouard, 1884), 93–94. The annales of Lyre have not been printed but are contained in Evreux, Bibliothèque municipale, ms. 60, ff. 2v–3r. Delisle notes that the original redaction of the annals of Bec ended in 1136. This is the entry where the hand changes in the annals of Lyre, suggesting that the annals were copied at Lyre very soon after that date. On the second annals, see Delisle, "Courtes annales," 94.

58. For the Rouen annals, see de Boüard, "Notes et hypothèses," 81; for an edition, see *PL* 147:273–80. Concerning the verse history of the archbishops, see *EH,* 3:xxvi. The text has not been printed, but it is available in manuscript, Rouen, BM, Y. 15.

ditional material intended to safeguard the prerogatives of the abbots of Saint-Ouen against their episcopal neighbor a few hundred
yards away.[59]

A number of Norman monasteries wrote works intended to
safeguard their property, their authority, or their privileges. Sometime around 1066, a monk of Saint-Wandrille wrote an account of
the discovery of the relics of St. Wulfran to counter the claim of
the monks of St. Peter's in Ghent that they had the authentic relics.[60] Just before 1100, a monk at Fécamp wrote the *Book of the
Revelation, Construction, and Authority of the Monastery of Fécamp
[Libellus de revelatione, aedificatione et auctoritate monasterii Fisca-
nensis]*, a history of the monastery up to its reform by William of
Volpiano, arguing for the monastery's full, Cluniac-style exemption from episcopal control.[61] Bec also produced a small history in
defence of its liberty, this time from lay control, which began with
the foundation of the monastery by Herluin and ended with the
death of Abbot Boso in 1136.[62] When Robert of Torigni became
the abbot of Mont Saint-Michel, he either sponsored or personally
wrote a number of works intended to enhance that monastery's
reputation and to protect its possessions: a chronicle of the abbots

59. On the composition of the *Deeds of the Archbishops of Rouen*, see Appendix
2 of this text.

60. Jean Laporte, ed., *Inventio et miracula sancti Vulfranni*, Mélanges de la Société de l'histoire de Normandie, 14th ser. (Rouen: A. Lestringant, 1938), 12–13,
suggests that the date for the composition of text was between 1074 and 1089. However, Elisabeth M. C. van Houts, "Historiography and Hagiography at Saint-
Wandrille: the 'Inventio et miracula sancti Vulfranni'" *Anglo-Norman Studies*, 12
(1990): 237, argues persuasively for 1053–54 as the date for the composition of most
of the text (that is, the text up to the *miracula*).

61. On the annals, see Laporte, *Annales de Jumièges*, 10, and the *Libellus: PL*,
151:701–24. The treatise was written for an Abbot William. Since it speaks of William of Volpiano as being of blessed memory, the William in question must be
William of Rots, abbot of Fécamp from 1079 to 1107. However, there is no mention
of any duke later than Robert the Magnificent, although he is mentioned largely as
a way of marking the death of William of Volpiano.

62. See Sally Vaughn, *The Abbey of Bec and the Anglo-Norman State, 1034–1136*
(Woodbridge, Suffolk: Boydell, 1981), 134–43. For the Latin text of the *Liberty of
the Monastery of Bec [De libertate monasterii Beccensi]*, see J. Mabillon, *Annales ordinis
sancti Benedicti* (Paris: Leonardo Venturini, 1740), 5:601–5.

of the monastery and the monastery's cartulary were begun during his reign.[63] Finally, the history of the monastery, written in the vernacular by William of Saint-Paer, was composed during Robert's rule and probably by his direction.[64] The charters show that Robert had a healthy respect for the importance of Mont Saint-Michel as a shrine, and the history was intended for the consumption of the pilgrims to the shrine.[65]

Norman institutions naturally also produced biographies of their illustrious figures. Within the circle of Bec, a number of abbots were commemorated, although these lives, generally written considerably after the deaths of their subjects, were not always composed in Normandy. The *Vita Herluini* of Gilbert Crispin was not written until some time between 1109 and 1117.[66] The *Vita Lanfranci* (the life attributed to Miles Crispin) was written much later, probably between 1140 and 1156. The lives of William and Boso, which are ascribed with greater certainty to Miles Crispin, were probably written about the same time.[67] No Norman life of Anselm was written, although Eadmer's biography was known there. Around 1150, the *Chronicon Beccense,* a monastic history, was begun. While not divided by the reign of individual abbots nor strictly concerned with them, the focus on the history of the mon-

---

63. For Robert's influence on literary culture at Mont Saint-Michel, see A. Dufief, "La Vie monastique au Mont Saint-Michel pendant le XIIᵉ siècle (1085–1186)," *Millénaire monastique du Mont Saint-Michel* (Paris: Bibliothèque d'histoire et d'archéologie chrétiennes, 1967), 1:125. On the abbots, see Rob. of Tor., 2: xvi–xvii. The first part of this work is also sometimes attributed to Robert. On the cartulary, see ibid., 2: xvii; also, Dufief, "La Vie monastique," 121.

64. Dufief, "La Vie monastique," 122–23. William only says that he wrote under Robert, but Robert cannot have been ignorant of his undertaking. See P. Redlich, *Der Roman du Mont Saint Michel von Guillaume de Saint-Paier* (Marberg: N. G. Elwert, 1894).

65. Dufief, "La Vie monastique," 119–20. Robert built a new complex of buildings on the south side of the monastery, which included a hostelry and infirmary.

66. Margaret T. Gibson, *Lanfranc of Bec* (Oxford: Oxford University Press, 1978), 195. For the text, see J. Armitage Robinson, *Gilbert Crispin,* 87–110. The second life of Herluin is based on it (Gibson, *Lanfranc,* 196).

67. For the Lanfranc life, see Gibson, *Lanfranc,* 196. For the text, see *PL,* 150:29–58. On William and Boso, see Vaughn, *The Abbey of Bec,* 117–133 for a discussion and translation of the lives. For the Latin texts, see *PL,* 150:29–58, 713–32.

astery meant that the abbots played an important role. In at least one version of the manuscript, the scribe replaced the portion of the chronicle covering the years 1034 to 1149 with the longer lives of the abbots, suggesting that in his mind the two works shared a central subject.[68] The same manuscript also contains a metrical history of the first seven abbots of Bec by Peter of Saint-Pierre-sur-Dives, written at the behest of Miles Crispin.[69]

A number of biographical works about local figures were also produced for Savigny, in the second half of the twelfth century. Stephen of Fougéres, the bishop of Rennes, wrote a life of Savigny's founder Vitalis, around 1168. Stephen, like Dudo of Saint-Quentin and William of Poitiers, had been a ducal chaplain and treasurer; he signed one of the charters he attested as "the precentor of Mortain," which was a collegiate church in the Avranchin not far from Savigny at which Vitalis had been a canon. Stephen also composed a biography of another local hermit, William Firmat (d.c. 1090), whose body was buried at Mortain. The biography of Vitalis was followed by a life of the second abbot, Geoffrey (d. 1139), written by a resident of the house.[70] Other lives of other local saints, such as Peter of Avranches and Haimo of Savigny, followed at the end of the century.[71] The beginning of this flowering coin-

68. L'Abbé Porée, *Chronique du Bec et Chronique de François Carré* (Rouen: Métérie, 1883), xviii; Porée offers an edition of the chronicle from 1149. See also *PL* 150:639ff., which contains the Achéry edition of a version of the chronicle from 1034 (but see also Porée, 119f. for the interpolations in the chronicle). On this text, see also Gibson, *Lanfranc of Bec*, 200.

69. *PL* 181:1709–18.

70. *Vitae Vitalis et Gaufridi*, ed. E. P. Sauvage, in *Analecta Bollandiana* 1 (1882): 355–410. *Vita Willelmi, AA SS* April, 3:336–43. For Stephen's obituary, see Rob. of Tor., 2:73–74. On Mortain, see *GC*, 11:511. For mention of Stephen in Henry II's charters, see R. W. Eyton, *Court, Household, and Itinerary of King Henry II* (London: Taylor & Co., 1878), 30, 53, 88, 92. For Stephen as bishop of Rennes, see *GC* 14:750–51. Although some scholars attributed the life of Geoffrey to Stephen as well, Sauvage argues that it must have been written by one of the brethren.

71. On Haimo and Peter, see *Analecta Bollandiana* 2 (1889): 475–560. The extant chronicle of Savigny appears to date from the thirteenth century at the earliest (see Étienne Baluze, *Stepheni Baluzii miscellaneorum, hoc est, collectio veterum monumentorum quae hactenus latuerant in variis codicibus ac bibliothecis* (Paris: F. Muguet, 1678–1715), 1:326–29.

cides with the long reign of Abbot Serlo (1140–84) under whose direction Savigny formally joined the Cistercian order and amassed considerable property.[72]

Finally, monks at many of the Norman houses wrote lives of locally important saints from the more remote past.

℺

From a distance, Norman historical writing seems to be well distributed across the two centuries of its production. No one center dominated the writing of history and although most historians were monks, secular clerics also wrote a few histories. However, at closer range, it is clear that the writing of history was more episodic, appearing at certain nodes of time and only in certain places. Dudo of Saint-Quentin's history was written when Richard I and Richard II were just in the process of extending their authority from the Seine valley and eastern Normandy into the west, organizing monastic reform, and monopolizing the Norman episcopate.[73] Similarly, the *Deeds of the Dukes* and the *Deeds of William* were both written in a similar node of increasing ducal authority in the period between 1050 and 1075 under the Conqueror. In times when ducal power contracted, little history was written in Normandy. Between 1026 and 1050, Richard III, Robert I, and William II were forced to contend with periodic rebellions against their authority, often led by their kin.[74] The work of Orderic Vitalis also exemplifies this trend. The *Ecclesiastical History* was begun and mostly written during the reign of Henry I who restored an order threatened during the reign of his brother, Robert II (1087–1106).[75]

---

72. See *GC*, 1:544–46.

73. The ducal family dominated the episcopate for most of the eleventh century, beginning with Robert (archbishop of Rouen, c. 990–1037), Richard I's son, who was succeeded at Rouen by his nephew Mauger, while Hugh the son of Raoul d'Ivry, Richard I's half-brother, became bishop of Bayeux. See Bates, *Normandy before 1066*, 100, and for noble control of the episcopacy more generally, see Bernard Guillemain, "Les Origines des évêques en France aux XI^c et XII^c siècles," in *Le istituzioni ecclesiastiche della "societas christiana" dei secoli XI–XII* (Miscellanea del centro di studi medioevali, VII) (Milan: Vita e Pensiero, 1974): 374–402.

74. *GND*, 98, 100, 103.

75. Robert's financial problems must have had something to do with the weak-

I am not arguing here that Norman historical writing was always part of the aftermath of crisis but that it was frequently a byproduct of crisis. Sometimes, histories were written in the midst of the crisis itself, like the *Norman Dragon*, which was composed during the Becket controversy, the struggle between Henry II and Louis VII over Henry's refusal to permit his sons to do homage, and a papal schism. Sometimes they appeared just before a crisis, like Robert of Torigni's redaction of the *Deeds of the Dukes*, produced in the uneasy days after Henry I's death when his daughter Matilda and her husband Geoffrey Plantagenet of Anjou were already troubling the Norman-Angevin border but before civil war had broken out. Crises produce change which is particularly difficult, as S. N. Eisenstadt has argued, for traditional societies to cope with since such societies often conceive of themselves as essentially unchanging. While change may be physically resisted, people may also reconsider or reiterate their traditions or even create new traditions.[76]

During periods of political crisis in Normandy, the authority of the duke tended to become weaker and the power of the Norman elite stronger. For example, the period of unrest between 1026 and 1050 saw the appearance of new elite families. Castle-building (although a more marked activity at the end of the eleventh century), feuding, and private wars all characterize the period. In these chaotic circumstances, the Church suffered particularly because of the inability of the duke to enforce the peace.[77] The reign of Robert

---

ness of his reign. Robert had access only to resources in Normandy, not to the riches of England. The monks of Saint-Pierre-sur-Dives in the diocese of Sées indignantly recorded in their cartulary that he sold the abbacy to Robert of Saint-Denis, "more a thief and a robber than an abbot" (*Gallia christiana*, 11, *Instrumenta*, 155). Unlike his parents and other predecessors, Robert did not become a great ecclesiastical patron (see Musset, "Le Mécénat des princes normands," 129). On the character of Robert's reign, see Bates, *Normandy before 1066*, 169; David Bates, "Normandy and England after 1066," *English Historical Review* 104 (1989) 868; Marjorie Chibnall, *The World of Orderic Vitalis* (Cambridge: Cambridge University Press, 1984), 28; *EH*, 4:146.

76. Eisenstadt, "Dynamics of Traditions," 452, 458ff.

77. On the new elite families, see Bates, *Normandy before 1066*, 99–100; on castles,

Curthose and the Anarchy (at least from 1138 to 1144 when Geoffrey Plantagenet of Anjou conquered Normandy in the name of his son, the future Henry II) again destabilized Norman institutions. The great histories of Normandy, which are closely associated with ducal power, appeared before and after these crises were resolved but not during them.

More local crises also generated historical writing, however. Many of the monastic annals and histories were written between 1066 and 1106, a period when the archbishops of Rouen were extending their authority over monastic Normandy and diminishing its prominence in religious life. Other local histories were responses to more specific threats or needs. Saint-Wandrille was defending its claim to possess authentic relics of St. Wulfran in the *Discovery of St. Wulfran*, but a monastery might also write a text, like the *History of Mont Saint-Michel*, to attract more revenues.

Just as history was not written at just any time, it was not written in just any place. Most historical activity took place close to centers of power, specifically in the circle around the dukes of Normandy, in the monasteries the dukes had founded, and in monasteries that were enjoying growth and prosperity. Jumièges was one of the earliest ducal refoundations; it enjoyed special privileges and was richly endowed, both before the Conquest and after. Fécamp, Saint-Wandrille, and Saint-Ouen were ducal refoundations, while Caen was a new house established by William the Conqueror. Mont Saint-Michel was reformed at Richard I's initiative. Houses like these were tied to the ducal authority from which they had received so many benefits, and the histories written there defended that authority.

Even monasteries that were not ducal foundations yet produced

---

114–15, 175; on feuds, 100–101. The Bellême family also seized the see of Sées during this period. (See *Gallia christiana*, 11:680). Developments of this kind were not limited to Normandy, of course, but were part and parcel of a process of change going on throughout northern France in the eleventh century during which the elite developed a new self-consciousness; on this subject, see Georges Duby, "Lineage, Nobility, and Knighthood," and "The Structure of Kinship and Nobility," in *The Chivalrous Society*, Cynthia Postan, trans. (Berkeley and Los Angeles: University of California Press, 1977), 59–80; 134–48.

histories were closely tied to the ducal family at the time of their historical productivity. The Conqueror added to the existing property of Saint-Evroul and his wife, Matilda, financed the rebuilding of the refectory needed to accommodate the growing number of monks at that house in the late eleventh century.[78] Henry I added to the possessions of the hermitage of Savigny in 1112 when he confirmed the donations made by the founder, Ralph of Fougères. The dukes had a quasi-familial interest in Savigny in that the first abbot, Vitalis, had been the chaplain of Henry's uncle, Robert of Mortain, but this slight connection does not explain the conspicuous generosity of the ducal family throughout the twelfth century to this institution, particularly during the reign of Henry II. For the dukes, the prestige of supporting a distinguished and widely-admired house established in their domain was probably more important.[79]

At Bec this pattern is particularly striking. Bec was a notable monastery almost from its foundation because of the prominence Lanfranc and Anselm brought to it as teachers and scholars. By the fourth decade of the twelfth century, it was no longer an important center for the study of theology and logic, but the pleasant afterglow of Bec's earlier celebrity hung over the monastery. It still offered a first-rate education and significant promotional possibilities for the men who took up the religious life there, and it actually enjoyed more royal/ducal patronage in the twelfth century than in the eleventh. Monks from Bec were frequently promoted in both Normandy and England. Monks admitted by William I of Bec (1094–1124) became bishops of Bayeux and Canterbury and abbots of St. Augustine's in Canterbury, Bury St. Edmunds, Préaux, Ivry, Conches, and of Bec itself. Bec's eminence did not falter through-

---

78. *Gallia Christiana*, II:820–21; Lucien Musset, "Le Mécenat des princes normands," 128.

79. *Gallia christiana*, 542, and *Instrumenta*, III; see also Jean-Marc Bienvenu, "De L'A-sociabilité à la sociabilité: De L'Érémitisme au cénobitisme dans la France de l'ouest aux XIᶜ et XIIᶜ siècles," in *Sociabilité, pouvoirs et société* (Rouen: Université de Rouen, 1987), 526. On ducal patronage, see Francis R. Swietek, "King Henry II and Savigny," in *Cîteaux* 38 (1987): 17–19.

out the twelfth century, for Robert of Torigni took note of the twelve Norman abbots in 1180 who were former monks of Bec.[80] Not surprisingly under these circumstances, Bec became prosperous. It acquired substantial properties in England, and Henry I and his daughter the "Empress" Matilda (d. 1167) were also important patrons of the monastery.[81] This seems to have been part of the pattern of ducal investment in the Risle valley and its tributaries, for the dukes also became patrons at Lyre which had close ties with Bec and Saint-Evroul.[82]

Thus historical writing occurred at the nexus of economic power, political authority, and literacy. The dukes of Normandy provided the center where power was most concentrated. Monasteries and bishoprics were centers of power in their own right, although they depended on the strength of that political center for protection. They requited that support in a number of different ways, but one of these was through the skills monopolized by the clergy, the writing of Latin texts. The most active centers of production were, not surprisingly, those with the most to lose. In that sense, Karl Morrison is correct that historical writing in the Middle Ages was about the realities of power, although that is probably true of all historical writing.[83]

The pattern of historical writing in Normandy raises the question of whether Normandy was typical of other territorial principalities in its production of history. Anjou makes a particularly

80. See *Gallia Christiana*, 11:227. For the shift in patronage at Bec, see Marjorie Chibnall, "The Empress Matilda and Bec-Hellouin," *Anglo-Norman Studies* 10 (1988): 36–37; Rob. of Tor., 2:90.

81. While Robert Curthose claimed authority over the house (at the request of the monks), the closer relationship dated from the beginning of the twelfth century. See Chibnall, "Matilda and Bec-Hellouin," 36–38. For Bec, see Donald Matthew, *The Norman Monasteries and Their English Possessions* (Oxford: Oxford University Press, 1962), 14. On Bec's English lands, see M. Morgan, *The English Lands of the Abbey of Bec* (London: Oxford University Press, 1946).

82. *Gallia christiana*, 11:644.

83. Karl Morrison, *History as a Visual Art*, 20, and elsewhere.

useful comparison, because as neighbors, the fortunes of Normandy and Anjou were tied together even before they were united under one ruler in 1144. Anjou coalesced as a county in the tenth century (about the same time as Normandy) through the efforts of counts Fulk the Good (942–60), Geoffrey Greymantle (960–987), and Fulk Nerra (987–1040). The relatively smooth upward ride of the counts was somewhat interrupted during the reign of Geoffrey Martel (1040–1060) who was in conflict with Henry I of France during the early part of his reign. This was followed by a civil struggle between Geoffrey Martel's nephews over the title which left Anjou considerably weakened, a situation from which the county did not recover in the eleventh century, although the authority of the counts was on the increase during the last years of Count Fulk le Réchin's life (d. 1109).[84] The counts also struggled against the bishops of Angers. The early history of the counts was one of struggle against the viscomital family that controlled the bishopric. However, during the second part of the eleventh century, the counts and bishops cooperated effectively.[85]

Like the dukes of Normandy, the counts of Anjou also created new monasteries and tried to dominate the old. Saint-Trinité of Vendôme was founded by Geoffrey Martel. The counts had a peculiarly strong hold on Saint-Aubin of Angers (although that hold declined over the course of the eleventh century), a repository of important records, and Saint-Florent in Saumur. Although the counts of Anjou did not originally control Marmoutier, when they acquired control of the Touraine in the late eleventh century, their influence over that monastery began to grow, as did the influence of Marmoutier over Angevin houses.[86] The power of the counts over their monasteries showed a similar pattern of reform introduced by the counts in the tenth century, followed by a decline of their power over their monasteries in the eleventh, and a rebuilding and extension of their power in the twelfth.[87]

---

84. Guillot, *Le Comte d'Anjou*, 1:124. 85. Ibid., 1:196–97.
86. Ibid., 1:173ff. 87. Ibid., 1:128, 162.

The first Angevin histories were composed in the last quarter of the eleventh century or in the early twelfth century beginning with the "annals of Renaud," which were continued to 1106.[88] These annals were probably contemporaneous with the annals of Saint-Trinité de Vendôme, with which they share a now lost source.[89] The later annals, written at various sites in Anjou, depend on these earlier texts.[90] Thus the earliest Angevin annalistic activity occurred at roughly the same time or perhaps a little later than that in Normandy and, as in Normandy, corresponded to political developments.

County history was also slightly retarded in Anjou compared to Normandy. The first history of Anjou proper, however, was written by Count Fulk le Réchin himself.[91] The Angevin tradition also contained an on-going history of the counts that was continually rewritten, the *Deeds of the Consuls of Anjou [Gesta consulum Andegavorum]*, which survives in five redactions. Much of this production is associated in the twelfth century with Marmoutier, which seems to have played the same role in Anjou that Bec played in Normandy as a center of historical writing and records.[92] Thus the

88. On this text, see Louis Halphen, *Recueil d'annales angevines et vendomoises* (Paris: Picard, 1903), xxxii–xxxiii. One of the manuscripts of the text was clearly drawn up at Saint-Maurice, but Halphen argues that there is no evidence to suggest that Renaud was working there. However, see also Bezzola, *La Formation de la littérature courtoise*, 2:327.

89. The source was probably composed at Saint-Maurice in Angers (the cathedral) around 1075 (Halphen, *Recueil*, xl ff.).

90. Annals were composed at Saint-Aubin of Angers, at Saint-Serge in Angers, and Saint-Florent in Saumur; the Saint-Aubin annals were copied several times. See Halphen, *Recueil*, vi, also xxii, for the *stemma codicum*.

91. Bernard Bachrach has speculated, perhaps correctly, that the Angevin family was already fairly literate in the tenth century. Bachrach, *Fulk Nerra, the Neo-Roman Consul, 987–1040: A Political Biography of the Angevin Count* (Berkeley and Los Angeles: University of California Press, 1993), 20–21. For Fulk's history, see Louis Halphen, *Chroniques des comtes d'Anjou et des seigneurs d'Amboise* (Paris: Picard, 1913), lxxxix–xc.

92. The surviving first redaction was by Thomas of Loches, chancellor to Fulk the Young (1109–29) and Geoffrey Plantagenet (1129–51). Another was composed between 1155 and 1173 by Breton d'Amboise, who was probably a canon of Saint-Florentin d'Amboise; it was written for Henry II, who was also the patron of Hugh

pattern of historical production looks rather similar for the counts
of Anjou and the dukes of Normandy. Norman historical production was spread out over a greater period and began earlier, but
Angevins wrote history in great quantity during the period in
which their counts were in the ascendent.

The counts of Flanders, who were also among the great lords
of the tenth century, patronized history early through the great
monastery of Saint-Bertin. There a priest named Witger composed
a genealogy for Arnulf of Flanders, a contemporary of William
Longsword of Normandy, between 951 and 959. In the twelfth century, there was a thriving production of comital history for the
counts of Louvain and Hainault as well as for the counts of Flanders.[93] Thus, historical writing appeared early in counties that
formed in the tenth century and maintained some territorial stability. It may also be significant that in the counties that produced
history, one lineage managed to remain in power over the course
of several centuries.

The pattern in Normandy, Anjou, and Flanders is at odds with
what happened in other counties. Some, like Berry and Picardy,
were fragmented for a long time.[94] In the linked counties of Blois/
Chartres and Champagne, the counts struggled to build their territories. Champagne developed later than some other counties,
consisting for a long time of a collection of rights and holdings
rather than a formal territorial base.[95] Nor did the counts have a

---

de Cleriis, the author of a treatise on the office of Seneschal of France, c. 1158. Two
versions of the history of the counts were produced by Jean of Marmoutier, along
with a biography of Geoffrey Plantagenet. For these texts, see Halphen, *Chroniques
d'Anjou*, vii–xlvi.

93. For this period, see Bezzola, *La Formation de la littérature courtoise*, pt. 3, 2:
408ff. Lambert of Saint-Omer wrote a genealogy c. 1120 of the counts; an anonymous writer produced a poetic genealogy for Charles the Good (d. 1127). Lambert's work was continued at Saint-Bertin after 1164 *(Flandria generosa)*, and this
later text was itself continued. Galbert of Bruges's account of the murder of Charles
the Good is only one of three extant narratives.

94. Elizabeth Hallam, *Capetian France, 987–1328* (London: Longman, 1980),
27–28.

95. Bur, *Comté de Champagne*, 311.

single set of rights in the county; these varied regionally.[96] In addition, the joined counties underwent a major crisis in mid-eleventh century. Part of the cause was the partition of the patrimony into two parts in 1034. Another was the alliance between Henry I of France and the counts of Anjou against the counts of Blois and Champagne.[97]

Whether this late formation was the reason or not, the counts of Blois and Champagne were not celebrated in any dynastic histories and its members mostly appear as side figures in the histories of others.[98] William the Conqueror's daughter, Adela, who married Stephen of Blois in 1081, was the recipient of numerous poetic and historical tributes, but many of these were framed with reference to her father rather than to her husband.[99] The later counts of Champagne, although important literary patrons, were not, apparently, patrons of history.[100]

Similarly, the dukes of Aquitaine and counts of Poitou, although powerful lords and sponsors of educational reform, were not patrons of historical writing and, one might argue, for similar reasons. Indeed, the first important historical work produced south of the Loire was the chronicle of Adémar of Chabannes, who wrote at Limoges in the 1030s.[101]

Thus, Norman historical writing grew out of Normandy's stability as a community. History appeared early in Normandy because Normandy coalesced as a political and social unit before many other French counties. History was written at the institutions with the most at stake in the economic and political stability of the county. When other counties achieved the same level of sta-

96. Ibid., 332–41.
97. On this crisis, see Bur, *Comté de Champagne,* 193–230.
98. Ibid., 479–86. This happened despite a well-established tradition of historical writing at Reims in the ninth and tenth centuries, which was, however, carried out under the auspices of the archbishops.
99. On Adela's patronage, see Bezzola, *La Formation de la littérature courtoise,* 2:370f.
100. See John Benton, "The Court of Champagne as a Literary Center," *Speculum* 36 (1961): 551–91.
101. Bezzola, *La Formation de la littérature courtoise,* 2:256–58.

bility, their rulers often became patrons of history as well. While by the thirteenth century, less powerful members of the elite would also become patrons of history, during the eleventh and twelfth centuries, the patronage of history was primarily confined to the families of the great territorial princes and the ecclesiastical centers that flourished under their aegis.

2   The Norman Comedy

*A*lthough Norman institutions produced a variety of histories, the great eleventh-century narratives of ducal and
provincial history were the works that helped shape how
all Norman writers thought about the past. Their power
resulted not only from their temporal priority but also
from the compelling stories they told about that past and
the meaning with which they filled it. For all historians
writing in the eleventh century, Norman history was a
comedy. However, they differed as to how that comedy
ought to be understood.[1] Some of these differences arose

1. Hayden White, *Metahistory: The Historical Imagination in Nineteenth-Century Europe* (Baltimore, Md.: Johns Hopkins, 1973), 7–11,
drawing on the work of Northrup Frye, suggested that modern historical writing uses four basic emplotments—comedy, tragedy, satire,
and romance—and their possible combinations. While White's work
primarily treats nineteenth-century historians, he stipulates that his real
concerns are the larger questions of historical knowledge (1). Moreover,
he suggests (although not explicitly) that only a few emplotments are
available (Frye was more categorical on this point). It is possible to fit
most medieval historical works into White's schema. For example, Dudo
of Saint-Quentin's *Customs* can be read as a comic romance. How-

from the differing ideologies of the historians (using that term in the broadest sense), but other variations arose from their preferences for one of the several modes of reading practiced in the Middle Ages. These diverse ways of reading texts presupposed rather distinct forms of historical argumentation.[2]

Medieval readers were trained through the dominant program of religious reading to read stories in four basic ways, literally *(historaliter)*, allegorically *(allegorice)*, tropologically *(moraliter)*, and anagogically *(mystice)*, that is, according to the letter of the text, with attention to recursive patterns and correspondences with other narratives, for moral and exemplary meaning, and for clues to divinity. Of these four, the first three were primary. While all three were theoretically possible for any scriptural text, in practice not all texts were easily read in all possible ways.[3] Each of these modes of reading produced its own kind of meaning. Hugh of Saint-Victor talks about those types of meaning as letter, sense,

---

ever, other aspects of White's analysis of modern historical writing do not fit well with medieval texts, particularly his linking of certain ideological stances with each type of plot.

2. White, *Metahistory*, 29–31, suggests that certain ideological stances have an affinity with certain plots and certain modes of argumentation so that ideology, plot, and argumentation all work together to produce meaning. For example, liberals are drawn to write satiric histories, radicals tragic history. Similarly, liberals are drawn to contextualist argument and radicals to mechanistic modes of explanation. These modern ideologies have no strict medieval counterparts.

3. On these ways of reading, see Erich Auerbach, "'*Figura*'" in *Scenes from the Drama of European Literature* (New York: Meridian, 1959), esp. 28ff.; see also Beryl Smalley, *The Study of the Bible in the Middle Ages*, 3d ed. (Oxford: Blackwells, 1983), 2–3 (on allegory). When Hugh of Saint-Victor talked about the three-fold ways of understanding scripture, he named history, allegory, and tropology (Hugh of Saint-Victor, *Hugonis de Sancto Victore Didascalicon de Studio Legendi*, ed. Charles Henry Buttimer [Washington, D.C.: The Catholic University of America Press, 1939], 95, 5:2). In his own discussion of the ark of Noah, Hugh separated these three modes of understanding from the fourth, the mystical understanding (Mary Carruthers, *The Book of Memory: A Study of Memory in Medieval Culture* [Cambridge: Cambridge University Press, 1990], 44). On the problem of reading texts on different levels, Hugh commented that while it was possible to read some texts in all three ways, it could not be done in every case. God was like a fine musician who used different effects, so that some works needed to be read in a spiritual manner and others in a literal or moral way (*Didascalicon*, pp. 95–96, 5:2).

and sentence. As Hugh reminded his readers, the point of reading was not to consider the words of scripture but to arrive at the meaning, the *res* of which the words were only a sign.[4]

I doubt that medieval readers abandoned these biblical modes of reading when they approached other kinds of texts. Certainly the Norman historians wrote narratives that, while they might be read in more than one mode, were each best suited to be read in one of the three. Which of the three each historian chose reflected the ways in which he thought history had meaning; in other words, to select the way one wanted one's history to be read amounted to a kind of historical argument. The manner of reading the historian preferred depended on what each historian felt to be the "big story" of his time, itself a function of particular historical circumstances. The force of each narrative depended not only on the uses to which each story and each mode of reading might be put but also on the degree to which each historian was able to render his narrative coherent.

The story Dudo of Saint-Quentin told about the Norman past in his *Customs of the Dukes* was an old but extremely powerful one: a people chosen by God won with God's help a kingdom of their own. This romance was one of the plots of Jewish scripture and had a secular variant in the *Aeneid*. It was also the basic plot of ecclesiastical history as chronicled by Eusebius in his *Ecclesiastical History* and as applied to the Anglo-Saxons in Bede's *Ecclesiastical History of the English People*.[5] The Norman dukes, like the Hebrew rulers of old, had to lead their people both into the promised land and out of paganism, and like their ancient predecessors, the dukes found the former task easier than the latter. Thus Norman history was allegorically prefigured in the experiences of other peoples.

Although Dudo wrote a serial biography, his history escaped the episodic qualities of that form through its strong teleology and emphatic closure. First, he described the dukes as representing a progression of merits. Hasting, the first, was an unregenerate pa-

4. Hugh of Saint-Victor, *Didascalicon*, 126–29 (6:9–11), 96 (5:3).
5. On comedy and romance, see White, *Metahistory*, 8–10.

gan. Although employed by God as a scourge, Hasting was divinely prevented from establishing a permanent Viking settlement. Rollo, his successor, was one of God's elect; although his baptism came, like Constantine's, toward the end of his life, he received divine assistance throughout his career. William Longsword, the third duke, became a powerful patron of the Church, but he was murdered before he could establish either order within Normandy or autonomy in relation to the duchy's French enemies. His son Richard the Fearless, however, was able to pacify all the warring elements of his society, to complete the conversion of his people to Christianity, and to create for Normandy an oasis of peace.

In addition to this linear progression, a subtle system of correspondences bound the biographies together so that the process of allegorical reading took place not only between the *Customs* and its antecedent text but within the *Customs* itself. Dudo arranged the four books of the *Customs of the Dukes* into two pairs of biographies in which the first prefigured the second, which represented both the recapitulation and the fulfillment of the first.

Dudo began his narrative of Hasting's career with his expulsion from Denmark. Polygamy has caused overpopulation, which requires a portion of the youth to become Vikings.[6] Hasting first devastates France, meeting little effective opposition. Acquiring ambition as a result, Hasting then decides to conquer Rome. Landing at the city of Luna, which he mistakes for Rome, Hasting discovers that he is unable to take it by force. Instead, he employs guile; pretending to be dying, he asks to be baptized. He then has his armed men carry in his "corpse" on a bier for burial in the city. Once inside, the Vikings slaughter the unprepared citizens. Enraged when he discovers he has not captured Rome after all, Hasting returns to France, but he no longer prospers. He last appears in the *Customs* fighting on the side of the French against Rollo and losing.[7]

Rollo's career also begins with his expulsion from Denmark, but

6. *De moribus,* 129, 130.
7. On the siege of Luna: ibid., 132–5; Hasting's last battle: 154–6.

unlike Hasting, Rollo resists this forceable ejection. Like the citizens of Luna, he is defeated by trickery.[8] A divine message then tells him to go to England. The English quite naturally assume that this Viking has come to attack them, although Rollo has no such intention. He is forced to defend himself and through his fortitude is able to make peace with and win himself a powerful ally in King Athelstan. Athelstan offers Rollo both baptism and a share of his kingdom, but Rollo, aware that his destiny lies elsewhere, refuses both offers and leaves for France.[9] He is accepted peacefully into Rouen, but the French leadership attacks his stronghold continually. Rollo responds by rampaging through France until the French are forced to come to terms with him. The king cedes him Normandy and Brittany.

As Rollo is an inversion of Hasting, so the career Dudo ascribes to Rollo is an inversion of that of Hasting, both in its general features and in certain specific events. For example, Hasting's siege of Luna is twice recapitulated by Rollo. The first time is when Rollo is at the court of King Athelstan. When Rollo sends emissaries to the king, his envoys use the same language as Hasting's envoys to Luna.[10] In both cases, the messengers announce the peaceable intentions of their lord. Rollo's messengers are, however, telling the truth. While Hasting requests baptism from the citizens of Luna, Athelstan initiates the proposal that Rollo accept baptism. Hasting seizes by force and blasphemy from Luna what Athelstan freely offers and Rollo piously refuses. Finally, Hasting's capture of Luna also prefigures, again in an inverted form, Rollo's recep-

8. Ibid., 142–43. In Dudo's account, Rollo is a Dane, although our best evidence suggests he was Norwegian. Searle, "Fact and Pattern in Heroic History," 125, suggests that this change of ethnicity is deliberate on Dudo's part, so as to associate Rollo with the Danish Norman chieftains of western Normandy in the tenth century. It is an elegant suggestion.

9. Ibid., 145, 147–48.

10. Cf. *De moribus*, 133, "Vestram urbem nec ferro depopulari, nec praedas venimus pagi vestri ad naves nostras deducere. Non nobis ea vis tot periculis fatigatis. Sequestram nobis pacem, precamur, date; quae nobis necessaria sunt liceat emere" with *De moribus*, 147, "Non autem regnum tuum depopulabimus, nec praedas usquam raptas ad naves vertemus. Vendendi atque emendi sequestram pacem petimus." The gist of both speeches comes from the *Aeneid*.

tion into Rouen. Rouen throws open its gates to Rollo, whereas Luna resists Hasting, but Dudo in his narrative had something more in mind. Whereas Hasting thinks he has come to Rome but has not, Rollo does comes to a new Rome (the etymology of *Rodomus*, one of Rouen's Latin names, was often given as *domus Romanorum*, the home of the Romans). Rollo dies as ruler of this new Rome, while Hasting dies not even possessed of a false Rome.[11]

The third and fourth books of the *Customs* employ more parallelisms of this sort, not, however, to demonstrate the differing moral worth of William Longsword and Richard the Fearless, who were both Christian leaders and God-fearing men. Instead, Dudo contrasts them to illustrate their progress in eradicating paganism and establishing Norman autonomy. In this task, Richard was more successful than his father.

Dudo cast William Longsword, who was venerated as a martyr in Normandy, in the mold of the *puer senex,* a common type of holy man in the late Carolingian period. William's sanctity and chastity are apparent from his early childhood, and he is so committed to the latter that he must be forced by his followers to marry so as to produce an heir.[12] Wishing to be "peaceable and well-intentioned in all things," William prefers to negotiate rather than to use force.[13] In other words, William interprets his Christian obligations to mean that he must conform to monastic canons of behavior. This interpretation of his duty nearly destroys Normandy and ultimately brings about William's own death.

The stories Dudo relates about William illustrate this point over and over again. For example, in William's first test as duke, he is confronted by a rebellion against his authority. Unwilling to use force against Rioul, the leader of the rebels, William tries instead to negotiate, a tactic Rioul interprets as weakness. Indeed, William goes so far as to decide to flee Normandy; on hearing this sugges-

---

11. When he asks the soldiers of Rollo's band whether they have ever heard of a Viking named Hasting, they answer that he began well but came to a bad end (*De moribus*, 154).

12. Ibid., 179–80, 185.   13. Ibid., 188.

tion, one of his followers, Bernard the Dane, not only refuses to accompany him but accuses him of effeminacy. William is so enraged by the accusation that he charges into battle with only three hundred followers; he nonetheless wins a stunning victory over the rebels. Immediately after the victory, William receives tidings of the birth of his son Richard.[14]

This story addresses most of the themes that run through the second part of the *Customs*. Rioul's pretext for rebellion is that William is spending too much time with his French relatives. However, Dudo also makes explicit reference to Gideon's victory over the Amalekites in his poem commemorating William's triumph over Rioul; since the Amalekites were gentiles, Dudo subtly suggests that Rioul and his followers were pagan.[15] This linkage between participation in the French world and conversion to Christianity appears elsewhere in the *Customs*. Dudo plays with this theme in the second book by granting Archbishop Franco of Rouen—the name emphasizing his French ethnicity—a role that he did not play historically in the conversion of the Normans.[16]

For Dudo, there was no shame in the Normans learning their Christianity from the French. However, other features of French character were distasteful. For example, the effeminacy and martial inadequacy of which Bernard accuses William go together in the French make-up. In Dudo's equation, martial prowess equals sexual prowess. Hence William's unwillingness to take up his arms is the counterpart of his chastity, which is a form of effeminacy in

14. Ibid., 188–91.

15. Ibid., 191; Judg. 6–8. Later in the text, Dudo comments that William "led pagans and unbelievers by his gifts and words to the cult of the truth faith," (193). While converting pagans is praiseworthy, however, one cannot stop with words. Richard I, who is for Dudo more perfect than his father, is willing to attack those who will not convert; when the persistent pagans lose, they must then go elsewhere (286–87).

16. See Olivier Guillot, "La Conversion des Normands peu après 911," *Cahiers de civilisation médiévales* 14 (1981): 200f. Franco was a bishop of Rouen, but sometime after 909, not between 876 and 911 as Dudo has it. The entire role Franco plays in Dudo's narrative, Guillot concludes, is a symbolic fiction.

the eyes of the Normans. It is no coincidence, then, that when William Longsword has proven his manhood in battle against Rioul, he receives a second gauge of his manhood: the birth of his son. In the anecdote which follows his account of Rioul's rebellion, Dudo elaborates upon this association between sexual and military prowess. When William of Poitou asks to marry William Longsword's sister, the Norman duke jokingly refuses because the Poitevins "are fearful and incompetent at arms."[17] The implication is that William of Poitou will also be sexually incompetent.

What helps to produce William Longsword's confusion about how he ought to behave is that he is convinced that there is only one appropriate kind of Christian behavior, the monastic life for which he longs. Martin, the abbot of Jumièges, explains to him when he expresses a desire to enter that monastery that the demands of the theoretical life and of the practical life are different and that one born to the latter should not seek to enter the former. William, however, refuses to listen.[18] William sees his efforts to make peace with Rioul without bloodshed as part of his Christian duty but as one born to the practical life and secular office, William would better fulfill his Christian duty by conquering pagans.

William Longsword's incomprehension of the gulf that separated the Christian ruler from the monk shapes his actions throughout the third book. After his victory over Rioul, when the duke comes to act as intermediary between the German emperor and French king, he comes without the display and magnificence appropriate to such an occasion. For this he is mocked by the Saxons present at the council. William's Norman soldiers, who cannot take such ridicule lightly, begin a destructive rampage that threatens to undermine the talks. When William sends an emissary to command his troops to stop, they refuse to listen, but when he sends his envoy back carrying the duke's sword as a badge, his men go meekly back to their barracks. The sword has a golden hilt and is studded with gold knobs and gems, so William has both made up for his initial lack of display and made manifest the symbol of his

---

17. *De moribus*, 192.   18. Ibid., 201.

authority, his "long sword."[19] Far from abandoning desires in-
appropriate for his station, however, William subsequently announces his intention to become a monk at Jumièges. This un-
seemly desire, this "unheard of and monstrous proposal," threatens to leave Normandy without a defender.[20]

William's humility and peaceableness set in motion the events
leading to his death. When Arnulf of Flanders proposes that the
hostilities between them be resolved by a peace parley between the
two men, William embraces the opportunity because "no offering
is so acceptable to God as the increase of peace." Because he meets
with Arnulf at a place and time of Arnulf's choosing, Arnulf is
easily able to arrange to murder William.[21]

Some of Dudo's clerical contemporaries would have seen a ruler
like William Longsword as ideal, incorporating into secular life the
mitigation of violence that the Church had already begun to preach
in Dudo's lifetime as the Peace and Truce of God. Odo of Cluny
(d. 942) wrote in praise of Count Gerald of Aurillac (d. 909), who
like William Longsword embraced peace, charity, and celibacy in
lay life and longed for the monastery. Dudo's ideas about peace,
however, do not derive from the Peace of God, which was not
promulgated in Normandy or Vermandois until the mid-eleventh
century. Nor did he share the Cluniac view of appropriate lay conduct, even though his stay in Normandy overlapped with that of
William of Volpiano. Dudo's ideas about the responsibilities of the
Christian ruler were more in line with Carolingian than Cluniac
sensibilities. For Dudo, William's espousal of monastic ideals prevented him from carrying out his primary duties—the strengthening of the Church, the extirpation of heresy and paganism, the
promotion of justice, and the maintenance of the peace—all of
which demanded a certain bellicosity.[22]

---

19. Ibid., 197.   20. Ibid., 201–2.

21. For the quotation, see ibid, 206; for William's betrayal and death, see ibid,
202–2, 207–8.

22. On the Peace and Truce of God in Normandy, see J.-F. Lemarignier, "Paix
et réforme monastique en Flandre et en Normandie autour de l'année 1023: Quelques observations," in *Droit privé et institutions régionales. Études historiques offertes*

Just as Rollo's life corrects the errors and excesses of Hastings's, so Richard's life is a commentary on and correction of the errors of William's. The first part of the fourth book of the *Customs* addresses the consequences of William's disastrous piety. Richard I, still a minor at the time of his father's murder, is for a time a hostage in the hands of Louis IV of France, and Normandy nearly loses its independence. Considerable Norman guile is necessary to save the situation. Bernard the Dane reappears in this part of the narrative, again embodying the true Norman spirit as the wily negotiator who foils Louis IV's designs on Normandy and who forces the king to recognize Richard as the duke of Normandy.[23]

The much different character of Richard's rule is apparent from the moment he begins to rule in his own right. Richard's first challenge after assuming his authority, like William's, is to deal with a potential usurper, Raoul Torta. Rather than permitting Raoul the initiative, Richard seeks out Raoul, escalating his demands for concessions until he forces Raoul and his family to go into exile. His decisiveness is a warning to his followers, who "seeing that he had so prudently exiled the leader of the army, feared him greatly."[24] Richard's aggressiveness produces the peace that William's tractability could not.

à Jean Yver (Paris: Presses Universitaires de France, 1976), 443–68. See also Michel de Boüard, "Sur les origines de la trêve de Dieu en Normandie," *Annales de Normandie* 9 (1959): 169–89 and M. R. Bonnaud-Delamare, "Les Institutions de Paix dans la province ecclésiastique de Reims au XIᵉ siècle," *Bulletin philologique et historique du comité des travaux historiques et scientifiques* (1955–56): 143–200. On the Peace of God in general in France around the year 1000, see Hans-Werner Goetz, "La Paix de Dieu en France autour de l'an mil: Fondements et objectifs, diffusion et participants," in *Le Roi de France et son royaume autour de l'an mil,* ed. Michel Parisse et Xavier Barral i Altet (Paris: Picard, 1992), 131–43. On Gerald of Aurillac, see Odo of Cluny, *Vita Geraldi, PL,* 133:639–704. On Dudo's thoughts on the duties of the ruler, see Shopkow, "The Carolingian World," 30, and at greater length in "Norman Historical Writing," 87–89.

23. *De moribus,* 225ff.

24. Ibid., 248–49. Raoul appears to be the seneschal (or an equivalent officer of the household), an impression reinforced by his cognomen, *torta,* a round cake or loaf. The similarly of the names, Rioul and Raoul (Riulfus and Radulfus) in Latin, suggests the possibility that one was twinned from the other to create a parallel.

In his dealings with his "foreign" enemies, Richard is again more aggressive, and hence more successful, than his father. He successfully avoids two potentially lethal traps and several attacks on his possessions. Indeed, Richard in the second case, when he is told that the attack of the enemy is imminent, calmly notes that breakfast has been prepared and suggests that he and his men offer it to God. He thus acts out both the fourth and fifth verses of the twenty-third psalm, not only walking in the valley of the shadow of death and fearing no evil (and Dudo specifically uses Richard's epithet "the Fearless" *[imperterritus]* here) but also sitting down to a table in the midst of his enemies.[25] Like Rollo, Richard wears down his enemies through constant raids, and they are forced to sue for peace. Here Richard is again more effective than William. When, at the end of the *Customs,* Thibaut of Chartres, who has harried Normandy with royal help for some years, wishes to sue for peace, Richard awaits a genuine change of heart on Thibaut's part, then he makes Thibaut come to him for reconciliation. Richard's subsequent reconciliation with the lords of France follows the same pattern. They must sue for peace and conclude the pact publicly at a time and place of Richard's choosing, in contrast to William Longsword's acquiescence to Arnulf.[26]

Richard also corrects his father's inclination to fraternize with and subordinate himself to the French. William compromises the independence of Normandy by strengthening his ties to the French throne and by making a humiliatingly subservient promise to support the French king:

Indeed, now and as long as I live, I will diligently carry out what you order. You will rule the realm of France and other realms which your father, grandfather, great-grandfather, and great-great-grandfather ruled, as I lead and help and preside over all things. . . . Those you wish to raise, I shall raise up. Those you wish to destroy, I shall fling to the ground.[27]

In contrast, Richard rules Normandy like a king or as if Normandy were an allod.[28] This princely independence was part of the original

---

25. Ibid., 271; Ps. 23:4–5.
27. Ibid., 199.

26. *De moribus,* 279–80, 281ff.
28. Ibid., 250, 265.

Norman condition as Dudo depicts it. Rollo's father had never done homage or served any king, and when Rollo had to do homage for Normandy, he refused to kiss the king's foot, delegating this distasteful task to one of his followers.[29] Richard's reign restores this state. Richard's Norman independence is reinforced by his mastery of his father's tongue. He is entrusted from birth to the bishop of Bayeux so that he can grow up knowing the language of his heritage, but Richard can move easily in the French world as well through his mastery of the "mellifluous sweetness of palatine discourse."[30]

In the end, Richard embodies the perfect Christian ruler. Richard, like William Longsword, founds a monastery, Fécamp, out of piety, but he does not wish to become a monk there; he requests that he be buried under the eaves of the building, a petition that neatly describes a desire to be as close as possible to the Church without actually being inside.[31] Richard also extirpates the last vestiges of paganism in Normandy, first by preaching a lengthy sermon that converts large numbers of pagans and then by inducing the new converts to fight and expel the remaining pagans from Normandy.[32] When he personally sees to the conversion or expulsion of his pagan followers and eradicates paganism from Normandy, Richard is responding implicitly to a rebuke by the bishops of France that he has permitted pagans to attack Christian churches.[33] In giving up his alliances with pagans, Richard abandons the Viking past, a past incompatible with Christian life. Another abandonment of pagan tradition in favor of Christian practice comes at the end of the *Customs,* when Richard enters a Christian marriage with his "Danish" wife Gunnor, after the death of his Christian wife, Emma. In relinquishing the keeping of concubines, Richard discontinues the Nordic custom of concubinage, with its resulting overpopulation, the cause of the Viking invasions in the first place.[34]

29. Ibid., 141, 169.
30. Ibid., 221–22, 230.
31. Ibid., 200–201, 290–91.
32. Ibid., 283–88.
33. Ibid., 282ff.
34. Cf. ibid., 129. "For these people, too aflame with wanton lust, ravishing

In Dudo's narrative, Norman history culminates in the reign of Richard, whom Dudo describes as the embodiment of the Beatitudes of the Sermon on the Mount.[35] Thus, the lives of the dukes form a progression leading up to the ideal ruler. This drive of Dudo's story toward its conclusion gave the *Customs* a satisfying completeness. Yet the power of Dudo's message came not just from its narrative wholeness but also from the ruthlessness with which he omitted anything irrelevant to his tale. Most notably, Dudo has little to say about the larger scene of French politics. The Capetians are the ghosts that haunt the shadows of the *Customs*. The two references to the deposition in 922 of Charles the Simple and the usurpation of his throne by Robert, the father of Hugh the Great and grandfather of Hugh Capet, are both placed in the context of Norman concerns and alliances. Dudo mentioned the coronation of Hugh Capet only as a way of explaining how he himself ended up in Normandy.[36] All the material in the narrative is associated with Dudo's four Norman leaders; he attributed famous deeds performed by other Vikings to his heroes.[37] Furthermore, all matters concerning the dukes which would not contribute to Dudo's plot were left out; Dudo said nothing about Richard I's reign between the mid-960s and the construction of Fécamp around 990. All of the information Dudo conveyed was unambiguous; for example, he asserted that all of Normandy was granted to Rollo, even though he had probably read the chronicle of Flodoard which contradicted this.[38] Dudo's observation of the unities of place and ac-

---

multitudinous women by coupling [with them] in notable squalor, generated therefrom innumerable offspring, accomplishing this through the disgusting union of illicit marriage."

35. Ibid., 293–94.

36. Ibid., 173, 251, 294. In fact, the first reference to the Robertian usurpation is mentioned only obliquely, and since the Normans were not involved, Dudo refuses to tell what happened.

37. On this borrowing, see, for example, H. H. Howorth, "A Criticism of the Life of Rollo as Told by Dudo of Saint-Quentin," *Archaeologia* 45 (1880): 245 and Henri Prentout, *Étude critique sur Dudon de Saint-Quentin et son histoire des premiers ducs normands* (Paris: A. Picard, 1916), 207.

38. Flodoard's chronicle dates the grant of Avranches and Coutances during the

tion lent his text the clarity of epic or of scripture. What Dudo created, in short, was a powerful founding myth of the Normans.

Both the compelling quality of Dudo's text and the fact that it was the only source for most of tenth-century Norman history made it the standard for all the works which followed. Dudo began Norman history with the arrival of Hasting in France and established 876, when Rollo sailed up the Seine to Rouen, and 912, when he was baptized and invested with Normandy, as the critical dates of Norman history.[39] Most historians followed him in this. But Dudo also influenced the ideological presentation of Norman history. For him, Norman history was both triumphal and providential. If Norman history was divinely ordained, by implication this also had to be true of all of human history. Not all later historians agreed either with this view of Norman history or of history in general, but because of the power of Dudo's narrative and his temporal priority in the field of Norman history, all were forced to respond to his vision.

The big stories of Dudo of Saint-Quentin's day and of the history he wrote were the survival and success of Richard I and the disappearance of paganism. Richard and Normandy came close to perishing at two points in his career: first, shortly after the murder of William Longsword in 942 when Richard became a ward/hostage of Louis IV of France and then in the 950s when his ill-advised campaign against Thibaut of Chartres could have finished Richard off. In the first case, Richard survived only with the help of Hugh the Great, while in the second, Norse pagan allies were crucial.[40]

---

reign of William Longsword (Flodoard of Reims, *Les Annales de Flodoard,* ed. Philippe Lauer [Paris: A. Picard, 1905], 55); however, in defence of Dudo, see Bates, *Normandy before 1066,* 9–10. On Dudo's use of Flodoard, see Shopkow, "Norman Historical Writing," 50–53.

39. *De moribus,* 151, 170. See, for example, *Annales de Jumièges,* 51; *Courtes annales du Bec,* 95.

40. *De moribus,* 227–31; 270ff. While Dudo says that Thibaut initiated the hostilities, Richard I was probably the aggressor in this case (Bates, *Normandy before 1066,* 14).

Richard's close calls and the successful reestablishment of Christian institutions in Normandy made it attractive for Dudo to cast Norman history in providential terms—it was a story for which there were almost unavoidable paradigms.

The rather different approaches taken by Dudo's successors reflect a society with different religious, political, social, and intellectual presuppositions from those of the late tenth and early eleventh centuries.[41] In Dudo's world, the ecclesiastical and the secular intermingled. Rulers were, in the ordinary course of their duties, responsible for the well-being of the Church. Consequently, Dudo shows the Norman dukes sponsoring reform, donating to churches, founding monasteries, and converting pagans, a role they played historically.[42] The powerful role the Norman dukes played in religious life in the late tenth and early eleventh centuries corresponded to the relative weakness of religious institutions. By the mid-eleventh century, however, the separation of the clerical and the lay spheres was hardening. The responsibility for good monastic order and orthodoxy, which had been the duty of the Carolingian monarch (and of the duke of Normandy in Dudo's vision), slowly moved into the sphere of the Church alone. William II embraced but co-opted the Peace of God, turning it into a secular peace, the Peace of the Duke.[43] The Norman dukes by no means abandoned the notion of overseeing the Church. William the Conqueror, for example, kept a tight rein on the Church, but he made the appropriate acts of deference to the popes and often acted indirectly through ecclesiastical figures.[44] The increasing distinction between the laity and the clergy also manifested itself in the rising tide of protest against clerical marriage, a key point of

41. Dudo's views are more representative of late Carolingian ideas than of the newer ideas being promulgated in the early eleventh century. On this subject, see Shopkow, "Carolingian World," 19–37.

42. Ibid., 29–30.

43. See Jean Yver, "Les Premières institutions du duché de Normandie" in *I Normanni e la loro espansione in Europa nell'alto medioevo* (Spoleto: Centro di studi sull'alto medioevo, 1969), 1:359–60.

44. Bates, *Normandy before 1066,* 190ff; 201–4.

papal reform which was also espoused in the council of Rouen in 1063.[45]

There was also during the course of the eleventh century a gradual move toward the formalization of Norman political institutions, although even at the end of the century these were still fairly rudimentary. The number of officials in the ducal household grew, and they were increasingly socially diverse; there was a Norman chancery after 1066.[46] The number of men described as ducal *fideles* greatly increased in the same period, and that group comprised the most powerful men in Normandy.[47] The way the powerful thought about themselves was also changing. In Normandy, as elsewhere, a nascent military aristocracy was developing family pride and a group identity.[48] Although informal ties and charisma were still important in the mid-eleventh century, relationships within society were becoming formalized, even as they retained much of their earlier fluidity.

These societal changes were paralleled by a rising current of naturalistic thought in the eleventh century. Historians were less likely to see God as the *reason* for history, and more likely to see God as the *meaning* of history. Dudo's kind of strongly providential history was replaced by histories in which the course of events unfolded without constant divine intervention.[49] All of these changes encouraged Dudo's successors, William of Jumièges and William of Poitiers, to read Norman history differently.

Dudo's big story, conversion and triumph, was old news fifty

---

45. See Mansi, *Sacrorum conciliorum collectio,* 19:1027–30.

46. Bates, *Normandy before 1066,* 154–55; 161.

47. Ibid., 170–72.

48. Ibid., 158–60 and *passim.* See also Duby, "The Nobility in Medieval France," in *The Chivalrous Society,* 94–111, for the development of a noble class in France in general.

49. See Alexander Murray, *Reason and Society in the Middle Ages,* corrected ed., (Oxford: Oxford University Press, 1985), 8f. for a discussion of rationalism in medieval thought. On the shift from typological history to naturalistic development, see Funkenstein, *Heilsplan und natürliche Entwicklung,* 10. Funkenstein places this shift in the eleventh century (ibid., 69). Dudo's contemporary, Ralph Glaber, represents the typological sort of history, while Frutolf represents the less apocalyptic view of history (ibid., 77ff., 85f.).

years later. The big story of the 1050s was a new comedy of survival, this time the triumph of William II over rebels inside of Normandy and a coalition of French enemies on its borders. This was not a religious triumph—these were all battles among Christian princes—but a political triumph. In Dudo's text, the power of the dukes derived from God, perhaps because the alternative was to derive it from the kings of France through the tie of fidelity. To Dudo, the subordination involved was vaguely degrading. Consequently, he parodied the act of swearing fidelity by having Charles demand that Rollo kiss his foot, rather than his mouth, during the ceremony.[50] For William of Jumièges, writing a half century later, there was no shame attached to fidelity, and so he depicted the dukes not only swearing fidelity but acting as *fideles*.[51] For William of Jumièges, these human institutions propagated political order and legitimacy. In a similar fashion, human actions propelled history forward.

For Dudo, the problem that shaped Norman history was the devil's continual opposition to the advancement of God's chosen people. Normandy's enemies are not just evil men, they are demonically inspired.[52] For William, the patterns of Norman history derived from a strictly political issue, succession, which is not problematic in Dudo's narrative at all. When Dudo of Saint-Quentin was writing, *more danico* or informal marriage was still a living institution, and Dudo presented the "Danish" marriages as they were viewed by the Norman dukes themselves, that is, as unions with some official standing. The offspring of these informal unions were eligible for the ducal office. The attitude toward the

50. *De moribus*, 169. The kiss of peace was just entering the ceremony of commendation; see R. Boutruche, *Seigneurie et féodalité*, 2d ed. (Paris: Aubier, 1968), 1:209. Dudo may have intended to parody this innovation.

51. For example, Rollo willingly swears fidelity to Charles the Simple (*GND*, 28). For two instances where Norman dukes assist the king of France when requested to do so on their fidelity, see ibid., 90f., 105.

52. *De moribus*, 148, (the devil tries to swamp Rollo in a storm); 189, (Riulf is said to be made drunk by the furies of diabolical fraud); 203ff., (the devil begins the plot against William that ends in his murder); 208, (William's murderers are inspired by the devil).

children not produced by Christian marriages in Normandy, however, was beginning to change by the early eleventh century. Richard II had only Christian wives, and "Danish" marriages for the dukes became a thing of the past. William II's mother, Herleva, was not Robert the Magnificent's formal concubine but his lover. Legitimacy of birth in Christian terms was not an absolute necessity in 1035, when William II succeeded his father, but illegitimacy made it possible to pass over a candidate for succession. When Robert the Magnificent succeeded his brother, Richard III, in 1027, Richard's illegitimate son, Nicholas, later the abbot of Saint-Ouen in Rouen, was passed over.[53] The duke's illegitimacy also made it possible to challenge his authority; the early part of William II's reign was spent fighting off the claims of legitimate relatives like Guy of Brionne and William of Talou.[54] William of Jumièges, therefore, needed to justify William II's succession by an appeal to contemporary ideas of authority. He had to accomplish this without overt reference to William the Conqueror's illegitimacy, a point on which the duke reportedly was touchy.[55] He rewrote Dudo's version of history to do this.

William of Jumièges used the history of Richard I as a template for the succession of the Conqueror. His account regularized the "Danish" marriages of Rollo and Richard I. William had Rollo repudiate his "Danish" wife, Poppa, when he married his Christian wife, Gisela, only to take Poppa back after Gisela's death. William mentioned Richard I's "Danish" wife, Gunnor, only when he described her later Christian marriage to the duke. However, he reported explicitly that William Longsword's marriage to Richard

53. Nicholas is not mentioned in William's version of the *GND*, but an interpolator, writing some time after 1092, added a short passage on Nicholas (ibid., 99). On the manuscripts with this interpolation, see van Houts, *GND* (2), I:96–98.

54. Ibid., 119–20, 122f. Orderic Vitalis, writing early in the next century, has Roger of Tosny refuse to serve the Conqueror explicitly because of his illegitimacy and adds that William was despised by all the Norman nobility, but especially the family of "the Richards," i.e. by his kin (*GND*, 157). However, Searle has argued that the issue was not William's illegitimacy but rather a struggle within the ducal kin group over power (*Predatory Kinship*, 184 and *passim*).

55. See Orderic's comments about the seige of Alençon, *GND*, 171.

I's mother, Sprota, was "Danish."[56] This "Danish" marriage thus conveniently becomes an issue in the succession of Richard I. When Richard I is a ward (and hostage) at the court of Louis IV of France, the king accuses Richard of being "the son of a prostitute, who had stolen another woman's man," and he threatens to mutilate the boy.[57] Louis here makes an oblique reference to a figure seldom mentioned in Norman histories but known through other sources, Leutgarde, William Longsword's Christian wife, to whom the duke was married at the time of his death. Dudo had omitted any mention of Leutgarde, although Bernard of Senlis, whom Dudo gives a role in helping Richard I to claim his birthright, was probably her cousin.[58] Although William of Jumièges does not insist on the parallels between Richard I and William II, a medieval reader, trained to see recurring patterns, would have spotted them. Like Louis IV, Henry I forgets that William II's father, Robert, had helped him secure his throne. Instead of protecting his young vassal, Henry betrays him by seizing the castle of Tillières.[59] William II was never a French hostage, but he too was at the center of life-threatening intrigue in which members of his entourage died, and he too suffered from French royal hostility.[60]

The principle that underlay the political legitimacy of these dukes was the right of their fathers to designate their successor. Dudo of Saint-Quentin described the dukes' designation of their successors succinctly. In contrast, William of Jumièges emphasized it: William's description of the designation of William Longsword is one of the few places where the later historian is more rhetorical

56. Ibid., 31, 68; 33.

57. *De moribus*, 229; *GND*, 48.

58. *De moribus*, 231; on Bernard of Senlis, see Dhondt, *Naissance des principautés terrioriales*, 119–20 and n. 5.; on Leutgarde, see Fauroux; *GND*, 35 and n. 1. The prominant role played in this history by Bernard of Senlis is one of the ways in which Dudo's Vermandois background makes itself felt in the *Customs*.

59. *GND*, 104–5, 117. However, David Bates suggests that the capture of Tillières was part of a punitive expedition against Waleran of Meulan, who had taken refuge with the Beaumonts (*Normandy Before 1066*, 74).

60. Ibid., 116.

than Dudo. In this passage, William of Jumièges articulated the idea that the duke alone chose his successor. The historian used direct speech in this passage, a rarity in the *Deeds*.

"It is my responsibility," he [Rollo] said, "to put him in my place, and it is yours to keep faith with him."[61]

William of Jumièges treats most of the subsequent successions casually, but when he comes to the succession of William II, he again describes the designation at length.[62]

In stressing designation, William was describing a practice of the Norman dukes (and other princes) known through charter evidence. Although the decision may not have been the duke's alone, the dukes often ensured the succession of their choice by associating the candidate with them during their lifetimes.[63] Richard III was styled count when he appeared in ducal charters before Richard II's death, and William II, although he bore no title in the charters, appears designated as Robert's successor.[64] The emphasis William of Jumièges gave to designation as the act that constituted the duke arose from challenges to this traditional system. By the turn of the twelfth century, illegitimacy was becoming an impediment to succession and legitimate male primogeniture was, under normal circumstances, the rule. Henry I was able to grant his illegitimate son, Robert of Gloucester, a lofty title, but he did not attempt to have Robert accepted as his successor. By then, only God could make an heir.

61. Ibid., 31; cf. *De moribus*, 173.
62. For the succession of Richard III, see *GND*, 97. For that of Robert, see ibid., 100. With Richard III the system of designation broke down, for William of Jumièges says only that Richard died leaving Robert as his heir. The method of selection must have involved some consultation of the nobility, for William goes on to say that everyone called upon Robert to become the duke. Had Richard's son, Nicholas, been older it is conceivable that he might have been chosen. On the designation of the Conqueror, the historian says, "Placing before them his son William, then about seven years old, the only one he had begotten and whom he had chosen to be his successor, he demanded most insistently that they choose him as their lord in his place, and that they select him as leader of the army" (ibid., 111).
63. Searle, *Predatory Kinship*, 170 and *passim*, argues that the family must have participated in the selection of the heir.
64. Fauroux, *Recueil*, 176, no. 55; 184, no. 60.

The increasing frequency with which important Norman lords were tied to the duke by the ties of fidelity also provided ammunition for William of Jumièges's defense of the political authority of the Conqueror. Rebels against William II might have had legitimate claims to ducal authority by blood, but in each case William stressed that the rebel was violating his oath of fidelity. When Guy of Brionne rebels against his cousin, he is forgetful of the service he voluntarily took on by swearing his oath to the king. Lest the reader miss the point, the word William uses to describe this service is "*electissimo,*" an intensive form of "chosen" or "voluntary."[65] Thus William emphasized fidelity to bolster the legitimacy of Norman rule, the very bond that Dudo had struggled to de-emphasize for the same reason.

William of Jumièges began the *Deeds* at the very time when William II had validated his disputed claim militarily. It was a literary corroboration of the Conqueror's claim to authority.[66] However, the criteria for legitimate authority that William of Jumièges developed also had the happy result of providing a paradigm to legitimate Norman authority over England in 1066. Though his blood claim was dubious, the Conqueror was designated the heir to the English throne by Edward the Confessor, a designation afterward confirmed by vows of fidelity.[67] The Conqueror's claim to the throne of England was additionally strengthened (although not created) by the fact that Harold, his chief rival, had already sworn fidelty to the duke as future king.[68]

Although William of Jumièges built his argument on parallels, just as Dudo of Saint-Quentin had, the parallelisms in the *Deeds* are not allegorical but are intended to establish precedents. Whereas Dudo's story was a recapitulation of the story of the chosen people, it was not directly connected to the history of any other people. Its ability to convince the reader derived from the reader's

65. *GND*, 123.
66. See above, p. 000 and p. 000, n. 000.
67. *GND*, 132, 136.
68. Ibid., 132–33; Harold is accused of perjury in regard to his oath and is said to act "*infideliter.*"

acquaintance with other stories of this type, which affirmed that God did in fact act in the world in this predictable fashion. In contrast, the arguments in the early part of the *Deeds of the Dukes* are directly connected to the succession crisis of the 1030s and 1040s. William by implication argues that the succession in 1035 was appropriate because in Normandy this was how succession had been traditionally handled. Thus the *Deeds of the Dukes* begs to be read historically, as an account of Norman traditions, rather than allegorically as an account of God's behavior.

This does not mean that God is absent from the *Deeds of the Dukes,* but he plays quite a different role from the one he plays in the *Customs.* William of Jumièges several times invoked God as an explanation for historical events. For example, he remarked that Edward the Confessor's childlessness—which forced him to choose William II of Normandy as his successor—was the will of God.[69] William also attributed the English loss at Hastings to divine punishment for English connivance in the murder of Alfred, Edward the Confessor's brother.[70] In contrast to Dudo's work, however, in which God and the devil continually intervene in mortal matters, William of Jumièges invoked God sparingly and as an explanation of those things for which there is no convincing human explanation.

The difference between William's and Dudo's visions of Norman history is clear in their respective treatment of the ducal saint, William Longsword. Dudo's view corresponds to his notion of Norman history as providential. The duke was marked from birth by God; he is a *puer senex.* In contrast, William of Jumièges depicts William Longsword before his conversion as a conventional military leader. If he hesitates before attacking Riulf, it is so he can

69. Ibid., 132. William may here be cognizant of a tradition that first appears with Osbert of Clare's life of Edward, that Edward died a virgin. The *Life of King Edward,* at least partly written by a contemporary of William, but completed by 1100, refers to Edward's chastity but does not specify anything about his marriage (see Frank Barlow, ed. and trans., *The Life of King Edward Who Rests at Westminster,* 2d ed. [Oxford: Oxford University Press, 1921], xxx–xxxiii, 92 and n. 230).

70. *GND,* 135. He made a few other similar references: ibid., 85, 102, 110, 114, 123, 138, 139.

mull over his options.[71] Longsword's conversion to the monastic life involves a sudden change of heart, which occurs when the duke is in the midst of that most typical (and manly) of aristocratic activities, hunting boar. During the hunt, Duke William meets two monks who have settled at the deserted site of Jumièges. The monks offer him a charity offering of barley bread and water, but, in his pride, the duke spurns their humble offering. Divine chastisement is immediate, and he is knocked down by a huge boar. The duke recognizes this as punishment for his sin, and he returns, not only accepting the monks' charity but promising to rebuild the monastery.[72] William of Jumièges's account reflects a new socioreligious phenomenon, the increasing visibility of adult conversions to the monastic life occurring in the late eleventh century. Herluin, the founder of the abbey of Bec, was an adult convert of this type, and Guibert of Nogent spoke of such conversions as a trend in the late eleventh century.[73] These trends were felt in literature as well; in new epics, heroes acquired an afterlife as monks. Orderic Vitalis tells this kind of story about William of Gellona, immortalized in the epics as William of Orange, and the chronicler of Novalesa claimed that Walter of Aquitaine had retired to that house.[74] Recasting the conversion of William Longsword as a *moniage* story permitted William

---

71. Ibid., 33–34.

72. Ibid., 39. Dudo also told the story of the spurned charity offering, but he placed it after abbot Martin of Jumièges refused to receive the duke as a monk in the newly founded Jumièges. The duke spurned charity in anger; his punishment was a bellyache, which did not, however, make him give up his design to become a monk (*De moribus*, 202).

73. John F. Benton, *Self and Society in Medieval France: The Memories of Abbot Guibert of Nogent*, (reprint, Toronto: University of Toronto Press and the Medieval Academy of America, 1984), 54–63, esp. 62–63. Orderic Vitalis, *EH*, 3:226, describes the chaplain, Gerold of Avranches, haranguing the knights and perhaps inspiring them to similar conversions.

74. Ibid., 3:218ff.; *Chronicon Novaliciense, MGH SS*, 7:73–133; the story of how Walter came to be a monk is told on p. 86. Other epic heroes came to enjoy a literary retirement to monasteries in the twelfth century. On these texts and their social context, see Jean Batany, "Les 'Moniages' et la satire des moines aux XIᵉ et XIIᵉ siècles," in *Les Chansons de geste du cycle de Guillaume d'Orange*, vol. 3, *Les Moniages, Guiborc*, ed. P. Menard and J.-Ch. Payen (Paris: Société d'Édition d'Enseignement Supérieur, 1983), 209–23, particularly 214–15.

of Jumièges to affirm the duke's sanctity, while preserving the boundaries between the lay and clerical states.

William's retreat from viewing Norman history as providential also affected the way he depicted the Normans as a group. While William, like Dudo, lauds the warlike character of the Normans— Norman women, he says, are as warlike as the men—the Norman character is less important than individual actions and political problems in explaining history.[75] This change, too, reflected cultural shifts in Normandy. By the mid-eleventh century, the Normans spoke French; the strong ties with Scandinavia that Normandy had enjoyed in the early part of the century disappeared.[76] William knew that St. Olaf had spent some time in Rouen about 1014, a stay he depicted as a military alliance, but he was almost completely ignorant of the Scandinavian kingdoms.[77] In his eyes, the Scandinavians were not kin but aliens, for he says that William Longsword sent Richard I to Bayeux to learn Scandinavian so he might be able to speak both to his own men and to foreigners.[78] Not surprisingly, Bernard the Dane plays a much reduced role in the *Deeds;* Bernard of Senlis replaces him as the mastermind of Norman independence.[79]

In re-emplotting Norman history in these ways, William of Jumièges retained the formal structure, serial biography, and the chronology that Dudo established. However, for the fulfillment Dudo depicted at the end of Richard I's reign, William had to substitute an alternative *telos.* If van Houts is correct, the first version of the *Deeds* was completed before 1063 and ended with the triumph of William II at Varaville in 1057, that is, with his repulsion of the French threat and the restoration of the duchy to something like the happy independence described by Dudo at the end of the *Customs of the Duke.*[80] The Norman Conquest of England, how-

75. *GND,* 77.
76. See Bates, *Normandy before 1066,* 237 and *passim.*
77. *GND,* 85.
78. Ibid., 41.
79. Ibid., 51.
80. van Houts, *GND* (2), I:xxxii–xxxiii.

ever, meant that this was no longer the high point of William II's career, and the narrative had to be reopened.

The Conquest brought with it new glory but also new troubles. The king faced rebellion within his family, among his most important vassals, and on the part of his new subjects. In the absence of any other way to end his text neatly, William of Jumièges happened on an ingenious solution: he brought his narrative to a close by looking past William II to his son Robert Curthose, the future duke of Normandy. William II designated Robert as his successor before the Conquest, so the historian was able to begin Norman history with one Robert (Rollo's baptismal name) and to end it with another. This revised ending, however, was in turn undermined by events. Robert Curthose, although designated as his father's successor, fell from favor, and William was forced to take out his reference to Robert, although he added no new material to this later version of the text.[81] In removing the potentially objectionable material, William also removed the closure he had created. Unlike the earlier books of the *Customs,* the biography of William simply ended in the middle of the Conqueror's reign. Thus, the teleological simplicity of Dudo's work gave way to a more open-ended and contingent narrative, with only the formal closure of an envoi to William the Conqueror. A later writer, troubled by the lack of closure in the book, appended a small narrative, *On the Death of William,* to the *Deeds,* thus at least ending the last biography with the death of the subject.[82] Still, William, like Dudo, saw Norman history as triumphant and saw his own times as the apogee of Norman glory.

The third of the early Norman historians, William of Poitiers, did not structure his biography of the Conqueror to demonstrate that God caused history to happen as Dudo had argued, although

81. *GND,* 143; on Robert's designation and rebellion, see Bates, *Normandy before 1066,* 249–50. On William's versions of the *Deeds,* see van Houts, *GND* (2), I:xxxii–v.

82. On the *De obitu Willelmi,* see van Houts, *GND* (2), I:lxiii–lxiv.

William certainly saw God as an actor in history. Nor was William of Poitiers particularly interested in Norman succession problems or politics, as William of Jumièges was, although again, the issues of succession comprised an important part of the *Deeds of William*. Instead, William of Poitiers's biography was an exemplary life, illustrating the responsibilities of the Christian ruler. Whereas the *Customs of the Dukes* was to be read allegorically and the *Deeds of the Dukes* to be read historically, the *Deeds of William* was cast in a tropological mode, where the character of the individual was the most important issue. This mode of reading, however, derived only partially from Christian readings of the past. The other component was classical biography.[83]

For William of Poitiers, as for classical historians, character was a static attribute.[84] In the course of the *Deeds of William*, the Conqueror's worth is gradually revealed by a series of political and moral tests. Each success brought with it an external change in dress, as William began with simple warrior's raiment and ended wearing royal regalia but with no essential internal change of character. William of Poitiers attributed to the Conqueror a full panoply of virtues, including the classical virtues of prudence, justice, temperance, and fortitude.[85] And just as for classical historians, for William the character of a man's reign reflected his own character and the private virtues he practiced affected public life. Since William of Poitiers wished both to praise his ruler and to present a portrait of the ideal Christian ruler, he attributed to the Conqueror all the virtues he saw as desirable in a ruler both for the ruler's salvation and for the good of his realm.

For example, William of Poitiers attributed to the Conqueror

83. Cf. *Agricola*, 1, where Tacitus connects the deeds and characters of distinguished men.

84. See, for example, Suetonius, *Tiberius*, 26, 42. Whereas a modern writer might talk about Tiberius's growing corruption by power, Suetonius describes Tiberius as having concealed his evil character in the early part of his reign and then revealed it.

85. *GG*, 12, 220–222. On the cardinal virtues in the Middle Ages, see Murray, *Reason and Society*, 133. For William's possession of them, see *GG*, 40, 44, 48, 96, 130, 138, 148 (prudence); 118, 130 (justice); 88, 98 (fortitude); 210 (temperance).

the virtue of clemency, the only historian to do so. Elsewhere, William II was depicted as a notably violent man. William of Poitiers had a classical precedent for clemency—it was a characteristic of Julius Caesar to whom the Conqueror was extensively compared in the *Deeds of William*. However, the duke's clemency is also presented as a religious stance; the Conqueror refrained from imposing the death penalty out of respect for God.[86] William of Poitiers was a supporter of the Peace and Truce of God, which the Conqueror sponsored in Normandy, the aim of which was to mitigate the terrible violence of tenth- and eleventh-century society. He was thus desirous of having his hero behave in accordance with the spirit of the Peace.[87]

The duke's self-control or chastity similarly had a public manifestion. It revealed itself in his control over his family and subjects, but it was also evident in his equity. In its original Roman use, the term equity described the mitigation of legal severity.[88] However, William of Poitiers meant something different, the selection of an appropriate punishment for a particular transgression, a consideration encompassing the seriousness of the crime, the state of the criminal, and the need for a deterrent.[89] Equity also implied legal blindness to inequalities of estate and wealth among those who are to be judged; consequently, according to the historian, the duke was no kinder to his kin than to anyone else, nor did he allow his Norman troops any greater license than those of other peoples.[90]

86. For a lengthy explicit comparison of the Conqueror to Caesar, see *GG*, 246–54, but there are many others scattered throughout the text. For clemency, see Suetonius, *Divus Julius*, 75. On clemency, see *GG*, 58; 90; 210, 238; 232. According to William of Jumièges, on the other hand, William the Conqueror had a well-developed appreciation of the power of terror, as at Alençon, where he burned the town to the ground and mutilated some of the citizens (*GND*, 126).

87. See *GG*, 118, on the truce of God.

88. Foreville, "Aux Origines de la renaissance juridique," 56–61. On William II's control over his family and subjects, see *GG* 112, 120, 132. On chastity, see *GG*, 120; 216.

89. Cf. Jonas of Orléans, *Jonas d'Orléans et son "De institutione regia": Étude et texte critique*, ed. J. Reviron (Paris: Librairie philosophique J. Vrin, 1930), 145.

90. Cf. Sedulius Scotus, *De rectoribus christianis* in H. Hellman, *Sedulius Scotus* (Munich: C. H. Beck'sche Verlagsbuchhandlung, 1908), 49; *GG*, 128–30, 232.

Thus, the ruler's character ultimately controlled the character of his subjects, and character drove the engines of history. William of Poitiers argues that because Harold was a tyrant, the English people before the conquest were perfidious and fickle, fierce, xenophobic and cruel. Accustomed to tyranny, they could not see the Conquest as their liberation. The Bretons too were like their masters: immoral, pleasure-loving thieves. The contrary was true for the Normans. Like their duke, they were lawful, bold, obedient, and valorous.[91] But national characteristics, because they were dependent upon the moral qualities the ruler encouraged in his people, were not assigned by God or innate. During the course of the *Deeds of William,* the duke has to teach his wild and rebellious subjects obedience and submission by beating down those who rebelled against him. The causes of this wildness lie outside of the narrative, but William of Poitiers may well have been thinking of chaotic conditions of the 1030s and 1040s. English barbarism was caused by relative isolation from the continent; the inhabitants of that part of England closest to the French coast, Kent, were less savage, and under King William's careful rule, all the barbarian English become civilized and less contemptible.[92]

In his views on the importance of the character of the ruler and the effect that his character had on the ruled, William of Poitiers did not only draw on classical biography. The role he described for the Christian ruler was in harmony with St. Augustine's thought. The qualities of equity and clemency William ascribed to his hero were also prescribed for the Christian ruler.[93] William of Poitiers likened the Conqueror's respect for the Church to the emperor Theodosius's deference to the monk John; and Theodosius's humility and penance before St. Ambrose for the destruction of Thessalonica cannot have been far from William's mind.[94] While

91. For the English: *GG,* 228–30; the Bretons: *GG,* 108–110; the Normans: *GG,* 38, 112, 192, and *passim.*

92. Ibid., 20, 64, 240; *EH,* 2:256 (this passage probably came originally from the lost portion of the *GG*).

93. Augustine, *City of God* (Turnholt: Brepols, 1955), 5:24.

94. *GG,* 128. Cf. Augustine, *City of God,* 5:26.

in the *City of God*, Augustine was not primarily interested in providing a blueprint for the Christian ruler, he devoted a few pages to the subject. He commented, for instance, that conquest was justified by the injustice of the conquered. Consequently, William of Poitiers expatiated upon the injustice of the counts of Anjou in their rule over Maine as part of his justification for the Conqueror's conquest of the province.[95] The influence of Augustine can also be seen in the duke's constant awareness of his accountability in the afterlife and his enjoyment of "felicity," a combination of good fortune, equanimity, and faith that characterize the good Christian and successful ruler.[96]

William of Poitiers also followed Augustine in arguing that evil men were the true authors of wars. The duke's enemies fail to share his virtues; they are characterized by the opposites of the Conqueror's virtues: injustice, impiety, and cruelty. Whereas for William of Jumièges, Guy of Brionne's primary vice is infidelity, in the *Deeds of William* the infidelity itself arises from Guy's corruption; his baseness encompasses not only ingratitude toward his ducal benefactor but also attempted fratricide.[97] At the end of their lives, the villains of the *Deeds* are forced to contemplate their own responsibility for their misfortunes.[98]

Thus the *Deeds of William* and the *Customs of the Dukes* have similar themes: how God rewarded the leaders of the Normans for their piety and uprightness by permitting them to escape from the attacks of their enemies and to rule their lands unchallenged, and both works have a panegyric and highly rhetorical cast. However, whereas Norman history in Dudo's work has the inevitability of divine predestination, William of Poitiers emphasizes not divine power but human moral choices; where he differs from Augustine

95. Augustine, *City of God*, 4:15. *GG*, 86–88.

96. The concept of felicity comes from St. Augustine. For further discussion of this notion and of the influence of St. Augustine's thought on William of Poitiers, see Pierre Bouet, "La 'Felicitas' de Guillaume le Conquérant dans les *Gesta Guillelmi* de Guillaume de Poitiers," *Anglo-Norman Studies* 4 (1982): esp. 38–44.

97. *GG*, 16, 20.

98. Ibid., 60–62, 84.

is in believing human moral choices to have intelligible consequences in history.

Like both of his predecessors, William of Poitiers saw Norman history as a comedy. Despite periodic adversity, the Normans advanced steadily in power and merit until they reached the pinacle of success in his own time. Like William of Jumièges, however, William of Poitiers did not achieve closure in the *Deeds of William*. He literally failed to close it because he failed to finish it, but it is difficult to see how he might have finished his work and still managed to maintain the comedic vision of Norman history he fashioned. While the Conqueror's reign was hardly untroubled before 1075, after that date he had to deal, among other things, with the rebellion of his son Robert Curthose. While such developments were easy to account for in a strictly Augustinian scheme, for Augustine was quick to point out that only divine history was truly intelligible to human beings, the *Deeds* is not fully Augustinian in that the author implies that virtue and vice receive their deserts in mortal life. Thus, these later developments would have undermined William's portrait of the Conqueror. Had William continued, he would have had to explain these later failures and to have acknowledged that the Normans were perhaps in decline. Instead of reevaluating the shape he gave Norman history and perhaps abandoning comedy for tragedy or satire, William of Poitiers put down his pen.

3 ❧ The Glorious Norman Past

*H*istorians writing in Normandy before 1100 painted the
Norman past in the triumphant colors of victory over adversity and potential ruin. Satisfying though these stories
obviously were (for people kept copying them), however,
historians writing the history of Normandy after 1100 did
not narrate the history of their own time in comic terms.
While it is tempting to say that this was because events
of the twelfth century were not easy to cast as comedy,
that would be to presuppose that history actually comes
preformed as a story, rather than having to be fashioned
into a story by an historian. It is possible to conceive of
a triumphant Norman history written in 1154, when
Henry II united Normandy and England once again under a single ruler, yet no one in Normandy wrote such a
history.

The Norman historians of the twelfth century did not
deny the legacy of Dudo of Saint-Quentin, William of
Poitiers, and William of Jumièges. However, while the
latter group of historians depicted their own times as the

high noon of Norman greatness, the twelfth-century historians tended to see the Norman glory days as lying in the past. Their own days at best represented a continuity with the past; more commonly, they saw the present as an age of decline. The twelfth-century historians of Normandy altered the legacy of earlier writers by giving their stories a tragic fall, a nostalgic coloration, by setting the Normans in the context of a larger history of the world, or by a combination of these treatments.

Orderic Vitalis, like William of Poitiers whose work he admired, adopted a tropological reading of history, but he turned the earlier historian's understanding of Norman history on its head. His characters were neither unalloyed villains nor unflawed heroes and thus his view of the historical process was more nuanced than William of Poitiers's. In keeping with this complexity of vision, Orderic presented Norman history as having a comedic potential which turned to tragedy because of Norman moral failings. He subverted William of Poitiers's account at the very point when the earlier historian's hero reached the pinnacle of his career, at the coronation of William the Conqueror.

Orderic's account of the coronation is largely borrowed from the *Deeds of William.* He follows William of Poitiers in saying that during the coronation, the bishops presiding asked the Normans and English inside the church to acclaim the king, but the Norman soldiers outside, hearing cries in English, assumed that the king was being attacked and set fire to the city. Orderic then added that all the laymen left the church to put out the fire, and only the clergy was left to finish the coronation, as the trembling king stood by.[1] What William of Poitiers presented as a simple misunderstanding, without long-term consequences, Orderic recast as the moment when a potentially great alliance began to go wrong. That the incident occurs because the Normans cannot understand the language of the people they have conquered is symbolic of Norman arrogance and unwillingness to learn from others. Also significant was the new king's fear, something William of Poitiers does not

1. *EH,* 2:182–84.

and would not have mentioned. The Conqueror's fear of his new subjects leads him to see conspiracies against him everywhere and thus to persecute the English harshly. It also leads him in 1075 to acquiesce in the judicial murder of Waltheof, who was unjustly accused of treason. After this, Orderic comments, the Conqueror had no further victories, and neither did his Norman followers.[2] Thus, the end of the story is already contained in the beginning.

The sentiments Orderic expressed obliquely in his account of the Conqueror's coronation, where he was dependent on the already established narrative of William of Poitiers, he voiced explicitly in his narrative of the Conqueror's funeral, where he did not need to follow any other source. Although Orderic certainly drew some of the material from oral accounts enshrined in collective memory, the funeral story so closely mirrors Orderic's account of the coronation that the resemblance cannot be coincidental.[3] Orderic relates that when the king died, his followers fled home in panic to protect their property, while his attendants carried off everything of value in the house. Because of the rapid dispersion of the household, no one could be found to prepare the body and bring it to Caen for burial. A local soldier finally agreed to do this out of charity. Then a fire broke out during the funeral mass, and those present went to put it out, leaving the body in the church with only monks to complete the office. When the funeral procession reached the graveyard, and the presiding bishop, Gilbert of Évreux, asked those present to forgive the dead king for any wrong he might have done them, a man named Ascelin immediately came forward, claiming that the land upon which the abbey stood had been illegally seized from his family. He permitted the burial to go forward only when the assembled bishops gave him partial compensation for the land and promised the rest of the money later. Finally, the coffin proved too small for the king's body, and it burst

2. Ibid., 2:350.
3. *GRA*, 2:461, gives an account of the funeral similar to Orderic's. However, William may have known Orderic's work (see *EH*, 1:89; 2:270, n.1).

when it was forced into the box, sending noxious fumes rolling over the spectators.[4]

In Orderic's exegesis, the Conqueror's funeral represented a reversal of the fortunes of William's life and revealed his flaws. Those retainers he had advanced abandoned him once he was dead, highlighting William's folly in raising "new men" to power. Orderic, with his firm monastic notions of order and functions, several times denounced the raising of the lowly. The moral lesson of this posthumous ingratitude did not escape him.[5] Next Orderic pointed out the irony of one who in life had enjoyed unlimited wealth, but who in death was dependent on charity. Here, William was being reproved for his avarice, for the wealth he enjoyed had been stripped from England, a fact Orderic also frequently laments.[6] Next, although William in life enjoyed many domains acquired illicitly, in death he was unable to find the six feet of earth necessary to bury him until symbolic atonement was done on his behalf to Ascelin, a representative of the many men disinherited by the king. Finally, Orderic made reference to the bursting of William's body which had been so well nourished; this is his only reference to something other historians were more forthright about—the king's enormous girth in his later years. The noxious smell, upon which Orderic does not otherwise comment, also clearly prefigured the troubles which plagued Normandy under William's successors, a sort of reverse of the odor of sanctity.

The sequence of events in each of the two rites is the same, and the figural relationship between the scenes permitted Orderic to bring out the moral resonances with relatively minimal commentary. He commented that the fire at the coronation portended England's destruction, and therefore did not need to say that the fire at the funeral presaged a similar trial for Normandy. Having remarked when he narrated the deathbed scene of the Conqueror that the Church always stood by him because he was always its

4. *EH*, 4:100–108.
5. For some of Orderic's comments on new men, see ibid., 6:16.
6. Ibid., 2:266–68.

defender, he did not need to point out that at both coronation and funeral the clergy alone among William's subjects did not desert him.[7]

The ordinary reader might derive general lessons from Orderic's narrative of these incidents, but, while using the same moral strategy as the earlier historian, Orderic was also making a specific refutation of William of Poitiers's portrait of the Conqueror. Orderic concurs with William of Poitiers about the Conqueror's piety, which was the reason he was able to ascend to the throne, but Orderic undermines William's presentation of the Conqueror as a clement monarch. To the later historian, the Conqueror's more notable characteristics were his pride and cruelty, traits which ultimately curtailed his success. Whereas William's tale was one of moral ascendency, Orderic's was one of moral failure.

Given his markedly more negative reading of the character of the Conqueror, it is not surprising that Orderic also read the Conquest in a darker manner. William of Jumièges and William of Poitiers had celebrated the Conquest as the triumph of a superior people over an inferior one. Orderic, an Englishman defending his people against the negative insinuations of these earlier historians, argued that they were courageous, trustworthy, peaceable. He particularly resented Norman assertions of religious superiority, remarking shortly that the Normans could learn much from the example of English saints. The apparent rusticity of the English at the time of the Conquest resulted from a decline caused by the Danish invasions of the eleventh century.[8] The English lost at Hastings not because of a lack of valor or national sins but because God was punishing Harold for his vices.[9] Orderic thus followed William of Poitiers in seeing the moral qualities of rulers as determining the fate of their followers.

Orderic did not demonize the Normans, to whom he conceded some positive characteristics drawn from the traditional view in-

---

7. Ibid., 2:29, 184.
8. Ibid., 2:218, 244–46, 324; 4:16, 4:126.
9. Ibid., 2:134–38, 170–72.

herited from Dudo and the Williams. They were innately warlike, audacious, and courageous, attributes also delineated by earlier historians. However, these great gifts were counterbalanced by flaws earlier historians did not acknowledge, such as avarice, greed for power, inconstancy, frivolity, and a taste for wrong-doing. Orderic likened the Normans to a frozen wind that killed the tender flowers of the south and to a viper's brood.[10] In this spirited defence of the English and equally forceful condemnation of the Normans, Orderic responded to the depictions of the English as inferior and effeminate offered by William of Poitiers and William of Jumièges.[11]

To Orderic what gave the trajectory of Norman history (and after the Conquest, English history) its frequently tragic cast was the varying ability of Norman rulers to control the destructive impulses of the Norman character. Orderic Vitalis framed his understanding of the lessons of Norman history in a speech made by William the Conqueror on his deathbed to his feckless son, Robert Curthose:

If the Normans are disciplined under a just and firm rule they are men of great valour, who press invincibly to the fore in arduous undertakings and, proving their strength, fight resolutely to overcome. But without such rule they tear each other to pieces and destroy themselves, for they hanker after rebellion, cherish sedition, and are ready for any treachery. So they need to be restrained by the severe penalties of law, and forced by the curb of discipline to keep to the path of justice.[12]

---

10. For the Normans' positive characteristics, see *EH,* 4:16, 36; 5:26; 6:454, 468. Dudo's image of Christian Normans is strongly positive: they were exceptional, bellicose, and skillful (*De moribus,* 198), practiced in war (275), and wiser than other folk (244). The treachery and savagery that Dudo portrays in Hasting are, to the historian, not manifestations of his Normanness but of his paganism (see *De moribus,* 141). William of Poitiers's view is very much like Dudo's, except that he also sees the Normans as intrinsically law-abiding and obedient (*GG,* 38, 242, 250). For the Normans' negative characteristics, see *EH,* 2:214; 3:14, 98; 4:14, 40; 5:24, 246; 6:332, 450, 457. For a more extensive discussion of these "gentile" characters and a comparison of Orderic's view with that of other Norman and English historians, see Shopkow, "Norman Historical Writing," 338–52.

11. *GG,* 184, 260; *GND,* 77.

12. *EH,* 4:83; see also 3:99 and 5:24. This and all other citations from the *Ec-*

William's successors provided a frequently distressing demonstration of this argument. Robert Curthose, who in the work of Orderic's contemporaries was sometimes depicted as a flower of chivalry, was the sort of weak ruler against whom his father had warned, a morally weak, foolish, and extravagant man.[13] A hermit in Germany has a vision in which Robert appears as a wanton cow (the gendering of Robert in this vision as female and hence weak and vice-ridden is deliberate).[14] Through Robert, Normandy is punished for its faults, for his reign allows the turbulent, the cruel, the disruptive and striving elements of Norman society to run amok.[15] Henry I, in contrast, offers both England and Normandy a reprieve from misrule, by embodying the manly virtues his brother lacked, particularly wisdom and the love of justice.[16] Like his father, Henry had the vices one would expect of the masterful leader, but Orderic carefully minimized them in the narrative. Orderic was aware of charges of cruelty against Henry, but he had the king refute them cogently. Orderic acknowledged that Henry was libidinous to a fault, but his other references to vices Henry shared with his father, such as his avarice, his favoring of new men, and his savage protection of his hunting rights, Orderic mentioned only obliquely.[17]

Fittingly, Orderic's account of Henry I's death and funeral demonstrates the difference between Henry and his father. Henry restored lands to men who had lost them (thereby avoiding a potential scene like that kicked up by Ascelin at the Conqueror's funeral). He allotted money for his household and thereby forestalled the desire of his followers to loot. The nobility swore to

---

clesiastical History are from the translation by Margery Chibnall, unless otherwise noted.

13. For Orderic's comments on Robert Curthose, see *EH*, 2:356; 3:96–98, 102; 4:92, 110, 114, 124, 146; 5:26, 30, 305; 6:56.

14. Ibid., 3:104–6.

15. Ibid., 5:300–302, 4:146.

16. For Henry's virtues, see ibid., 2:214; 4:250, 252; 5:294, 300, 316, 318; 6:14, 96, 98, 200, 248, 354; 6:14, 96, 176, 450.

17. On Henry's vices, see ibid., 6:16, 96, 100, 176. For his refutation of charges of cruelty, see ibid., 6:284–8, 352–4.

accompany the body to its final resting place, and twenty thousand people followed it to Rouen. The body was filled with balsam, so it would not stink as his father's had done. Finally it was escorted by monks to Reading. Disorder followed the king's death, but that disorder did not invade his funeral.[18]

Orderic seems not to have expected moral perfection in a ruler, for despite his description of Henry's flaws, he calls the king the "glorious father of his country" and depicts his reign as a peaceful and happy one. Since Henry's reign was marked by periodic rebellions, some of them in the area around Saint-Evroul, Orderic's statements about Henry clearly reflect the historian's general moral outlook rather than a historical reality.[19] However, like William of Poitiers, he drew parallels between the king's private behaviour and public consequences. If for Orderic the Conqueror's reign was less successful than it was for William of Poitiers, it was because Orderic disagreed with William's description of the Conqueror's character, not because he disputed the essential moral argument. The potentially negative consequences of the character flaws of the ruler again emerge at the end of the *Ecclesiastical History* in Orderic's various depictions of Stephen. Orderic describes Stephen early in his career as rejecting the advice of elders and preferring the counsel of sycophants. When he first becomes king, Stephen neglects his Norman responsibilities, thus breeding unrest and violence. As king, his kindliness is a liability and weakness that causes

18. Ibid., 6:448–50. Chibnall (*EH*, 449, n. 5) comments that the intent of having the nobility swear not to abandon the body may have been to avoid a debacle like that at the Conqueror's funeral, but it seems possible to me that this detail was deliberately inserted by Orderic to stress how different Henry's edifying obsequies were from those of William the Conqueror. One knows a man's character by the manner of his death. Orderic's account is in direct conflict with the narrative of Henry of Huntingdon, *HA,* 256–58, which tells how Henry's body oozed noxious liquids after death, despite being heavily salted, and links this to his splendor and gluttony before death.

19. *EH,* 4:94, 6:180, 450. See Green, "King Henry I and the Aristocracy of Normandy," 163–64, and "Lords of the Norman Vexin," in *War and Government in the Middle Ages,* ed. John Gillingham and J. C. Holt (Woodbridge, Suffolk: Boydell, 1984), 47–61. Much of the evidence for the difficulties of these rebellions comes from Orderic's work.

his subjects neither to fear nor obey him.[20] Orderic's depiction of Stephen parallels his depiction of Robert, who abandoned his Norman responsibilities to go on crusade and who was similarly more inclined to listen to adulators than the wise. As Orderic ended his history, Stephen, like Robert before him, was in prison.[21] Thus, the *Ecclesiastical History* depicts Norman history as a process of rise and fall, in which cycles of Norman well-being were followed by tragic and painful periods of decline, a pattern from which the Normans seemingly could not escape.

Most of the *Ecclesiastical History* is concerned with things Norman and English. However, Orderic went beyond his predecessors in placing the story of the Normans in the context of all of Christian history by prefacing his account of contemporary history with a lengthy chronicle beginning with the Incarnation. This chronicle forms nearly a third of the text of the *Ecclesiastical History*.[22] By doing so, Orderic implicitly commented that the story of the Normans was only one story of many peoples unable to live consistently under God's law. There were exceptions to this lamentable human fate. Indeed, Orderic interrupted the Norman tragedy to relate a story of marvelous triumph, the story of the First Crusade (book nine of the *Ecclesiastical History*). The moral clarity of the Crusade, however, was an exception to the generally more muddy waters of ordinary human existence.

Naturally, Orderic could not offer exegesis on the entire wealth of material he placed in his *Ecclesiastical History*. Instead, he left the reader to discover the meaning of history independently by contemplating the great tableau.[23] Neither Norman history nor history

20. *EH*, 6:206, 456–68, 522.

21. Ibid., 6:551.

22. The entire edition of Orderic's history is *PL* 188:15–984. The first two books occupy cols. 17–229.

23. Morrison, *History as a Visual Art*, 80–91 and elsewhere, argues that historians deliberately presented their material in series of tableaux, like those of narrative painting, the gaps between which were to be filled by the readers through protension and memory. While this does not seem to apply equally well to the work of all historians, it makes sense in connection with Orderic, whom Morrison explicitly discusses in this connection.

in general could arrive at closure and while it might offer moral meaning for the astute, it could not offer any promise of security or happiness. Orderic ended with the ultimate moral lesson that history might teach: that there was security only in God.[24] Orderic's dark moral view of human history can be read as a delayed response to the optimistic moralism of William of Poitiers.

৶

Robert of Torigni's continuation of the *Deeds of the Dukes* stood apart from Orderic's essentially tragic and William of Poitiers's triumphant characterizations of Norman history. Like William of Jumièges, Robert read the past mostly literally, and so his history was an account of human actions and their results. He had read the histories of Dudo and Orderic, but he embraced neither the allegorical schemata of Dudo, nor the moral inclinations of William of Poitiers and Orderic. True to his emphasis on the literal, Robert rarely commented on the events he narrated in any of his historical works. For example, when in his continuation of the *Deeds of the Dukes,* he tells about the White Ship disaster of 1120 in which Henry I's only legimate son drowned along with many of the young members of Henry's court, he says only that up until this point, fortune had smiled on Henry. In contrast, Orderic Vitalis made it a moral story of the proud brought low, reporting that most aboard were drunk and refused to permit priests to bless the ship; the proud nobility perished while the son of a butcher survived, because the rough hides he wore kept him warm.[25]

Where Robert did offer interpretations of events in his continuation of the *Deeds,* they have the ring of stories in general circulation, rather than the personal reflections that characterize Orderic's moral ruminations. For example, he advanced two theories about William Rufus's death: that his death was retribution for the accidental slaying of Rufus's brother Richard (who was also struck

24. *EH,* 6:550f.
25. *GND,* 281; *EH,* 6:296–300.

down in a hunting accident in the New Forest), or that it was re-payment for Rufus's destruction of villages and churches when he expanded the forest.[26] Many opinions of Rufus's death must have been in circulation. Some of these appear in the work of other historians, where they are often accompanied by stories of portents and visions that preceded the king's death.[27]

Most of Robert's interpolations into the *Deeds,* however, reflect pragmatic concerns. He added many genealogies by way of ex-plaining Normandy's complex politics. He also added to the *Deeds* material from the *Customs* that William of Jumièges had chosen to omit.[28] There are several possible explanations for this reinterpo-lation of material. One possibility is that Robert wished to include all possible information about the Norman past in his version of the work. Another, however, is that Robert felt a kind of nostalgia for a golden past when the Normans enjoyed divine guidance and purpose. Robert does not argue for any particular direction to the history of his own times; the eighth book of his *Deeds of the Dukes* has no particular closure. It ends in 1135, but not with the death of Henry I, because after reporting that death, Robert goes on to report a few other stories: an anecdote about how Gunnor came to be married to Richard I (he first admired her married sister, who cunningly sent Gunnor to the duke's bed in her place) and the death of the abbot of Bec, among other things.[29] Elisabeth van Houts's description of the *Deeds of the Dukes* as a "history with-

26. *GND,* 279.
27. See, for example, *GRA* 2:333 and 376–78. In the earlier passage, William of Malmesbury basically reports what Robert also reports. In the later passage, how-ever, he reports an apparition of the devil, St. Anselm's foreknowledge of William's death, William's dream that he is being bled and his blood covers the sky, and a dream by a monk that William was bitten on the arm by a crucifix. Also *HA,* 232, reports that blood flowed from the earth in Berkshire a little before his death.
28. Genealogies: the Bellême-Montgomery family (*GND,* 320–22); the Beau-monts (324); the Giffards (324–25); the Warennes (328); and the Mortemers (328); all of these families claimed descent from Richard I's wife, Gunnor. Robert also provides genealogies for the dukes of Flanders and counts of Hainault (285–86), the FitzOsberns (287–88), the de Montforts (292–93), and the kings of France (301–2). For these interpolations, see van Houts, *GND* (2), 34–50; 54–56; 60–62; 66–72.
29. *GND,* 316–20, 322–23, 334.

out an end" is a particularly apt one for Robert's version of the *Deeds*.[30]

For his most important other work, Robert emulated Orderic's strategy in that he set Norman history within the context of universal history, but here again Robert passed up the opportunity to perform either allegorical or tropological exegesis on his material. Although Robert remarked in his introduction that chronicles enabled readers to recognize the meaning of portents so that they might identify the sins for which they were about to be punished and avoid God's wrath (a clearly figural way of reading events), he offers no generalized exegesis of signs. All the omens he interprets are explained only in specific terms. For example, he explains that the comet of 1106 signals the imprisonment for life of Robert Curthose, but the historian does not discuss comets in general. Similarly, the host that broke in the hands of Bishop Alexander of Lincoln when he was about to offer King Stephen communion portended King Stephen's ruin, but this logic is not extended to other accidents during the mass.[31]

Robert's comments on the meaning of historical events are very brief when they occur. For example, he reported that Robert Curthose failed to prosper because he refused the crown of Jerusalem which offended God. (While other historians, including Henry of Hungtingdon (Robert's probable source), also noted that Robert had been offered but spurned, the crown of Jerusalem, Robert of Torigni alone links this refusal to Curthose's later fate.[32]) On sev-

30. van Houts, "A History without an End," 106–18. van Houts has argued (*GND* (2) 1:lxxxix–xc) that Robert's first intention was to end in chapter 33, with the death of Henry I. However, once he decided to continue the work, he seems to have had no particular end in mind. van Houts points to one and a half blank columns at the end of Robert's manuscript as evidence that he planned to come back to this work later.

31. Rob. of Tor., 129, 221. Robert did not always choose to explicate portents. When four white circles appeared around the sun in 1104, Robert comments only that it was a sign of things to come (Rob. of Tor., 1:126).

32. Rob. of Tor., 1:91, 87, 128. For other sources which mention the legend that Robert refused the crown of Jerusalem, see *HA*, 236; William of Malmesbury, *GRA*, 2:608–9; and Geoffrey Gaimar, *L'Estoire des Engleis,* ed. A. Bell, Anglo-Norman Texts, 14–16 (Oxford: Blackwells, 1960), 183, ll. 5761–5764. For this legend, see C. W.

eral striking occasions, however, Robert refrains from making just this sort of comment. When he mentions the demise of William Rufus, Robert comments that at his death the king held three bishoprics and eleven abbeys in his own hands, and that whatever displeased God and his servants pleased the king. As a suggestion that God struck the king down, it is oblique.[33] It is worth noting that Robert does not even allude to the alternative explanations he offered in the *Deeds of the Dukes*.

In the chronicle, as in his version of the *Deeds of the Dukes*, Robert avoided arguing for any large patterns in history, and contented himself with small stories that reflected the concerns of his day. His narrative contained several accounts of transsubstantiation miracles where the bread and wine of communion appeared to communicants as flesh and blood.[34] Such miracles were common in the twelfth century as the doctrine of transubstantiation was more widely taught and known. However, Robert may have been particularly interested in them because Lanfranc and Guitmond, transsubstantiation's most articulate defenders in the eleventh century, had, like himself, been monks at Bec. Robert also recounted four cases of ritual murder of Christian children by Jews; the increasing intolerance within Christian society of any deviance meant that the blood-libel was widespread during the twelfth century.[35] The last part of the chronicle contains more miracle stories than the earlier part. Their greater length and liveliness suggest that Robert in his last years may have been increasingly interested in the miraculous, although it is also possible that the prevalence of miracle stories may be a byproduct of Robert's methods of gathering information.[36]

David, *Robert Curthose* (Cambridge: Harvard University Press, 1920), 114 and n. 135.

33. Rob. of Tor., 1:91.   34. Ibid., 2:104–6.

35. Ibid., 2:27–28, 66–67. On the rise of the blood libel, see R. I. Moore, *The Formation of a Persecuting Society* (Oxford: Blackwells, 1987), 36–38.

36. Other miracles include a lengthy account of the miraculous resurrection of a woman at Roc-Amadour (Rob. of Tor., 2:99–102), a vision seen by Stephen of Fougères (ibid., 2:73–74), the story of the conversion of the mother of Kilidge Arslan II (ibid., 2:106–7), and the appearance of the Virgin at Puy (ibid., 2:126).

The chronological structure of the chronicle organized the contents so that Robert did not need to worry about coherence. He was thus free to include material that was less obviously significant or serious. Robert was not averse to including the occasional humorous anecdote. One wonderful tale, which is also revealing about Norman naming patterns, relates that when Henry the Young King, Henry II's son, held court in Normandy as the future duke for the first time, some Williams in his entourage procured an eating chamber into which only Williams were permitted to enter. Many Williams chose to eat with Henry, but 110 Williams ate in the William room.[37] Apart from these small narratives, Robert's chronicle concerns itself primarily with events in all their seeming randomness: the comings and goings, births, milestones, and deaths of the great men and women of his world.

Although Robert had made his own contribution to the eleventh-century tradition of serial biography by continuing the *Deeds of the Dukes,* Robert's chronicle, like the *Ecclesiastical History* of Orderic, is evidence that it was increasingly undesirable to write Norman history in isolation from the history of other realms. The effect of Orderic's integration of Norman history into a larger whole, however, was rather different from the impact of Robert's combination of Norman and universal history. In the *Ecclesiastical History,* Orderic minimizes Norman history, reducing it to its proper stature by setting it in the context of other people's histories. Orderic, after all, started by writing Norman history and added the universal history afterward. In contrast, Robert introduced the Norman and English past into the great chronicle tradition of Eusebius-Jerome-Sigebert from which they had been omitted. Robert, therefore, was claiming the Normans to be a great people, who belonged in a great history. To render the Normans more significant, Robert had to extend their history before the arrival of the Vikings. To do so, however, he had to shift away from the eleventh-century notions of how the Norman community was constituted which had

37. Rob. of Tor., 2:31.

been accepted by previous Norman historians, including Orderic Vitalis. For Dudo of Saint-Quentin (and most subsequent Norman historians, whether they wrote Norman history or some more local sort of history), Normandy came into being with the confluence of the Vikings, the territory of Normandy, a ruling family, and religious conversion. When Robert says that he added into Sigebert's chronicle materials concerning Normandy, he was speaking of Normandy primarily as a geographic territory. He added things like the succession of archbishops of Rouen and other bishops.[38] While this was a tribute to Normandy's perceived territorial stability, it was also a sign of the weakening power of the eleventh-century triumphant narrative.

This weakening was also accentuated by a second shift of emphasis in Robert's chronicle. Eusebius had organized his chronicle around independent monarchies, prefacing each yearly entry with the regnal years of the rulers. Jerome, Prosper, and Sigebert continued this practice, although Sigebert listed only the rulers of Germany, France, and England (beginning in 1066). To incorporate Norman history into this scheme meant that Robert had to stress England, which was a kingdom, rather than Normandy, which had an independent existence but which was not ruled by a king.[39] A token of this shift of focus was Robert's decision to begin the original part of his chronicle with the coronation of Henry I in 1100; Henry did not become duke of Normandy until 1106. It was a tacit acknowledgement that Henry's royal title overshadowed his ducal one.[40]

More importantly, however, Robert did not see his chronicle as telling only the history of the Normans, or even the history of the Normans and English, although most of the information in the original part of the chronicle concerned these two peoples. Rather, he was taking his place in the Eusebian tradition of universal

38. Ibid., 1:94–95.
39. Bates, "Normandy and England after 1066," 863–64. Robert also had to list only one Anglo-Saxon royal lineage and to ignore others. On this point, see below, p. 169.
40. Rob. of Tor., 1:96.

chroniclers. He must also have expected that others coming after him would continue his work, just as he had continued Sigebert's and Sigebert had continued Jerome's.

While it is impossible to say why Robert shifted away from dynastic history—why, for example, although he lived until 1186, he did not continue the *Deeds of the Dukes*—there are some tantalizing possibilities. While Normandy maintained its territorial contours and its legal identity, its fate was bound up with other territories from 1144 on, when Geoffrey Plantagenet of Anjou became Normandy's duke. Normandy continued to have an active duke (Henry II spent as much time in Normandy as anywhere else).[41] However, that duke was Angevin in the male line at a time when people in Normandy and England were developing more restrictive senses of identity. It is suggestive that after Robert completed his version of the *Deeds of the Dukes,* when he was no longer writing Norman regnal history but had turned to his chronicle, he urged Gervais of Saint-Cénéri to write Angevin regnal history.[42] Furthermore, Normandy was also increasingly peripheral in the far-flung possessions of her dukes. The traffic across the channel after 1150 was more likely to run from England to Normandy than from Normandy to England.[43] To write a chronicle was to be able to avoid having to make sense of these changes in Norman experience and of Normandy's place in the world. The annual breaks in the narrative confounded story-telling and story was replaced by chronology as the organizing principle of the text.[44] Robert included some of the same information in his chronicle as he did in his version of the *Deeds of the Dukes,* but it appeared without an interpretive framework, and thus was essentially "un-

41. Bates, "Rise and Fall of Normandy," 31–32.
42. Rob. of Tor., 2:339.
43. Bates, "Rise and Fall of Normandy," 29, 33.
44. Schmale, *Funktion und Formen,* 82–83, has argued that what mattered in chronological works was not the particular events included but the depiction of the passage of time. Hayden White has made a similar argument ("The Value of Narrativity in the Representation of Reality," *Critical Inquiry* 7 (1980–81): esp. 14–15. That the primary concern was to describe the passage of time explains the inclusion in some annals of "blank" years.

digested."[45] The frame of reference for including certain information for including certain information and excluding the rest lay outside the material itself, inside Robert's mind and the minds of his contemporary readers.[46]

℞

When Robert of Torigni refused to tell a story, he also refused to speculate upon the meaning of the Norman past. The author of the last Latin narrative history of Normandy, Stephen of Rouen, however, rose to the challenge of assigning meaning to events in Normandy. Stephen was uninterested in the moral readings of the past provided by William of Poitiers and Orderic Vitalis.[47] Instead, he returned to the earliest mode in which the story of Normandy had been cast, the allegorical reading of Norman history favored by Dudo of Saint-Quentin but with two differences. First, he was aware that Norman history could not be isolated from that of the surrounding peoples, so he recapitulated the internationalism of Robert of Torigni's chronicle. Second, Dudo's reading of the Norman past had been charged with religious significance, which Stephen replaced with a secular and ultimately more pessimistic counterpart: the theory of the "*translatio imperii,*" the change of ruling dynasties.[48] The natural rulers of Europe in this scheme were the descendents of the Trojans, first the Romans, then the Franks, and finally the Danes. This notion of historical causality had its origins in both the triumphalism of Dudo of Saint-Quentin, who was the first to tell the story of the Trojan descent of the Normans, and a classicism Stephen shared with William of Poitiers.[49] Like

45. On digestion as a widely used medieval metaphor, see Carruthers, *The Book of Memory,* 166–68; Morrison, *History as a Visual Art,* 56.

46. This displacement of the central subject from the text to the reader or compiler is a common feature of annals and chronicles. On this issue, see Louis O. Mink, "Everyman His or Her Own Annalist," *Critical Inquiry* 7 (1980–81): 780.

47. He shows no evidence of knowing either man's work.

48. See, for example, *DN* 722 (III:324). Stephen uses the term "transfer of thrones."

49. *De moribus,* 130. Descent from peoples from classical times, not only the Trojans, was a common claim by medieval historians. Widukind of Corvey thought it possible that the Saxons were descendants of the soldiers of Alexander the Great;

Dudo, Stephen saw God's hand in determining the passage of authority from one people to another, although for Stephen, as for other twelfth-century writers, God worked through natural agencies like climate.[50] Like William of Poitiers, Stephen was inspired by the precedent of imperial Rome and was forceful in making the analogy between the Normans and the Romans. William the Conqueror is a second Caesar; so is Henry II. Rouen is the "city of Caesar," while Robert Guiscard, the Norman conqueror of southern Italy, is said to have brought the victorious eagles with him to Sicily.[51] Stephen insisted on the imperial status of Henry II's mother Matilda, as though to underline the fitness of her son ruling an empire.[52]

What made this story of bright beginnings tragic, however, was that Stephen's protagonist, Henry II, failed to live up to his potential by making Normandy independent of France. Dudo had rationalized Norman independence from the king of France by stressing that Normandy came to the Normans as a gift of God, and that the dukes had never become royal *fideles*. Fidelity had become too natural an institution by the later twelfth century for Stephen to revive that argument, but he arrived at another, rather ingenious historical argument, based not on the authority of the dukes of Normandy, nor even on their royal status as kings of England but on a denial of the Capetian claim to enjoy legitimate authority. The Capetians deposed the Carolingians, despite a clear

---

the theory of the Trojan origins of the Franks was first put forth by Fredegar (Widukind of Corvey, *Widukindi rerum gestarum Saxonicarum*, ed. G. Waitz [Hannover: Hahn, 1882], 4; Fredegar, *Chronicarum quae dicuntur Fredegari scholastici libri quattuor, MGH, Scriptores rerum Merovingicarum*, 2:93).

50. On climate, see *DN*, 610 (I: 487–90). On naturalistic explanation, see Funkenstein, *Heilsgeschichte*. For an extended discussion of this issue in the work of Stephen's contemporaries, Henry of Huntingdon, William of Newburgh and Richard of Devizes, see Partner, *Serious Entertainments*, 212–30.

51. See, for example, *DN*, 604 (I:311); 602 (I:273–76); 604 (1:324). A roughly contemporary poem, "Rothoma nobilis" (Charles Richard, *Notice sur l'ancienne bibliothèque des échevins de la ville de Rouen* [Rouen: Alfred Peron, 1845], 37), makes a comparable play on "Rome" and "Rouen" and echoes the opening of the famous poem "O Roma nobilis" as well.

52. See, for example, *DN* 599 (I:219) and 617(I:669).

warning from the Pope that no one should presume to replace the lineage he has installed.[53] As usurpers, the Capetians were not legitimate authorities, and Henry II was not obligated to recognize them as his overlords in any of the lands that had belonged to Charlemagne (Stephen explicitly enumerates Henry II's territories as belonging among Charlemagne's conquests).[54] Stephen depicts Louis VII of France as a new Childeric, ripe for overthrow.[55] The German emperors, in contrast, were legitimate heirs of Charlemagne. While Frederick Barbarossa could have claimed France on that basis, Stephen depicts him as willing to cede that authority to Henry II.[56] Stephen's polemic advances an argument both for Norman independence from France, a resurrection of Dudo's assertion, and for a conquest of France by Normandy, a new opportunity for Norman glory.[57]

However, by the end of the *Dragon,* Stephen's hopes are frustrated. After toying with the possibility of a German alliance, Henry II permits his sons to do homage to Louis VII for the lands they will hold of the king after their father's death. Equally bad, Henry partitions his lands among his sons, thereby breaking up his empire. The division of the patrimony was for Stephen always a sign of weakness; he attributed the decline of the Carolingian

53. Ibid., 670f. (II:133–414). Here, as in many places in the *Norman Dragon,* Stephen has made a historical error. He names the pope who deposes Childeric as Stephen, but it was Zacharias who deposed Childeric.

54. Ibid., 672 (II:361–62) and 673 (II:373–74, 387–89).

55. See, for example, ibid., 681 (II:585–86).

56. Ibid., 720 (III:245ff.).

57. The *Draco* is one of the few sources from the period which shows much interest in Germany. The monks at Bec must have been aware of the negotiations afoot between Henry II and Frederick Barbarossa with which the canonization of Charlemagne was intimately tied. On these issues, see Peter Munz, *Frederick Barbarossa: A Study in Medieval Politics* (London: Eyre and Spottiswood, 1961), 242ff. The monks' awareness would have been heightened by their close connection with Henry's mother, Matilda, the widow of Henry V, whose marriage to the German monarch established friendly literary ties between Germany and England, and which brought among other things, a copy of Ekkehard of Aura's chronicle to Normandy. See Hans Eberhard Meyer, "Staufische Weltherrschaft? Zum Brief Heinrichs II von England an Friedrich Barbarossa von 1157," in *Friedrich Barbarossa,* ed. Gunther Wolf (Darmstadt: Wissenschaftliche Buchgesellschaft, 1975), 184–207.

empire to its division among the sons of Louis the Pious.[58] When Normandy and England had been held by different men, when William the Conqueror gave Normandy to his son Robert Curthose and England to his son William Rufus (who was succeeded by his brother Henry I), and again when Geoffrey Plantagenet conquered Normandy for his son, the future Henry II, and Stephen of Blois held England, there had been bloodshed. Stephen firmly believed in absolute male primogeniture, for when he speaks of the war between Henry I and his brother, he implies that Robert Curthose was in the right because of his prior birth.[59] Just as William of Jumièges's acceptance of fidelity resulted from social changes, Stephen's insistence here on male primogeniture also reflects the success of that ideology in the twelfth century. Many of his contemporaries would have agreed with him that dividing a patrimony led to the decline of a family. Hence Stephen anticipated a further decline of Norman greatness in the next generation, since Henry II had already made clear his intention of dividing his territory among his sons.

Since history unrolled in an inevitable succession of ruling peoples, however, the Norman decline was, in a sense, a foregone conclusion. All peoples in the end vanished into the past, into history. The *Norman Dragon* is punctuated with references to great past heroes whose deeds no longer had currency. Charlemagne, after all, left no lasting empire, and the triumphs of Arthur were also long in the past. Stephen's theory of history, which was composed of cycles of dominance, presupposed the decline of Norman greatness eventually, if not as a direct consequence of the actions of Henry II. Thus Stephen's celebration of the deeds of the Normans is not triumphant but nostalgic for a glorious past. He clearly hoped that the Normans would maintain their tradition of greatness despite his knowledge, derived from reading history, that even the greatest of peoples were destined to fall.

The nostalgia for the past so strongly exhibited in the *Norman*

58. *DN*, 674 (II:407–14).
59. Ibid., 649 (I:1508–9).

Dragon and implicitly present in Robert of Torigni's version of the *Deeds of the Dukes*, the sense (also embraced by Orderic) that the high point of Norman history lay in the eleventh century and not in the twelfth, seems to have been characteristic of Norman attitudes of the mid to late twelfth century. Henry II commissioned Norman regnal histories in the vernacular, but the historians he chose, Wace and Benoît of Sainte-Maure (contemporaries of Stephen of Rouen), never managed to bring their histories beyond 1100. Even the name Wace gave his history, the *Romance of Rollo*, harkened back to the earliest period of Normandy's existence. The annalistic traditions at most Norman monasteries became extremely attenuated. The short annals of Bec trailed off in 1183. The annals of Jumièges underwent a long period of mediocrity before reviving at the end of the century. Most other monastic annals trailed off in the years following the conquest of Normandy by France. Clearly much of the impetus for writing history had disappeared.

Even outside of historical writing, however, the eleventh century seems to have exerted a strong emotional pull on twelfth-century Normans. In book production, for instance, Norman monasteries were conservative, illustrating the books that were copied in the scriptorium with an artistic vocabulary already established in the eleventh century. A similar phenomenon pertains in architectural style. Normandy did borrow some features from English architecture, but it also remained quite conservative, engrossed in what Lindy Grant has called "architectural autism."[60] Historians, then, seem to reflect a wide-spread attitude in Normandy that the good days were the old days.

What is visible at the end of the twelfth century, then, in Nor-

---

60. Lawrence, "Anglo-Norman Book Production," 93; Grant, "Architectural Relationships between England and Normandy," 121, 124ff.. "Otherwise [apart from its planned double ambulatory], Fécamp epitomises the inward-looking nature of twelfth-century architecture in Normandy. Its design harks back, it seems to me quite self-consciously, to its splendid Norman predecessors of a century earlier. . . . It seems to have struck a chord in the duchy, establishing the accepted elevation for all Gothic buildings of pretension for the next fifty years" (125–26)

man historical writing is an imaginative failure on the part of Normandy's historians. The eleventh century had provided satisfying narratives about the early period of Norman history. However, twelfth-century writers were unable to extend the earlier narratives successfully to encompass their own period or to propose alternative stories about the past. Unable to glorify the present, historians either celebrated the past or stepped outside the Norman narrative entirely.

4 ❧ Truth

*T*o achieve their visions of history, Norman historians were discriminating in the information they placed in their narratives. Sometimes they coped with disadvantageous information, as modern historians might, by explaining it away. Other commonly accepted medieval practices, particularly the omission of pertinent but inconvenient information, the alteration of what sources reported, and the wholesale creation of information to suit the story, are not acceptable in modern historical practice. While some medieval historians were able to fashion satisfying works without much recourse to invention, the narratives of others owe their power to the willingness of their authors to perform extensive manipulation and fabrication of their materials. Dudo of Saint-Quentin's *Customs of the Dukes* is a remarkably shapely narrative. However, little that Dudo reports would satisfy a modern historian's criteria for factualism. As Dudo was not a modern historian, it would be foolish to hold him to modern standards. However, since medieval historians held with Isidore of Seville that history was an account of things that had truly happened, it is appropriate to ask to what standard of historical truth Dudo and other medieval historians might have adhered.

The concern for historical truth was often expressed by medieval historians. Sometimes the references to it were perfunctory and topical.[1] In other cases, historians anticipated the criticism of their readers that they had not met some notion of truth. Lambert of Ardres, for instance, clearly expected to be attacked for beginning his history of the counts of Guines (1202) two hundred years before any of his sources. He knew himself to be vulnerable to the criticism that he was not an eyewitness of the events he narrated, as Isidore had suggested the best historians were, and his defence of his work was geared to addressing that issue. His defiant response to the critics was to ask whether anyone was prepared to doubt Moses for writing about events that occurred 2242 years before the flood.[2] The preference for eyewitness accounts rather than oral traditions underlay one notion of historical truth (not one espoused by everyone), but there were others.

Not all of the Norman historians expressly considered the question of historical truth. One who did was the Anonymous of Fécamp whose introductory remarks touch on many ideas of how history might be true or false. He subscribed to the notion that history's primary characteristic was its truth, but how historical truth was to be secured and established for readers was a complex matter.

In this book I have not falsely placed anything false. Truly, I have written down sacred histories, known by the faithful narrative of men of old, kept in the bosom of tenacious memory by their followers and carried down to our times by the diligent report of succeeding men, and I have set them down in writing for the dignity of the church of Fécamp and the benefit of the brothers reading. Therefore, following the authority, not of all but of a few of the reasonable narrators, I placed the miracle of the stag

---

1. On this issue, see Guenée, *Histoire et culture historique,* 350ff.

2. Lambert of Ardres, *Historia comitum Ghisnensium,* ed. Johannes Heller, in *MGH SS* 26:557.

at the beginning of the book and imitating the excellent diligence of the chronicles, I set this down as the first revelation of Duke Ansegisus. For I have truly declared that Fécamp was adorned from this ancient beginning, not with the name of the glorious and unsullied Virgin Mary, as some would have it, but with that of the holy and indivisible Trinity. My judgment was that I should incline toward that opinion which would incur no ignominy of falsehood. Every church, whether named in honor of this or that saint is founded, constituted, and dedicated in the name and under the protection of the holy and indivisible Trinity.[3]

The Anonymous had limited written sources at his disposal in writing the history of his monastery, particularly for the period before the late tenth century. Dudo of Saint-Quentin, for example, was interested only in Richard I's foundation at Fécamp and not the church that preceeded it. However, he mentioned that there was a church dedicated to the Trinity on the site before Richard I founded the monastery, a scrap of information the Anonymous wrung as much out of as he could.[4] This lack of written evidence did not overly concern him, however, for oral evidence was so acceptable that he made no reference in the introduction to any other kind.

More significant was the conflict among the traditions about Fécamp that the Anonymous was weaving together into a history. The majority of witnesses reported that Fécamp had originally been dedicated to Mary. The Anonymous seems aware that one method of finding the truth would be to report what the majority of the witnesses had said, but this would not have served the author's argument well.[5] Instead, the author followed the minority

3. *Libellus de revelatione*, 702.

4. *De moribus*, 290.

5. The Anonymous argued that the site at Fécamp was chosen as a sacred place by the Trinity at the time of the Incarnation. Thus the actual foundations on the site were a series of "revelations" rather than acts of human will and desire. The implication of this process was that since the church enjoyed a divine foundation, it should not be subject to the authority of the merely human archbishops of Rouen. The author knew that his monastery had been reformed by William of Volpiano, who had presumably secured a Cluniac-style exemption from episcopal authority

report, and offered an elaborate explanation for why this was acceptable practice. The witnesses were "reasonable" men, and their rationality made them worthy of credence. More important was the second rationale for selecting this testimony. The author justified his choice by offering a rather ingenuous statement that he had taken the morally safest course, since all churches are "really" governed by the Trinity, whatever saint they happen to be dedicated to. In other words, his narrative expressed a higher truth than a merely factual veracity. Thus notions of truth were flexible for him and might be selectively applied.

The anonymous author defends the truth of his narrative in a number of ways. First and most simply, he asserts that he is speaking the truth, denying that either he or the stories he tells are false. He similarly characterizes his sources as "diligent" or "faithful." He twice in this short passage uses the word "true" or "truly." He also emphasizes the chain of oral tradition, suggesting that it was unbroken, when the discontinuities in the monastery's history and the gender change of its inhabitants made this improbable. The implication is that he, like Lambert of Ardres, was aware of the vulnerability of a second-hand account. In addition, he appeals indirectly to the authority of the Bible. The term he uses for the stories he wrote down, *sacras historias* (holy stories) was resonant, for the Bible itself was *sacra historia*. This identification with the Bible was natural given that the *Authority,* like the Bible, was a chronicle of the acts of God. Finally, he likens his history to the "excellent diligence of the chronicles," by implication making a claim that his work, through its devotion to chronology, had the same sort of authority.

The author of the *Authority of Fécamp* was not alone in his uneasiness about the issue of truth in history. While Dudo of Saint-Quentin, whose position in relation to truth is intriguing, made no reference to the issue, the later eleventh-century Norman his-

---

for the house. In fact the monastery based its legal case against the archbishop on the charter purportedly procured for the house by that saint. However, the Anonymous, while referring to William's actions at the end of the history, made a distinctive, and temporally prior, second case.

torians, William of Jumièges and William of Poitiers, explicitly addressed the question. The twelfth-century Norman historians were similarly diverse in the degree to which they were explicit about their concern for historical truth and in the ways they achieved it in their narratives.

Part of the problem was that there was no agreed-upon criterion for historical truth in the Middle Ages. In fact, there were several concurrent notions of truth. One criterion was whether something was widely believed to be true. Suzanne Fleischmann suggests we should consequently think about history in the Middle Ages as what was collectively believed. According to this notion, a dishonest historian would be one whose account was not consonant with commonly held beliefs.[6] Because collectively held beliefs were expressed in histories, history was less divorced from memory than it is today, and memory, which included things that never happened, like epic tales, tended to jumble the imagined and the experienced together, making the distinction between "history" and "fiction" less clear. What people remembered was nevertheless true.

Another notion of truth was derived from Augustine, for whom the virtuous intentionality of the writer or speaker guaranteed the truth of the words, a truth which was then perceptible through the charity of the readers or listeners.[7] Earlier medieval historians translated Augustine's notion of truth into a verbal guarantee of the good character of their witnesses. For example, Gregory of Tours describes his witness for the miracles of St. Lupicinus as an eighty-year old priest (an authority by both age and vocation), who spoke under oath.[8] Bede similarly stressed the credibility of

6. Fleischmann, "On the Representation of History and Fiction," 278–310, and especially 305. Paul Veyne makes the same argument for all pre-modern history in *Did the Greeks Believe in Their Myths?*

7. Stephen G. Nichols, *Romanesque Signs: Early Medieval Narrative and Iconography* (New Haven, Conn.: Yale University Press, 1983), 39–40. Jan Ziolkowski has pointed out to me that Augustine makes the same point in *On Christian Doctrine* that he makes in *Confessions* 10:3.

8. Gregory of Tours, *Vita patrum*, in *Les Livres des miracles et autres opuscules de Georges Florent Grégoire* (Paris: Renouard, 1862), 3:308. The oath suggests an anxiety

Abbot Albinus, a deeply learned man appointed to his office by Theodore and Hadrian, who in Bede's time were venerated as saints.[9] The same assurances were transferred to written sources when these became more common than oral sources. Robert of Torigni's respect for the work of Jerome and Eusebius derives not only from the antiquity of the work but also from the authors' saintly character, and he follows Augustine in also seeing the good will of the readers as crucial to the appropriate reception of history.[10] This notion of truth appears as well by implication in the defence by the Anonymous of Fécamp of his text. What makes the author's assertion that the churches of Fécamp had always been dedicated to the Trinity true was his intention to speak the truth (albeit the higher truth) about the foundation.

While the credibility of a witness was one guarantor of truth, another was the consonance between secular events and the divine template or between events in the past and events in the present. Ralph Glaber conceived of truth in the former way, probably under the influence of Eriugena's philosophy.[11] Writers operating under this notion of truth might alter or omit the factual data to encourage it to resemble the template, as Bede did.[12] How much shaping of the evidence was permitted was indeterminate and depended on the writer's purpose and expectations for an audience. For example, the author of the biography of a saint in certain periods might feel free to borrow miracles told about one saint to adorn a life of another as

---

about the credibility of his narrative. Walter Goffart, *The Narrators of Barbarian History (A.D. 550–800): Jordanes, Gregory of Tours, Bede and Paul the Deacon* (Princeton, N.J.: Princeton University Press, 1988), 137, argues that Gregory was well aware of the strain of incredulity among his readers, which the function of his narratives was, in part, intended to counteract.

9. See Bede, *Bede's Ecclesiastical History of the English People,* ed. B. Colgrave and R. A. B. Mynors (Oxford: Oxford University Press, 1969), 2.

10. Rob. of Tor., 1:92–93. "There is a useful purpose in these things [i.e. histories], just as in other treatises, which, although it is hidden from fools and buffoons, is apparent to the studious and the insightful."

11. On Glaber, see Stephen Nichols, *Romanesque Signs,* 8ff.

12. See Goffart, *Narrators of Barbarian History,* 242, n. 37, and 272. On the larger question of Bede's perspective, see C. W. Jones, *Saints' Lives and Chronicles in Early England* (Ithaca, N.Y.: Cornell, 1947), 80–93, esp. 91–92.

the saints were all sustained by one life.[13] The second method of gauging truth, the expectation that events in the past would resemble those in the present, was also commonly used. Verisimilitude might be used to assess and modify accounts of the past. Historians might also use verisimilitude to decide how to fill in gaps in histories or to give accounts a more satisfying shape.[14]

Historians used all of the above criteria for truth as it suited them, and consequently they not only produced strikingly different works from one another but also disagreed about the truthfulness of others' writing. The reception of Geoffrey of Monmouth's *History of the Kings of Britain* demonstrates this very clearly. Robert of Torigni, who read the book within a few years of its completion, was an enthusiastic partisan of this history and noted Geoffrey's election as bishop of St. Asaph in his chronicle.[15] He liked it so much, he introduced it to Henry of Huntingdon, when that historian passed through Bec in 1139 on his way to Rome.[16] Henry of Huntingdon, in contrast, was somewhat more cautious, saying he was astounded to find writings *(scripta)* on the early history of Britain, having already searched in vain for something on the subject when he was composing his own history. There is a note of polite skepticism in his words.[17] Orderic Vitalis also accepted Geoffrey's work as genuine, copying a portion, the prophecies of Merlin, into his text.[18] The English historian William of Newburgh, however, made a lengthy attack on Geoffrey's history which consumes most of the prologue of his *English History*. Geoffrey's stories are repeatedly called "lies" *(figmenta)* and "idle tales" *(fabula)*. Geoffrey is "our story-teller" *(fabulator noster)*; the prophecies of Merlin, which appear toward the end of Geoffrey's history, are simply

13. Gregory of Tours, *Vita Patrum*, 132–34.
14. On verisimilitude, see Veyne, *Did the Greeks Believe in Their Myths*, ch. 2, esp. 24ff.
15. Rob. of Tor., 1:265.
16. Rob. of Tor., 1:96, 97–98. Only the versions of Henry's letter describing his discovery of Geoffrey's text that are appended to Robert's chronicle mention Robert by name.
17. Ibid., 1:96–98.
18. See *EH*, 1:47. The text appears *EH*, 6:380–86.

"falsehoods" *(fallacia)*. These are contrasted with the "honest name of history" *(honesto historiae nomine)* and the "truth of history" *(historiae veritas)*.[19]

For the historians who accepted the *History of the Kings of Britain* as genuine, Geoffrey's adherence to the formal standards of historical writing—the use of a historical style and his attribution of his material to a written source—made his work unquestionably true. These are the criteria the author of the *Authority of Fécamp* invoked when he referred to the unbroken chain of witnesses to the events he described and when he claimed to work as chroniclers do. This formal criterion is one that twelfth-century historians were increasingly interested in, for they once again began to talk about different sorts of history.

In the twelfth century, historians began to add another criterion for historical truth to the existing ones, namely that written sources were preferable to oral sources. Modern scholars differ as to when oral testimony was no longer as acceptable as a document. Brian Stock sees that development as occurring in the eleventh century with the growth of textuality. In contrast, Michael Clanchy has argued that in law, oral testimony was still preferred to written evidence at the end of the twelfth century, partly because of the problem of forgery. Since it was difficult to establish the authenticity of a document, the oral was consequently often considered more trustworthy. Mary Carruthers has also placed the privileging of the written later. She sees the turning point coming with the systematic organization of memory around the middle of the thir-

---

19. William of Newburgh, *Historia rerum Anglicarum*, in *Chronicles of the Reigns of Stephen, Henry II, and Richard I*, vol. 1, ed. Richard Howlett (London: Her Majesty's Stationers, 1884), 12–18. The word *veritas* appears six times in this passage, twice alone, three times with *"historica"* or *"historia,"* and once with *"res gestae."* William might have been thinking of I *Tim.* 4:6–7, where Paul contrasts the "words of faith and of good doctrine" which Timothy is to follow, with the "foolish old-wives' tales" *[aniles fabulas]* which he was to avoid. By using the word *"fabula,"* William may also be contrasting history and fable, which for Isidore and those after him, were mutually exclusive categories. Gerald of Wales also attacked Geoffrey of Monmouth's work, but he offerred no argument for his position, whereas William of Newburgh based his rejection of the *History of the Kings of Britain* on the fact that Geoffrey's account did not accord with those of Bede and Gildas.

teenth century.[20] It seems logical that the acceptance of the authority of the written varied according to circumstances. Historians, however, unlike lawyers, do not seem to have been so much concerned with the problem of forgery. Instead, they were troubled by the tendency of oral traditions to grow and become embellished. The written seemed to provide greater stability and consequently to be more trustworthy. The accusation raised against Geoffrey of Monmouth was not that his source lied but that he had no source to begin with. In the eleventh century, this accusation would have carried much less weight—the Anonymous of Fécamp, as I have said above, was not worried that he had only oral sources but that others would be aware that his narrative diverged from some of them.

The Norman historians drew on all of these notions of truth, but each historian gave them different weights. Dudo of Saint-Quentin came closest to embracing an Eriugenian notion of truth, the idea that historical events had to follow a divine template.[21] This way of viewing truth was implicit in the allegorical view. Dudo's narrative was pinned down by two great and indubitable facts: when the Normans arrived in Normandy, they were pagan, and when Dudo was at Richard I's court, they were Christian. They had become so, and become French-speaking as well, while still maintaining a distinct regional character. His task was to supply the stories to show how this happened.[22] The inventions in the

20. Brian Stock, *Listening for the Text,* (Baltimore, Md.: Johns Hopkins University Press, 1990), 36 and 46; also and more extensively Brian Stock, *The Implications of Literacy* (Princeton, N.J.: Princeton University Press, 1983). Michael Clanchy, *From Memory to Written Record: England, 1066–1307* (Cambridge: Harvard University Press, 1979), 210–11. Carruthers, *Book of Memory,* 150. She also points out that many of the features customarily associated with "oral" societies continued to be true of literate society (10–12).

21. While it is unlikely that Dudo had read Eriugena, he had read Heiric of Auxerre's *Vita sancti Germani,* which presents portions of Eriugena's philosophy. On Heiric and Eriugena, see Edouard Jeauneau, "Heiric d'Auxerre disciple de Jean Scot," in *L'École carolingienne d'Auxerre de Murethach à Remi, 830–908* (Paris: Beauchesne, 1991), 353–70.

22. For Dudo's many factual "errors," see Prentout, *Étude critique sur Dudon de Saint-Quentin.*

Customs of the Dukes are never without parallels in other texts, although the nature of the parallels varies.

In some cases, Dudo borrowed stories told about other people. For example, when he had Rollo endow the churches of Normandy after his baptism, Rollo was imitating Constantine's granting of gifts to the Church in the *Donation of Constantine*. Constantine demonstrated how great leaders behaved when they converted to Christianity, and Rollo had to conform to this model of behavior. Dudo was so anxious to be thorough about this that he had Rollo endow Jumièges, a church which Dudo, because he recounted the story of its refoundation, knew had ceased to exist by the beginning of the tenth century.[23] When the role of a historian was to report what was said or what was commonly believed, such inconsistencies did not necessarily reflect badly on a historian's truthfulness. Vincent of Beauvais, for example, included inconsistent accounts in his *Speculum historiale* without feeling the need to choose between them or explain away the inconsistency.[24]

Dudo also filled in gaps in his narrative by borrowing suitable stories about other Vikings from his sources. For example, Dudo says that as part of the pact of 911 by which Rollo was ceded Normandy, Rollo was also given Charles the Simple's daughter, Gisela, as a spouse. This story comes from the Saint-Vaast annals, where it is told about Gotfried who married Charles the Fat's daughter, Gisela.[25] Here, Gotfried's experience is a model for the ways kings dealt with Vikings, and it established a paradigm for peace between

23. *De moribus*, 171, 200. "Then he built Jumièges, marvelous to say . . ." (200).
24. See Monique Paulmier-Foucart, "Ecrire l'histoire au XIIIᵉ siècle: Vincent de Beauvais et Helinand de Froidmont," *Annales de l'Est*, ser. 5, 33 (1981): 64, for a discussion of Vincent of Beauvais's similar lack of concern for consistency.
25. Howorth, "A Criticism of the Life of Rollo," 245; Prentout, *Étude critique*, 207; C. Dehaisnes, ed., *Les annales de Saint-Bertin et de Saint-Vaast* (Paris: Jules Renouard, 1871), 312. The Saint-Bertin annals mention the cession of Frisia to Gotfried but not the marriage. The annals do say, however, the Charles asked Hasting to intercede with Gotfried to make peace. (ibid., 288.) Since Hasting is asked to negotiate with Rollo in the *De moribus* (154), it seems clear that Dudo based his account of Rollo in part of Gotfried's career. For Rollo's campaign in Frisia, see ibid., 149ff.

enemies. Thus Dudo's story satisfied the criterion of verisimilitude—this is the way Vikings behave.

A third sort of invention supplied events which were not strictly required by a prototype nor needed to fill in blanks but instead underlined the significance of Norman history. For example, Dudo says that when Rollo sailed from England to Normandy, the devil whipped up a storm to prevent him; Rollo calmed the waves through prayer. This incident is drawn directly from the life of St. Germanus, who in the earlier story was travelling to England to dispel Pelagianism. The story was not necessary to the narrative (and indeed William of Jumièges omitted it entirely), but it underlined the significance of Rollo's journey and Dudo's notion of the ways in which history was meaningful.[26] Of course, the devil would oppose the conversion of any group of people to Christianity, since the loss was his. Previous experience had shown that the devil did not take such defections lying down, and he would certainly attack when Rollo was most vulnerable, on the sea. These inventions made the history of the Normans conform not so much to specific stories told about others as the larger and insistent pattern of salvation history.

Dudo also strove in his "discovered" evidence to make political and social relations in the Norman past reflect his personal circumstances. For example, he gave Richard I's "uncle," Bernard of Senlis, a large role as one of Richard's protectors during his minority. Senlis belonged, in the tenth century, to the family of the counts of Vermandois, Dudo's lords, and Bernard was a common name in the family. Giving Bernard of Senlis a prominent role permitted Dudo to link his older patrons with his new patrons, despite their previous political disagreements.[27]

---

26. *De moribus*, 148–49. On the relationship between Heiric of Auxerre's work and the *Customs*, see Shopkow, "The Carolingian World," 72–75 and *passim*.

27. Bernard of Senlis would not, however, have been Richard's uncle. He may have been a cousin of Herbert II of Vermandois and thus kin to William Longsword's Christian wife, Leutgarde. However, Leutgarde was not Richard's mother. On Bernard of Senlis, see Dhondt, *Naissance des principautés territoriales*, 119 and n. 5; Bur, *Comté de Champagne*, 88 (Table 2). Since Bernard of Senlis nearly always

In his invention of stories about the Normans, Dudo may seem to be violating the only unavoidable requirement of history, that it be true. However, Dudo operated throughout on the assumption that past histories provided a vocabulary of true stories that reflected the way history unfolded in the past and continued to unfold. If Constantine was converted by a vision which led to his baptism and the conversion of the Roman empire, Rollo, whose conversion similarly entailed the Christianizing of his people, would also have been inspired by a vision. Indeed, Rollo's vision makes reference to Constantine's.[28] Thus, in making decisions about the contents of his history, Dudo was guided by the requirement that the present must recapitulate the past and that the past must resemble the present. He had no desire to present "facts" but only for his readers to see the Norman rulers as the civilized people he had found them to be.[29] For him, as for the author of the *Authority of Fécamp,* these greater truths were more important than facts.

Dudo's successor, William of Jumièges, while equally likely to use verisimilitude as a standard for truth, submitted the contents of the *Customs of the Dukes* to drastic editing to satisfy his rather different ideas about historical truth:

> In truth I omitted from the course of this history the genealogy of Rollo, who was born of pagan parents, and many things done in his pagan state until he was reborn into holy infancy in the salutary font of baptism, and also his dream along with many things of this sort, believing them to be completely adulatory and to have no semblance of honesty or utility.[30]

In part, William's skepticism may have been aroused by his knowledge of other sources. William omits any account of the

---

acts in concert with Bernard the Dane, I suspect that the latter was twinned from the former.

28. See below, p. 151.

29. Fleischmann, "On the Representation of History and Fiction," 289–90, cites Stephen Nichols who comments that in much medieval history, the uniqueness of historical events is subordinated to their resemblance to previous or scriptural models.

30. *GND,* 2.

"treaty" of Saint-Clair-sur-Epte—one of Dudo's real masterpieces —possibly because the Saint-Bertin annals, which he may have known, said nothing about it.[31] However, he accepts many things Dudo says that are similarly not found in other sources. Therefore, William's objections to Dudo's narrative cannot arise from what we would understand to be historical criticism. One aspect of Dudo's work which seems to have aroused William's suspicion was its unabashedly exuberant rhetoric. In the later eleventh century, historians came to avoid the high style, preferring instead the middle style, perhaps in imitation of the Bible's *sermo humilis*.[32] In contrast to Dudo's baroque language and complex narrative, William's story is explicitly spare:

not adorned with the elegant weightiness of the rhetoricians, nor with their venal sheen or brightness of polished speech, but in the unadorned style, composed intelligibly in simple speech for any reader to understand.[33]

William's reference to venality is part of the traditional attack on rhetoric, which was seen as giving the user the slippery ability to alter every argument to suit any possible stance. Such denunciations of rhetoric were common among historians.[34] Dudo's employment of the high style was a sign of his adulatory intentions, for if he had meant to write no more than the truth, he would have written plainly. This criticism of Dudo's work, partly explicit and

31. William mentions Bjorn Ironsides, who appears there, in connection with Hasting (*GND*, 8, 16). Bjorn is named as the leader of the Seine Vikings in the Saint-Bertin annals under the year 858 (Felix Grat, Jeanne Vielliard, Suzanne Clémencet, eds., *Les Annales de Saint-Bertin* [Paris: Klincksieck, 1964], 76–77). There is no record that the Saint-Bertin Annals were in Normandy, but since the monks of Jumièges fled to Haspres in Flanders during the Viking invasions, and since the monastery had ties with Saint-Vaast where the Saint-Bertin annals were continued, William may have known these annals or known something of their contents.

32. On *sermo humilis*, see Erich Auerbach, *Literary Language and Its Public in Late Latin Antiquity and in the Middle Ages,* trans. Ralph Mannheim (Princeton, N.J.: Princeton University Press, 1965), 21–66.

33. *GND*, 1.

34. On the subject of rhetoric, see Nancy Partner, "The New Cornificius," 5–59, esp. 22–3; Guenée, *Histoire et culture historique,* 215ff.

partly implicit, is effectively an attack on Dudo's character, and since the truth of a narrative depended on the character of the speaker, Dudo's narrative was thus suspect.

Still, William could not throw out Dudo's narrative entirely, since it was the only written source for the tenth century in Normandy. If history was what people said and believed about the past, Dudo's work was information William could not afford to discard. Thus just as Greek historians set out to purge myths of their fictive elements, William set out to correct Dudo's work, using the tool of verisimilitude and making the past conform to the present— William's present.[35] William rescued Dudo's history from its lapses by reformulating or omitting Dudo's stories and by emphasizing different things, as when he stressed the importance of fidelity as a bond to hold society together or when he recast Dudo's hagiography of William Longsword.[36] His own experience of human behavior and motives led him to change some stories as well. For example, rather than accepting Dudo's explanation that Hasting's actions were motivated by frustration, William suggests that Hasting returned to France after the sack of Luna because he could no longer hope to take Rome, his original goal, by surprise.[37] Such reasoning also led him to omit all of Dudo's stories set before Rollo's conversion that made Rollo seem too Christian, although he retained Dudo's story that Rollo endowed churches after his baptism. However, whether William reworked Dudo's material because it did not describe the world as he knew it or because he was a more shrewd psychologist, his disbelief arose not because he disapproved of Dudo's methods or because of the discrepancy between Dudo's account and the meager sources available but from aesthetic considerations. In other words, while modern scholars criticize the way other historians use evidence, for William, the availability of evidence and the way it was used were not the means

35. Paul Veyne, *Did the Greeks Believe in Their Myths?*, 23ff.
36. See above, pp. 71, 87–89. For a lengthier discussion of William's concern for fidelity and proper social order, see Shopkow, "Norman Historical Writing," 182–85.
37. *De moribus*, 135; *GND*, 16.

by which the truth of a narrative was assessed. In fact, William did not comment on Dudo's methods at all.

William of Poitiers raised explicitly the comparison of the truth of history with the lies of the poets to which William of Jumièges had referred obliquely. The historian, William remarked, must tell what is true, while the poet is free to invent. The historian must include no tales for which he has insufficient evidence, lest the whole work be thrown into disrepute. William must limit himself to the simple but truthful praise of his hero.[38] The *topos* of the prolixity and lies of the poets versus the truthfulness and concision of the historians was old long before the Williams invoked it, but William of Poitiers's use of it is clever. The historian often cites the poets while rejecting their narratives and thus is able to show his erudition while insisting on the purity of his history. Thus Xerxes and Agamemnon keep company in one case, and William of Poitiers remarks that both Rome and Troy would have proven equally vulnerable to a hero like the Conqueror.[39] But for all that, William's rejection of the lies of the poets is a cliché; it is a statement of policy about the nature of history.

This policy did not prevent William of Poitiers from modeling events and the characters of the people he discussed on stories from other texts. William's account of the surrender of Domfront after the destruction of Alençon echoes Caesar's sack of Gomphi and the subsequent surrender of Metropolis.[40] The panic caused by rumors of the duke's death at Hastings recapitulates a similar moment at the battle of Cirta as recounted by Sallust in which the Romans fall back because they believe Marius has died. William of Poitiers must have been thinking of the earlier incident when he remarked that even experienced and fearless troops have been known to retreat when they believe their leader to have been killed. However, the duke's tactics to rally his troops come courtesy of Suetonius's biography of Julius Caesar.[41] Again like Caesar, the

---

38. *GG*, 44. See also ibid., 184, 200, for other references to the topos.
39. *GG*, 162, 208.
40. Julius Caesar, *De bello civile*, 3:80–81; *GG*, 40–44.
41. Sallust, *De bello Iurgurthino*, 101.11; *GG*, 188–90; ibid., n. 3. William of Poi-

Conqueror is not superstitious and does not pay any attention to omens. He merely laughs when he dons his cuirass backwards. Like Sulla, he puts his friends in his debt.[42]

Like Dudo of Saint-Quentin, William apparently did not subscribe to the notion that events are singular or unique, the view of the past that underlies modern historical writing. However, the two historians used materials from other histories in different ways. William was more subtle than Dudo. He seldom introduced a story from the past wholesale, instead inserting short allusions into longer, independent stories. Whereas Dudo's repetition of stories from earlier histories was tied to his allegorical notion that history had to repeat itself, William of Poitiers uses his borrowings mostly to illustrate moral points. For instance, William said that the Bretons lived on meat, milk and thievery, were ignorant of agriculture and practised polygamy, using language borrowed from descriptions of the Numidians and Germans by Sallust and Caesar.[43] What William probably meant by this was to provide a likeness rather than the one-to-one correspondence the modern reader would expect, namely that like the Numidians, the Bretons were rustics and fated to be conquered by a superior and more civilized enemy. For medieval philosophers this sort of likeness, which they called *adaequatio,* was a sort of truth.[44] To a reader not familiar with the classical texts or this more qualified notion of truth, however, William's words were misleading. They not only obscured the differences between the remote past and the present as William of Jumièges's work did, but they also seemed to be saying something specific about one group of people, when they were really making a general statement about certain kinds of people. This anachronism may have resulted from the indifference of historians to the

---

tiers is the first to tell this story about the battle, a story which found its way into many subsequent tellings, including the Bayeux Tapestry. It is possible, therefore, that William effectively made the story up.

42. Suetonius, *Divus Julius,* cap. 59; *GG,* 182. Sallust, *De bello Iurgurthino,* 96; *GG,* 26.

43. *GG,* 109, n. 4; 110, n. 1.

44. On adequation, see Carruthers, *Book of Memory,* 24–25.

distinction between the past and the present, as Schmale has argued, but it is also the consequence of a preoccupation with meanings beyond the literal.[45]

In the vexed question of truth, therefore, William stood somewhere between Dudo of Saint-Quentin and William of Jumièges. Like Dudo, William of Poitiers had no compunctions about inserting details from histories about peoples other than the Normans into his text, even though for the most part his borrowings from the writings of the past were a way of imparting traditional wisdom. However, like William of Jumièges, he verbally embraced a commitment to make his history true. In fact, part of his argument for the superiority of his hero over ancient heroes is that William the Conqueror was celebrated in a history, while accounts of older heroes were poetic and thus lies.[46] He claims several times in the narrative to be telling the truth, although each of these protestations that he was speaking the truth was made when his material was most dubious. Consequently, the protests seem disingenuous.[47] Telling the truth, however, did not mean that William of Poitiers felt compelled to tell everything he knew. Where he commits what would be sins for modern historians, they tend to be sins of omission rather than commission.[48] Therefore, while

45. Schmale, *Funktion und Formen*, 66. Schmale suggests that medieval historians were barely able to grasp historical change as change because the past and present were so thoroughly bound together in their minds. There is another way of looking at the problem, however, suggested by Carruthers, *Book of Memory*, 168–69 and elsewhere. For most of the Middle Ages, reading and memorizing (and writing, by extension) were the mechanisms by which the individual internalized experience, which was not distinguished from personal experience; it was then available to be turned into moral action. That process of internalization itself blurred the distinctions of time and space.

46. Jeannette M. A. Beer, *Narrative Conventions of Truth in the Middle Ages*, (Geneva: Droz S. A., 1981), 13.

47. Ibid., 19–21; all of Beer's chapter on William of Poitiers, "Truth and the Authorities," is extremely helpful on this issue.

48. Among the omissions: the rather suspicious deaths of Walter and Biota of Mantes, both at Rouen (*EH*, 2:312), the duke's savage punishment of those who had mocked him at Alençon (*GND*, 126), and the controversy surrounding the marriage of the Conqueror and Matilda. One rather astonishing sin of commission

William of Poitiers knew that history was defined by its truthfulness, he applied the notion of truth with more latitude than William of Jumièges or indeed modern historians would.

The twelfth-century Norman historians continued to operate within an environment in which there was no consensus about what constituted historical truth and in which historians were either more or less concerned about the issue. Orderic Vitalis was probably the most concerned of any of the Norman historians about history's truth, for he assures the reader continually that he is telling the truth, that he writes truthfully *(veraciter)* or with a truthful pen *(veraci stilo or veraci calamo)*. He uses these terms to describe his witnesses and sources as well.[49] The term *verax*, like the term *veraciter*, invariably refers to the character of the witness rather than the witness's information, as when Orderic says that he heard a story from "truthful" monks who lived at Jumièges, or mentions "truthful" men who knew of a miracle of St. Judoc, or speaks of "truthful" pilgrims who said there had been a million Christians at a particular battle during the Crusade.[50] It is not surprising that Orderic, as a moralist, embraced the Augustinian notion that truth was derived from character. Unlike his contemporary William of Malmesbury, who reported everything he heard but warned his readers about that which he considered dubious, Orderic never reported anything he considered to be untrue.[51]

Truth also depended on the impartiality of the historian. For Orderic, the truth of history was compromised when the historian

---

is his comment that the duke carefully avoided nepotism, given that three of his episcopal appointees came from his own family (*GG*, 128).

49. *Veraciter*: *EH*, 1:130, 137, 150, 175, 177, 190, 191; 2:150, 156, 304, 320; 3:6, 210, 214, 302, 324; 4:72, 106 (twice); 5:6, 188, 190; 6:8, 358, 388, 450. *Veraci stilo*: ibid., 1:162, 177. *Veraci calamo*: ibid., 2:188.

50. Ibid., 2:18, 2:160, 5:336.

51. As, for example, when William remarks that some said that the Conqueror had beaten Matilda to death with a bridle for injuring his mistress (*GRA*, 2:453). William continues, saying that he cannot credit this story, and he thinks it grew up because of the estrangement between Matilda and William over their son Robert (cf. *EH*, 3:102–4).

wrote for a patron. Orderic defends his ability to write truthfully at the end of the third book on these grounds:

> In the following books, I will tell more of King William and will record without adulation the unhappy fates of the English and Normans, since I await remuneration neither from victors nor vanquished.[52]

Orderic may be consciously echoing William of Jumièges's denunciation of Dudo of Saint-Quentin here, for he uses the term adulation to describe the historian's distortions of the past as William did, but the belief that patronage or partisanship corrupted the purity of history was common among twelfth-century historians. William of Malmesbury echoes these sentiments when he says that as a man of mixed descent he is best suited to write truthfully about the relationship between the Normans and English.[53]

Orderic also agreed with William of Jumièges that truth arose from a rejection of rhetorical artfulness. Orderic declared his intention to write simply, calling himself a simple son of the Church.[54] This is not an apology for a rustic style or a modesty topos but an offering of his credentials; Orderic nowhere in his work apologized for his manner of presentation and frequently defended the importance of his labors. When he used the term simple, he meant both clear and unpretentious, even humble, and by espousing simplicity, he distanced himself from the eloquent men who wrote to please William the Conqueror; again, he echoed William of Jumièges.[55] While other historians rejected artifice, Orderic's embrace of simple language seems directly connected to the aesthetic of the Bible and its *sermo humilis*. While most historians in the Middle Ages viewed the Bible as history, its influence on Orderic was particularly profound in that he saw historical writing as sharing in its holy character. The Bible, like

---

52. *EH*, 2:188–89. The substance of the translation is Chibnall's; I have altered her wording slightly.
53. *GRA*, 2:389.
54. *EH*, 1:130.
55. Ibid., 2:190.

all truthful histories, was written for the praise of God, not of mortal men.[56]

Orderic's concern for truth, however, did not lead him to develop a critical apparatus for recognizing it in his sources. Although both William of Poitiers and William of Jumièges wrote to please the Conqueror, and William of Poitiers's work was highly rhetorical, Orderic used the work of both men. Thus, even though the *Deeds of the Dukes* and the *Deeds of William* should both have been suspect, these texts had authority in Orderic's eyes because they were written down. Orderic was the first Norman historian to privilege the written over the oral, and he thus represents the emergence of a new criterion of truth. For him, once a text was written down, it came with a certain guarantee of truth. In contrast, Bede, whose work Orderic in some ways emulated, made no distinction between the oral and the written.[57] Consequently, Orderic seems to have accepted pretty much all the written texts that came to hand. (Orderic only explicitly rejected one written text, although he may have rejected others without comment.)[58] For example, he accepted Geoffrey of Monmouth's work as at least partially genuine, for he included the prophecies of Merlin, one of Geoffrey's more extravagant passages, in his own work. This reverence for the written was tied to his perception that the past was slipping away through both the destruction of documents and the neglect of their creation and thus being lost to ecclesiastical history; hence the large numbers of epitomes of other works in Orderic's history.[59] In collecting together these fragile materials, Orderic was also following old notions of history, that whatever people have said about the past is important.[60]

56. See *EH*, 1:48–54 for Chibnall's comments on the influence of the Bible on Orderic's writing. Henry of Huntingdon, a contemporary of Orderic, refers to the Bible as a historical standard (*HA*, 2). See also Hugh of Saint-Victor, *Didascalicon*, 115, where Hugh names the eleven books of the Bible that are historical in the strict sense.

57. See Stock, *Implications of Literacy*, 76f. on Orderic's attitude to the written. See Bede's comments to Ceolwulf on his sources, *Ecclesiastical History*, 2–4.

58. *EH*, 3:306.

59. See below, pp. 163, 203–4.

60. See Veyne, *Did the Greeks Believe in Their Myths?*, 6.

Among the stories that people told about the past or wrote about the past were miracle stories, which Orderic accepted without demur. For some writers, however, the miraculous was in the process of becoming largely "unhistorical," as there was a growing preference for naturalistic, as opposed to supernatural, explanation. The uneasiness some people felt in the face of the miraculous, and particularly the miraculous performed by a living saint, is vividly demonstrated in Stephen of Fougères's *Life of Vitalis of Savigny*.[61]

Stephen's unease had several causes. One was that his only written source, apart from the death roll of Vitalis, was a vernacular text, which Stephen seems to view as somewhat obscure for he mentions that in translating the work into Latin, he is making it available in "more manifest" letters.[62] Another source of anxiety was the use of oral accounts that might not be corroborated, twice forcing Stephen to make direct disclaimers that he had made anything up. In this case he also invokes the character of those who have told him the story.[63] Stephen enjoins even the doubters to listen to the life of Vitalis, so that they may acquire faith. In this reference to the doubters, Stephen acknowledges a current of disbelief in his own time.[64] In one case, he defiantly announces that he believes in a miracle himself.[65] When the issue of doubt comes

61. See André Vauchez, "L'Influence des modèles hagiographiques sur les représentations de la sainteté, dans les procés de canonisation (XIIIe–XVe siècle)," in *Hagiographie, cultures et sociétés* (Paris: Etudes Augustiniennes, 1981), 587, and *La sainteté en Occident aux derniers siècles du Moyen Age* (Rome: Ecole française de Rome, 1981).

62. *Vita sancti Vitalis*, 364. On his use of the death roll, see ibid., 380.

63. Ibid., 376. "Let no one suspect that these things are invented by us because of the novelty of this great matter which we have inserted here, because we have described not our own matters but those proven and transmitted to us by the testimony of the faithful." Stephen repeats almost the same thing in the following chapter (376).

64. Ibid., 377.

65. Ibid., 369. "I shall say, I shall say what I think. I do not judge that he lacked the spirit of prophecy, who was able to predict the horrible death of a man and foil the machinations of the devil." Both Stephen's repetition of "I shall say" *(dicam)* and his use of the first person pronoun, *ego,* with the verb *existimo* as an intensifier offers a challenge to those who might judge differently.

up, Stephen appeals to the precedent established by the Bible, arguing that God could surely repeat in modern times anything that happened in the past. This criterion of authenticity is the same as that employed by Dudo of Saint-Quentin, although Dudo never makes explicit reference to it. However, the number of times Stephen invokes the precedent suggests that some of his contemporaries no longer felt that biblical narratives resembled historical ones.[66]

It would be a mistake, however, to see Orderic's concern with historical truth or Stephen's awareness of an increasing skepticism toward the miraculous as imposing serious constraints on twelfth-century historians. The later Norman historians used essentially the same criteria of truth as the earlier ones, adding to these rules only the reverence for the written. Like Orderic, Robert of Torigni tended to believe in the veracity of what he read. Consequently, he interpolated into his version of the *Deeds of the Dukes* much of the material from the *Customs of the Dukes* that William of Jumièges had chosen not to use. Dudo's written account, by virtue of being written, well-known, and old, had a certain degree of authority. However, unlike Orderic, Robert had no particular objection to orally transmitted material. Robert included in his interpolations material that had circulated in oral form, such as legendary genealogies of prominent Norman families.[67] Robert reported miracles, whether he knew them through written accounts or oral transmission. In fact, he reported more miracle stories and gave more space to the miraculous toward the end of his chronicle,

66. See ibid., 361, 365–66, 369, 374–76, 378. Interestingly, these questions of truth do not arise in the life of William Firmat. However, William was a hermit and not the founder of an order. The Savigniacs thus had a stake in the narrative Stephen created for them, their own traditions handed down from Vitalis's disciples. Stephen's unease may derive as much from the possibility of conflicting traditions as anxiety over truth.

67. For the genealogies, see *GND*, 258, 320. At least one of the stories, which tells how Richard I fell in love with Gunnor's married sister who agreed to a tryst but sent Gunnor in her place, clearly belongs in the romance tradition of *Tristan*. The genealogies, however, were not frivolous; they were necessary to explain the complicated politics of twelfth-century Normandy, as Searle, *Predatory Kinship*, 102 has pointed out.

where he relied on oral accounts, than at the beginning, where he used primarily written sources.[68] Writing simply and clearly in all of his works, Robert concurred with William of Jumièges about the appropriate style for the historian. He does not seem to have chosen his sources with a critical eye but rather according to which text would fit in the space he wished to allot to it. Robert used Dudo's work extensively in his revision of the *Deeds of the Dukes* where he wanted a more ample narrative. His use is sparing in his chronicle, however, where the narrative is abbreviated. Thus, Robert's criteria for the inclusion or exclusion of material seem aesthetic and formal, rather than critical or methodological.

No singular criterion for truth was indispensible, however, not even the avoidance of rhetoric, for Stephen of Rouen wrote a strikingly rhetorical text, in poetry no less. Indeed, the purpose of his text seems sometimes to be to teach rhetoric. When he recounts the siege of Toulouse, Stephen has Henry debate whether to attack the city in which his liege, the King of France, is staying. The reader is told little of the content of the speech; instead, Stephen outlines the form.

The king, like an orator, calls together his legions. The nobility of the realm was present, as were the leaders of the army. As the deliberative argument demands, he proposes, distributes, and recites most usefully. He begins, narrates, confirms and refutes. He concludes, and upon these four propositions he bases his arguments: whether he should overthrow the city and the king enclosed within; whether he should capture him alive, and let the count and city [of Toulouse] fall; whether he should urge those enclosed within the walls to betray the city; or whether he should wait to capture the city when the king was not there. When he had argued these four things, the speaker touched on each and brought everything together in an epilogue.[69]

Henry's conclusion, as is proper for the deliberative argument, depends on what is most honorable for him to do rather than what

---

68. See Partner, *Serious Entertainments*, 216–18, for a discussion of the English historians and naturalistic explanation. On Robert of Torigni, see Shopkow, "Norman Historical Writing," 422–23.

69. *DN*, 608–9 (I:441–52).

was most expedient, while his troops urged a more practical course of action.[70] Thus, the reader of the *Dragon* can learn the proper way to approach a deliberative argument, although not what specific arguments were advanced on this occasion. Stephen also provides examples of demonstrative argument, or the speech of praise and blame, and he mentions forensic argument.[71] The *Dragon* contains many letters and much direct speech. Of a total of 4,386 lines, almost 1,300, or about one-third of the whole, contain direct speech of some sort.

Because his text was filled with divergences from other sources, Stephen's work epitomizes what other historians meant when they talked about the lies of the poets, because his text was filled with divergences from other sources. For example, the council at which Octavian (anti-pope Victor III) anathematized Alexander was not held at Mainz, as Stephen reports, but at Pavia.[72] It was not Saint Oswald's head which remained uncorrupt after his death, as Stephen reports, but his arm, as Bede, Stephen's source, told him.[73] One suspects that the needs of scansion may have motivated these sorts of changes. However, Stephen was also willing to slip from history into fable in a way that was as evident to his contemporaries as to modern readers. The most striking case where he does this is when Stephen tells how King Arthur, upon hearing that Henry II had attacked Brittany, sent a letter from the Antipodes threatening revenge. Henry was amused by the letter and sent a mockingly respectful reply, promising to rule in Arthur's name. Stephen makes it clear that he himself does not believe in the story of Arthur's survival or return, yet he includes the story anyway, almost certainly as a way of linking his work with that of Geoffrey of Monmouth's *History of the Kings of Britain,* which Stephen used as a source and to which he made reference in his title. He probably also wished to attack those who believed that Arthur would return.

70. Cf. Quintilian, *Institutionis oratoriae libri duodecim,* III, 4, 6.
71. *DN,* 617–18, 667.
72. Ibid., 731 (bk. 3, cap. 9).
73. Ibid., 615 (I:625); Bede, *Ecclesiastical History,* 230. For other inaccuracies, see Shopkow, "Norman Historical Writing," 468–69.

Nevertheless, the story makes a great set piece and demonstrates the epistolary art.[74]

What is striking in this passage is not that Stephen accepted Arthur as a historical individual but that he reported an incident that he clearly did not believe to have happened. If there was something distinct about history from other sorts of composition, even the small matter of history being about true things that really happened, Stephen did not care. Despite all of the grammatical and rhetorical information Stephen conveys in the *Dragon,* he never invoked Isidore's distinction between argument, fable, and history; a fine argument might be made that his history was a mixture of all three, a bastard form.

Twelfth-century historians, therefore, used largely the same criteria as eleventh-century historians to establish the truth of their own narratives and of the works they read, and they used these criteria with similar freedom. No uniform method of ensuring history's truth emerged. A standard of this kind could only have emerged from a community of historians and readers sufficiently uniform in their methods and expectations and sufficiently powerful to dictate which works were acceptable and which were not. Communities of readers and historians, however, were often isolated from each other, and neither historians nor readers would be dictated to. While historians occasionally criticized each other for transgressing against the truth, the success of a history was independent of this consideration. The dubious *History of the Kings of Britain* of Geoffrey of Monmouth exists in some 215 manuscripts and in numerous vernacular translations. It was still being copied into the fifteenth century, because it was deeply satisfying to readers, some of whom may have thought it fabulous but did not care.[75] In contrast, Orderic's *Ecclesiastical History,* a text by a historian who

---

74. *DN,* (II:945–1282). For the relationship between the *Norman Dragon* and the *History of the Kings of Britain,* see Shopkow, "Norman Historical Writing," 497–500.

75. See Julia C. Crick, *The* Historia Regum Britanniae *of Geoffrey of Monmouth: IV. Dissemination and Reception in the Later Middle Ages* (Cambridge: D. S. Brewer, 1991), xi–xvi, for a list of the manuscripts.

thought seriously about history's truth and who worked hard to make his history true within the constraints of his criteria for truth, had little success in capturing an audience. If history was a sort of literature that made a truth-claim, the degree to which each history could substantiate that claim was less important to readers than other considerations.

5 ❧ Methods, Models, and Sources

*F*or medieval historians, the truth of history did not reside in the methods of historians but in the historian's character, language, and intentions. The contrast with the modern notion of historical truth, which avoids the issue of the historian's character and instead focuses on methods, could not be more striking. While a few historiographers of the modern period have concerned themselves with the ways history is or might be true, most practicing historians are more concerned with how one should go about the work of writing history.[1] Under the currently

---

1. Among the philosophers who have wrestled with the epistemological problems presented by history, see, for example, Louis Mink, "History and Fiction as Modes of Comprehension," *New Literary History* 1 (1970): 541–58; writings on the objectivity question such as Peter Novick, *That Noble Dream: The Objectivity Question and the American Historical Profession* (Cambridge: Cambridge University Press, 1988); and Thomas Haskell's response to it "Objectivity Is Not Neutrality: Rhetoric vs. Practice in Peter Novick's *That Noble Dream*," *History and Theory* 29 (1990): 129–57; the writings of Hayden White; and Nancy Partner, "Making Up Lost Time: Writing on the Writing of History," *Speculum* 61 (1986): 90–117. The writing on methods predates these

accepted methodology, a historian must be aware of all of the relevant primary and secondary literature and privilege the primary over the secondary. The historian must demonstrate an adequate knowledge of the languages of the pertinent sources. Sources must be cited and cited accurately. Historians begin to learn these methods as students when their work is critiqued by their teachers. As professionals, their work is subject to peer review, which punishes not only deliberate or accidental transgressions against historical methodology but also regulates which stances historians may take toward their work, which opinions and interpretations may be expressed, and which topics are appropriate for research.[2] In other words, modern historians belong to a guild which enforces its standards, producing works of formal and methodological uniformity. As long as a text adheres to these standards, its "truth" will not be questioned, only the abilities of its author.

The guilds that supervise the academic professions have a nineteenth-century origin.[3] Medieval historical writing developed in the absence of such an enforced uniformity of methods, sources, and models. In the eleventh century, other studies did begin to

kinds of considerations; one could argue that the modern discussion of historical methods begins with Jean Bodin.

2. Peter Novick gives an account of a recent case in which a historian was punished for transgression against history's methodologies (the David Abraham case) in *That Noble Dream*, 612–21. For a discussion of how peer review censors certain opinions, albeit in a discipline other than history, see Carole Blair, Julie R. Brown, and Leslie A. Baxter, "Disciplining the Feminine," *Quarterly Journal of Speech* 80 (1994): 383–409. These authors describe how "Referee #2 marks us immediately as 'unprofessional' and 'anti-intellectual,' indicating that he or she is 'embarrassed' for the academic field for producing persons who have written 'the single worst piece of "scholarship"' that he or she has ever reviewed. Both reviews further specify the stances and attitudes that 'professionals,' 'intellectuals,' or 'scholars' must demonstrate in order for these roles to designated as approved identities within the discipline" (398). Peer review determines which projects will be funded: Patrick Geary in *Phantoms of Remembrance* notes the words of a reviewer who recommended that his project be rejected. The process is not always recognized by participants as one of gate-keeping.

3. On this subject, see the essays in Thomas L. Haskell, ed., *The Authority of Experts: Studies in History and Theory* (Bloomington: Indiana University Press, 1984).

develop a disciplinary apparatus in the schools, and within these disciplines, particularly theology and law, scholars began to create the critical techniques that became the foundations of historical criticism. Historical criticism was familiar to university students by the end of the twelfth century. Historians, however, did not work in the schools for the most part, nor did they embrace the teachings of other disciplines.[4] Thus, when they sat down to write history, historians operated more or less on their own. The histories and other texts each historian read created a "horizon of expectations," the parameters within which the historian had to situate a history.[5] When historians had access to a large number of histories, they might come to see history as something like a genre and begin to develop some critical approaches to writing it. However, there was nothing forcing a historian to use one model or another, to consult one set or sources or another, to prefer particular methods, or even to limit his or her models to historical works.

Dudo of Saint-Quentin's work demonstrates the implications of the freedom with which historians could write in the late tenth and early eleventh centuries. He used many models, some histories, some not, using some a single time, relying on others to a greater extent. His models influenced not only the form of his text and its language but also the stories he told and the meaning to be imputed to them. The *Customs,* therefore, represents a text with complex antecedents. Dudo knew no classical history and little classical literature, but he was deeply imbued with the work of Virgil. Most of the texts he knew were those of the Carolingian curriculum, which may have influenced his choice to write in *prosimetrum.*[6] Carolingian writers encountered this form in the *Consolation of Philosophy* and the *Marriage of Mercury and Philology,* which were be-

---

4. On the development of these techniques in law, see Donald Kelley, "Clio and the Lawyers: Forms of Historical Consciousness in Medieval Jurisprudence," *Medievalia et Humanistica,* n.s. 5 (1974): 25–49. Cf. Nancy Partner, *Serious Entertainments,* 186–87 on the frequency with which histories were read in formal or educational settings and the effects this had on historical writing generally.

5. Jauss, "Literary History as Challenge," in *Aesthetic of Reception,* esp. 19–22.

6. On Dudo's education, see Shopkow, "Carolingian World," 21f.

ginning to be read widely in the ninth century.[7] While many histories contained poetry, often in the form of epitaphs or small decorative pieces, and historical poetry continued to be written at least through the twelfth century, history was only rarely written in *prosimetrum*.[8] One of the few other contemporary examples was the *Antapodosis* of Liutprand of Cremona, with which Dudo was probably not acquainted. *Prosimetrum*, however, had some important characteristics which recommended it to Dudo; it permitted him to show his mastery of a variety of complex meters (Dudo used hexameters, glyconics, catalectic dactylic trimeters, adonics, distichs, pherecrateans, asclepiads, and mixtures thereof) and to use the poetry to comment on the action described in the prose.

Dudo crammed this literary sampler into an common historical form, the serial biography. Serial biographies, sometimes called *gesta* by scholars,[9] were primarily used for ecclesiastical history, al-

---

7. Pierre Riché, *Ecoles et enseignement dans le Haut Moyen Age* (Paris: Picard, 1989), 249.

8. For example, Paul the Deacon's history of the bishops of Metz contains the epitaphs of the Carolingian women buried at Metz (Paul the Deacon, *Gesta episcoporum Mettensium*, G. H. Pertz, ed., *MGH SS* 2:265–67); Robert of Torigni's version of the *Deeds of the Dukes* contains epitaphs (see *GND*, 315), as does Henry of Huntingdon's *English History*. Lambert of Ardres decorates the introduction of his history of the counts of Guines with poetry, some quoted from classical sources and some original, (Lambert of Ardres, *Historia*, 558–59). The first book of the anonymous life of Edward the Confessor was also prosimetrical, while the second book was prefaced with a poetic debate between the poet and his muse.

Poetic history was common in the Carolingian period: the Annalista Saxo and Ermold Nigel both wrote in poetry. On Carolingian poetic history, see Alfred Ebenbauer, *Carmen Historicum: Untersuchungen zur historischen Dichtung im karolingischen Europa*, (Vienna: Wilhelm Braumüller, 1978). However, poetic history did not totally disappear later. The *Song of the Battle of Hastings (Carmen de Hastingae Proelio)*, whether an eleventh or a twelfth-century work, was written in poetry. On the controversy over dating, see L. J. Engels, "Once More: The *Carmen de Hastingae Proelio*," *Anglo-Norman Studies* 2 (1980): 3–14 and R. H. C. Davis, "The *Carmen de Hastingae proelio*," *English Historical Review* 93 (1978): 241–61. Stephen of Rouen wrote the *Norman Dragon* in heroic couplets. Gilles of Paris wrote his poetic history of Charlemagne, the *Carolinus*, a little before 1200, and William le Breton wrote a poetic history of Philip II of France, the *Philippide* in the early thirteenth century.

9. I use "serial biography" in preference to "*gesta*" because the term is simply

though the progenitor of the form, Suetonius's *Twelve Caesars*, was secular. These works consist of a series of biographies of the office holders of a diocese or monastery. The most widely known ecclesiastical example was the serial biography of the popes, the *Liber pontificalis*. Dudo may also have encountered the form at Liège, where a serial biography of the bishops was underway at the end of the tenth century.[10] Although the abbots and bishops whose lives were commemorated in serial biographies were not related to each other, serial biography was closely related to genealogy, a very basic form of history.[11] Its adoption in this case was appropriate not only because the Norman dukes belonged to a biological lineage but also because Dudo saw the dukes as religious leaders as well as political leaders.

Dudo found antecedents for a coherent salvation tale in many places, among them Jewish scripture, but one of his most powerful models was the *Ecclesiastical History of the English People* of Bede, which, like the *Customs* is both an ecclesiastical and a gentile history.[12] In both narratives a barbarian people came to a new land, won it from the original inhabitants, and were gradually converted

---

descriptive and makes no assumption about the contents or the generic status of this kind of work.

10. Heriger of Lobbes began the *Gesta episcoporum Leodiensium* under orders of bishop Notker (972–1008); it was then continued by Anselm. However, Heriger may not have begun before 990, when Dudo had already made his first trip to Normandy. See Heriger of Lobbes, *Gesta episcoporum Tungrensium, Traiectensium, et Leodiensium,* ed. Rudolf Koepke, *MGH SS* 7:135, 145.

11. See Michel Sot, "Historiographie épiscopale et modèle familial en occident au IXᵉ siècle," *Annales: E. S. C.* 33 (1978): 435; see also Howard Bloch, "Genealogy as a Medieval Mental Structure and Textual Form," in *La Littérature historiographique des origines à 1500* (*Grundriss der Romanischen Literaturen des Mittelalters,* vol. 11, pt. 1) (Heidelberg: Carl Winter Universitätsverlag, 1987), 135–56, and Gabrielle Spiegel, "Genealogy: Form and Function in Medieval Historical Narrative," *History and Theory* 22 (1983): 43–53.

12. The evidence for Dudo's knowledge of Bede is indirect, but he seems to know Bede's story about Gregory the Great and the Angles/Angels (*Ecclesiastical History,* 132–34), because in Rollo's first vision, in which he is told to go "*ad Anglos,*" his vision is interpreted by a Christian as telling him to become baptised and go "*ad Angelos*" (*De moribus,* 144–45). Bede's history was one of the most widely read histories in the Middle Ages and is still extant in more than 150 manuscripts.

to Christianity. This process in each case took time and there were setbacks, but once the conversion was complete, both peoples demonstrated through the peace and prosperity of their realms that they were divinely favored. Bede's history ends with peace and religious unity, as the last of the Irish converted to Roman Christian religious practices.[13] Bede's neat conclusion may have influenced Dudo's decision to end his story in the 960s with the establishment of peace between the duke and his French enemies and the conversion of the last pagan Normans, rather than recount the Norman history of his own time.[14]

The main difference between Bede's and Dudo's views was that in Dudo's history the dukes were the primary actors. Very few clerics are named in the *Customs*, although unnamed members of the clergy acted as messengers, and a chorus of unnamed bishops appears in the fourth book.[15] Rollo's conversion, unlike Aethelberht's, was not brought about through the intercession of any saint but through a vision, while the individual responsible for the conversion of the last Normans was Duke Richard I.[16] In Bede's work, however, the men and women who advanced Christianity in England were primarily members of the clergy whose lives were interwoven throughout the *Ecclesiastical History*. No book of the *Ecclesiastical History* is defined by the life of any one individual. Instead the books are organized around the ebb and flow of Roman, Irish, and Anglo-Saxon missions among the pagans.[17]

13. Bede, *Ecclesiastical History*, 552–54.

14. *De moribus*, 287–90ff.

15. Franco, the archbishop of Rouen is named (*De moribus*, 152, 168, 170), as is Martin, the abbot of Jumièges (ibid., 201ff.) For "the bishops of all of France," see ibid., 277.

16. For Aethelberht's conversion, see Bede, *Ecclesiastical History*, 76–78. King Edwin did have a vision before his conversion, but it was a vision in which bishop Paulinus of York appeared to him. Paulinus eventually converts Edwin in person (ibid., 178–82).

17. Book one, for instance, ends with the arrival of Augustine's mission in England. Book two ends with the failure of the first Roman mission in Northern England. Book three recounts the successful Irish mission in the North and the replacement of Irish Christianity by Roman; the Synod of Whitby stands at the center of the book. All of book four belongs to the reign of Theodore of Canter-

For the individual biographies in the *Customs*, Dudo turned to still other models. Virgil's *Aeneid* was the primary model for Dudo's life of Rollo.[18] However, Dudo invoked the epic as early as the first book of the *Customs*, where it underlay the story of Hasting's capture of Luna. This anecdote is modeled after the siege of Troy with Hasting's own body being the Trojan horse.[19] Since in this anecdote, Hasting was cast in the role of the treacherous Greeks, not the victimized Trojans, Dudo's use of the *Aeneid* reenforces Hasting's role in the narrative as an antitype to Rollo by highlighting the false ways in which Hasting seems to recapitulate the life of Rome's heroic progenitor and contrasting his iniquity and depravity with Rollo's purity and virtue. It is Rollo who is a true figuration of Aeneas. Rollo's voyage to England parallels Aeneas's adventures in Africa; Rollo's envoys to King Athelstan speak in the words of Aeneas's messengers to Dido.[20] While Rollo's final settlement in Rouen and marriage to Gisela, a French princess, is based on its Viking antecedent, the marriage of Gotfried to Charles the Fats' daughter,[21] the story is also clearly resonant of Aeneas's settlement in Italy and marriage to Lavinia. Like Aeneas, Rollo has a descendent who brings to fruition the foundation of a new empire: as Romulus founds Rome, so Richard builds Fécamp. The imitation is reenforced by Dudo's assertion that the Normans were descended from the Trojans.[22]

Useful though the *Aeneid* was to him, however, Dudo seems not to have felt that it was fully satisfactory as the prototype for

bury, with whose election it begins, but the contents vary. This book and book five are more chronologically than thematically organized, although the fifth book contains accounts of the Irish conversion to Roman practices and the missions of the Anglo-Saxons on the continent.

18. For a fuller discussion, see Shopkow, "Norman Historical Writing," 99–104.

19. *De moribus*, 33–35.

20. Ibid., 147; *Aeneid,* I:55ff. Hasting's envoys to Luna also used nearly the same words (*De moribus,* 133). For more on Dudo's relationship to the *Aeneid* and some intriguing comments on Virgil satire, see Emily Albu-Hannawalt, "Dudo of Saint-Quentin: The Heroic Past Imagined," *The Haskins Society Journal* 6 (1994): 111–118, esp. 113f.

21. *De moribus*, 169.

22. Ibid., 130.

the life of a man who converted to Christianity and spawned a Christian lineage. Therefore, some of Rollo's actions are also modeled on the Emperor Constantine of the eighth-century *Donation of Constantine*. In this case, Dudo reworked the contents without quotation from his source. Perhaps Dudo knew the story without having read the text. However, Dudo's debt to the *Donation* is unmistakable.

In the *Donation,* the still-pagan Constantine, suffering from leprosy but having refused the remedies offered by his magicians because they involve murdering a child, has a vision in which St. Sylvester appears to him with St. Peter. The pope promises him a cure which is effected when Constantine is baptized. In gratitude, Constantine gives extensive gifts to the heirs of St. Peter, among them the governance of the western Empire. Dudo recast the elements of the *Donation* somewhat when he applied them to Rollo. Rollo does not suffer from leprosy but only has a dream in which he does; when in his dream he washes himself in a fountain, he is cured. A Christian in his entourage interprets the vision to mean that Rollo will be cleansed of the disease of paganism by being baptized. When Rollo finally does convert, he, like Constantine, gives gifts to the Church. Although he favors the churches of Normandy first, he also gives land to Saint-Denis because Denis was the apostle of France.[23] Dudo echoes the Constantine story again when he has Richard I promise to fight, "armed with the banner of the holy cross," a reference to Constantine's banner, the *labarum.*[24]

When it came to the third and fourth books of the *Customs,* Dudo again employed new models, this time from hagiography. The life of William Longsword owes much material to the *Life of St. Lambert,* the seventh-century bishop of Liège, while the life of Richard the Fearless is dependent in part on the *Life of St. Germanus,* the great bishop-missionary of Auxerre. Dudo quoted both

---

23. Ibid., 146–47, 170–71. For the donation, see C. Mirbt, *Quellen zur Geschichte des Papsttums,* 5th ed. (Tubingen: J. C. B. Mohr [Paul Siebeck], 1934), 107–12.

24. *De moribus,* 271.

works in the third and the fourth books, but in general he drew on the life of Lambert the martyr when writing about the murdered William, and the missionary who stamped out England's Pelagianism was paired with the duke who (in Dudo's depiction) stamped out paganism.[25]

Other models were used more fleetingly, as when Dudo drew on Gideon's victory over the Amalekites to shape his account of William Longsword's triumph over Rioul.[26] There are also stories that have epic echoes. William Longsword's promise to uphold Louis IV against his enemies bears a strong resemblance to the promise of William of Orange to do the same for Louis the Pious in the epic *Coronation of Louis*. The coincidences—both heroes are named William, both promise to protect weak kings named Louis who ultimately prove ungrateful—make the linkage very tempting, although difficult to prove.[27]

While Dudo found models aplenty, sources presented a much greater problem. There is some evidence that Dudo used the Saint-Bertin annals and Flodoard's chronicle, and he may have known the *History of the Franks* written at Sens [*Historia Francorum Senonensis*].[28] However, most of the information in these annals concerned Viking raiding, and there was a long silence in the sources from 942 on.[29] No doubt the members of the ducal family told

25. For the influence of saints' lives on the *De moribus*, see Shopkow, "Carolingian World," 20, 23–24, 27f.

26. See above, p. 72.

27. See Ernest Langlois, ed. *Le Coronnement de Louis, chanson de geste du XIIe siècle*, Les Classiques français du Moyen Age, 2d ed. (Paris: Honoré Champion, 1925), 22:8 (*laisse* 13, ll.217–24); 55 (*laisse* 41, ll.1744–46). The oldest manuscript of the *Coronation* comes from 1130 at the earliest. Nonetheless, some version of the *Coronation* may well have been in oral circulation in the early eleventh century. In fact, it is peopled by late tenth-century figures. The villains are Richard the Old (the epic face of Richard I of Normandy) and Ascelin (in the *Coronation*, Richard's son but clearly tied to Ascelin/Adalberon of Laon who betrayed Charles of Lorraine, the last Carolingian, into the hands of the Capetians). In other words, Dudo made the Normans the heroes of a story in which they were otherwise depicted as the villains.

28. Printed in *MGH SS*, 9:364–69. For a fuller discussion of this sort of factual source, see Shopkow, "Norman Historical Writing," 50–53.

29. Searle, *Predatory Kinship*, 61.

Dudo stories about the early days; he credits Richard I's half-brother, Raoul d'Ivry, with being the "narrator" of his work, although his term, *relator,* can also mean appellant, in which case he meant only that Raoul urged him to write.[30] He also observed the Norman life of his day and extrapolated.[31] But for the history of the Normans, from the crucial migration period of the late ninth century and to the middle of the tenth century, Dudo did not have much material to work with, and thus he borrowed stories from other texts which, because his notion of truth was both verisimilar and allegorical, was not problematic for him.

Whereas Dudo had to put together a congeries of models and to struggle with the dearth of sources for early Norman history, William of Jumièges had both a model and a source ready-made in Dudo's text. Indeed, he adopted the serial biographic form from the *Customs,* and most of the events he narrates in his first four books came from Dudo of Saint-Quentin's work. Nevertheless, William also seems to have had access to oral sources not otherwise known to us. For instance, of all the early Norman sources, only the *Deeds of the Dukes* names Gerloc, the daughter of Rollo who married William of Poitou.[32]

However, William of Jumièges's stylistic ideas about history were not drawn from Dudo's work but from what William referred to as chronicles. William twice called his own work a chronicle.[33] By this he may have meant, like the author of the *Authority of Fécamp,* that he kept his narrative in temporal order, supplying the reader with "time-marking" events (the deaths of kings and emperors and the successions of the archbishops of Rouen) which substituted for dates. He may also have meant what Gervais of Can-

---

30. *De moribus,* 125. See J. F. Niermeyer, *Mediae latinitatis lexicon minus* (Leiden: Brill, 1984), 905, for *relator.* Dudo describes Raoul making just such an appeal (*De moribus,* 119–20). William of Jumièges says that Raoul commanded Dudo to write (*GND,* 2), which suggests William understood the term *relator* not as narrator but as appellant.

31. See van Houts, "Scandinavian Influence in Norman Literature," and Searle, "Fact and Pattern in Heroic History."

32. *GND,* 34–35. Gerloc was also known as Adela.

33. Ibid., 1, 143.

terbury meant later on, that his work was written in a straightforward and uninterpretive way.[34] In practical terms, what the *Deeds
of the Dukes* shares with chronicles and annals is a concern with
actions rather than character, brevity of discussion, lack of description, and a lack of structural coherence, all of which mark a para-
tactic style.

Because events were narrated under the heading of the year in
which they occur, annalistic histories tended to present all events
as isolated incidents. Parts of one story might be told in several
places. While the *Deeds of the Dukes* does not offer that fragmented
a narrative, nearly every chapter of the text is autonomous, and
where a story overspills the chapter division, it does so into a con-
secutive chapter. Although William of Jumièges makes no references to hagiographic conventions, this style of writing was common in these texts, which were designed to be read in the refectory
or as part of the liturgy or to be given to the monks to read in the
short intervals for such activity during the monastic day. The contrast with Dudo's text, in which many of the stories are narrated
with great amplitude, is striking.[35]

William of Jumièges not only avoided the poetry, the rhythmic
and rhyming prose, and the rhetorical flourishes of his predecessor
that he found so suspect. He also eschewed the use of direct speech.
When Dudo used speech it was to reveal the character of the
speaker and occasionally to edify the reader, but it was seldom in
order to advance the action of his narrative. When William of Jumièges did use direct speech, it was always to bring the narrative
forward by supplying necessary information compactly or by causing action.[36] William employed no apostrophes, poetic or other-

34. Guenée, *Histoire et culture historique,* 206.
35. For instance, Dudo's account of the struggle between Rioul and William
Longsword occupies five pages of the printed edition (181–91), and the passages of
prose between poems could be longer than this. Dudo did not otherwise divide
the books.
36. Direct speech is used very sparingly in the *Gesta* in comparison with the *De
moribus*. A certain number of speeches are drawn directly from Dudo's text, for
instance, the interchange between Rollo and Hasting at Hasdans (*De moribus,* 154;
GND, 22). Some of the speeches in the *De moribus* become part of the narrative of

wise, and he edited down Dudo's extensive panegyrics to more restrained versions.[37] The *Deeds*, therefore, was a version of the *Customs* reshaped to an entirely different historical aesthetic.

William of Poitiers brought to his history yet another set of models, the classical histories he encountered at Poitiers. Among the classics, William's favorite author was Caesar (he had read both the *Gallic Wars* and the *Civil War*), but he also knew the works of Sallust, Tacitus (the *Agricola*), Suetonius, Plutarch, Statius, and Lucan.[38] The use of classical histories as models was not new in the eleventh century; Carolingian writers were sometimes influenced by classical historians, as Einhard was by Suetonius. However, classical models were only being widely rediscovered in the late tenth century. One of the first historians to do so was Richer of Reims who wrote in a neo-Sallustian style.[39]

Classical histories were rhetorically and formally different from medieval histories, and their authors were generally more sophisticated about history. A medieval writer dependent on classical sources might imbibe some of this different aesthetic.[40] To a degree William of Poitiers was influenced in his formal notions of history by the classical histories he read. From classical history he borrowed the notion, probably reenforced by Isidore, that the best history is that which is written by a contemporary or eyewitness.[41]

---

the *Gesta*, such as Bernard the Dane's reproaches to William Longsword (*De moribus*, 183–84; *GND*, 33), while others become indirect speech, like Hasting's lies to the citizens of Luna (*De moribus*, 133; *GND*, 15). Others are left out entirely, like William Longsword's joking insults about the Poitevins (*De moribus*, 192). For Dudo's use of direct speech, see ibid., 283–85, 170; for William's, see *GND*, 56, 71.

37. See, for example, GND, 70–71, where William makes a brief reference to Dudo's long description of how Richard I embodied the Beatitudes (*De moribus*, 293–95).

38. *GG*, xxxviii–xliii. Lucan and Statius were considered historians in the Middle Ages; see Eva M. Sanford, "The Study of Ancient History in the Middle Ages," *Journal of the Hisotry of Ideas* 5 (1944), 24 and note 8.

39. See Robert Latouche, "Un Imitateur de Salluste au X^c siècle: l'Historien Richer," *Annales de l'université de Grenoble*, n.s. *Lettres-droit* 6 (1929): 289–305.

40. For example, Sanford, "Study of Ancient History," 23, argues that Livy, Sallust, and Suetonius not only furnished material for Lampert of Hersfeld's annals but also helped him arrive at a more sophisticated notion of history.

41. *Isidore*, Etymologies, 1:40.

From it he also acquired at least a formal and rhetorical notion of history's generic distinctness; the topos of the poets versus the historians is a classical one. Classical texts also provided William of Poitiers with the vocabulary of historical stories and of character sketches with which he embellished his main source, the *Deeds of the Dukes* of William of Jumièges. Just as William of Jumièges had stripped Dudo's narrative of its shining rhetoric, so William of Poitiers adorned William of Jumièges's plain prose.

William of Poitiers did not confine his borrowings to stories from classical history. The *Customs of the Dukes* also inspired William of Poitiers. When William tells how the Conqueror becomes separated from his fleet while crossing the channel and, instead of panicking, orders a meal to be spread, the obvious model for his actions is Richard I who orders his troops to partake of a meal while they are surrounded and outnumbered by their enemies.[42] Likewise, the envy that the young duke William attracts for his stalwart defence of King Henry and the rancour roused against him in the king by those envious of the duke recall the difficulties faced by both William Longsword and Richard I.[43] Finally, when the historian turns to the attacks of the French monarch upon Normandy, he has Henry echo the accusations of Louis IV and Lothar against Richard I, that the duke ruled Normandy like a king.[44] The use of apostrophes may also derive from Dudo's model, for, as in Dudo's work, they have a dramatic function—to point to the futility of resisting the will of God—and they also serve as transition devices.[45]

This interspersion of models is not surprising given that William of Poitiers was conscious of the important difference between the heroes of the classical past and his protagonist, namely that the duke was Christian. It is precisely because he is Christian that William the Conqueror is superior to his pagan counterparts, and for that reason he merits *felicitas*, the divine gift to the Christian ruler.

42. *GG*, 164; *De moribus*, 271.
43. *GG*, 22, 28; *De moribus*, 199, 205, 250, 265.
44. *GG*, 66; *De moribus*, 250, 265.
45. *GG*, 10–12, 114, 206–8, 228–30.

Augustine, the historical moralist, lies behind this aspect of William of Poitiers's work.[46]

The Norman historians of the eleventh century were forced to cope with limitations—in models, in sources, in paradigms to follow—and were forced to make the best of them using their own judgments and experience. The mind of each historian was a repository for a limited number of texts which provided not only the framework supporting an edifice of history and the planking installed upon the frame but also the instructions as to how to proceed with construction. What was available to historians depended on where they were educated and where they worked. As a man educated at one of the preeminant intellectual centers of the tenth century, Dudo came to Normandy primed with a typically Carolingian body of texts, a deep knowledge of the *Aeneid*, a florid compositional style, and a love for poetry, all of which found expression in his work. William of Poitiers, also the product of a notable school, brought an entirely different corpus, a markedly classical one, to bear on his historical endeavor. William of Jumièges possessed yet another mental library, one shaped by monastic education rather than the elaborate rhetorical training of the schools.

What the works produced by these early historians make clear, however, is that these limitations in sources and models were not necessarily a point of weakness but instead lent strength to the narratives. These writers operated in an environment of scholarly freedom. The *Customs of the Dukes* is more compelling than it could ever have been had its author had to trouble with sorting through sources. The *Deeds of the Dukes* told its stories as cleanly and clearly as the hagiographies William would have encountered at every turn in monastic life. Only the *Deeds of William* seems weak or ineffectual as a literary work, for which William of Poitiers's love of classical histories may have been partly to blame. William's desire to demonstrate his erudition—albeit to the glory of his subject—frequently gets in the way of him telling his story well. The classical histories he read were sometimes marvels of effective narra-

46. See above, pp. 93f.

tive, but William seems not to have learned this particular lesson from them.

William of Jumièges seems to have had the most limited resources at his disposal, probably because he was cloister-educated and because eleventh-century Norman institutions had limited offerings. The catalog of Fécamp's library in the later eleventh century suggests that most of what monks read there was spiritual, liturgical, patristic, and hagiographic texts. There were only three works of history to guide the anonymous author of the *Authority of Fécamp*.[47] The early twelfth-century catalog of the chapter library of Rouen lists basic grammar and rhetoric texts, along with Ovid, Virgil, Donatus, Juvenal, Cicero, Terence, and Homer (probably the *Ilias latina*). There were a few liturgical books in the collection but little of the hagiography that was so prominent in monastic libraries, and few patristic texts.[48]

In the twelfth century, Norman institutions were significantly richer in their literary possessions, adding classical Latin texts and books on the natural sciences, medicine, history, and music to traditional texts for *lectio divina*.[49] Fécamp acquired the *Natural His-*

47. H. Wolter, *Orderic Vitalis* (Wiesbaden: Franz Steiner Verlag, 1955), 5, argues that Cluny has been unfairly charged with hostility toward history, but the quantity of Cluny's histories is not large, nor is Ralph Glaber, the example Wolter uses, a typical Cluniac. On Fécamp's curriculum, see Emile Lesne, *Histoire de la propriété ecclésiastique en France*, in *Les Écoles de la fin du VIIIᵉ siècle à la fin du XIIᵉ* (Lille: Facultés Catholiques, 1940), 5:115. On the library, see *CG*, 1:xxiv. The works are an ecclesiastical history (probably Eusebius) the *Historia tripartita*, and Bede's *De temporibus*.

48. The cathedral probably owned such books but kept them in a different place, and hence they do not appear in this catalog.

49. This discussion is based on the extant library catalogs for Normandy. For Fécamp (c. 1050 and 1150), see *CG*, 1:xxiv–xxvi; for Lyre (c. 1150), see ibid., 2:380–83; for Bec (after 1163), see ibid., 2:385–98; for Saint-Evroul (c. 1150), see ibid., 2:468–69; for the cathedral at Rouen, see ibid., 1:x–xiii. The only lists from Saint-Wandrille are for the ninth-century library and the fourteenth-century library. (See Ferdinand Lot, *Études critiques sur l'abbaye de Saint-Wandrille* [Paris: Librarie ancienne Honoré Champion, 1913], xliii). No complete list is extant for Jumièges, although there is a list of books donated by Abbot Alexander in the late twelfth century (*CG* 1:xx). There once were catalogs for Mont Saint-Michel, Caen, Jumièges, and Savigny that are now lost (ibid., 1:xx). There is only a fifteenth-century catalog from the chapter of Bayeux (ibid., 10:272f.). In addition to these lists, G. Nortier, *Les Bibliothèques*

tory of Solinus, a medical text, and the histories of Josephus, Josippus, Orosius, and Hegesippus, as well as a Norman history (either Dudo of Saint-Quentin's or William of Jumièges's work) during the course of the twelfth century.[50] A copy of Adelard of Bath's astronomical works has survived from Mont Saint-Michel's library, although the library catalog has not.[51] Bec had an unusually good collection of historical and classical texts, owning the histories of Josephus, Eusebius, Paul the Deacon (the *History of the Lombards*), Hegesippus, Orosius, Trogus Pompeius, Henry of Huntingdon, Geoffrey of Monmouth, Gildas, Nennius, Gregory of Tours, Baudry of Bourgueil, Fulcher of Chartres, William of Jumièges, Eutropius, and Suetonius. Bec also held Einhard's life of Charlemagne, a life of Alexander the Great, and the *Tripartite History*. Its classical collection included Quintilian, Macrobius, Palladius's treatise on agriculture, Vegetius, various works by Cicero and Seneca, Priscian, some Plato and commentaries on him, and Sallust. It shared these riches with its neighbour Lyre, and possibly with Saint-Evroul as well.[52] At Saint-Evroul, the scriptorium was active, and the library's historical collection grew through the efforts of the historian, Orderic Vitalis, among others. Still, the twelfth-century catalogue of the library shows only moderate historical holdings—Eusebius, Bede's *Ecclesiastical History*, Josephus, Paul the Deacon, the *Liber pontificalis*, and the lives of Herluin and Anselm, as well as Orderic's own history. The real strength of its library was *lectio divina*.[53] Jumièges's library was an exception, in that Jumièges's acquisitions seem to have been few in the earlier twelfth century, only to pick up by the

---

médiévales des abbayes bénédictines de Normandie (Paris: Bibliothèque d'histoire de d'archéologie chrétiennes, 1971), 194–231, gives a table of works that are either still extant or are known to have been available in the libraries of Fécamp, Bec, Mont Saint-Michel, Saint-Evroul, Lyre, Jumièges, Saint-Wandrille, and Saint-Ouen.

50. *CG*, 1:xxv–vi.

51. Nortier, *Les Bibliothèques*, 194.

52. For Lyre, see Nortier, ibid., 145; on Saint-Evroul, *EH*, 2:xvii. For catalogs, see *CG*, 2:380–83, 468–69.

53. See *EH*, 1:24 for a list of works Orderic copied.

end of the century when library growth had slowed at other monasteries.[54]

Twelfth-century writers were consequently more aware of possible models for their work. They had a larger number of sources available to them, particularly histories of areas outside of Normandy, and they were more likely to seek out works they had heard of but had perhaps never read. In short, they were confronted with more answers to the question of how to write history. These greater resources did not mean, however, that historical writing became in any sense uniform during the twelfth century. History was written for such diverse audiences and purposes and in such varying circumstances that no one answer to the question of how to write history was definitive, just as no one notion of historical truth prevailed.

Orderic Vitalis was inundated with potential models and sources, both because he had access to English libraries and histories and because there were more historical works in Norman libraries. Beginning around 1100, writers in England began a sustained outpouring of historical writing unmatched elsewhere in Europe.[55] Much of this writing Orderic did not know—he was not familiar with the works of William of Malmesbury, probably the most prolific of the English historians of the earlier twelfth century. However, he did know the great chronicle of Worcester, based on Marianus Scotus and continued by John of Worcester, which became one of his models.[56] Another model was the historical writing of Bede—ethnic pride probably played a role here—not only his *Ecclesiastical History* but also the long universal chronicle that formed part of Bede's *On Times [De Temporibus]*. Orderic also turned to the oldest work in the Christian Latin historical tradition, the *Ecclesiastical History* of Eusebius. Following the examples

54. Nortier, *Les Bibliothèques,* 145, 176.

55. For a discussion of the implications of this burst of historical writing, see Southern, "The Sense of the Past," 246–56. The catalog from Saint-Evroul was written after Orderic's time, since it includes his work, but some of the texts it lists must have been available to Orderic.

56. *EH,* 1:58, 89.

of these three prototypes, Orderic titled his history—which began with the life of Jesus—the *Ecclesiastical History*. Many other works also influenced Orderic's history, but these three writers gave shape to his ideas and fired his ambitions.

Each of Orderic's models had an impact on part of the history, but with a work as monumental and diverse as the *Ecclesiastical History*, no one work could influence the whole. Two of the models were narrative—the ecclesiastical histories—while two were annalistic. Orderic managed to incorporate both types of history by prefacing his narrative history with a chronicle in two books, an awkward resolution. Although the inspiration for the inclusion of the life of Christ came from Marianus Scotus, the authorization to do so came from Eusebius who declared that ecclesiastical history must begin with the dispensation of Christ.[57] Orderic quoted documents and canons when he had them, also in imitation of Eusebius, who depended heavily on documents to authenticate and enrich his history, and Orderic's concern for the whole Christian people, not just the English or the Normans, clearly stems from the Eusebian tradition. The influence of Bede was pervasive in Orderic's history for obvious reasons, not least their common English origins. Another reason was Bede's versatility; his writing of chronological works, saints' lives, the serial biography of his abbots, and his history of his own people authorized Orderic to combine all of these sorts of narratives into his own work, while Bede's autobiographical comment at the end of the *Ecclesiastical History* in turn sanctioned Orderic's comments about his own life at the conclusion of his work.[58]

57. Eusebius Pamphili, *Eusebius Pamphili's Ecclesiastical History,* trans. Roy J. Deferrari (New York: The Fathers of the Church, 1953), 1:37. "For he who intends to hand down in writing the story of the Church's leadership would have to begin with the very origin of Christ's dispensation." Lives of Jesus were unusual; see *EH* 1:49–50. There was a tradition of reluctance to supplant the Gospels themselves. Sulpicius Severus refuses to paraphrase the Gospels in his *Chronicle,* a rewriting of the contents of Jewish and Christian scripture, directing the readers to the original. Marianus was the first to break with the Latin tradition. Vernacular versions of the life of Christ were written for a different audience, one with no access to the Gospels.

58. *EH,* 6:550–56; Bede, *Ecclesiastical History,* 566–70.

Orderic's material for the narrative part of his history, however, was in some ways less promising than Bede's, in that the story he had to tell lent itself less to jubilation than to contemplation. Both Bede and Eusebius were interested in the establishment of orthodox Christianity and in the trials and tribulations of a church faced with pagans and heretics, but they were writing from the vantage point of a process that could be depicted as complete and successful. Orderic's subject matter was more problematic. The history of the Normans and English tended toward tragedy in Orderic's perception. Nor was Orderic's larger concern for Christian history any less fraught with complications. In Orderic's time, the population of Europe was largely Christian and overwhelmingly orthodox; only the First Crusade offered the kinds of dramatic possibilities and certainty available to Eusebius and Bede, and then only temporarily as the crusaders squabbled among themselves and gradually lost what they had won. Whereas Bede managed to organize his material so that the events themselves and their meaning were simultaneously apprehended by the reader and so that his presence managing the story was virtually invisible to the reader, Orderic was not so lucky (or perhaps so skillful). His story was not the kind of grand narrative advanced by Bede, perhaps because he could not make it conform to this kind of model. Orderic was therefore reduced to performing a kind of spot exegesis. As he presented each part of his narrative, he sometimes paused to offer the moral meaning of the events afterward. The reader, instead of being pulled forward through the text as the meaning unfolded, seemingly naturally and by itself, was instead made conscious of the author's interpretive efforts, and might well wonder about the meaning of those events Orderic chose not to explicate.

Perhaps because of his many models, none of which had attempted or quite suited what Orderic wanted to do, Orderic did not evolve a strategy fully to integrate the parts of his history. Orderic was certainly not the only medieval historian to create a fragmented text. Karl Morrison has argued that historians did so deliberately, leaving it to their readers to bring together the scattered elements of their narratives. Nancy Partner suggests, in contrast, that such unstructured narratives are more likely to be the result of unfamiliarity with classical rhetorical principles than the rejection of narrative coherence.[59] I agree with Partner that the incoherencies of medieval histories are probably not deliberate. However, when Morrison draws attention to the role of the historian as a compiler, he points to an important factor. Dudo of Saint-Quentin did not write a marvelously coherent history because he had a deep acquaintance with classical history, although R. W. Southern has placed him among the medieval classicists.[60] He wrote a coherent history because he was not working as a compiler and was not forced to attempt to integrate works of varying character. On the other hand, compilation alone did not necessarily lead to incoherent histories. Robert of Torigni's chronicle, which is a compilation, hangs together well because he was willing to tailor his sources for his own use. Orderic, in contrast, saw his work as a repository for texts that might be lost. One of his aims was to preserve some measure of integrity for each of them.

This choice had both advantages and disadvantages. Had Orderic chosen a more coherent form, he would have had to sacrifice some of the richness of his history. An annalistic form would have eliminated the redundancies of his text but would have made exegesis, which depends on the knowledge of the configurations of the story, difficult. The biographical-regnal structure favored by his Norman predecessors and some of his English contemporaries would have placed undue emphasis on mortal government and detracted from the ecclesiastical import of the history. Nonetheless, because it lacks generic coherence, the *Ecclesiastical History* falls into an amorphous configuration from which only the last books, which are chronologically arranged and largely uninterrupted by epitomized texts, escape.[61]

Robert of Torigni used a different strategy to cope with the

59. Morrison, *History as a Visual Art*, 80–81 and elsewhere; Partner, "The New Cornificius," 18.

60. Southern, "The Classical Tradition," 191–92.

61. See *EH*, 1:48–63, for the literary sources of the history; ibid., 1:63–77 for the documentary sources.

riches he wanted to transmit to posterity. He assigned different sources to different works of his own. Of all the Norman historians, he was the most sensitive to the formal qualities of histories. Whereas Orderic used loose terminology to describe histories and jumbled together different types, each of Robert's works was distinctive.[62] The differences between Robert's version of the *Deeds of the Dukes* and his *Chronicle* cannot be attributed simply to Robert's growing maturity as a historian, as Chibnall suggests, or to his finding his own voice, for his histories are not entirely separate; parts of his revisions of the *Deeds of the Dukes* do find their way into the chronicle.[63] What distinguished one of Robert's works from another was that each work conformed to the rules for a subgenre of historical writing.

Robert's expansion of the *Deeds of the Dukes* demonstrates his ideas about the nature of narrative and regnal history. At the time of writing, Robert had limited sources for his additions: apart from the *Customs of the Dukes*, Orderic's *Ecclesiastical History* seems to have been the major source, although Robert used the life of Herluin by Gilbert Crispin, Eadmer's life of Anselm, and Miles Crispin's life of Lanfranc as well.[64]

Material from these sources was blended into Orderic Vitalis's version of the *Deeds of the Dukes*. In making his interpolations, Robert was aware of the need for narrative continuity, and he privileged that over chronology. Therefore, his account of the daughters of the Conqueror and their offspring was not interpolated into the seventh book of the *Deeds,* the book that dealt with William the Conqueror but appears after the death of Henry I. Its purpose is to explain the succession of Stephen, and it thus appears in contiguity with that event.[65] Just as Robert included new material per-

62. For Orderic's use of terminology, see above, p. 20, n. 52.

63. Majorie Chibnall, "Orderic Vital et Robert de Torigni," in *Millénaire monastique du Mont Saint-Michel,* (Paris: Bibliothèque d'histoire et d'archéologie chrétiennes, 1967), 2:136.

64. On the relationship between the *EH* and Robert's work, see M. Chibnall, "Orderic Vital et Robert de Torigni," 133–39. On the lives of Herluin, Anselm, and Lanfranc, see *GND,* 235, n. 1; 244, n. 2.; and 240, n. 1.

65. *GND,* 316–19.

tinent to the family history of the dukes, he refrained from interpolating into the *Deeds of the Dukes* material that did not concern the reigning family. The result was a cohesive, if somewhat episodic, narrative.

While medieval historians did not often explain why they arranged their materials in particular ways or which materials were appropriate for inclusion, we are fortunate in Robert's case to have a clue. Around 1152, Robert wrote to Gervais of Saint-Céneri, encouraging Gervais to write a history of the Angevin and Mançeaux counts and giving him precise instructions for proceeding. First, Gervais was to give the names, genealogies, successions, and regnal years of each of the counts of Anjou, as well as their more worthy deeds. The material Robert added to the *Deeds* all falls within these categories of information. Then Gervais was to include a brief history for the counts of Maine in the entry on Fulk Nerra, for Fulk acquired the office by marrying into the family. Robert thus describes his own decision about the placement of his material concerning the Conqueror's daughters. At the conclusion of the letter, Robert refers Gervais to his own version of the *Deeds of the Dukes* as an example.[66]

In writing his chronicle, Robert used somewhat different criteria for organization and contents. First, he had to choose a base text, and he considered and rejected the chronicle of Marianus Scotus. Robert does not say why, but he may have preferred not to work with a historian as clearly idiosyncratic as Marianus. Marianus's chronicle grew out of a study of *computus,* which suggested to him that the dating generally in use was incorrect; everyone else was off by seventeen years.[67] Perhaps more important than the disadvantages of using Marianus's chronicle, however, were the advantages of using Sigebert's. Robert clearly liked the idea of taking his place in the long and respected tradition established by Eusebius, to whose work he granted the inviolability normally only

---

66. Rob. of Tor., 2:339–40.

67. Ibid. On Marianus, see van den Brincken, *Lateinischen Weltchronistik,* 166–73.

commanded by Scripture.[68] Sigebert's chronicle was highly controlled; the entries did not vary in length significantly from year
to year. Finally, Sigebert's chronicle was fairly comprehensive, giving regnal years of important monarchs even when the entries
themselves were fairly attenuated.[69] As a framework, Sigebert's
chronicle was nearly perfect.

In his interpolations in the first part of Sigebert's chronicles,
Robert included anything to do with Christian Neustria or Normandy. In so doing, Robert was borrowing from Norman popular
culture and monastic tradition, for most of the important Norman
monasteries (Bec was the notable exception) claimed Merovingian
roots and some of the founders of Norman monasteries had widely
spread cults.[70] The thread of continuity in Norman history was
created by the archbishops of Rouen and the saints of Normandy:
Taurin, Nicaise, Wandrille, Evroul, and Ouen. These were names
that every Norman was familiar with, saints everyone had come to
think of as Norman, but who were Norman as defined by a geo-
graphical, rather than an ethnic, criterion. For the English additions as far as 1138, Henry of Huntingdon's *History of the English,*
which Robert acquired only after he completed his redaction of
the *Deeds,* was a major source, often quoted in lengthy passages
verbatim, so it is possible to think of the early part of Robert's
chronicle as having a skeleton drawn from Sigebert of Gembloux,
fleshed out with Henry of Huntingdon and a few Norman histories. There are a few other sources, but Robert did not rely on them
as extensively.[71]

68. Rob. of Tor., 96. "Truly I say it is indecent to add anything extraneous to
the writings of those men of such authority, Eusebius and Jerome."
69. Ibid., 1:94.
70. See Fournée, "Le Culte populaire des saints fondateurs d'abbayes pré-
normandes." Some of the saints were only venerated at one place in Normandy, as
Waningus was at Fécamp (although he was also venerated in Picardy) (ibid., 78).
Others, like Evroul, were venerated widely throughout the province (ibid., 68–69).
71. For other sources, see the *Chronicon Beccense* and Baudry and Fulcher's histories of the First Crusade. See also Robert of Torigni, *The Chronicle of Robert of
Torigni, Chronicles of the Reigns of Stephen, Henry II, and Richard I,* vol. 4: Rolls
Series, 82, ed. R. Howlett (London: Eyre & Spottiswoode, 1889), xxvi f.

Eusebius, Jerome, and Sigebert seem to have provided Robert with a sense of what belonged in a chronicle, as opposed to other sorts of history. Eusebius had commented at the beginning of his *Ecclesiastical History* on the summary nature of chronology and the fuller narrative of history.[72] In keeping with the sorts of entries he observed from Sigebert, Robert announced that he would include "the names and successions of the dukes and some of their more illustrious deeds, and all the names of the archbishops of Rouen and some of the bishops of that same province . . . and the same for the English kings, of whom he [Sigebert] makes no mention."[73] He also added entries of a sort which had interested Jerome, notes about the works and lives of fellow scholars, such as Ivo of Chartres and John of Salisbury, and stories of miracles, in other words, records of public events and deeds.[74] Whenever possible, Robert liked to arrange the material in chronological order within the yearly entries, and he did so consistently in his continuations of the chronicle (the entries for 1153 and later). Robert began each entry with the location of the Christmas court—the Anglo-Norman year began at Christmas—and followed events as they occurred throughout the year; his variations from strict chronological order probably arose from faulty information or poor memory. In the earlier entries, where he had no way of knowing how the events of the year were themselves ordered, Robert generally presented his sources in a seldom varying sequence: extracts from Henry of Huntingdon's *English History* came first, followed by Fulcher of Chartres, and only afterward by fully original entries, thereby creating a hierarchy of authority within the entry.

Where his sources contained speeches, Robert systematically deleted them, although he had included a few speeches in his in-

72. Eusebius, *Ecclesiastical History*, 1:37.
73. Rob. of. Tor., 1:95.
74. The Bec library had a copy of Jerome's *De viris illustribus* with Gennadius's additions (*CG*, 2:389), but Jerome also included such information in his chronicle and this seems a likely model for Robert's interpolations; Robert may have been aware that Sigebert imitated Jerome in creating a work in this genre himself (Sigebert of Gembloux, *Catalogus Sigeberti Gemblacensis monachi de viris illustribus: Kritische Ausgabe,* ed. Robert Witte [Bern: Herbert Lang, 1974]).

terpolations into the *Deeds*.[75] Similarly, Robert deleted much of the poetry contained in Henry's history, leaving only the epitaphs and these much edited. Of the twelve poems that are contained in the chronicle, only four are longer than four lines; three of the four commemorate abbots of Bec, while the fourth is the epitaph of Henry I. Henry's epitaph also appears in the *Deeds of the Dukes*, but it is abbreviated in the chronicle.[76] Further evidence of Robert's sense of what was appropriate to each of the subgenres in which he worked was his reluctance in the chronicle to make personal references, even where he appears as an actor.[77] Finally, each entry was relatively brief—he seems to have preferred concise entries of restricted length, varying from one to five pages in the printed edition, even at the end of his chronicle where other chroniclers tended to become more prolix. In contrast, his additions to the *Deeds of the Dukes* amplified that text considerably. Thus, the differences between the chronicle and the *Deeds of the Dukes* seem deliberate—different models led to different formal structures. The sort of information that went into Robert's *Deeds of the Dukes* was more restricted than that which went into his chronicle, but he was free to treat the material more fully and to pay more attention to narrative principles than chronology.

Robert's awareness of formal generic constraints is even clearer when we consider the annals of Mont Saint-Michel, if he was indeed the author of this text. The annals are very brief; Robert's portion, the years from 1136 to 1173, covers only one page in the printed edition.[78] The entry for 1171 is typically laconic:

75. See, for example, *GND*, 205, 209, 268.

76. Rob. of Tor., 1:75–76 (Lanfranc), 1:203 (Boso), 1:249 (Letard), 1:196 (Henry); *GND*, 315; and *HA*, 254–55.

77. He generally refers to himself in the third person, even doing so when mentioning his own literary reputation (Rob. of Tor., 2:58). He uses the first person only three times (ibid., 2:74, 2:90, 2:116). This is not a feature of the chronicle alone, however; in none of his works is Robert's person obtrusive.

78. Rob. of Tor., 2:207. For a description of the manuscript, Avranches, BM, #211, see ibid., 2:209ff., *CG*, 10:94, and Charles Samaran and Robert Marichal, *Catalogue des manuscrits en écriture latine portant des indications de date, de lieu ou de copiste*, vol. 7, *Ouest de la France et Pays de Loire* (Paris: CNRS, 1984), 77, (hereafter cited as *Manuscrits datés*).

King Henry crossed into Ireland and subjugated it for the most part to himself. St. Thomas, the archbishop of Canterbury, was martyred in the church of the Holy Trinity at Canterbury, and God magnified him, not only in curing the sick but even in the resuscitation of the dead.[79]

In contrast, the entry in Robert's chronicle begins with Henry's Christmas court, then refers to troop movements from North Africa into Spain, various deaths and the comings and goings of the great, the canonization of Thomas, marriage negotiations, and a pogrom at Chartres, a six-page entry in the printed edition.[80] There was a hierarchy of events then, from the most important, the ones to be included in annals which would truly signify the year, and lesser events which might find their way into chronicles.

Robert made the contents appropriate to the form, but he was essentially a compiler, working by preference with the words of others. He almost never altered his sources; at best he occasionally added information to a passage with a parenthetic phrase or sentence, or a commentary on the material, most commonly remarking on a portent or omen. He seldom divided up the passages he drew from his sources, unless there was a clear division in the entry itself and the division of the material would not destroy the sense of the passage. In consequence, although his sense of form was fairly well developed, he was not a strong presence in his own works, as Orderic Vitalis and William of Poitiers were.

Robert's use of his sources suggests that his tolerance for historical complexity was not great. For example, in the entries he culled from the *English History* of Henry of Huntingdon, Robert shows no understanding of the English political situation before the unification of the English kingdoms. Much of the material for the English entries comes from Henry's summaries at the end of each book. In these summaries, Henry gave the successions for all the English kingdoms, but Robert gave only that of the kings of Kent. It would not be incorrect to see Robert's additions to Sigebert's chronicles up to 851 as being the product of pre-selected and

79. Rob. of Tor., 2:228–29.
80. Ibid., 2:25ff.

interspersed catalogs. Whereas Orderic presented history in all its untidy complexity, Robert's aim seems to have been to schematize and to produce a general outline, a textbook, rather than a dissertation.

Still, that Robert recognized these formal dimensions to historical writing, that he had a clear idea of the sort of material that ought to be included in any given type of history and the organization proper to particular genres, suggests that historical writing as a distinct enterprise was clear in his mind in a way that it seems not to have been for many, perhaps most, of his contemporaries. Surely the marvelous library at Bec, partially Robert's creation, and Robert's many years as a practicing historian helped to form this consciousness.

Given that history was not taught as a distinct discipline, however, and that even in Robert's time each historian learned how to write it anew, Robert's insights were not transferred to his contemporary and fellow-monk of Bec, Stephen of Rouen. Stephen worked in the same rich library as Robert, but the texts that influenced him were entirely different. He includes a broad variety of material in the *Dragon,* such as the *Treatise on Consideration* of Bernard of Clairvaux, the *Treatise of Garcia* (the famous medieval satire on Sts. Silver and Gold), Quintilian, Vegetius, Gratian, Cicero, and the *Song of Roland.* He had at least a passing knowledge of a large number of classical, contemporary, and hagiographic works.[81] He makes elaborate classical references. Childeric, for instance, who claims to be a believer in Christ, Stephen jokes, is better friends with Bacchus and Ceres (i.e. is a drunkard).[82] The reader is constantly bombarded with parenthetical information. Thus, when Stephen tells of the coronation of Louis VII by Pope Innocent, he cannot resist mentioning Innocent's great knowledge of the laws of Justinian, which leads Stephen into a reference to Gratian.[83] Whereas Robert exercised great control over the con-

---

81. On Stephen's reading, see Shopkow, "Norman Historical writing," 469–72.
82. *DN,* 665 (II:154–54).
83. *DN,* 650–51 (Bk. I, cap. 33).

tents of his histories, and even though Orderic was generous in including epitomes of texts about the past, Stephen put in anything that interested him. He seems to have written in a stream of consciousness in which one text suggests another, neither of them necessarily historical.

In form, the *Norman Dragon* also departs from the twelfth-century conventions so well embodied by Robert of Torigni. While Latin historians had mostly abandoned poetry as a medium for historical writing, Stephen embraced it, casting his work in the form of a classical epic, beginning in *medias res*. While history and epic might not be incompatible in many ways—and perhaps William of Poitiers and Dudo of Saint-Quentin may have conceived of their works as epic—the convention that history was to begin at the beginning and then go to the end was so strong that no other historian, to my knowledge, used an epic temporal scheme. More interesting, however, is that Stephen does not make reference to the writing of history at all. His opening remarks discuss how to compose poetry and the parts of rhetoric.[84] Stephen's research methods also suggest his very casual interest in history: out of the riches of the Bec library, he seems to have relied on a single volume for all of his principal historical sources, although he was clearly widely read.[85] To have a wonderful library at one's disposal did not necessarily mean that one would use it.

The writing of history in Normandy did change from the early eleventh century to the end of the twelfth century but not uniformly. Historians worked in an environment of freedom in which they chose their own sources and used them as they saw fit. One sort of change was that historians gradually began to do more re-

84. On the issue of the uneasy marriage of poetry and history, see Ebenbauer, *Carmen Historicum,* particularly 301–11, a section which Ebenbauer entitles "Poetry between Discovery and Lies." On the prefatory comments of historians, see Bernard Guenée, "Histoire, mémoire, écriture. Contribution à une étude des lieux communs," *Académie des Inscriptions et Belles-Lettres, Comptes rendus* (1983):441–56.

85. *DN,* xxv; *CG,* 2:392. That volume contained the interpolated *Deeds of the Dukes,* Einhard's life of Charlemagne, the life of Alexander, a letter about India allegedly written by Aristotle to Alexander the Great, an abbreviated history of the French kings, Geoffrey of Monmouth, and Nennius.

search. Both Robert of Torigni and Orderic Vitalis went out of their way to find sources they had heard about. Robert sent to Beauvais for a copy of Sigebert's chronicle, while Orderic notes with satisfaction at one point that he was copying a work that was not widely available.[86] Robert of Torigni's sensitivity to genre is evidence of a second change, a growing notion of how histories should look and sound. Histories should be written in the middle style, rather than the high style, should employ reputable sources, and have a sobriety of appearance. This emerging consciousness probably contributed to Geoffrey of Monmouth's success as a historian, because he imitated these conventions. It was not necessary, however, to subscribe to any of these ways of viewing history. In his individual way, Stephen of Rouen confidently wrote a history that operated within a different horizon of expectations from most other historians writing in the twelfth century.

86. Rob. of Tor., 2:341; *EH,* 2:148.

6 ❧ The Purpose of History

I was frequently at the side of the remarkable Duke Richard, the son of Marquis William, during the two years before his death, for I wished to offer him the duty of my service because of the innumerable benefits with which he deigned to enrich me, although I was quite without merit. Coming to me one day, he began to embrace me with the arms of pious love, and to entreat me with sweet words and to cajole me with pleasant pleas, and then to protest and swear in charity, that I should satisfy the longstanding desires of his heart, if I possibly could: namely, that I should describe the customs and deeds of the land of Normandy and the laws his ancestor Rollo had established in the realm. I was dumbstruck, as though I had lost my mind, and resisting for several days, I refused his petitions. At last, however, moved by so many entreaties and worn out by so many supplications, I bent my spirit to take the great weight of this task on my shoulders. . .

My ignorant pen had not really completed the first parts of the work when, alas! lachrymose fame announced that Richard, the first citizen of the whole world, had died. I would have put everything aside in sorrow for this prince because of my excessive weeping and intolerable lamentation (which tortured not only my heart but also my body's members), had not the matter been taken up by the peerless son who survived him, the Patrician Richard, and the notable Count Raoul. Both insisted with pleas that I carry out what Duke Richard of memorable life had ordered by his request, and they swore that the project I had promised him to carry out, which was now debased by the vice of deception, should not be polluted by the filth of falsehood but should go forward as far as the greatest depths of my understanding permitted. Bowing to their prayers and orders, I pursued the work.[1]

Thus Dudo of Saint-Quentin explained the genesis of his history of the Norman dukes. He wrote because Richard I and Richard II asked him to, and they paid him for the work. Because a copy of the charter by which Dudo donated them to the monastery of Saint-Quentin is still extant, we know of two properties Dudo received for his various services to the dukes. But Dudo's words do not explain why the two Richards asked him to write a history, only that they thought history worth writing. He says nothing about how the dukes intended to use this history, what it meant to them, or even what it meant to him beyond a great deal of labor.

These questions arise, because Dudo of Saint-Quentin's *Customs of the Dukes* was written for members of a society not seemingly much in need of written histories. Only five charters are extant from the reign of Richard I, Dudo's first patron, suggesting that contemporary Norman society was not much dependent on writing.[2] The Normans before 1000 still operated in the primarily oral mode that characterized much of early medieval lay culture. Some later ducal charters confirmed monastic donations originally made orally by Rollo or William Longsword. Important transactions were carried out face to face or through the mediation of physical objects, a practice which continued even after the writing

1. *De moribus*, 119–20.
2. Fauroux, *Recueil*, ##1–5. In contrast, Richard II left some fifty extant acts (ibid., ##6–57).

of charters became more common.[3] The anecdote Dudo tells about Duke William I's "long sword" illustrates this orality; the duke had to authenticate the authority of his emissary with his sword. The overwhelmingly oral nature of Norman society also meant that it was difficult to alienate property, as Eleanor Searle has pointed out. The need for writing was not pressing until the eleventh century when the increased complexity of Norman society and law required a more frequent recourse to written documents.[4]

As far as Norman lay society of the early eleventh century was concerned, a history like the *Customs* had no precedents. For one, it was in Latin, and Latin played only a very limited role in daily life. The knowledge of Latin was largely confined to the monks of the few functioning monasteries and the clerical circle surrounding the archbishop of Rouen. Members of the laity carried out their transactions primarily in French, although the Scandinavian population of western Normandy in the region of Bayeux and Caen clung to their own tongues until the early eleventh century, perhaps because of a continual influx of immigrants from Scandinavia.

As a text, the *Customs* was probably different from what the Scandinavian inhabitants of Normandy were used to as well. Although the *Customs* has epic qualities—and may draw on French epic narratives—it was a long and complex text. Although epics are often thought of as the literature of primary oral societies, in Greece and elsewhere lengthy epics first appeared with the adoption of writing.[5] If the Vikings followed the same pattern as other peoples whose acquisition of literacy can be documented, their oral narratives were probably not like the later lengthy written sagas but

3. Tabuteau, *Transfers of Property*, 7, 121ff.
4. On William's "long sword," see above, pp. 73–74. Searle, *Predatory Kinship*, 166; see also Jack Goody, *The Logic of Writing and the Organization of Society* (Cambridge: Cambridge University Press, 1986), 18; Tabuteau, *Transfers of Property*, 42, on the development of Norman charters. On the growth of dependence on writing in England, see Clanchy, *From Memory to Written Record*, esp. chapter two, "The Proliferation of Documents," 29–59.
5. On epic, see Jack Goody, "Africa, Greece and Oral Poetry," in *The Interface between the Oral and the Written* (Cambridge: Cambridge University Press, 1987), 78–109, esp. 84–86, 92–93, 106–7.

more like the shorter lays. Whatever Viking stories sounded like, however, the *Customs* so clearly belonged to Latin traditions of written texts that it is unlikely that it had more than a passing resemblance to familiar stories the Norman elite may have told each other.[6] Therefore, in commissioning a written Latin history, Richard I was demanding a new sort of artifact for his culture.

In part, Richard may have done so in response to the rapid and unsettling changes affecting Norman society during the late tenth and early eleventh centuries. While the Scandinavian component of Norman society diminished, ties with other parts of France were increasing as the Norman dukes married into French noble families and became involved in French politics.[7] These alliances, however, had a limited impact on the internal structures of Norman society. No children seem to have resulted from the unions of William Longsword and Richard I with their French wives Leutgarde and Emma.[8] Nonetheless, the dukes not only acted like French territorial princes in their dealings with Norman neighbors, they also embraced Frankish practices of rule when these were appropriate; this too must have been unsettling to their Norman followers.[9]

6. Here I am disagreeing with Eleanor Searle, "Fact and Pattern in Heroic History," who argues that Dudo was producing a Latin version of a saga.

7. William Longsword appears in Flodoard in the circle of Hugh the Great (d. 956), Herbert II of Vermandois (d. 943), William I of Poitou (d. 963), and Arnulf I of Flanders (d. 964), all of whom were great independent princes striving to increase their territory and assert their autonomy. He made alliances with these families, marrying Herbert's daughter Leutgarde and marrying his sister to William of Poitou. Like these other potentates, William sometimes defied Louis IV (936–954), although from 940 until his death, he was loyal to the king (Bates, *Normandy before 1066*, 10). Richard I survived his minority thanks to the support of Hugh the Great, whose daughter, Emma, he married. Richard appears in one charter as a vassal of Hugh's son, Hugh Capet, and he supported the latter against the last Carolingian rulers of France, although he seems not to have been very active in politics during the last three decades of his reign Normandy (Bates, *Normandy before 1066*, 14, 25, 27).

8. The marriages may have been unconsummated, or the offspring of these marriages may not have been considered for succession and therefore would not have been mentioned by historians (Searle, *Predatory Kinship*, 94).

9. William recreated the mint at Rouen, and began a Carolingian-style palace at Fécamp. The early leaders of Normandy assumed the title of count—there was

The spread of Christianity, with which the dukes were deeply involved, was also richly productive of conflict. Contemporary sources do not speak about whether the tenth-century dukes enforced adherence to Christianity. The chronicler, Flodoard, however, a contemporary of the events he described, reported that after William Longsword's death, there was widespread apostasy in Normandy which was combined with revolts against French overlordship. The apostasy suggests that some Normans had converted either unwillingly or only because they felt it conferred some advantage on them.[10] Dudo of Saint-Quentin put the formal end of paganism only a generation before he came to Normandy; paganism may have quietly hung on in parts of Normandy into his day, along with all the hostilities a quasi-forceable conversion may have occasioned.

The religious reform programs embraced by Richard I and Richard II must also have had unsettling effects, although these are harder to judge. The Norman clergy was not celibate: Richard I's son Robert, the archbishop of Rouen, was married and was succeeded as count of Évreux by his son. This behavior was normal in the early eleventh century, but reformers were already trying to put an end to it.[11] Monastic reform, which reorganized monastic customs and changed monastic personnel, sometimes met with resistence, although the Norman sources don't provide evidence of this. The laity was less directly affected by reform movements, but the reformers did not limit their activities to regulating the behavior of the clergy. The Flemish reformer, Richard of Saint-

---

a Carolingian count in Rouen until 905—along with what was left of Carolingian government in the region (Bates, *Normandy before 1066*, 10–11). However, see Searle, *Predatory Kinship*, 45, who points out that Flodoard never uses the title count to describe William Longsword. On the palace, see Annie Renoux, "Palais capétiens et normands à la fin du Xᶜ siècle et au début du XIᶜ siècle," in *Le Roi de France et son royaume autour de l'an mil*, ed. Michel Parisse and Xavier Barral i Altet (Paris: Picard, 1992), 179–91. Renoux suggests that the dukes of Normandy were the only northern princes to employ the Carolingian palace system, although they abandoned it in the course of the eleventh century (ibid., 179) and probably did not have the same notion of the palace as contemporary Capetians (ibid., 187–89).

10. Flodoard, *Annales*, 88–89.

11. *GND*, 159, 293; Bates, *Normandy before 1066*, 228.

Vannes, for example, who was a friend of Richard II, was a proponent of the Peace of God which he unsuccessfully urged Richard II to institute in his province, albeit after Dudo had completed his history.[12] Barbara Vopelius, in her study of the *Customs*, thought that Dudo's work was intended to criticize clerical reform. While her case is not entirely convincing, it is reasonable to expect that religious reform also caused some anxiety.[13]

These rapid political, social, and religious changes in the tenth and the early eleventh centuries created in Normandy opportunities for what the anthropologist, Victor Turner, called "social dramas."[14] Social dramas occur when individuals or groups perceive a disruption of traditions that threatens their place within a group or society. Social dramas may arise because of rapid economic change, political alterations, or from invasion. In these circumstances, power often shifts hands, creating perceived status incongruities. Some groups may feel, as a result, that their social identity is threatened. People can attempt to regain their lost status or hold onto a new, higher status in a number of ways. Those who feel themselves to be harmed by change may attack those whom they see as causing it. They may also seek mediation of some kind. This might take the form of performing reconciliation rituals. For example, Stephen White suggests that when a relative was not consulted over a donation of family property, that relative was effectively treated as a non-family member. The reconciliation rituals during which the individual gave consent and received a countergift reenforced the individual's status as a family member and person of note.[15] In the eleventh century, people had increasing

---

12. For Richard II and Richard of Saint-Vannes, see the latter's biography in *AA SS*, June, 2:469. For this first appearance of the Peace of God in Normandy, see J.-F. Lemarignier, "Paix et réforme monastique en Flandre et en Normandie autour de l'année 1023."

13. Vopelius, *Studien zu Dudo von Saint-Quentin*, 482ff.

14. See Victor Turner, "Social Dramas and Stories about Them," *Critical Inquiry* 7 (1980): 141–67. Cf. Eisenstadt, "Dynamics of Traditions," which offers a more cogent explanation of why social dramas arise and how people respond to such dramas, depending on the level of society from which they originate.

15. Stephen White, *Custom, Kinship and Gifts to the Saints*, 108–12.

recourse to legal action. Finally, both those given the advantage by change and those who were disadvantaged by it might sponsor the writing of history. Histories of this kind mediate, naturalize, and explain experience, either as it is or as it ought to be.[16]

A social drama may take place at any level of society: at the level of the kingdom or territory, within a social class, or in a small community.[17] The English initially responded to the Norman Conquest of England with scattered uprisings, but these were soon replaced by other forms of resistance, the most striking and prolonged of which involved historical writing. R. W. Southern has suggested that the English burst of historical writing in the first half of the twelfth century should be seen as a way to resolve the tensions created by the Conquest.[18] Similarly the Franco-Flemish elite of the late twelfth and early thirteenth century, whose activities have been analyzed by Gabrielle Spiegel, were also deeply enmeshed in a social drama. They suffered economically as the bourgeoisie of the towns began to outstrip them financially. Most maintained the opulence of their lifestyles only by borrowing, a practice that led to further impoverishment. At the same time, the king of France posed an increasing threat to Flemish autonomy. The response of the nobility was partly political—most allied themselves, disasterously, to the kings of England—but they also commissioned the writing of histories that argued for their lost autonomy from the French king and for the special moral worth of the nobility.[19]

16. This has been Yerushalmi's explanation for the pattern of Jewish historical writing (Yerushalmi, *Zakhor*, 36–40). The Crusades and the consequent attacks on Jewish communities represented such a dramatic break with previous Jewish experience that they could not be absorbed through the normal recourse to biblical paradigms, so the community turned to historical writing. The outburst of historical writing in the fifteenth century following the expulsion of the Sephardim from Spain was a similar interpretive effort. On mediation, see Turner, "Social Dramas," 149. See also Veyne, *Did the Greeks Believe in Their Myths?*, 11, who argues that the modern historical consciousness arises from controversy, hence from the mediatory aspects of history.

17. Eisenstadt, "Dynamics of Traditions," 455. Although Eisenstadt speaks only in terms of changes and innovations, these kinds of changes clearly belong in the category of "social dramas" posited by Turner.

18. Southern, "The Sense of the Past," 246–49.

19. Spiegel, *Romancing the Past*, 11–54 ("The Historical Setting").

The case of Bury Saint-Edmunds reveals how social dramas can be enacted within a single small community. Most of the social drama in the monastery was generated internally. There was a continuing struggle between the obedienciaries and the abbot, who was extending his sphere of authority over monastic property; between the monastic learned, who felt that they were being pushed out by the less pious brothers educated in the schools, and the school-educated, who resented men they regarded as uneducated; between the noble and the common; and between the young and the old. This power struggle manifested itself overtly during elections or other crises but also covertly. For example, the obedienciaries evaded the authority of the abbot by borrowing money without his permission, endangering the economic stability of the monastery. In addition to these internal battles, the monastery had an ongoing struggle to maintain its authority over its *fideles* and tenants.[20]

Various methods were employed to mediate this social drama. As far as the external problems were concerned, the abbot expelled the monastery's creditors—Bury's Jewish community—from the town, although the king protected the Jewish community's accounts receivable. The monastery took those who challenged its rights to court on more than one occasion. Internal responses to the crisis were more varied. There was what may have been an attempt on the abbot's life (or Abbot Samson believed that on at least one occasion his monks wanted to kill him). Monks publicly reported their dreams, since dreams were often considered symbolic and/or prophetic. These dreams were then given explicitly political interpretations. In one case, the abbot reported and interpreted one of his own dreams, only to find that some of the monks had their own and more negative interpretation of it. Finally, the abbot attempted to bolster his own charisma by opening

20. Jocelin of Brakelond, *Chronicle*. For conflicts among the brothers, see, for example, the comments of the monks during the election of Samson, 11–15; on the debts of the monastery, 1–4, 29; on the struggle over property and rights between the abbot and convent, 72–73, 99f.; on challenges by the tenants and struggles with outside claims of rights, see 28, 50f, 57f., 65f.

the shrine of St. Edmund and touching the body, an action for which Edmund had punished a previous abbot with palsy.[21] We know about this whole social drama, however, because Jocelin of Brakelond, a monk at Bury, wrote an eyewitness account of the events. Jocelin was inclined toward the abbot's position, but he was deeply troubled by the continuing failure of the monks to resolve their situation and did not hold his abbot blameless. At least one brother in the monastery read the text while Jocelin was writing it.[22]

Tenth-century and early eleventh-century Normans similarly responded in a variety of ways to the cultural forces changing their society. In the 940s, Norman pagans responded to the arrival of Christianity by rebelling. William of Jumièges describes a similarly violent incident from early in the reign of Richard II. Peasants all over Normandy, he says, held conventicles over their loss of rights over the woods and waters of Normandy, for the elite were in the process of appropriating these rights. The peasants never had the opportunity to take direct action. Instead, Richard II's uncle, Raoul d'Ivry, fell upon one of these conventicles and made examples of the emissaries sent to him by the rebels by chopping off their hands and feet.[23] Such violent responses to conflict did not preclude the use of subtler means, such as the writing of history.

Dudo's history is an eloquent testimonial to the anxieties among the Normans created by the changes in their society and the activities of their rulers. The contents of Dudo's *Customs of the Dukes* make it clear that one of its functions was to put forward the case for ducal policy in the social drama generated by the rapid social changes in tenth-century Normandy. Dudo acknowledged Norman ties with other territories and depicted the Norman rulers as playing a grand role—probably greater than their true role—in French politics. For example, he depicted William Longsword as

21. Ibid., 45–46 (expulsion of the Jews); 51–52, 57–59 (court cases); 31f., 119 (Samson's fears for his life); 110–11 (a dream and its several interpretations); 114 (the opening of Edmund's shrine); xviii (on the punishment of Abbot Leofstan).

22. Ibid., 105; for Jocelin's doubts, see 81, 105, 129.

23. *GND*, 73–74.

organizing the return of Louis IV from England in 936, whereas the *History of France* from Sens, which is roughly contemporary, credited William, Archbishop of Sens, and Flodoard attributed this action to Hugh the Great.[24] At the same time, however, he presented the association between the Norman rulers and French princes as voluntary and stressed the independence of Normandy from royal control, thereby rendering the policies of the dukes more palatable.

Dudo also argued in favor of Normandy as a Christian territory by depicting the Viking conversion to Christianity as an integral part of Norman success. By describing Rollo as hospitable to Christianity even before his conversion, Dudo makes that conversion the completion of a divinely destined journey, rather than a requirement to which Rollo acquiesced so he might receive seisin of Normandy; indeed, Dudo argued that God granted Rollo success because he was destined to become a Christian. Thus the *Customs* stressed the legitimacy of the dukes' actions in forcing their Norman followers to convert at the same time as it de-emphasized the persistence of paganism in western Normandy, presenting paganism as a continual import, rather than an indigenous system of beliefs, and covering up the role of paganism in the troubles following the assassination of William Longsword.

While the anxieties arising from the advent of Christianity were part of the background to the writing of the *Customs,* the arrival of Christianity also helped create conditions propitious to the text's reception. The growth of Christian institutions led to an increased use of written records in Normandy. The dukes relied on members of the clergy to compose documents for them. Dudo in his capacity as ducal chancellor produced at least two of Richard II's extant charters.[25] Once present in the ducal court, however, members of the clergy probably acted as ducal advisors on more matters than religion. For example, Richard II's contemporary, William V of

24. *De moribus,* 193–94; *Historia Francorum Senonensis,* 366; Flodoard, *Annales,* 63.

25. Fauroux, *Recueil,* #13, 86–89; #18, 100–102.

Poitou (d. 1030) asked Fulbert of Chartres about his obligations as a lord and those of his *homines casati*.[26] By these means, clerical ideas about lay conduct were conveyed to secular lords. This sort of clerical advice was highly traditional: when in the *Customs*, Dudo had Abbot Martin of Jumièges explain to William Longsword that he was responsible for the protection of the clergy and people against the pagans and for law enforcement, and that he could not abandon this charge to become a monk, he was offering the same sort of advice to his ruler as the authors of Carolingian mirrors of princes did.[27]

Although in his introduction, Dudo presents the commission as being completely the duke's idea and describes himself as stupefied and unwilling to undertake the work, it is also possible that the history was originally Dudo's idea. The reticence Dudo expressed about writing was a standard example of the *trepidatio* variant of the modesty topos.[28] Dudo's expression of this topos was masterful; his account of Richard I's plea that he write a history of the Normans used verbs of delicately increasing force *(trahere, mulcere, detestari, jurare)* imitating the supposedly escalating vehemence of the duke's entreaties to splendid effect. While Richard, feeling his reign to be successful and grown conscious of the permanence of writing and its ability to disseminate information widely, might have requested that Dudo create some sort of written panegyric, it was Dudo who through his education was acquainted with the traditions and models of such histories, and who was familiar with Bede's *Ecclesiastical History of the English People* and perhaps some other "national" histories such as Jordanes's *Getica* or Paul the Deacon's *History of the Lombards*. He was in a better position than Richard I to comprehend the possible uses of a history of the Normans.

26. Behrends, *Fulbert of Chartres*, 90–92. C. Stephen Jaeger, *The Origins of Courtliness* (Philadephia: University of Pennsylvania Press, 1985), has argued that this clerical influence was responsible for the rise of courtly culture.

27. *De moribus*, 201. See Shopkow, "Norman Historical Writing," 87–88.

28. See E. R. Curtius, *European Literature and the Latin Middle Ages*, trans. Willard R. Trask (New York: Harper, 1963), 83–84.

It seems unlikely, however, that Dudo anticipated his history being used to instruct the Norman laity about their history. The *Customs of the Dukes* was not accessible to anyone who was not an accomplished Latinist and was not written so as to make translation into the vernacular easy. Its rhythmic prose and complicated metrical passages would have lost their artistry in the translation; some of the copyists of the text chose to omit the poetry, perhaps because of its difficulty.[29] Therefore, the *Customs* does not seem intended to indoctrinate Normans but to serve other functions. However, simply because Richard I and Richard II could not read the *Customs,* it does not follow that they could derive no benefit from having it written.

For us, reading and writing are inextricably linked, but medieval readers were not always writers and not all writing was written to be read. For example, monasteries kept necrologies, lists of the names of dead monks and sometimes of donors. Saint-Evroul's roll of donors and friends of the monastery, however, was not read but placed on the altar and those listed were prayed for in a general way.[30] Thus the roll itself represented the dead; presumably God read it. Another similar monumental use of writing was the mortuary roll; when the monks of one institution wrote a poem for the dead abbot of another, they participated in a funerary ritual in which the existence of the written contribution mattered more than the content of the contribution. Indeed, since the same poems were often used on many different mortuary rolls, the emphasis was clearly more on participation in the commemorative ritual

---

29. Huisman, "Notes on the Manuscript Tradition," 123, argues that Dudo's first edition probably lacked the poetry. I am, however, inclined to believe that the poetry was original, since the manuscripts that omit the poetry contain at least the three poems which advance the action of the text (*De moribus,* 148, 149, 182). These three poems, at least, must have been in the original version, and if these three, why not all the rest? The quotations from Dudo's sources can be found in both prose and verse; in one case (182), Dudo follows his source, the *Vita sancti Lamberti* of Stephen of Liège as it moves from prose to poetry. Therefore, the versions in which the poetry and dedication are absent seem to me to be abbreviated versions of the originally longer text, rather than early versions of a text later expanded.

30. Chibnall, *The World of Orderic Vitalis,* 67.

than on making an original literary contribution. After circulating, the roll became a monument to the dead person, while the act of circulating the roll created ties between monasteries.[31] Either a necrology or a mortuary roll might be read—Stephen of Fougères used the mortuary roll of Vitalis in writing his biography—but such a document was important even if no one ever picked up the text to read it.[32]

While Dudo assuredly wanted the *Customs* to have readers, the text, like these rolls, also had a monumental and symbolic function. To see how this was so, we need to think of Dudo's history (or any sort of writing) as a kind of message. Roman Jakobson suggests that messages function in a number of different ways. They refer to something, that is, they have a content (which Jakobson terms the "context"). They are written in a code, that is, a language. They represent a contact between the sender and the recipient of the message. And the form the message itself takes matters as well.[33] All four aspects of the message can be meaningful, although the sender may emphasize one over the others, and all are simultaneously present in every message.

While I have discussed the *Customs* thus far primarily in terms of its contents, its code and contact mattered as well. Although Dudo's patrons could not decode the *Customs*—they did not read and probably did not understand Latin—the very fact that the *Customs* was written in Latin symbolized the importance of the dukes. To have a history written in Latin was to emphasize one's Christianity and one's cultivation. To be the patron of such a work was to be princely; to have such a history written about one's territory was testimony to its importance. Dudo provided this service to the Norman rulers as earlier historians had done for other Germanic groups such as the Anglo-Saxons and Goths, who were lauded by histories bearing the same sorts of messages at approx-

31. On mortuary rolls, see Léopold Delisle, *Rouleaux des morts du IXe au XVe siècle* (Paris: Renouard, 1866).

32. On Stephen's use of the mortuary roll, see Stephen of Fougères, *Vita sancti Vitalis*, 380.

33. Jakobson, "Closing Statement: Linguistics and Poetics," 353, 355–57.

imately the same stage in their assimilation to Latin Christian culture.[34]

The book as an object also had a particular resonance. When the duke gave his presentation copy of a manuscript to a favored monastery, as patrons usually did, the book became symbolic of the relationship between the institution and its benefactor. In giving the book, the donor emphasized the relationship between himself and the monastery, just as the historian in writing the book also emphasized the contact between himself and his patron.[35] In a monastic library, in which there might be only a hundred books, the history would represent a substantial contribution to the treasure possessed by the institution. The book, like any other valuable gift, further set up chains of mutual obligation.[36] When other institutions in the province copied such a book, these institutions demonstrated not only their own wealth but also expressed their solidarity with and interest in their rulers. The importance of these symbolic messages sent by a book as an object is difficult to assess. However, other territorial princes within the next century found it useful to have such histories of their lordship written, despite the limited reading audience the work might have. In this way, even an illiterate patron benefited from the writing of a history.

I am not arguing here that the contents of the *Customs* were unimportant. The messages the text conveyed by its existence were accompanied by the messages conveyed by its words. These messages were about, among other things, Norman legitimacy and assimilation into the culture of Christian Europe. Although lay readers might not have been able to read the text, the clerical audience, which controlled and wrote history, could be reached and influenced by the

34. Schmale, *Funktion und Formen*, 23f.

35. Dudo twice makes reference to that relationship himself in *De moribus*, 118–20, 295.

36. On the costs of books and their value, see Rosamund McKitterick, *The Carolingians and the Written Word* (Cambridge: Cambridge University Press, 1989), 135–37; 148ff. On the associations set up by the gift between monastery and donors, see Stephen White, *Kinship, Custom, and Gifts to the Saints*, 158f. (White here draws on the anthropological literature on gift-giving, primarily Mauss and Evans-Pritchard.)

text. This audience, particularly readers outside of Normandy, held views of the Normans that were sometimes quite derogatory. Richer of Reims, Dudo's contemporary, might have called the Norman rulers *duces pyratarum*—leaders of the brigands—but Dudo gave an alternative portrait of Richard as a cultivated Christian monarch.[37] The *Customs* defended the authority of the Norman dukes, as the works produced for the early Carolingians had attempted to legitimize their growing power.[38] Not only that, but Dudo's version of Norman history contained a covert warning; it would be foolish to assail a leader who dealt as handily with his enemies as Richard I, since Richard forced King Lothar of France, Lothar's brothers-in-law, Otto I (the German emperor) and Bruno (the archbishop of Cologne), and the wily count of Chartres, Thibaut I the Cheater, either to sue him for peace or to suffer defeat. Thus the *Customs* conveyed its meaning both through its existence as a book and through its existence as a text.

In addition to the ways the *Customs* might have been intended to benefit the Norman dukes, however, there were ways in which Dudo might have expected to benefit himself. Although the work was conceived at the Norman court, the *Customs* is not dedicated to any Norman but rather to Adalberon, the bishop of Laon.[39] While Dudo might have sent his work to Adalberon because of a previous acquaintance, he explicitly stated his hope that Adalberon would become his patron. Dudo's argument was based on Adalberon's learning, which Dudo praised in the opening pages of his text. Adalberon was certainly formidably well-educated. He had

---

37. Richer of Reims, *Histoire de France,* ed. R. Latouche (Paris: Société d'édition "Les Belles Lettres," 1964), 1:104, 156; 2:328.

38. The first, second, and third continuations of the chronicle of "Fredegar" and the *Gesta regum Francorum* were produced under Arnulfing auspices. Among the works written to please the family once they had come to power were Paul the Deacon's *Gesta archiepiscoporum Mettensium,* the *Royal Frankish Annals,* Angilbert's *Carmen de Carolo Magno,* and Nithard's *Histories.* The *Royal Frankish Annals* in their earliest form were not official; some of their continuations were.

39. Not all manuscripts contain the dedicatory introduction (see Huisman, "Notes on the Manuscript Tradition," 125–26). Generally the versions which have the dedication also contain the poetry.

also wavered in his support of the new Capetian lineage, as had the counts of Vermandois, Dudo's initial patrons. Adalberon was therefore able to appreciate both the artistry and the political sentiments of the *Customs*.[40] Dudo's expressed hope was that "those things which seem obscured in this book by its shadows might be brought into the light" by the bishop, in other words, that Adalberon would help his book circulate by correcting its errors and lending it his name.[41]

However, as a bishop, Adalberon also had the power to offer preferment to those who pleased him. Dudo's possibilities of advancement in Normandy were limited, for the important ecclesiastical offices of his day went either to members of the ducal family, to other local notables, or to reformers brought in from abroad. If Dudo wished to advance, he might well need a new and third patron, who might become interested in a candidate by a judicious gift.

There is no evidence that Adalberon helped Dudo find any higher office or even read the *Customs*. Nonetheless, the *Customs* may indeed have helped Dudo to advance, at least indirectly. Scholars have assumed that Dudo's donation to Saint-Quentin of the two benefices he acquired in return for his service to the Norman dukes provided an incentive to his monastery to choose him as dean of the congregation. His service to the house of Vermandois, of which his lord, Albert, had been the lay abbot, must have helped as well.[42] Dudo's sturdy history may also have contributed to his success by earning him a literary reputation which would have been attractive in a monastic leader. After all, Guibert of Nogent attributed his election at the end of the century as abbot of Nogent to his growing eminence as a scholar.[43]

---

40. *De moribus,* 118. Vopelius, "Dudo of Saint-Quentin," 250ff., has argued that Dudo was a student at Reims and probably met Adalberon who was also a student there. I have argued in "Carolingian World," 25–27, that Dudo was educated at Liège and not at Reims.

41. *De moribus,* 118.

42. On the former supposition, see Vopelius, *Studien zu Dudo von Saint-Quentin,* 100; on Dudo's service, see *De moribus,* 295.

43. Guibert of Nogent, *Autobiographie,* ed. and trans. Edmond-René Labande (Paris: Société d'édition "Les Belles Lettres," 1981), 166.

Although the *Customs* illustrated the usefulness of history for recipients, readers, and authors and made it easier for later writers to embark upon the writing of history, its existence alone did not provide the incentive to write new histories. Later histories arose from their own set of circumstances. Particularly relevant to the production of the histories that came after the *Customs* was an increase in the level of Latinity in Normandy. The use of Latin charters in Normandy increased dramatically in the course of the eleventh century, and while these were generated by the ecclesiastical institutions that benefited from them, they do attest to growing facility with both Latin and writing.[44] The eleventh and twelfth centuries were the period in Europe in which Latin came closest to being a living language. It was still no one's native tongue, but it had a vitality and energy drawn from an increasing number of speakers (who were also generally readers) and was not yet seriously challenged in the sphere of writing by the vernaculars.[45] The new readership was one motivation for the return to the writing of history.

Political and social circumstances in Normandy also arose to encourage new historical production around the middle of the century. With the reign of Robert the Magnificent, Normandy entered a period of turbulence that ended only around 1050. New families appeared among the Norman elite and challenged ducal authority. The most powerful families began to build castles in defiance of the ducal monopoly over this activity, although castle-building became frequent only at the end of the eleventh century. The fierce competition between families developed into feuds and private wars. In these chaotic circumstances, the Church suffered particularly because of the inability of the duke to enforce the peace.[46] During this period of unrest, it is not surprising that monasteries did not produce much writing of any kind apart from charters; they were too busy attempting to survive. However, after Wil-

---

44. Tabuteau, *Transfers of Property*, 7, table 1.

45. See Richter, "A Socio-Linguistic Approach," 71.

46. On new families, see Bates, *Normandy before 1066*, 99–100; on castles, 115–15, 175; on feuds, 100–101.

liam II's triumph over his Norman enemies at Val-és-Dunes in 1047 and the French at Mortemer in 1054 and Varaville in 1057, peace was restored, permitting clerics to devote their energies to the process of restoration and renewal. This restoration was followed hard upon by the Norman Conquest, which not only increased Norman resources but also encouraged the Normans to rethink who they were. All of these experiences provided rationales for historical writing.

At Jumièges, "certain good men" urged William to take up the task of historical writing.[47] William mentioned their existence only at the end of his history, and he did not say who they were or whether this was a commission or merely encouragement. The former seems more likely, since monks almost never wrote history spontaneously.[48] By mentioning these men at the end only, William avoided detracting attention at the beginning from the dedication to the Conqueror, but they seem to have been the force behind his history and not the man to whom the work was dedicated.

Nevertheless, the history was probably intended from the start for presentation to William II. Orderic Vitalis emphasized this point when he included at the beginning of his autograph of the *Deeds of the Dukes* a pen and ink drawing of William presenting his book to the Conqueror.[49] William of Jumièges and his monastery were not the only ones to offer this kind of tribute to the new king, for William himself mentions "men illustrious for their knowledge of letters" who surrounded the king, while Orderic Vitalis mentions that other men, such as Guy of Amiens, also bore literary gifts to the Conqueror.[50] William of Jumièges and his patrons may have hoped, as did other bearers of tribute, to receive some tangible benefit from the duke for their efforts.

Like the *Customs,* the *Deeds* mediated a social drama. It did so most obviously in the treatment of the succession crisis, where its

47. *GND,* 143.
48. Garand, "Auteurs latins," 95.
49. *EH,* 2:78; Rouen, BM, Y. 14, 116r.
50. *GND,* 1; *EH,* 2:184f.

author defended the succession of William II. By implication this defense included a justification of the duke's other policies; for example, the firm hand he took against his nobility, although most of what we know about this issue comes not from William of Jumièges's version of the *Deeds* but from Orderic's.[51] The *Deeds* presented the growing dominance of certain noble families and the increasingly complex organization of society as a *fait accompli,* which masked the dislocations of the transition. William's comments about his own labors and those of others are revealing; he described other writers as defending the city with drawn blades and his own book was offered as "a little wall."[52]

Unlike Dudo, however, who had little to say about how he viewed history apart from the implication that history was to preserve memory (an issue I will return to below), William of Jumièges advanced abstract reasons for reading and writing it. Since William criticized Dudo because portions of the *Customs* offered "the appearance neither of honesty or utility," he clearly expected history to be useful.[53] One of its uses was to offer a series of examples from which readers might learn if they chose, the time-honored moral function for history.[54] Among the examples the *Deeds* contained were practical lessons in lordship. The *Deeds of the Dukes,* like the *Customs,* may have been intended as a sort of historical mirror for princes. William had a more abstract notion of history's importance as well, this time for the monastic reader. The monk who wrote history, according to William, made the virtues and deeds of great people, which were known to God, equally well-known on earth, thereby allowing humanity to partake of divine knowledge.[55]

---

51. See *GND,* 185, for example.
52. Ibid., 2.
53. Ibid.
54. Cf. Livy, *The Early History of Rome,* trans. Aubrey de Selincourt (Harmondsworth, Middlesex: Penguin, 1960), 18: "The study of history is the best medicine for a sick mind; for in history you have a record of the infinite variety of human experience plainly set out for all to see; and in that record you can find for yourself and your country both examples and warnings: fine things to take as models, base things, rotten through and through, to avoid."
55. *GND,* 2.

The *Deeds of William* appeared at nearly the same time as the *Deeds of the Dukes,* but William of Poitiers's work seems to have been written with somewhat different ends in mind. William of Poitiers was not interested in defending William II's succession, which he dealt with briefly and early in his text; the social drama the *Deeds of William* engaged was the Conquest. While the English had to come to terms with their dramatic defeat at Hastings, the sudden domination of their institutions by foreigners, and the subordination of their language and culture, the Normans too had to adjust to changes brought about by the Conquest. They had to assimilate a windfall that dwarfed their old holdings and suddenly shifted the center of gravity away from Normandy across the channel and which brought them into contact with people who were proud of their own quite different cultural traditions. This cultural conflict may explain the harshness of William of Poitiers's language about the English and his insistence that only by conforming to Norman notions of behavior might they become "civilized.[56] William of Poitiers also offered a quasi-legal justification of the Conquest for anyone who might feel in need of it.

It seems likely that William of Poitiers, who was so deeply imbued with classical history, also had absorbed some of the classical rationales for the writing of history. This is a surmise, for the preface of the *Deeds of William* is missing and any comments William might have placed there are gone as well. However, because William had read the *Agricola* of Tacitus, he was acquainted with Tacitus's ideas on the subject. Tacitus lauded biography in traditional terms for its exemplary value, but he also presented it as a duty of the individual to write about conspicuously egregious individuals. Further, he depicted his biography of Agricola as a "testimony to present happiness" through its account of past turmoil.[57] William of Poitiers might easily have seen himself as occupying the same circumstances as Tacitus, to be writing in a glorious time following

56. See above, pp. 93, 100–101.
57. Tacitus, *The Life of Cnaeus Julius Agricola,* in *The Complete Works of Tacitus,* trans. A. J. Church and W. J. Brodribb (New York: Modern Library, 1942), 677–78.

upheaval and to have before him a similarly appropriate subject; he might thus have felt obligated to commemorate the Conqueror for posterity.

Medieval historians often invoked the desire to preserve information for memory when they wrote history. History was often described as *memorabilia,* things worthy of memory. Like a text, memory was often described as being a book or table.[58] History in the Middle Ages depended to a far greater degree on memory than it does today, because so much of the testimony that found its way into history came from oral traditions and hence was a product of collective memory. Texts also became objects of memorization. For instance, Ralph of Diceto created symbols for the different sorts of historical events he narrated in his chronicle, not only as an index to events but probably also to aid the memory in retaining the information.[59] Funkenstein has likened the relationship between memory and history to the one between *parole* and *langue;* memory is a series of utterances reflecting only some of the rich possibilities of history.[60]

These connections between memory and history obscured for medieval writers the ways in which the two were different. Events that were truly important to communities were not forgotten, even if they were not written down. When he came to write the *Deeds of the Dukes,* William of Jumièges was able to draw on the collective memories of his community for events a century earlier because the history of the community was something that mattered to the monks. Monastic communities functioned as places of memory, not only for the monks but for the larger community of their donors. The monastery kept alive the memories of those who had enriched it as well as praying for them; indeed, the two functions were inseparable.[61] The information contained in monastic histories or annals was often considerably

---

58. Carruthers, *Book of Memory,* 16–32.

59. Clanchy, *From Memory to Written Word,* 142–43; on similar sorts memory systems, see Carruthers, *Book of Memory,* 86, 108ff.

60. Funkenstein, "Collective Memory," 7.

61. See Geary, *Phantoms of Remembrance,* 68, 72–80.

less memorable than the genealogies and legends preserved at monasteries. For instance, the regnal dates of rulers and their successions or the date of remote battles was not crucial to monastic life or rituals, and consequently such information was often marginal to the identity of the community, which would naturally be more interested in its own leaders, their activities, and monastic events. Moreover, the material the historian preserved for memory did not necessarily come from memory. It sometimes consisted of new or invented memories. The "memories" Dudo of Saint-Quentin immortalized were his own memories from the materials he had read and from his own experience, not necessarily Norman memories of the past. (In a sense, his work was designed to challenge the socially generated memories of opposing groups.) In the process of writing a history, the historian decided not only what ought to be remembered but also structured how the material was to be remembered, offering as a substitute for personal, social, and self-referential memories external and abstract written accounts. As the collectivities in which memories resided changed, histories preserved memories that would otherwise have been forgotten and continually reintroduced them to society. The vision of Normandy proffered by Dudo's *Customs of the Dukes* far outlasted the disappearance of the late Carolingian society he wrote for and about.[62]

Medieval historians were unconcerned about most of the ways that memory was different from history; our awareness of the differences between the two comes out of modern theory about memory, which stresses the objective existence of something written on paper and the more intangible and sometimes ephemeral presence of ideas carried only in the mind. These historians did not care much about this distinction. However, they were very much aware that much about the past, if it depended entirely on the passive operations of memory, would be forgotten as events from the past

---

62. These features of memory and history are discussed by Nora, "Entre mémoire et histoire," esp. xxv–xxxiv; see also Funkenstein, "Collective Memory and Historical Consciousness"; Yerushalmi, *Zakhor*; and Halbwachs, "Historical Memory and Collective Memory," in *The Collective Memory*, 50–87.

waned in importance within memory. To counteract the process of forgetting, the historian took an active role, creating a new object based on what was remembered but which was itself no longer, strictly speaking, a memory, since it no longer required anyone to do the remembering. This new object, this history, passed on the contents of the memory (although those contents were no longer subject to the transformative actions of memory). This process by which memories were turned into something different was a common process in medieval Europe, where memories might become rituals or books or other kinds of objects.[63]

Once the memories had been turned into these commemorative objects, the memories themselves might pass away, while their representatives continued to exist. Once this happened, the commemorative objects might become the means through which people might memorize a past they no longer carried in their heads, that is, become a means of instruction. They might also become a means by which existing memories might be reprogrammed with new meanings.

This was one potential function of the *Deeds of William*. In commemorating the Conquest, William of Poitiers was writing for a society which remembered the events. However, in the process of creating a monument to their achievements, William also told his readers what meaning they were to assign to the Conquest and how they were to assign to it and how they were in the future to justify their possession of their new lands. While the Conqueror was clearly the focus of the commemoration since his merits made this expansion possible, the historian presented him as the center of a named community of shared experience. William of Poitiers took pains to mention most of the important courtiers, including the duke's counselors and those who accompanied the Conqueror across the Channel.[64]

The *Deeds of William*'s moral function was also tied to the question of memory, for memory was conceived of as being moral. Not

---

63. See, for example, Carruther's *Book of Memory*, 1–6.
64. *GG*, 148, 194–966.

only did memory provide a vocabulary for history, it also provided a formulary of action for the individual. Mary Carruthers describes how in at least one case, an individual used a historical text as a commentary upon her actions. When Heloise assumed the veil at Argentan, she used the words of Cornelia from Lucan's *Pharsalia* to rebuff those attempting to persuade her not to. In so doing, Heloise was drawing on the "ethical memory" situated originally in the text but enacted by Heloise.[65] William of Poitiers clearly hoped that his text would provide the same kind of "ethical" memories for his readers. This hope was intrinsic in the writing of tropological history.[66]

William of Poitiers generally put the memories he was trying to preserve into a moral context, but his audience might well have been more interested in the heroic function of memory, the preservation of the memory of great deeds both as examples and as a source of pleasure. Eleventh-century audiences, even monastic audiences, had epic heroes before their eyes. While the *Deeds of William* is also commemorative in this more secular sense, for it does chronicle great deeds, its author was more interested in the character of the Conqueror than his glorious conduct in battle. In fact, his narrative frequently describes the Conqueror as heroic, without narrating the actions that made him so.

While the great Norman narrative histories of the eleventh-century filled certain easily identifiable intentional niches, the functions of the Norman annals, begun at the same time William of Jumièges and William of Poitiers were writing, are harder to perceive. The annals were by their form narrative in only the most limited way. Because their contents derived in part from other annals, and because the annalists changed over the years, even when they engaged in narrative or in narrative sketches they offered a compilation of different viewpoints and agendas. The information they provided was frequently of perplexing import. In addition to notices about the births, coronations, perambulations, and de-

---

65. Carruthers, *Book of Memory*, 181–83.
66. See above, p. 67.

mises of kings and other notables, they offered notations about the weather and other highly local phenomena.[67]

What were these texts supposed to mean? Schmale has argued that annals were fundamentally different from other sorts of historical writing. Whereas other forms of history in the Middle Ages served theology, were written to demonstrate the great play of God's actions in the universe, and were part of grammar or rhetoric, annals served chronology and were subject to the quadrivium. To write an annal was to take note of the passage of time.[68] This hypothesis would explain the writing of annals in Easter tables and the appearance of annals in conjunction with computus texts.

There are problems, however, with these suppositions about annals. There is only limited evidence that annals were thought to belong to the quadrivium or that their purpose was the description of time. Isidore of Seville did place his comments about chronicles in his book on time. It is also true that many annals are found in manuscripts with computus materials—the Lyre annals came to rest beside a treatise on computus, a calendar, and Bede's *De temporibus*. Moreover, Bede's work, which contains a chronicle as well as a discussion of computus and the measurement of time, may have set the precedent of grouping such texts together.[69] However, not all annals appeared in manuscripts with computus texts. The two medieval manuscripts that contain the annals of Jumièges also include the chronicle of Robert of Torigni and the history of Henry of Huntingdon, so that whoever organized the manuscript thought the annals belonged with the narrative histories.[70] In addition, annals continued to be written long after standardized Easter tables made the study of computus obsolete. Furthermore, as descriptions of the passage of time, annals seem rather want-

67. See, for example, the entries for 859 and 871 in the annals of Jumièges (Laporte, *Annales de Jumièges,* 49).

68. Schmale, *Funktion und Formen,* 70–78. Hayden White makes a similar argument about the annals of Saint-Gall in "The Value of Narrativity in the Representation of Reality," 13.

69. The Lyre annals are contained in Évreux, *Bibliothèque municipale,* ms. 60, 2v–3r. For the manuscript, see *Manuscrits datés,* 464; also *CG,* 2:437–38.

70. Laporte, *Annales de Jumièges,* 16ff.

ing. Some annals numbered all the years, even if they noted events only in a few, but some annals simply noted a scattering of events and the years in which they occurred.

If, however, annals were intended to have some other practical significance, both the variable nature of annals, the kind of entries they contain, and their proliferation in Normandy between 1060 and 1106 make more sense. The Norman annals were not generally detailed or specific enough to serve as complete or even satisfying accounts of the past, but they could be used as markers of relative time for ecclesiastical purposes. Because they are physically experienced, great winds and cold winters are the sort of events that live well in memory; more important events might be temporally anchored to these lesser and more local phenomena. For example, a monastery might know that it began a building program after a great wind destroyed most of its outbuildings or that it received a certain donation during the reign of a particular duke. Annals might then assist the clergy in dating their undated documents in preparation for defending their property. Establishing title was crucial during two periods of Norman history, after 1050 and after 1106, when Norman institutions attempted to retrieve property lost during periods of weak ducal control. Histories and annals were also quite useful as an aid to forgery, to which monks sometimes had resort.[71]

In the twelfth century, when some monasteries kept much more abbreviated short annals, the property acquisitions of the monastery were noted in the annals themselves, offering another sort of proof of possession. Some monasteries also organized their documents into cartularies, which might have a strongly historical flavor. Even though charters were not dispositive documents, the material in cartularies was useful evidence in legal battles over rights, since, through at least the twelfth century, the settlement of property disputes tended to involve adjudication and compromise rather than strict adherence to abstract legal requirements.[72]

71. See Tabuteau, *Transfers of Property*, 216–17, 220.
72. Tabuteau, *Transfers of Property*, 212; see also 213f. for a discussion of how

Most monastic cartularies began with a brief history of the abbey, which served not only to attest to the circumstances under which the abbey had come into being but also to the properties which were part of the endowment. The cartulary of Saint-Pierre-sur-Dives, for example, contained a narrative history of the abbey from its foundation. It related that an anonymous woman had predicted that the land upon which William of Eu was building his house would become a house of God and that William's widow Lesceline did in fact donate the land to create a monastery. It reported the countess's gifts to the monastery and how these were jeopardized during the reign of Robert Curthose. The account ended with Henry's restoration of the monastery in 1108.[73]

Clerical property also came in forms other than real estate. The authors of the *Discovery of Saint Wulfran* and the *Authority of Fécamp* were both defending less tangible, but no less valuable, kinds of property. Both works were offered as testimony in controversies with potentially serious consequences. In the case of Saint-Wandrille, the monks were making a claim to hold authentic relics of St. Wulfran, against the assertion on the part of the monks of St. Peter in Ghent that the saint's body had never been returned to Normandy after the Viking invasions. Saint-Wandrille stood to lose an important spiritual patron, whose miracles were no doubt a source of identity and consolation to the community, and whose

---

charters were used as evidence in Normandy. On the settlement of disputes, see Fredric L. Cheyette, "Suum cuique tribuere," *French Historical Studies* 6 (1969), esp. 293; Susan Reynolds, "Law and Communities in Western Christendom, c. 900–1140," *American Journal of Legal History* 25 (1981), 214–16.

73. *Gallia christiana*, 11, *Instrumenta*, 154–55. The historical character of English cartularies has been argued by Genet, "Cartulaires, registres et histoire," 95–129. Genet calls attention not only to the historical content of the cartularies but also to the methods of composition used by those compiling them and the functions cartularies served. Geary, *Phantoms of Remembrance* ("Archival Memory") takes this argument beyond the English examples used by Genet and suggests that this historical dimension explains the summary character of some cartularies *(Traditionsbücher)* and the tendency of the monks to recopy old cartularies rather than consult the original documents anew. (At Saint-Denis, the original charters were destroyed to make forgeries, and Geary argues that this was probably also done at other monasteries with a similar desire to create a new past for themselves.)

presence not only added to the community's prestige but undoubtedly added to the community's resources. For example, in 1053, during a drought, the body of the saint was brought to Rouen; although the author does not say so, the many miracles worked by the saint were probably accompanied by many donations. The clergy of Laon raised money to rebuilt their cathedral after its destruction in 1112 by parading the relics they possessed through the land, and Guibert of Nogent described this as a common practice.[74] In the case of Fécamp, the monastery's independence from the bishop included a number of quasi-episcopal prerogatives including the ordination of priests and control over other churches.[75]

Works of history created as adjuncts to legal or quasi-legal controversies were different from other histories, in that they were geared toward advancing a very specific argument about property—rights and relics were as much property as land—in aid of which the authors were more likely than other historians to consult or incorporate charters. The author of the *Discovery* used two undated charters to suggest that the celebration of the translation of St. Wulfran (the return of his relics to Normandy) was earlier than it in fact was.[76] Ironically, because they were producing salvos in a controversy and not simply trying to record common report, the authors of these works came closer to using modern methods of historical research than sometimes quite orthodox historians did. Consequently, they produced a sort of forensic argument. While such histories had an immediate use, however, they were of interest only within their communities. The two manuscripts of the *Discovery* were both written at Saint-Wandrille; all of the complete manuscripts of the *Authority of Fécamp* were also composed at that monastery.[77]

Not all of the lesser histories of Normandy were limited to

74. Laporte, *Inventio*, 38ff. Cf. Guibert of Nogent, *Confessiones*, 3:12.

75. Bates, *Normandy before 1066*, 193–94.

76. van Houts, "Historiography and Hagiography at Saint-Wandrille," 240–41.

77. On the mss. of the *Discovery*, see van Houts, "Historiography and Hagiography," 235–37, and 237, n. 29; on the *Authority of Fécamp*, see Arnoux, "*Libellus de revelatione*," 138–43.

strictly instrumental functions. While the *Acts of the Archbishops of Rouen* identified the benefits that different archbishops had brought to the See, sometimes quite specifically, it was also concerned with the history of the spiritual life of the diocese.[78] The writing of the history, both the *Acts* and the annals of Rouen, was part of the reorganization of archiepiscopal authority begun by Maurilius. The annals showed the unbroken traditions of the archiepiscopal See and contained an implicit argument for the authority of the archbishops over the province. The *Acts* was more explicit, beginning with a description of the ecclesiastical province. The *Acts* conveyed, in its assessment of past archbishops, the uncompromising advocacy of clerical reform: it praised Richard I's son, Robert, for abandoning his wife at the end of his life and condemned the nepotism that had led to the election of Maurilius's predecessor Mauger.[79] Thus the function of the *Acts* as an ethical model was much like that of the *Customs of the Dukes* or the *Deeds of the Dukes,* only with an ecclesiastical application. The benefits offered by such works were no less real for being intangible.

The *Ecclesiastical History* of Orderic Vitalis provided a meeting ground between pragmatic views of history and more abstract ones. It began as an instrumental monastic history. Saint-Evroul, like Saint-Pierre-sur-Dives, had lost property during the reign of Robert Curthose; as part of Henry I's reimposition of order in the province, Robert of Bellême was forced to return property he had seized from the monastery. Roger of Le Sap, in asking Orderic to write a history of the monastery with particular attention to its acquisitions of property, was providing evidence of ownership for the future, should it be necessary.[80]

78. For example, Archbishop Grimo was said to have built fountains on the Iton, which he gave to the diocese along with their appurtenances, but he also gave the people an example of good works. His successor, Ramfred, gave the villa of Cramisiacum, but Archbishop Gilbert is said only to have ruled his diocese honorably and decently. (Rouen, *Bibliothèque municipale,* Y. 27, 17r, 17v).

79. Ibid., Y. 27, 18v; Bates, *Normandy before 1066,* 31.

80. *EH,* 4:146, 1:32.

Orderic carried out Roger's instructions, but his own views of history came into play, causing him to change the nature of his work. With the possible exception of Robert of Torigni, Orderic had read more histories than any other Norman historian. Furthermore, he was peculiarly well placed by the circumstances of his life to be aware of the cultural conflicts created by the Norman Conquest of England. English and a speaker of Anglo-Saxon from birth, he came to reside at a monastery in Normandy where he had to learn French. The monks renamed him Vitalis because they could not or would not pronounce his English name, Orderic.[81] He used the name the Norman monks had given him, but he preserved his "unpronounceable" English name in at least one rubric of his book and in his account of his coming to Normandy.[82] These circumstances must have quickened his desire to make sense of the turbulent history of Normandy and England, and perhaps to reflect on the meaning of history itself.

In Orderic's view, as in William of Jumièges's, history was the record of God's actions and hence worthy of study; this is the theological justification for history that is often averred to be the basis of medieval historical writing. Thus, the hand of God was active in Orderic's narrative, punishing, rewarding, and transforming people, a theme also explored in many of the prologues to the books.[83] Since history was more than just a series of examples—it is a record of the acts of God and, therefore, a record of truth—accuracy was crucial to Orderic; thus Orderic's concern for truth arose from his sense of the function of history.[84] For Orderic, the events of the past were texts which he, and some of his contemporaries like Hugh of Saint-Victor, hoped might ultimately prove readable.[85] They could not be read, however, if they were not preserved.

81. Ibid., 6:554.

82. Ibid., 2:190.

83. See particularly the prologue to book six, *EH,* 3:214, where Orderic stresses God's control over both rise and decline and affirms that a chronicle which writes truthfully of the world as it is both praises the Creator and reflects his acts.

84. See above, pp. 135ff.

85. See R. W. Southern, "Aspects of the European Tradition of Historical Writ-

While the twelfth century produced an abundance of documents, people in earlier centuries had not relied to the same degree on the written and had not produced as much writing. Orderic was fully indoctrinated into world of the written word, and he assumed that people in the past had relied on writing as he did. Thus he tended to presume that writings from the past had simply been lost through error or catastrophe. For example, in referring to the miracles of St. Evroul, he explained that the book which contained the original version of the stories had been accidently burned, and he invokes the destruction of written documents elsewhere in his text as well; while some of these texts might have existed originally, others probably did not.[86] Orderic's sense of these losses must have been heightened by the discontinuities of Norman history. No Norman monasteries had histories continuous from the date of foundation to the twelfth century. At best each Norman monastery that was a refoundation of a Merovingian or Carolingian institution had a few early historical texts, such as the ninth-century *Deeds of the Abbots of Fontenelle* (Saint-Wandrille).

These discontinuities were highlighted in works like the *Discovery of St. Wulfran,* which describes the rediscovery of long lost relics, or in works like the *Authority of Fécamp,* which tells how the site upon which the monastery was built was repeatedly discovered and forgotten. Indeed, the author of the *Discovery* also began with a poem that emphasized both the loss of knowledge and the way the disappearance of that knowledge led to the physical loss of the saint's body.[87] Orderic tells two stories of the rediscovered past himself: the discovery of the body and the subsequent miracles of St. Iudoc and the discovery of the chapel of Saint Evroul.[88] These kinds of stories are not only found in Normandy; however, in Normandy the destruction wreaked by the Vikings heightened the sense of discontinuity. For Orderic, who had seen the English his-

---

ing: 2. Hugh of St. Victor and the Ideas of Historical Development," *Transactions of the Royal Historical Society,* ser. 5, 21 (1971): 159–79.

86. *EH,* 3:291. See also 3:292, n. 1 for Chibnall's comments on this sort of story.

87. Laporte, *Inventio et miracula,* 21.

88. *EH,* 2:156–64, 76–78.

torical tradition in its vigor on his trips to England, a tradition which stretched back unbroken through the Anglo-Saxon Chronicle and Bede to the fifth century, this gap in Norman history would seem even more striking.[89] Hence Orderic's history itself became a repository of all-too-fragile texts:

> I am happy to mention these books in this record so that would-be readers may seek the manuscripts out for themselves, for they are the fruits of great learning, and are hard to come by. They have been written by men of this age, and are not yet widely circulated.[90]

This lack of wide circulation no doubt encouraged Orderic to include epitomes of other works in his own, reasoning that these other works might not be readily available to his audience. And thus Orderic wrote his own history, for:

> with the loss of books, the deeds of men of old pass into oblivion, and can in no wise be recovered by those of our generation, for the admonitions of the ancients pass away from the memory of modern men with the changing world as hail or snow melt in the waters of a swift river, swept away by the current, never to return.[91]

Orderic's two memorial purposes are somewhat different from each other. The latter might be said to be commemorative, in the same way that the *Deeds of William* and much other history, was commemorative. This sort of commemoration was bolstered by Orderic's explicitly theological purpose. However, Orderic's interest in preserving the *writings* of the past, while it might contribute to people's memories of the past, was also a literary one; it was not just the contents but often the forms in which the material was found that Orderic preserved. His history, then, embodied a program of study.

The loss of knowledge of the past was in the twelfth century a

---

89. Although William of Malmesbury, Orderic's exact contemporary, expresses his dismay at the lapse of 223 years between the end of Bede's history and the beginning of Eadmer's history, his point is partly directed at decrying the rhetorical inadequacies of times past (*GRA*, 1:2).

90. *EH*, 2:189.   91. Ibid., 3:284.

much-invoked topos. Wace repeated it a generation after Orderic to glorify the role of the clergy in preserving the fame of the past.

For all die, both cleric and layman, and their fame after their deaths will have short duration if it is not put in a book by a clerk; it cannot live or last through any other means.[92]

But Orderic was not concerned with mere human fame, as Wace was, nor was he content with once invoking the topos of the labile world of history and lost exempla. Instead, his concern for the loss of the knowledge of the past runs as a current through his entire history. In this Orderic's work was not typical history but indeed was rather more philosophical than most histories were.

In presenting history as an object for exegesis, Orderic was tacitly accepting history as a form of knowledge about the world. He was not totally alone among his contemporaries in this, for from the late eleventh century, there was a growing belief that God operated in the world not through spectacular interventions but through natural processes, and that, therefore, worldly events might reflect the divine purpose. However, not all historians, even if they tacitly accepted such a position, articulated it. No other Norman historians made manifest in their work such an understanding of history, although Robert of Torigni made reference to it. At best, for writers like William of Poitiers or Stephen of Rouen, history provided models for action. For Orderic, history was not simply a guide to action but to apprehension. When he rebuked the Normans for abusing the English—

O fools and sinners: why did they not ponder contritely in their hearts that they had conquered not by their own strength but by the will of God and subdued a people that was greater and more wealthy than they were, with a longer history.[93]

---

92. Wace, *Maistre Wace's Roman de Rou et des ducs de Normandie*, 2 vols., ed. Hugo Andreson (Heilbronn: Verlag von Gebr. Henninger, 1877–79), 1:13.
93. *EH*, 2:269.

—he was chastizing them for a false valuation of the world, based on their ignorance of history.

Implicit in Orderic's statement was also the notion that learning, rather than military prowess, made a people great. Orderic several times made reference to Norman illiteracy and lack of learning before the Conquest, which was part of his argument that the Normans were inferior to those they had conquered.[94] The knowledge of history was an important indication of cultivation. Orderic's English contemporary, Henry of Huntingdon, argued that history separates men from beasts, who know nothing of their pasts; this philosophical justification, that history is linked to human consciousness, is, while not the same as Orderic's, similar in its cultural implications.[95] In his valuation of history as a way of understanding and as a positive good in itself, independent of the instrumental purposes it might serve, Orderic, of all the Norman historians, comes closest to modern abstract attitudes about the value and purpose of history.

If Robert of Torigni had a much less philosophical notion of history than Orderic, he nonetheless valued history highly enough both to write numerous histories and to patronize others. It is possible that Robert's initiation into the writing of history came through an order from his abbot to compose the first part of the anonymous chronicle of the abbots of Bec.[96] This work, like other ecclesiastical serial biographies, fulfilled a number of functions. One of these was certainly the securing of the property and prerogatives of the monastery. This it had in common with other serial biographies, such as the *Acts of the Archbishops of Rouen*. However, like the earlier work, the *Chronicle of the Abbots of Bec* also chronicled the monastic culture of Bec, telling members of the community how to see their past; in that way it was also commemorative. Robert's sponsorship of renewed historical writing at Mont Saint-Michel should be seen at least partially in similarly practical terms. The histories he sponsored there served pilgrims and the

94. Ibid., 2:2, 166; 3:120, 290, 334.   95. *HA*, 2.
96. Rob. of Tor., 2:xvi–xvii.

needs of the monastery to document its past. In a similar vein he also ordered the compilation of the monastic cartulary.[97]

However, unlike Orderic Vitalis who renounced the hope of personal remuneration for his services to history, Robert was shrewdly aware of the pragmatic benefits that might accrue to the writer of history and the political uses of history as well.[98] In his letter to Gervais of Saint-Céneri, Robert remarked that he heard that Gervais had been freed from secular concerns (what he meant is unclear) and now enjoyed religious leisure. Robert recommended that he use this time to write a history of the counts of Anjou (Henry II was the count of Anjou). It is not clear why Robert chose Gervais to compose the history; perhaps Gervais came originally from Bec, Robert had business with him, or Robert knew Gervais to have an interest in history. If the latter was the case, this was not the point Robert touched on in his letter. Instead, he concentrated on the possibilities of advancement Gervais might enjoy if he were to write a history. He himself would be Gervais's debtor, but Gervais might also hope for some ducal promotion once his work had drawn the duke's favor. As for circulation of the work, Robert would take care of that.[99]

Two things are interesting about Robert's comments in this letter. The first is that the letter offers a partial insight into Robert's own success. While he was of noble family, and thus might expect advancement, his promotion to prior of Bec, probably in 1149, came after his first historical works had been written.[100] His reputation was the reason monks at Mont Saint-Michel elected him as abbot, and it probably helped him win Henry II's confirmation for this appointment to what was a very important abbey both strategically and, as a major European pilgrimage site, financially.[101] The second interesting feature of the letter is Robert's offer to help circulate Gervais's work. While Robert's intrinsic interest in history was certainly sufficient for him to do so—we know

97. Ibid., 2:xvii.
99. Rob. of Tor., 2:338f.
101. Ibid., 2:iv.

98. *EH*, 2:188.
100. Ibid., 2:iii.

that he helped build the historical collection of books at Bec—he may also have had plans for the work himself, perhaps to enhance his own advancement, as did the men who urged William of Jumièges to write the *Deeds of the Dukes*. In any event, Robert's letter to Gervais emphasized the instrumental uses of history over the value of its contents.

However, there was another side to Robert's interest in history. Like Orderic, although without Orderic's insight or compassion, Robert was committed to the larger enterprise of historical writing for disinterested reasons as well as pragmatic ones. Henry of Huntingdon's epitome of the work of Geoffrey of Monmouth seems to have begun in a discussion between Henry and Robert about sources for the writing of history. The passage in Henry's text that describes this encounter may have been composed by Robert, but it does not really matter. The more important point is its depiction of Robert as "a seeker and assiduous collector of both divine and secular books," who was pleased to talk history with other historians.[102]

Robert's comments both in his letter to Gervais and in his historical works also touch on more disinterested reasons for writing history. He was strongly aware that in writing history he was participating in a tradition and felt that there was an obligation on the part of those who came after to continue what others had begun.[103] In his letter to Gervais, Robert also mentioned this commemorative aspect of history.[104] In the preface to his chronicle, Robert invoked the moral function of history, that people might

102. The version of the letter which contains this passage is included in Robert's chronicle. The independent versions of the letter do not mention Robert by name. Robert may have inserted the reference to himself into the letter when he copied this material at the beginning of the original part of his chronicle. On the version of the letter that appears in Henry's work, see Edmond Faral, *La Légende Arthurienne, études et documents, première partie: Les Plus anciens texts*, 3 vols. (Paris: Honoré Champion, 1929), pt. 1, 2:18 and n. 18, and *HA*, xxi, n. 1; for Robert's version, see Rob. of Tor., 1:98.

103. *GND*, 266. This is offered as an explanation of why he cannot skip over Robert and William Rufus, whose deeds were unedifying, and go directly to Henry I.

104. Rob. of Tor., 2:339–40.

imitate the good and avoid the bad, when they had before them examples of both. He also held up the example of Moses and other biblical writers both as examples of historians and as an argument for the ecclesiastical value of history.

While Robert did explain the purpose of history, it is clear that he was not that interested in the issue of history's applications beyond political utility. He liked collecting information more than thinking about how it might be used. Although he described history as revealing God's will through signs, omens, and portents, he did not feel it to be his job to delineate the engines of the plan himself. His job was to provide the tableau for contemplation, as Karl Morrison has argued medieval histories were intended to do.[105] Although Robert did not say this, explanation came not out of history, but rather it arose from other disciplines, such as philosophy or theology. Despite a broad concern for learning (he wrote introductions to at least two non-historical works in the library, a copy of Pliny and a copy of the *Liber Floridus*), he never described history as having a philosophic or contemplative value as Orderic did; history was always presented as a tool to be used to ends other than itself.[106]

Robert's contemporary, Stephen of Rouen, was even less reflective about the purpose of history, perhaps because he had such a clear notion of why he himself was writing. The *Norman Dragon* is a polemic, intended to convince Henry II to abandon his policy of reconciliation with Louis VII and to adhere to the imperial position in the papal schism of 1159. Its disputatious purpose may well explain Stephen's lack of concern about faithfully reporting what his sources had said. His text was different from that of the other Norman historians in other ways as well. Whereas other Norman historians put the emphasis on the contents of the work and its symbolic functions, Stephen shifted the emphasis away from the message itself and toward its recipient, giving the work a strongly hortatory character.[107] Of course, the *Dragon* offered something

105. Ibid., 1:92; Morrison, *History as a Visual Art,* 28.
106. Rob. of Tor., 2:342–43.
107. See Jakobson, "Closing Statement: Linguistics and Poetics," 355. Jakobson

in addition to its historical content and entertainment, which Stephen might have hoped would make it useful; it also provided instruction in rhetoric and composition, and thus might be enjoyable for students to read. Stephen was here imitating his earliest predecessor, for in some manuscripts the *Customs* contained *scholia* on metrics and the transliteration of Greek terms. (Dudo may well have written these *scholia* himself in imitation of the *scholia* contained in the *Life of Saint Germanus,* one of Dudo's important stylistic models.)[108] Although the pedagogical function of a historical text was collateral and Stephen makes no explicit mention of this purpose for his text, classical histories were often used in the schools to teach rhetoric, which was probably why William of Poitiers had read so many of them. Stephen's contemporary, Godfrey of Viterbo, recommended his history as a more "wholesome" reading for children than fiction.[109]

---

sees this stress (which he terms conative) as being best expressed by the imperative mood. Imperative sentences, he notes, cannot be queried as to their truth. While the truth of Stephen's narrative could certainly be questioned, it also had an imperative force that might lead a reader to ask whether the course of action he advocated was sensible but was less likely to lead the reader to ask whether his account was true.

108. For the *scholia,* see for example, *De moribus,* 126, nn. 1 and 3; 127, n. 4; 128, n. 6. The *scholia* appear in three of the earliest manuscripts, Rouen BM Y. 11. (Lair's "R"), Phillipps 1854, now in the Berlin Staatsbibliothek (Lair's "M"), and Cambridge, Corpus Christi College 276 (Lair's "C"). All three manuscripts date from the eleventh century and contain the dedicatory letter to Adalberon and the poetry. See Huisman, "Manuscript Tradition," 123. The different meters of Heiric of Auxerre's *Vita sancti Germani* were noted in *scholia* in one manuscript, Paris *BN* 13757, as were transliterations of Greek words and commentaries on Eriugenian philosophy. John Marenbon, *From the Circle of Alcuin to the School of Auxerre: Logic, Theology and Philosophy in the Early Middle Ages* (Cambridge: Cambridge University Press, 1981), 115, raises the possibility that the glosses on the *Life of Saint Germanus* were written by Heiric or at his direction (the manuscript is not in Heiric's hand), but Edouard Jeauneau, "Heiric d'Auxerre," 357, argues forcefully that this manuscript must be close to the exemplar and the glosses selected by Heiric. Not all the manuscripts of the *Life of Saint Germanus* have all the scholia (perhaps not even BN 13757), but several have some of the material (ibid., 357–58). It is not necessary for Dudo to have read a fully annotated version of the text for him to have imitated Heiric.

109. Schmale, *Funktion und Formen,* 76.

While Stephen of Rouen's polemic was unusual among the Norman histories, it is understandable given the many possible functions of historical writing. Norman histories were written to fulfill some functions that their authors acknowledged: record-keeping, commemoration, or contributing to knowledge. History filled another of its functions tacitly: mediation and monumental representation. The Norman historians, and (medieval historians in general) were not articulate in justifying the writing of history, as one might expect given that history was not an object of formal study. Only Orderic Vitalis seems to have envisioned the possibility that history might be something more than an entertaining, modestly useful, literary genre, and even he did not fully clarify what it would mean for history to be a form of knowledge in its own right.

7 ⚬ Patrons and Other Readers

The Reception of the Norman Histories

I will truly treat the different events, both prosperous and adverse, which have happened in the course of thirty years, and will record them simply, for the information of those who come after, to the best of my ability. For I believe that there will be some men like myself, who will eagerly peruse the events and transitory acts of this generation in the pages of chroniclers, so that they may unfold the past fortunes of the inconstant world for the edification or delight of their contemporaries.[1]

The modest remarks cited above, which end the ninth book of Orderic Vitalis's *Ecclesiastical History,* encapsulate the hope of historians medieval and modern that their works influence the future by acquiring readers. Part of assessing history's importance, therefore, is finding out what sort of readers history found and what it meant to them.

Determining readers, however, is no easy matter. While Orderic clearly hoped for readers within his mo-

1. *EH,* 5:191. Translation Chibnall, somewhat altered.

nastic community, the audience he envisioned in the passage cited above was composed of other historians.[2] Because historians frequently quoted or mentioned the works they had read, or even if they did not, used evidence whose source can sometimes be identified, it is relatively easy to tell which historians were readers of the works of others. From the way each historian used his sources it is possible to determine what he thought of them: a source might be cited for some things but not for others; it might be altered or incorporated whole, all to suit the similar or differing purposes of the later writer, as Dudo of Saint-Quentin's vision of Norman history was transformed, avoided, and reinstated by later Norman historians.

Other readers wrote no texts of their own and thus are harder to identify. These readers might encounter a history in its original form or as a quotation, excerpt, epitome, or translation. Other "readers" might hear the text in whole or in part, or they may simply be orally informed of its contents. These oral modes of encountering the written were as important in their own way as reading, for texts "read" in this way might exert a powerful force on the minds of the hearers through the hearers' participation in a "textual community."[3] Individuals might memorize what they heard and then disseminate these ideas further. Thus works might have an influence far beyond those who encountered them in written form.

There are several splendid examples in Joinville's life of St. Louis of how a text might influence someone who had not read it or who had, perhaps, encountered it only in translation. In the first instance, Louis asked Joinville to define God, and he responded that God was "something so good that there cannot be anything better." Louis replied, "You've given me a very good answer; for it's precisely the same as the definition given in this book I have here."[4]

2. Roger Ray, "Orderic Vitalis and His Readers," *Studia Monastica* 14 (1972), 18–19.

3. Stock, *Implications of Literacy,* esp. 90ff.

4. Jean de Joinville, *The Life of St. Louis,* in *Chronicles of the Crusades,* trans. M. R. B. Shaw (Harmondsworth, Sussex: Penguin, 1963), 169; for the French, see

Joinville did not say what book Louis had in his lap, but the definition is that of St. Anselm in the *Proslogion*.[5] Although Joinville did not explain how he acquired this information, he had either read or been orally informed about Anselm's theology; both Joinville and Louis were part of the "textual community," the audience, of the *Proslogion*.

The second example of Joinville's readership involves historical information. Toward the end of his biography, Joinville compared Louis to the emperor Titus, who was wont to lament that the day was wasted if he had failed to do something good for someone. This anecdote about Titus came from Suetonius's *Twelve Caesars*, but Joinville remarked only that the story came from "old writings."[6] In the case of the definition of God, Joinville was seemingly unaware of the origin of his beliefs, and it seems likely that he acquired them through a human intermediary, a chaplain or other teacher, as part of catechistic or homiletic instruction. In this second case, however, Joinville knew that his information had been transmitted in writing, and it is possible that he was referring to something he himself had read; he might have encountered the anecdote in one of the many thirteenth-century translations of classical history.[7] However, this kind of information could be transmitted orally as well, for Joinville remarked that King Louis narrated history to his children, telling them stories of the good and bad deeds of kings and emperors, so that they would know what examples to imitate and avoid.[8]

Joinville's case highlights the difficulty of identifying most me-

---

La Vie de Saint Louis: Le Témoinage de Jehan, seigneur de Joinville, ed. Neil Corbett (Sherbrooke, PQ: Naaman, 1977), 88.

5. *Proslogion, capitulum* 3, PL 158:228. Anselm actually says "greater" *(majus)* rather than "better" in his most famous statement of the nature of God, but in *capitulum* 5, he does say, "You are thus just, truthful, blessed and whatever it is better to be than not to be" (ibid., 229).

6. Joinville, *Saint Louis,* 234 (translation, 342–43); Suetonius, *Titus,* 8.

7. On French translations of ancient history, see P. Meyer, "Les Premières compilations françaises d'histoire ancienne," *Romania* 14 (1885): 1–81; also Sanford, "The Study of Ancient History."

8. Joinville, *Vie de Saint Louis,* 228 (trans. 336).

dieval readers, since we know of his reading only because he was himself a writer. One way scholars have gotten around this problem is by identifying hypothetical or implied readers. Reader-response critics distinguish between at least two types of hypothetical readers, one type "constructed from social and historical knowledge of the time," that is, the reader who had reason to come in contact with the text, and the other "extrapolated from the reader's role laid out in the text," that is, the reader whose prejudices and interests are reflected in the text.[9] For the Norman histories, the former category contained both members of monastic communities, who copied the texts and who had access to them in their libraries, and the patrons or people to whom works were dedicated.

Advancing beyond the identification of implied readers, however, to speak confidently about actual readers is difficult. Part of the difficulty is the as yet still murky relationship between the patron of a work or the person to whom a work was dedicated (who might be different individuals) and its author. The purpose of commissioning a work, as I have argued above, was not necessarily to read it, nor was a dedicatee necessarily an author's patron. An author might dedicate a work on speculation in the hopes that the person so honored might become a patron or assist in the dissemination of the work, as Dudo did when he dedicated the *Customs of the Dukes* to Adalberon of Laon; these hopes might or might not be realized.[10] For example, Geoffrey of Monmouth dedicated his *History of the Kings of Britain* (c. 1135) to both Robert of Gloucester and Waleran of Meulan. Robert may have read it, and he may have assisted and promoted its circulation in Normandy.[11] However, Waleran was also educated and also had close associations with Bec, and with Philippe de Harcourt, who donated a copy of Geoffrey's text to Bec in 1164. Thus, Waleran may also have

9. Wolfgang Iser, *The Act of Reading* (Baltimore, Md.: Johns Hopkins University Press, 1978), 28.

10. See above, pp. 187–88. Adalberon of Laon was not Dudo's patron, as far as we can tell.

11. Around the time of the composition of the *Historia regum Britonum*, Robert spent much time at Bec (Faral, *La Légende Arthurienne*, 2:20).

been responsible for assisting the text's dissemination.[12] Finally, there is the question of language. While there is some likelihood that Robert of Gloucester and Waleran of Meulan were literate in Latin, one cannot assume that all lay dedicatees necessarily were; if not, such individuals "read" the texts dedicated to them only in translation, perhaps only in a paraphrased, oral version, if at all.

While it is difficult to determine whether those who had access to a text actually read it, it is equally difficult to identify the other kind of implied reader, the reader whose interests or world-view are apparently addressed by a given text. Authors' comments about readers are often commonplaces or quotations from other writers. For example, Dudo of Saint-Quentin remarked in one of his prefatory poems that he feared that "the Normans may crush the unwilling poet with a blow," which can be read to imply that Dudo expected the Normans to spurn his work. The line, however, is both a reworked quotation from an earlier source and a conventional sentiment and therefore not necessarily a comment on what Dudo expected from his audience.[13] In choosing old and elegant models, stories, and *topoi,* an author might well be attempting to guide the taste of readers or to edify them, but the author might also have selected the material because it retained some kind of currency. Whether a story was repeated simply because it was traditional or because, despite some antiquated ingredients, it still rang true (or both) is hard to say.

Furthermore, the author's choice of contents and forms might have resulted from the desire to speak to a particular audience or might have arisen from authorial considerations in which audience was not a factor. For example, Dudo of Saint-Quentin might have written in *prosimetrum* because he encountered the form in the life

12. James Westfall Thompson, *The Literacy of the Laity in the Middle Ages* (New York: Burt Franklin, 1960), 173. On the circulation of the *History of the Kings of Britain* in Normandy, see David Dumville, "An Early Text of Geoffrey of Monmouth's *Historia regum Britanniae* and the Circulation of Some Latin Histories in Twelfth-Century Normandy," *Arthurian Literature 4* (Woodbridge, Suffolk: Boydell and Brewer, 1985), 1–36, esp. 23–24.

13. *De moribus,* 120; Heiric of Auxerre, *Vita sancti Germani,* 1.31, *Allocutio ad librum.* The poem continues in the same vein, all borrowed from Dudo's model.

of St. Lambert, from which he borrowed extensively in the *Customs of the Dukes*.[14] He might equally well have liked it because it was a venerable philosophical and didactic form that could lend his work grandeur or because he could use the poetic passages to comment on the action in the prose part of his text. Bede refers to the way the Bible mixes poetry and history, and Dudo may have been thinking either of this passage in Bede or of the scriptural precedent.[15] He might, alternatively, have been attempting to entertain or impress educated readers with his mastery of poetry, while still retaining the advantages of a prose narrative, or he may have wanted to alleviate the potential tedium of his text through variety. His goals in relation to his readers may have been even more specific than that; Eleanor Searle has argued that Dudo shaped his history to approximate in Latin the Norse forms the Norman elite might have been familiar with.[16] Any or all of these considerations may have been important. It is therefore difficult to draw any firm implications about Dudo's audience from the form of Dudo's work.

There is a further problem with assuming too much about the readers who may be revealed by the clues about the readers in the text: we miss potential readers who are not signalled by the text. For example, the epics and romances are clearly directed toward the secular elite. These texts, with their martial and amatory themes and their general disregard for ecclesiastical attitudes would seem to be unsuitable for members of the clergy. Yet monks were interested in epics; the author of the *Chronicle of Novalesa* incorporated most of the *Waltarius* into his chronicle of the abbey (*Waltarius* was itself composed by a cleric), and included many stories also to be found in vernacular epics.[17] For all of these reasons, our notion of who read and who was intended to read a medieval text is always approximate. However, the clues left to readers in the text and the

---

14. See above, pp. 151–52.
15. Bede, *Ecclesiastical History*, 396.
16. Searle, "Fact and Pattern," 120–22.
17. *MGH SS*, 7:73–133.

environment in which the text circulated do provide resonant implications about who might have read the text.[18]

While individual readers are elusive, the relative number of manuscripts of a text that survived provides a gauge of its popularity. The strict numbers can be misleading, for the stability of monasteries means that texts that were of no great interest might have been preserved. Unread books, not subject to the wear and tear of reading, may have survived better than books whose contents were crucial to the lives of the monks. However, books not popular in monastic circles or not part of monastic official collections also might not be well preserved. Books that were lent were also vulnerable, and medieval monasteries did lend their books. Orderic Vitalis's work was a case in point. The missing third volume of the autograph corresponds to a portion of the text copied at Caen in the later twelfth century, which suggests the possibility that this volume was borrowed but not returned to Saint-Evroul.[19] Furthermore, manuscripts cannot testify to the dissemination of the information they contained. A text surviving only in a single manuscript or in a few copies might have been very important to a local community.[20] Finally, sometimes no manuscripts survive of a text that was popular for a time but later was superseded by other texts or lost the interest of its readers. William of Malmesbury and Ralph of Diceto read William of Poitiers' *Deeds of William,* which attests to a readership for the *Deeds* in England, but no manuscripts survive at all. Thus estimates of audience based on the numbers of surviving manuscripts are only approximate.

The condition and form of the manuscripts of a text also offer testimony about its readers. Manuscripts that were much read sometimes acquired marginalia or became dog-eared. Readers

18. Because of these problems, medieval reception theory tends to concentrate on the late Middle Ages where more is known about real readers. In a recent publication, *Mittelalter-Rezeption: Ein Symposion,* ed. Peter Wapnewski (Stuttgart: J. B. Metzlersche Verlagsbuchhandlung, 1986), most of the authors concentrate on the modern reception of medieval texts.

19. *EH,* 1:121.

20. Guenée, *Histoire et culture historique,* 255, suggests that this is the case with the three manuscripts of the annals of Genoa.

might correct errors or rectify omissions. For instance, they might fill in capitals where the illuminator had failed to do so. A book that was considered important might be illustrated, or given an attractive format with good margins. In contrast, a book that was not valued might have its margins cut away or pages cut out. While these sorts of indications refer only to the readers of one copy of the text, they suggest what other readers of other copies might have felt. No one line of inquiry about readers can be conclusive, but all of them together yield suggestive results when applied to the work of Norman historians.

Some of the Norman historians explicitly named their patrons or those they hoped would become patrons, the implied first readers of their texts, and expressly shaped their material to please these individuals. Dudo of Saint-Quentin's dedicatory letter to Adalberon began with adulatory comments about his erudition, followed by a demonstration of Dudo's acquaintance with mathematical and music theory. He began with an exposition of the number twelve (symbolizing Adalberon's ascent to the number of the apostles), then of the octave (composed of twelve half-steps). The purpose of this somewhat confusing display of Dudo's knowledge seems to have been to capture the good will, and hence the assistance, of his desired patron.[21]

Dudo also praised his Norman patrons in the body of his work. His poem to Richard II was both short and simple in its form, easy to translate. Most of its lines echo the opening, "O magnanimous, pious, modest man!" but Richard was asked to be mindful of the text and to feast his heart upon its contents.[22] Dudo also included a poem in praise of Raoul d'Ivry, which was based on an occasional poem of Fortunatus. The title of the poem named Raoul as a patron, while the poem itself compared him to Cato, Scipio, and Pompey.[23] However, Dudo saved his most explicit pleas that his book be read for Robert, the archbishop of Rouen. The first poem

21. *De moribus*, 116–18.
22. Ibid., 122.
23. Ibid., 125; Fortunatus, *Carmina*, in *MGH, Auctores Antiquissimi*, vol. 4, ed. F. Leo, 159, "De Lupo duce."

to him, enjoined him to "take up the deeds of your great-grand-father, memorable bishop, and take up the deeds of your wealthy grandfather." The second and third poems to him again asked him to receive the book.[24] Here Dudo paints a verbal picture of the archbishop, holding the *Customs* in his hands. In the last of his poems to Robert, Dudo addressed him *as* a reader, urging him to look to the merits of his father and past the poor text that described them.[25] Thus, while he acknowledged all of his patrons in writing, Dudo most pointedly addressed those who could read the text, Adalberon and Robert. Robert was probably the only member of the ducal family who could do so.

Dudo might have presented his text in other ways to meet the needs of his illiterate patrons. There is a tantalizing possibility that one copy of the *Customs* was illustrated. No illustrated manuscript of the text has survived, but one copy of the text made at Jumièges in the late eleventh century (one of the earliest surviving manu-scripts of Dudo's work) left spaces at irregular intervals, which might have been used for illustrations. The spaces were appropriate for ink drawings even if not suitable for illuminations. One of these spaces in the life of Rollo was filled in with a scratched drawing of two standing men pleading before a third, seated one; the text de-scribes the youth of Denmark pleading with Rollo to help them resist expulsion. If the scribe were copying an illustrated version of the *Customs*, his leaving of spaces makes some sense, and he may even have copied the scratched illustration from an inked original. There would be good reason to illustrate the presentation copy, given the illiteracy of its recipient; perhaps this was what the scribe of the Jumièges manuscript was copying.[26] Norman manuscripts generally confined their decoration to historiated capitals, and no Norman manuscript with this kind of extensive illustration cur-rently exists. If Dudo did create such a manuscript, he did so not

24. *De moribus*, 123, 11.1–2; 126, 11.6–7; 127, 1.10ff.

25. Ibid., 292.

26. Rouen, *Bibliothèque municipale*, Y. 11; the illustration is 8r. On this manu-script, see *Manuscrits datés*, 527; Huisman, "Manuscript Tradition," 127–30 (includes two plates of the spaces in the manuscript).

based on the kinds of books produced in Normandy in his day.[27] However, since the exemplar of the *Customs of the Dukes* has not survived, we cannot rule out the possibility that it was illustrated. If so, illiterate members of the Norman court may have had some access to the text after all.

Most of the readers of the text, however, were probably clerics. To judge by the manuscripts, the text was read in Normandy and England. Apart from the copy at Jumièges, mentioned above, Saint-Wandrille, Fécamp, and Saint-Evroul all had copies of the manuscript (Saint-Evroul's copy is now lost), and there may have been others; the provenance of the English manuscripts is as yet undetermined. This pattern makes sense. It was Normans in Normandy and England who would be most interested in Norman history. However, one of the manuscripts came from the monastery of Anchin, near Douai.[28] Anchin was a center of historical writing, but it was also not very far from Saint-Quentin; Dudo almost certainly took a copy of his work home to Saint-Quentin.

The only actual readers of the *Customs of the Dukes* who can be named are Norman and English historians and annalists. However, the anonymous readers of the *Customs* have also left significant traces, adapting the text to their own requirements as they copied it. For example, one manuscript tradition omitted all but three of the poems (the three that advanced the action of the story). Clearly the originator of this textual tradition either did not like the many apostrophes Dudo included or found the poems too difficult, because Dudo's manner of composition rendered the syntax of the poems particularly tortured. Dudo's poems were often based on the work of earlier poets. However, he demonstrated his independence by changing the meters of the poems. One of the works from

27. On Norman books, see Lawrence, "Anglo-Norman Book Production," 85–87. The rectangular spaces call to mind the spaces used for illustration in the Utrecht psalter and in the English manuscripts of the *Psychomachia*, which contained text both above and below the illustrations. On the *Psychomachia* manuscripts, see Elzbieta Temple, *Anglo-Saxon Manuscripts, 900–1066* (London: Harvey Miller, 1976), 69–72, plates 155–66. Pages 70–71 are missing in some copies of the text due to printing errors.

28. See Huisman, "Notes on the Manuscript Tradition," 125f.

which he borrowed, the *Life of St. Germanus* of Heiric of Auxerre, contained Greek words. Since Dudo probably did not know Greek, he had to rephrase the material in ways that would not require him to change the cases of the borrowed Greek words. His efforts to fit Heiric's lines into shorter or longer ones, often using different feet, complicated the grammar of the poems and rendered them more obscure.[29] Some manuscripts of the *Customs* show other signs of reading, such as marginalia and corrections.[30] Most of the manuscripts date from the eleventh and twelfth centuries suggesting that in this period Dudo's work was still important to possess, and perhaps to read as well.[31] The relatively rapid dissemination of the *Customs* may reflect ducal assistance in circulating it, which would make it an official history.

Of course, not all readers encountered Dudo's work directly. Dudo's influence was felt indirectly through William of Jumièges's *Deeds of the Dukes,* and even more forcefully through Robert of Torigni's interpolated version of that text.[32] He was also read and his material reproduced in the vernacular in Wace's and Benoît of Sainte-Maure's histories, which made him available in the French vernacular to readers in England. Even so, the *Customs* was never quite displaced by later versions of Norman history. In fact, one copyist preferred Dudo's text over that of his successor, William

29. On Dudo's compositional methods, see also Shopkow, "Norman Historical Writing," 60–77. Lucien Musset, "Le Satiriste Garnier de Rouen et son milieu," *Revue du moyen age latin* 10 (1954): 248, suggests that Dudo was influenced by the Hisperic style. In a sense, he was, but indirectly through Heiric of Auxerre, who was himself influenced by the Irish scholars in the Carolingian schools, particularly John Scotus Eriugena.

30. Rouen, *Bibliothèque municipale,* Y. 11, the Jumièges manuscript, also contains many corrections. For example, when fol. 61 was torn, someone copied the lost material from 61r onto 60v.

31. Ten of the fifteen extant manuscripts come from the eleventh or twelfth centuries. Huisman dates the lost manuscript from Saint-Evroul, (Alençon, *Bibliothèque municipale,* ms. 20), which also contained the work of William of Jumièges, to the thirteenth century.

32. For the Saint-Evroul manuscript, see *GND,* xxxii. On the dissemination of the *Deeds,* see van Houts, *GND,* 42ff. Robert of Torigni's version is the "F" redaction.

of Jumièges, and replaced the first four books of William's text with Dudo's.[33] The influence of Dudo of Saint-Quentin was thus felt very widely among those who wrote history in Normandy and probably among those who read it as well.

Like Dudo of Saint-Quentin, William of Jumièges directly addressed one implied reader of his text, William the Conqueror. In the introduction, the historian offered his work as a contribution to the construction of the Conqueror's memory, urging him, as Dudo had urged his patrons, to pick up the book. He ended with the fervent hope, also expressed by Dudo, that God would reward the Conqueror with salvation.[34] Thus William advanced the pro forma hope that his subject would read his words. The Conqueror was probably unable to read the *Deeds*, for most of the evidence points to his illiteracy. It is possible, however, since William's prose was straightforward, that portions might have been orally translated for him.

The conclusion of the *Deeds* referred more obliquely to another implied reader, Robert Curthose. The historian commented that he hoped to be able to write about Robert's deeds, through which the young man might "represent his great ancestors through his noble virtue as well as his name." (William here referred not only to the Conqueror's father, Robert the Magnificent but also to Rollo who took the baptismal name Robert).[35] William of Jumièges was tacitly offering Robert a text upon whose contents he might frame his actions. Robert possibly knew some Latin, since his brother, Henry, did. The most literate siblings, however, seem to have been Cecily and Adela, the latter of whom was frequently sought out as a reader by contemporary poets.[36]

William of Jumièges also made reference to another implied audience for his text: the ducal court. William's rather hyperbolic reference to the "illustrious men, learned in the skill of letters, who

33. For the chimerical manuscripts, see van Houts, *GND* (2), 1:lxi; also van Houts, *GND*, 30. This is the "A" redaction, extant in 4 manuscripts.

34. *GND*, 1–3.   35. Ibid., 143–44.

36. James Thompson, *Literacy of the Laity*, 167ff. See also Bezzola, *Formation de la littérature courtoise*, 2:370–82, 389–90.

encircling the city with their drawn swords, when they have destroyed the plots of the wicked, are vigilantly occupied in defending the bed of Solomon with the wall of divine law" may somewhat exaggerate the degree of literacy at the Conqueror's court.[37] However, there is evidence that the court was becoming professionalized. There were fewer counts and bishops who were in regular attendance and more viscounts and curial officials, both clerics and laymen.[38] While overall literacy may not have been much greater than in Dudo of Saint-Quentin's time, literacy was increasingly important for the Conqueror's administration in both England and Normandy, as written documentation became a normal part of bureaucracy. The trend, as Ralph Turner has shown, at least for England, was for greater Latin literacy among the laity.[39] Perhaps because of this increased demand for literacy, lettered men came seeking advancement or, like William of Jumièges, sent literary tributes to the Conqueror, so that the court became, if not precisely a literary salon,[40] a place where the learned hoped to sell their wares.

It was the *Deeds of the Dukes'* second audience, however, its monastic readers, whose labors made the text widely available in all its versions. There are sixteen extant manuscripts of the various versions of the *Deeds of the Dukes* from the twelfth century, with an additional six manuscripts from the thirteenth. Three copies of the text come from the late twelfth or early thirteenth century and cannot be dated more precisely, for a total of nineteen manuscripts. Like the manuscripts of Dudo of Saint-Quentin's *Customs,* the

37. *GND*, 1–2.
38. Fauroux, *Recueil*, 58; also L. Valin, *Le Duc de Normandie et sa cour* (Paris: L. Larose & L. Tenin, 1916), 103. On professionalization, see Fauroux, *Recueil*, 61–62.
39. Ralph Turner, "The *Miles Literatus* in Twelfth- and Thirteenth-Century England: How Rare a Phenomenon?" *American Historical Review* 83 (1978): 928–45.
40. See Bezzola, *Formation de la littérature courtoise,* pt. 2, 400–401. Apart from the poem of Guy of Amiens on the conquest, there was a poem, "*De rege Willelmo*," attributed to Serlo of Bayeux. There may also have been poetic tributes by Lanfranc, Fulk of Beauvais, Hugh of Langres, and Marbode of Rennes, some of whom were also literary correspondents of the Conqueror's daughter, Adela.

majority of these manuscripts were composed in Normandy and England. However, a copy of Orderic's recension made its way to Saint-Denis very shortly after it was written—three of the manuscripts come from that monastery—while one copy of William's uninterpolated text arrived at Saint-Victor by the early thirteenth century. There were ties between Normandy and Saint-Denis which may explain both the migration of the *Deeds* to Paris and the appearance in Norman libraries of French histories.[41]

There are several explanations for this wide pattern of dissemination, none of them mutually exclusive. van Houts has argued that the continuations of the *Deeds of the Dukes* were official, and many monasteries may have felt that acquiring a copy of the official version of Norman history was important.[42] The text was also open-ended. As van Houts has also pointed out, the *Deeds* was a framework onto which additional material could be hung without difficulty, whenever the text was recopied. Orderic Vitalis and Robert of Torigni did precisely that, as did the assortment of anonymous interpolators.

Another explanation is that the *Deeds* came to be viewed as a "basic" text, part of the complement of histories it was desirable to have. Many of the manuscripts that contain the text are historical miscellanies that included texts like Paul the Deacon's *Roman History*, the *Deeds of the Consuls of Anjou*, William of Malmesbury's *Deeds of the Kings of England*, the *Liber pontificalis*, the pseudo-Turpin Chronicle, and the life of Alexander the Great.[43] While the

41. For manuscripts, see van Houts, *GND*, 195–260; the Saint-Denis manuscripts are E2, E3, and E4; C2 was copied at Saint-Victor. On Saint-Denis's holdings in Normandy, see Bates, *Normandy before 1066*, 12, 32; also see Musset, "Mécénat des princes normands," 128.

42. On the continuations, see van Houts, "History without an End," 115, and also more generally, *GND* (2), 1:lxff. For Orderic's interpolations, see *GND*, 151–198 and van Houts, *GND*, 107–116; see also van Houts, "Quelque remarques," 213–22, for some valuable correctives about the Marx edition of these interpolations. For the anonymous interpolations, see van Houts, *GND*, 94–106; *GND*, 98–101, 106–109, 112–113. For Robert's interpolations, see *GND*, 199–334 and van Houts, *GND*, 117–129. On the official character of the continuations, see van Houts, "History without an End," 111, 115.

43. van Houts, *GND*, 208, 209–210, 215, 217, 226, 230.

texts copied with the *Deeds* varied, some manuscripts in which it is found were strongly historical in character. Of course, these manuscripts were in some cases assembled later, but whether originally copied together or later compiled, what these groupings indicate is that Norman history was seen as having a place within the broader scope of history. These collections may also have been seen as reference volumes. The *Deeds* was particularly well suited as a reference work because its straightforward Latin was accessible to only moderately accomplished readers of Latin. It was short, well-organized, and comprehensive; it covered Norman history from the beginning to the reign of William the Conqueror in under one quarter of the length of the *Customs;* and it was divided into books and short chapters that made movement through the text relatively easy.

Finally, the *Deeds* may have circulated widely because it provided pleasure for its readers. It was filled with the kinds of events that seem to have the most lasting currency: rebellions and battles. Its contents, therefore, were unlikely to become dated by shifts of taste. Its message retained currency, too. What William of Jumièges said of William the Conqueror was no less true of later rulers. They too had their peace and their wars, and medieval readers seem to have had a great appetite for the discussion of the latter.[44] It is worth noting that these features of the *Deeds* made it suitable for a somewhat different audience than the *Customs*. While some individuals may have read both texts with interest, some individuals were no doubt more attracted to one than the other. The somewhat greater circulation of the *Deeds* suggests that its appeal was broader, even though the *Customs* continued to circulate during the twelfth century.

The success of the *Deeds* and the *Customs* offer a stark contrast to the much more limited circulation of the *Deeds of William* of William of Poitiers and the *Ecclesiastical History* of Orderic Vitalis. Orderic Vitalis reported that William of Poitiers wrote for William the Conqueror, but whether he concluded this from reading a now lost part of the text or through conjecture based on William of

44. *GND*, 3.

Poitiers's connections or his biases, he did not say. The portion of the text of the *Deeds of William* that is still extant makes no mention of patronage or expected readers but the introduction and conclusion, the places in the text where historians normally addressed their patrons and explained their work, are missing. It seems unlikely, however, that the Conqueror commissioned the *Deeds* directly, for he seems not to have commissioned any of the works that were eventually offered to him and his illiteracy would have prevented him from reading this account of his own deeds.

There was, however, another possible patron for the *Deeds of William*, William of Poitiers's superior, Hugh, bishop of Lisieux. Hugh could have commissioned the work to please the Conqueror, who was his cousin as well as his duke, or perhaps even for his own reading; from Orderic Vitalis's account of him, Hugh was deeply concerned with learning.[45] Whether he took an active role in encouraging William of Poitiers to write the *Deeds of William* or not, the historian's passage on Hugh of Lisieux is by far the longest and warmest of his descriptions of the bishops of Normandy, and in this passage, he seems to have anticipated that Hugh would be one of his readers. Since William sometimes referred to Hugh of Lisieux here in the present tense, it makes sense that the bishop was alive when this portion of the narrative was composed. Orderic mentioned that William was prevented from completing his text by unfortunate circumstances; Hugh's death on July 17, 1077 may have been what he was thinking of.[46]

The potential patrons aside, two audiences are implied by the contents of the *Deeds of William*. The first audience, as for the works of William of Jumièges and Dudo of Saint-Quentin, was the ducal court. William of Poitiers named many individuals active in the court and in the duke's entourage at Hastings. They were no doubt pleased to be immortalized in this way.[47] In addition, long

45. *EH*, 3:20.
46. *GG*, 136–42. Most other descriptions are only a few lines long. See also *GG*, xix; *EH*, 2:184.
47. For example, William's counselors are named, as well as those who accompanied the Conqueror across the Channel (*GG*, 148, 194–96).

passages of the *Deeds of William* are about the questions that concerned laymen. For example, the text explores the obligations of a man toward his lord and the struggle of an individual to increase his patrimony with warlike deeds. The villains in the text were those deplored in a society held together by fidelity and lordship: oathbreakers and traitors like Walter of Mantes, Harold, and Conon of Brittany.[48] The actions of such men chipped away at the adhesive which held society together, and so the tale of their comeuppance might have been cathartic.

Moreover, the Conqueror appeared in the *Deeds of William* as the sort of leader fighting men could admire and emulate. He was endowed with prowess, strength, fortitude, courage, and foresight. The demonstration of this wiliness seems to be the point of an anecdote the historian related in which the Conqueror pretended to be his own seneschal when he received an emissary from King Harold; he managed thereby to get the message immediately but to delay his own response until he had time to deliberate.[49] The sense of group identity that William promoted in his narrative through his delineation of Norman characteristics may not have been embraced by this secular audience—I think it probably was—but the audience would have been flattered by the claims William advanced for Norman exceptionalism.

Despite William of Poitiers's sympathy with Norman aristocratic lay views, in other ways his work in the *Deeds of William* would have frustrated a secular audience. Even if they had been able to understand it, they would have put off by William's style of story-telling. The historian often undercut his potentially most exciting tales in the telling. For example, he begins one story by describing how, during the French royal campaign against Geoffrey Martel, young William II slips off with only four followers to seek adventure. He chances to meet fifteen of the enemy, whom he promptly attacks, wounding one and putting the rest to flight. The duke charges after them—but at this point, he disappears from the

48. *GG*, 88, 114, 106.
49. Ibid., 172–78.

narrative! William of Poitiers summarily turns to the Normans and their anxious search for their young ruler. The duke reappears in the story only when the action was over, bringing with him as captive seven of the fleeing fourteen men.[50] An audience accustomed to epics, where the thrust and parry of battle were rendered in loving detail, would have wailed with frustration at the omission of most of the exciting action.

The story of the Conquest had the potential to be a gripping one, and it proved to be so in the hands of contemporaries and later writers. Baudry of Bourgueil, one of the readers of the *Deeds of William*, borrowed William's motifs to write an elegant and trim account of the Conquest. His narrative of the building of William's fleet and its departure, which was as classical as William of Poitiers's, comprised only fifty lines, each of them succinct and delicate. William spoke of the same events in five or six dry pages. Baudry's battle of Hastings is full of the press of the crowd and the sudden shifts of fate; it is wisely built around the battlefield rumor that the duke had been killed. In contrast, William's account is, despite its length, vague.[51] It is perhaps unfair to compare the compact delivery of poetry to the *longeurs* of prose, but in a sense, in choosing prose over poetry and in avoiding much discussion of action, William chose not to cater to any desire for action on the part of his audience.

Instead, William concentrated on features of his text which would have appealed to a more literary audience. William's account of the battle of Hastings, instead of describing the action, offered a series of literary allusions that the learned might have enjoyed. Orderic Vitalis admired William of Poitiers's prose and copied lengthy passages from the *Deeds of William* nearly verbatim into his *Ecclesiastical History*. He was nearly alone, however, in this appreciation for William of Poitiers's work, and even he left out the

50. Ibid., 24–26.

51. Baudry of Bourgueil, *Carmina*, ed. K. Hilbert (Heidelberg: Carl Winter Universitatsverlag, 1979), 157–58 (ll.331–80) (on building the ships for the Channel crossing); *GG*, 150–52, 158–62. On the battle of Hastings, see Baudry, *Carmina*, 159–61 (ll.397–646); *GG*, 184–204.

classical references in his own work.[52] What William had clearly labored hard over may have been precisely the material that put his potential audience off. Moreover, even those with an appreciation for literary style might have liked juicier anecdotes.

More importantly, however, the *Deeds of William* was created in physical circumstances that had the tendency to limit the survival of texts. William did not belong to a monastic community but to a secular clerical community. In a monastic community, whatever was thought of a monk's writing, his book had a chance of being preserved and finding an audience, if only a local one. Orderic Vitalis's equally unpopular work managed to survive in just such circumstances. Works written by the secular clergy had a more precarious existence. They did not survive as well as those of monks, contributing to the dense clouds of anonymity that surround members of this group. Because the *Deeds of William* was unfinished, it seems unlikely that the author presented it to its subject, whose patronage might have contributed to its dissemination.

It is hardly surprising, then, that William of Poitiers's work was scarcely read. Only two writers on the Continent had read it, both in the early twelfth century: one was Orderic, who does not say when he encountered it, and the other was Baudry of Bourgueil, who had Norman connections.[53] A copy seems to have gone to England, however, and there the *Deeds* enjoyed a modest success.[54] Apart from William of Malmesbury and Ralph of Diceto, the author of the *Song of the Battle of Hastings,* whom I think was English, knew it as well.[55] It was the English manuscript which ensured the

52. *EH,* 1:58–59.

53. P. Abrahams, *Les Oeuvres poétiques de Baudri de Bourgueil* (Paris: Honoré Champion, 1926), 243f., n. 61.

54. If the historian is the William of Poitiers who was a canon at Dover (see above, p. 45), he may have taken a copy of his work with him himself.

55. Scholars have long known that the *Deeds of William* and the *Song* are closely related, but they have been unable to determine which came first. I have argued in "Norman Historical Writing," Appendix 2, that the *Song* seems to be a twelfth-century English text, rather than an eleventh-century French one. In brief, my arguments for the English provenance of the *Song* are three-fold. The first is essentially linguistic, based on the author's use of *Franci* to designate French speakers,

survival of William's text, for it made its way into the Cotton library, and there Duchesne made the transcription which is all that survives.[56]

The fate of Orderic Vitalis's *Ecclesiastical History* was similar to that of the historian whose moral leanings he shared. Like most earlier texts of Norman history, his *Ecclesiastical History* was commissioned; its commissioner, Roger of Le Sap, the abbot of Saint-Evroul, was an implied reader of the text. However, Roger commissioned a work which by its nature would have been of limited interest outside his monastery and its community: a monastic history. He most likely wanted a text the monks might consult should disputes over property arise, and he may also have expected the history to supply pious reading for his monks or to be available for consultation. As the quotation that begins this chapter demonstrates, Orderic was not fully content with this small local audience. He claimed for himself what he imagined to be the larger audience of those interested in history for its own sake. Just as Orderic was the only Norman historian to be aware of the possibility that history might be an important form of knowledge in its own right, he was also the only historian to articulate the kind of audience that this view of history would generate.

In reaching for the larger audience, Orderic did not abandon hope that he would also provide reading for his fellow monks. Both Roger Ray and Margery Chibnall have suggested, based on

---

improbable in a continental writer; the term *Normannus* is similarly loosely used. The second concerns passages of the *Song* that seem to echo scenes in the Bayeux Tapestry. N. P. Brooks and H. E. Walker, "The Authority and Interpretation of the Bayeux Tapestry," *Anglo-Norman Studies* 1 (1979), 9–18 have argued that a cartoon of the tapestry was extant in the twelfth century at Canterbury. My third argument is that the succession confusion of 1135 offers a rationale for a new treatment of the Conquest story. The debate on the dating of the *Song* has been extensive. For the arguments for an eleventh-century dating and attribution to Guy of Amiens, see Elisabeth M. C. van Houts, "Latin Poetry and the Anglo-Norman Court 1066–1135: The *Carmen de Hastingae proelio*," *Journal of Medieval History* 14 (1989): 39–62 and L. J. Engels, "Once More: The *Carmen de Hastingae proelio*;" for a summation of the arguments for a twelfth-century date, see Davis, "The *Carmen de Hastingae proelio*."

56. On the history of the manuscript, see *GG*, i–iiii.

the rhythmic qualities of Orderic's prose and the large number of speeches in the text, that the *Ecclesiastical History* was designed for reading aloud, either in the refectory or as *lectio divina* on the part of individuals.[57] Despite the style, Orderic seems not to have pleased the local audience. Ray has argued that in referring to his preference for writing about the miraculous, Orderic was responding to criticism from his fellow monks.[58] (While the *Ecclesiastical History* does contain miracle stories, there are not many compared to the hagiographies with which monks were so familiar.)

There are two other ways, however, to read Orderic's comment that he would have rather written about miracles. While it may have been a defence of history against local detractors, Orderic also may simply have been echoing what was by his time a historian's commonplace sentiment. Other historians like William of Malmesbury, Robert of Torigni, Hugh of Saint-Victor, and William of Jumièges felt it necessary to defend history as well.[59] The existence of such a commonplace does suggest that historians felt their work to be undervalued, but it does not mean that they were responding to specific criticism. Orderic's comments can also be explained not only as a defence of history but also as an expression of his view of the world around him. The theological commonplace about the aging of the world and its accompanying scarcity of miracles— already invoked by Augustine—was particularly in tune with Orderic's rather elegiac outlook.[60]

Orderic's advocacy of history does not seem to have convinced his fellow monks, for there are many indications that Orderic failed to find much of an audience in the Middle Ages for his *Ecclesiastical History*. His history did not survive in a complete form; most of it is extant only in a partial autograph. Its survival in autograph is

57. Ray, "Orderic Vitalis and His Readers," 21; Chibnall, *World of Orderic Vitalis*, 197.

58. Ray, "Orderic Vitalis and His Readers," 19.

59. *GRA*, 2:484; Rob. of Tor., 1:91–92; Hugh of Saint-Victor, *Didascalicon*, 6:3 (p. 115); see also above, pp. 191, 208–9; below, 251–52, 252n.14.

60. On the topos, see James Dean, "The World Grown Old and Genesis in Middle English Historical Writings," *Speculum* 57 (1982): 548–50. Cf. Augustine, *City of God*, 22:8.

one of the strongest indications that it was lightly read. The portion that does not survive in autograph, books seven and eight (concerning the history of Normandy in the later reign of the Conqueror and the reign of Henry I), were copied at Caen. This might easily have been done to supplement a copy of William of Jumièges's version of the *Deeds of the Dukes,* which would have ended in the middle of the Conqueror's reign. Orderic's treatise on the new orders, however, circulated separately from the rest of the text and more widely.[61] The autograph also offers some testimony about the few readers. It contains sparse marginalia by twelfth, thirteenth, and fourteenth-century readers, presumably monks at Saint-Evroul.[62] Apart from the readers who wrote in the manuscript and the copyist at Caen, Robert of Torigni read the text; William of Malmesbury may also have known of Orderic, even if he did had not read the *Ecclesiastical History* itself.[63] Indeed, it was not until the sixteenth century that Orderic found readers again and not until after the first edition in the early seventeenth century that he was recognized as a historian of unusual ability.

There are many possible explanations for the lack of popularity of the *Ecclesiastical History* in the Middle Ages. First, it was neither official, nor was Orderic at one of the monasteries with the strongest ducal connections. Thus Orderic's patronage was essentially local and his local readership was not enchanted. A second factor was that the task he eventually undertook was different from the one he had been assigned. While his abbots permitted him to continue his work and may even have been proud of his efforts, he had fulfilled the original assignment by around 1127, that is, he had completed the history of gifts to the monastery.[64] For the history of monastic bequests, the abbots had a use; for the larger universal history, they probably had no plans.

This absence of patronage seems to me to have been crucial, but there were other features of Orderic's history that may have rendered it less attractive to readers. The book was enormously long.

61. *EH,* 1:113.
62. Ibid., 1:120.
63. Ibid., 2:270, n. 1.
64. Ibid., 1:46.

If one did not want to read the whole thing, finding one's way through this extensive work was difficult. The mixing of genres in which Orderic indulged ensured that few readers would have been equally interested in all the contents of his history. Medieval notions of genre were looser than ours, but even by medieval standards, Orderic's work was quite a miscellany. The books of the *Ecclesiastical History* that were read most often, that is, the ones that were copied or which contain the most marginalia, are books seven through thirteen, the most coherent portion of the text. Orderic's modern editor, in fact, chose not to edit the books in their numeric order but dealt with the narrative of recent and contemporary history (books three and four and books seven through thirteen) and then turned to the monastic and universal histories which formed the remaining books.

Unlike modern readers, medieval readers had no guides to the text, no indices, and very few topic rubrics to make it easier to find material. Orderic's contemporaries wrote some notes in the margins to assist the reader but too few to overcome medieval readers' difficulty using this text as a source.[65] While readers could have chosen the *Ecclesiastical History* for slow, reflective reading, *meditatio* (Karl Morrison has argued that this was what Orderic intended), they clearly did not.[66] The monks of Saint-Evroul had many other choices for such reading in the rich collection of hagiography, *miracula,* and patristic texts that filled their library. For Orderic to find the kind of audience he envisioned, history had to become more meaningful and important to his audience. Finally, the failure of Orderic's history in conjunction with the failure of the *Deeds of William* suggests that history written in a tropological mode might not have appealed as well to readers as allegorical or literal history. The lack of success of the *Ecclesiastical History* in the Middle Ages was probably the result of a combination of all of these factors.

65. Ray, "Orderic Vitalis and His Readers," 18.

66. See Morrison, *History as a Visual Art,* 92–93; Ray, "Orderic Vitalis and His Readers," 18.

It was not until Robert of Torigni's version of the *Deeds of the Dukes* was composed that a text by a Norman historian again enjoyed substantial success. Some of Robert's histories seem to have been locally commissioned and intended for local consumption. It is thought, for instance, that Robert wrote his history of the abbots of Bec (if he is indeed the author of the *Chronicon Beccense*) at the behest of his superiors, and while it was continued into the fifteenth century, it seems to have been of largely local interest. The annals of Mont Saint-Michel, which Robert as abbot would have decided to continue himself, were similarly of interest to those at the monastery.

Robert's other works were a different matter, because they circulated very widely. However, the circumstances under which Robert wrote them are murky. His letter to Gervais of Saint-Céneri and his version of the letter of Henry of Huntingdon to Warren both suggest that Robert had the freedom to decide on his own tasks and to carry them out. The letter to Gervais also shows Robert's awareness that writing history was one way to attract patronage and advancement. Consequently, his works were carefully tailored at least not to offend the powerful. Robert's version of the *Deeds of the Dukes* was composed before his *Chronicle,* and we can see the shift in Robert's presentation of material as his need to appease his audience changed.

Robert's continuation of the *Deeds* dates from the end of the 1130s, a time when the issue of the English and Norman succession was neither fully resolved nor yet violently contested, and Robert could not afford to offend either of the parties laying claim to Normandy. Stephen of Blois was duke of Normandy until 1144, but Bec had close ties to Henry I's daughter, Matilda, that lasted through her lifetime. Not only did Bec enjoyed Henry's patronage, but Matilda gave the monastery significant donations in 1134 after the difficult delivery of her second son. At that time, Matilda vowed to be buried at Bec. When her father died in the next year, his heart, tongue and innards were buried at Pré (Bonne-Nouvelle) at Rouen, a Bec priory, while the rest of his body went to his foundation at Reading.⁶⁷ Robert also, no doubt, had personal reasons to be attached to Matilda. Robert of Gloucester, Matilda's half-brother and her most faithful supporter, was the lord of Torigni and perhaps Robert's patron in that capacity.⁶⁸ Matilda and her brother were the obvious recipients of a work that was expanded to include a biography of their father.

In the continuation of the *Deeds of the Dukes,* therefore, Robert picked a careful path between personal attachments and political necessities, never accusing Stephen of usurpation but taking equal care to assert that Henry I wanted his daughter to be his successor. On the crucial matter of whether the nobility swore an oath to accept Matilda as their queen, Robert said, rather ingenuously, that it was none of his concern. Still, he twice referred to Matilda as her father's heir.⁶⁹ Even though Robert was generally cool in his narrative toward Geoffrey Plantagenet, Matilda's husband, probably because of the disastrous effects of Geoffrey's raids on Normandy, Robert made him a descendent of the Capetian lineage, using this noble descent as a justification for Matilda's marriage into a comital family.⁷⁰

The *Chronicle,* because it was composed later, probably after 1153, was freer to accommodate what turned out to be the winning side. Robert added passages praising Henry I to the material he drew from Henry of Huntingdon. Robert could also afford to call Stephen's accession a usurpation, to assert that the nobility had indeed sworn an oath to support Matilda's candidacy for the throne, and to state unequivocally that Henry II, and his brothers, Geoffrey and William, were Henry I's rightful heirs.⁷¹ Where Robert had been reserved about Geoffrey Plantagenet in the *Deeds of the Dukes,* praising him only through his ancestors, in his obituary notice in the *Chronicle,* Robert praised Geoffrey in his own right, albeit carefully excluding himself from those who lamented Geoffrey's passing.⁷²

---

67. Rob. of Tor., 1:193, 198.　　68. *GND*, 306.

69. Ibid., 299–300, 319, 329.　　70. Ibid., 300–302.

71. For the praise of Henry I, see Rob. of Tor., 1:133: "*Cujus bonitatis fama . . . patuit dilata*"; on Henry II, see ibid., 1:199, 229f., 200; on the oath, see ibid., 1:199.

72. Ibid., 1:256.

While Robert's partisanship was often expressed by praise, as when he lauded Henry II on his accession, his partiality was as much a matter of what he did not say as what he did.[73] The most blatant of Robert's omissions was his failure to mention the Becket controversy at all while it was in progress. Robert referred to Becket's absence from England in connection with the coronation of Henry, the Young King, in 1170 and recorded Becket's return later that same year, but the four-line poem on Becket's death seems to have been added afterward, as was the chronicle's account of Becket's canonization.[74] Robert does mention Henry's penance for the death of Becket but in as favorable a way as possible. His account stresses Henry's humility, likening the king's patient suffering of a beating to Jesus's acceptance of scourging, attempting to garner as much sympathy for the king as possible. All references to Becket are cautiously brief.[75] This tact might have been appreciated by Henry II, who received a presentation copy of the final version of chronicle in 1184.[76] Henry II may actually have read the chronicle, for unlike many of his ducal forebears, he was literate in both French and Latin.[77]

The pattern of dissemination of Robert's chronicle resembles that of the *Deeds of the Dukes* and the *Customs of the Dukes*. The text was most likely to be found in major monasteries with close ducal associations and/or active interests in historical writing. Of the thirteen manuscripts from the twelfth and thirteenth centuries

---

73. Ibid., 1:287–88.

74. Ibid., 2:25 and n. 2. Delisle believed the manuscript in which these verses were written (Avranches, *Bibliothèque municipale,* 149) to be the autograph of the last recension of Robert's chronicle (see Rob. of Tor., 1:xlv f.). On the canonization, see ibid., 2:26 and n. 7.

75. On Becket's absence and return, see ibid., 2:18, 24. On the poem, see ibid., 2:25 and n. 1). On the canonization, see ibid., 2:26, n. 7. On Henry's penance, see ibid., 2:51. Other references, see ibid., 2:66, 83–84, 96.

76. Ibid., 1:xlvi.

77. James Thompson, *Literacy of the Laity,* 174ff. Walter Map, *De nugis curialium,* ed. Montague Rhodes James (Oxford: Oxford University Press, 1914), 237. "He was lettered for every appropriate purpose and use having knowledge of all tongues that exist from the French sea to the Jordan, that is, speaking French and Latin."

identified by Leopold Délisle, Robert's editor, the vast majority were from Norman monasteries. However, a copy of the first version of the chronicle was written at Reading, an establishment that continued to be important to the ducal family after the death of Henry I.[78] Another, now lost, manuscript was composed at the monastery of Valasse, which enjoyed the special patronage of Henry II's mother, Matilda.[79] Fécamp, Jumièges, and Saint-Wandrille had copies, while Savigny, which was in the midst of its burst of historical writing as Robert was writing, did as well. Lyre too had a copy, produced around 1220. Although Lyre did not produce any significant histories itself, it was a wealthy house, close to Bec, that had a habit of copying Bec histories.

Although Robert's version of the *Deeds* was not as popular as his chronicle was during the twelfth and thirteenth centuries, the dissemination pattern for Robert's version of the *Deeds of the Dukes* is very similar. Of the seven manuscripts from the twelfth or thirteenth centuries, one came from Reading, the rest from Normandy. The provenance of all the Norman manuscripts cannot be established; however, Bec's, Préaux's, and Jumièges's copies have survived and possibly the copy from Fécamp as well.[80] This lesser popularity makes sense, because Robert's version of the *Deeds* was competing with other redactions. Many monasteries must have already had a copy of the *Deeds of the Dukes* when Robert completed his work, and they would not have acquired another. Some did recopy it anyway, for two manuscripts are extant which contain both the combined texts of William of Jumièges and Dudo of Saint-Quentin as well as Robert's version of the *Deeds*.[81] However, most Norman monasteries would have possessed no major chronicles, and, therefore, Robert's chronicle filled an unoccupied niche. In addition, the scribes also copied the Eusebius-Jerome chronicle with the continuations by Prosper and Sigebert, and thus sup-

78. Henry II buried his son, William, there. See Rob. of Tor., 1:300; on the manuscripts, see ibid., 1:iii–liii.

79. *Gallia christiana,* 11:313.

80. On these mssanuscripts, see van Houts, *GND,* 229–41.

81. Ibid., 195–98.

plied their monasteries with a chronicle of great reputation and authority that began with creation. Robert's chronicle was an important part of the whole chronicle's appeal, however, because Robert's continuation was more successful than any other. No doubt Robert's own authority and reputation as the abbot of Mont Saint-Michel helped popularize his work in Normandy.[82]

Although Robert's histories contained material that a secular audience might have found interesting, particularly his noble genealogies, it is unlikely that many of his readers came from the secular sphere. As was the case with other Norman historians, his readers were from the ranks of the learned, those "well-intentioned people who love, await and demand" his work.[83] This general reference to Robert's hoped-for readers precluded no one, but the obvious readers would have been monastic. Indeed, the abbot of Bec sent an emissary to Robert in the 1180s asking for the updated material for his chronicle.[84] These were the people who might ruminate over the meaning of omens and contemplate the chronography, in other words, the sort of monastic reader I have already shown to be the major audience of Norman histories.

Robert's works did find readers. On the other hand, the *Norman Dragon* of Stephen of Rouen, his fellow monk, seems to have remained unread. We know little of Stephen of Rouen's intentions about his audience, for he, unlike Orderic or Dudo of Saint-Quentin, mentions no patrons and addresses no specific reader in his text. The purpose of the work implies an audience, for it argues for a particular royal policy—hostility to Louis VII and alliance with Barbarossa. It therefore seems logical that Stephen intended Henry II to be his primary audience, whether or not the *Dragon* was sent to Henry II. Its existence in a single manuscript (possibly an autograph), which also includes Stephen's poems, suggests it was not.[85]

---

82. See ibid., 229–60; Rob. of Tor., 1:liiif., and Guenée, *Histoire,* 265. Robert of Auxerre's work, another continuation of Sigebert, is extant in only six manuscripts (ibid., 261).

83. Rob. of Tor., 1:92.   84. Ibid., 2:340.

85. *DN,* x and n. 1.

One suspects that the *Dragon* was overtaken by the events of its day, as each of the causes Stephen embraced became moot. Stephen advocated Norman independence from France, but the poem ended with Henry's sons doing homage to Louis VII for the holdings they would inherit from their father. Henry abandoned his defiance of his lord, at least for the time being. Although Stephen opposed the partition of the Angevin empire, Henry, in permitting his sons to do homage for their inheritances, made clear his intention to divide his lands on his death. Stephen took the king's side in his quarrel with Thomas à Becket, but Thomas's murder in 1170, just after the *Dragon* was completed, made the support of the king's position in the controversy untenable. (In this case, Robert of Torigni's caution served better than Stephen's frank partisanship.) The king's admission of some guilt in the murder in 1172 and Thomas's canonization in 1173 rendered the case closed. The resolution of the Becket controversy took away Henry's most serious temptation to renounce his support of Pope Alexander III in favor of the rival set up by Frederick Barbarossa, another course of action urged by Stephen. Thus, the *Dragon's* topicality meant that it became dated very quickly, as polemics tend to do.

The disappearance of the issues that interested Stephen did not necessarily preclude the *Dragon* from finding other readers for other reasons, but both Stephen's own position and the nature of his text made this circulation unlikely. Here the absence of indications of patronage seems to be crucial. A number of Stephen's poems were occasional poems, and these were the kind of writing that might attract the attention of patrons. There was a lament on the death of Archbishop Theobald of Canterbury, a former monk of Bec; a commemorative poem on the death of Waleran of Meulan at Préaux (1166); a poem about Henry II as count of Anjou, various poems to acquaintances; and a poem on the election of an abbot of Mont Saint-Michel, which might have been for Robert of Torigni.[86] None of the poems commemorating the great is very per-

---

86. On Theobald, see *Dragon*, 220; Waleran, 189; Henry II, 199; acquaintances, 195, 218, 237, 239, 249, 251; Robert of Torigni, 224.

sonal, which suggests that Stephen had limited connections and therefore probably had no assistance in circulating his work. In other words, he was in much the same position that Orderic Vitalis was in; he was notable only in the context of his monastery.

Moreover, the *Dragon* itself was a problematic work because it confounded the generic expectations for history that were gradually emerging as a consensus in the later twelfth century. Historians increasingly taught their readers to expect that Latin histories would be written in prose, not in poetry, and would strive for an impartiality of tone rather than engage in satiric vituperation. Historians were expected not to create imaginary epistolary exchanges between long-dead heroes and living individuals. While many potential readers would not have known enough history to spot the numerous factual inaccuracies of the text, the Arthurian material signaled very clearly that the *Dragon* was not simply a history, as did its didactic preoccupations. It is possible that the *Dragon* was read locally as a "fun" way of reinforcing the lessons of rhetoric or as an example of satire, but it never transcended that purely local impact.

The dissemination of Norman histories in Normandy, then, seems to have depended in large part on the ability of the historian to make his name and work known; patronage seems to have been crucial to this process in nearly every case. The only apparent exception to this were the annals of Rouen. Through their association with the archdiocese, these must have taken on an official character, so that when someone at a monastery decided that it was important for the monastery to keep annals, the process naturally began by acquiring a copy of the annals of Rouen.

Even the works which circulated relatively widely were available largely in monasteries and read presumably primarily by monks. Most Norman histories, however, did not circulate very widely, and understandably so, for they were generally local in their point of view and in their interests. While works like the *Authority of Fécamp* and the *Discovery of St. Wulfran* discussed the history of Normandy at large, their purpose was to authenticate the narrative of local events. This was a normal expectation for a monastic writer. The Anonymous of Fécamp, after all, expected that the brothers would find his work useful.[87] This type of work generally survives in only one or two manuscripts and often in autograph. The *Acts of the Archbishops of Rouen*, for example, survives in two manuscripts, one from the archdiocese, the other from Saint-Ouen and both from the late eleventh century. The monks of Saint-Ouen obviously had an interest in acquiring this text, since their patron saint was one of the archbishops and because the archbishops were such powerful and close neighbors. Other monasteries were more distantly connected to the archdiocese and thus did not need to respond to the archbishops' salvo. They produced other texts to stress their independence.

How frequently were these minor historical works read? The copy of the *Acts* made at Saint-Ouen has no marginalia, and, although the text of the *Acts* ends on folio 13r and the catalog of the archbishops begins on 14v, thus leaving room for additions, no one felt it necessary to continue the text. The catalog was continued until the thirteenth century, but this continuation did not mean that the *Acts* were read. The manuscript itself has missing pages, suggestive of the hard use one would expect a lectionary to receive.[88] The archiepiscopal copy left no space for expansion of the text of the *Acts* for these are followed immediately by the metrical catalog, which (as at Saint-Ouen) was continued into the thirteenth century. Like the Saint-Ouen copy, the diocesan copy of the *Acts* is free of marginalia, although a vision of Archbishop Maurilius was added after the catalog and other parts of the book were much annotated.[89] Clearly then, these were texts that were of interest only for a limited time. Something similar might be said of the *Discovery of St. Wulfran*. Like the *Acts*, it is preserved in two copies, one fragmentary, both from Saint-Wandrille. Someone did find it useful to copy some of the material in the thirteenth century, but the text did not travel from the house that produced it.[90]

87. *Libellus de revelatione*, 702.

88. For example, there is at least one page missing between fols. 46 and 47 (Rouen, *Bibliothèque municipale*, Y. 41).

89. Rouen, *Bibliothèque municipale*, Y. 27, p. 41.

90. See van Houts, "Historiography and Hagiography," 235–37, for these manu-

The evidence has thus far suggested that the audience for history in Normandy was not large and that its desire for history was satisfied by relatively few works. A handful, most notably William of Jumièges's *Deeds of the Dukes* and its continuations, were copied many times and known to all historians writing Norman history on either side of the Channel. Other works, such as Orderic's *Ecclesiastical History,* were generally unknown, and most works served only local readers. That so many Norman histories survived in only one copy or two from the eleventh or twelfth century also indicates light readership, for heavily read texts were less likely to survive at all. Orderic's manuscript is a case in point for the first two books in particular, the universal history, show "little sign of use . . . although these contained many lives of apostles, prayers, and hymns that were ideally suitable for use in the Church on Saint's Days."[91] The volume that contains them is in excellent condition, as is the second volume, which contained the monastic history (the final page, which is blank, has been damaged). The fourth volume, which contained the last and most heavily annotated portion of the text sustained more damage. Among other things, the book had to be rebound (the gatherings are now out of order because of it).[92] The third volume, the one that was copied at Caen, is missing altogether. Thus, the readers left a path of destruction through the parts of the text they read.

Some of the manuscripts of other Norman histories offer further testimony through their design and decoration about the way histories were seen by those who copied them and those who later encountered these copies. Orderic's *Ecclesiastical History* was a plain manuscript, compared to some of the other books he copied, but it did have colored capitals. He also used colored capitals in his autograph of the *Deeds of the Dukes,* but, in addition, he decorated this book with a large initial "P" with an interlace pattern containing an illustration of William of Jumièges giving his book to

---

scripts, Rouen, *Bibliothèque municipale,* Y. 237 and Le Havre, *Bibliothèque municipale,* 332. See also, *CG,* 1:303, 2:332 and *Manuscrits datés,* 157.

91. Chibnall, *World of Orderic Vitalis,* 218.

92. *EH,* 1:118–20.

William the Conqueror.[93] The Jumièges manuscript of the *Customs of the Dukes* that left room for illustrations was designed as a fine book with generous margins (the marginalia are cut in half, so the existing outer margins are smaller than the original ones) and colored capitals. The names of Richard and William are rubricated with a red line where they appear, as though both were saints. However, the colored capitals were never finished, nor were any illustrations completed, leaving the book with a raw look. The designer of the book planned a beautiful object, but it was not important enough to anyone else to complete the project.

Norman manuscripts tended to be restrained in their decoration, and the historical manuscripts mostly follow suit. The *Acts of the Archbishops of Rouen,* now contained in the *Livre d'Ivoire* of the diocese, had initial letters touched up with red, but it is otherwise very plain. This text was thrown in with other things which might come in handy for the archdiocese—episcopal *acta,* offices and lives of the bishop-saints of the diocese, diocesan legislation, and copies of the oaths of the archbishops. The book was rather like a file of items the archbishops might need to look up from time to time rather than a book designed for reading.[94] The decision to decorate books was obviously a decision of time and money. When they needed to be cheaply and swiftly produced as, for example, during the period in the late tenth and early eleventh century when Norman libraries were expanding rapidly, decoration had to be limited.[95] It is reasonable to expect, however, that a manuscript that was continually read would be finished, i.e. the rubrics and initials would have been filled in, if only in ink.

Another indication of reading, glosses and corrections, betray the Norman histories as little used. Someone did at least check the copy of the *Customs of the Dukes* made at Jumièges, for text was inserted in several places in the book. Someone also indicated those

93. Ibid., 1:118–19; Rouen, *Bibliothèque municipale,* Y. 14, fols. 116r–139v. For a description of the manuscript, see *CG,* 1:294; *Manuscrits datés,* 321.

94. Rouen, *BM,* Y. 27. On this manuscript, see *CG,* 1:399 and *Manuscrits datés,* 327.

95. See Lawrence, "Anglo-Norman Book Production," 86.

things worth remembering by placing a large "N" (for *nota* or "make note of this") in the margin near them.[96] An assortment of hands continued, corrected, and added poems to the poetic catalog of the archbishops of Rouen.[97] However, many texts offered opportunities for continuation, commentary, or emendation of which no one took advantage. The annals of Lyre were written on a small gathering of two bifolios; the annals stopped on folio 3r, leaving the verso and the next folio blank for additions, but there are no entries after 1200.[98] When Norman historical manuscripts did acquire glosses, commentary was never copious in the way it might have been for a philosophical or school text. By these indications too, these histories were lightly read.

The final evidence are the complaints by Norman historians that their work was not read or might not be read, or their defences of history against those who said it was pointless or useless. Orderic's defences of history are the most explicit and vociferous. However, William of Jumièges's suggestion that his work was being ridiculed and Robert of Torigni's acknowledgement that there were those who harbored no favorable view of history are also significant. These defences of history do not mean that the general attitude toward history was hostile. However, they do suggest that the historians expected, like prophets, to be without honor in their own land.

96. See Rouen, *Bibliothèque municipale*, Y. 11, 5r, 31r, 61v, and 61r, and for "N" (for *nota*), see 17r. On *nota*, see Carruthers, *Book of Memory*, 107–8.

97. Rouen, *Bibliothèque municipale*, Y. 27, 39 where an additional poem on archbishop Rotrou is added; 40, ll.10–11 are written in over verses that had been scratched out.

98. Evreux, *Bibliothèque municipale*, ms. 60; on this manuscript, see *CG*, 2:437; *Manuscrit datés*, 464.

※ Conclusion: The Propagation of Historical Writing in Medieval Europe

*H*istories written in Normandy circulated in a skewed pattern. A few, the *Customs of the Dukes,* the *Deeds of the Dukes* (in all three of its major recensions), and the *Chronicle* of Robert of Torigni were widely available in Normandy and were well-known in England and also at some monastic centers outside of the Anglo-Norman realm where there was a marked interest in history. Each of these texts was at least quasi-official, commissioned by or for the duke and written either at the court or at a monastery with strong ties to the dukes. The dissemination pattern in Normandy and England reproduces the pattern of production: copies of these texts found their way to substantial monasteries with a stake in knowing (if not always adhering to) a duke's-eye view of Normandy's past. The Annals of Rouen, which might be said to have circulated widely within Normandy through the monastic annals copied from it, must have seemed similarly authentic and important (if not precisely official), as these annals issued forth from a seat of power (if not one entirely independent of the ducal circle).

Other histories were written and copied within a more limited radius. Many Norman histories did not circulate widely or perhaps at all. They were frequently written to cope with local crises or to foster local identity. However, although the works themselves might be of largely local interest, the institutions at which they were produced were neither poor nor obscure and were generally places where historical works of broader appeal were collected, if not produced. Historical writing accompanied the desire to secure, expand, and protect property at Savigny, Saint-Evroul, and Mont Saint-Michel.

Still, what is striking from the modern point of view is how limited all this historical activity really was. Although undoubtedly more historical manuscripts were produced than have survived and although whole texts may have been lost as well, history had a very small audience in Normandy, and the interest of that audience in history tended to be anything but spontaneous. Even granted that the time-frame within which I have examined Norman histories is also limited—a mere two hundred years or so—the somewhat marginal character of history is clear. History was one of the ways in which one might flex one's political muscle, but it was not, despite the resources evidently allocated to its production and dissemination, the main means by which dukes, abbots, or bishops asserted their authority.

The Norman pattern of the wide dissemination of a few works but the narrow circulation and light readership of most histories, recapitulates the position of Latin history in medieval Europe up to the thirteenth century. A few early medieval histories, such as the *Ecclesiastical History* of Bede (extant in over 150 manuscripts), the *History of the Lombards* of Paul the Deacon, and the *Tripartite History* of Cassiodorus (both these latter two surviving in over a hundred manuscripts), were widely disseminated and frequently consulted by other historians. A few later works managed to become similarly authoritative. The *Scholastic History* of Peter Comestor (c. 1160) also survives in a large number of manuscripts.

Much more common, however, was the survival of histories in one, two, or three manuscripts.[1]

In her study of autograph manuscripts, Cécile Garand found that most surviving eleventh- and twelfth-century autographs are histories. Garand has argued that history was preponderant among autographs because it was so seldom spontaneously written. Instead, history was often commissioned and assigned, a rather menial task to be performed by the *scolasticus* or director of the scriptorium. Important writers did not have to write out their own manuscripts; they dictated.[2] Orderic Vitalis's autograph seems to confirm Garand's points. He was important in the scriptorium, but he seems never to have held high monastic office, and his project was originally assigned to him.

History was marginal, I would argue, because of an incompatibility between the audience that had the most use for history and the form in which history was presented—the Latin language. The linguistic barrier created by Latin helped restrict the audience for history primarily to the most educated members of the clergy. But it was the laity and particularly the lay elite who were the greatest potential audience for history and whose patronage seems to have been responsible for the circulation of most of the Norman histories, and probably histories written in other regions.

In theory, the clerical audience was interested in history because it could serve theology. One medieval argument that was sometimes raised in defence of history—Robert of Torigni invoked it—was that by contemplating history the individual could come to understand the place of one's own times in God's plan. Robert was writing universal history, the genre which most clearly lent itself to this sort of contemplation, and which, from the eleventh century onward, was undergoing an efflorescence.[3]

1. See Guenée, *Histoire et culture historique*, 250–52, for a table of manuscript survivals of selected histories. For manuscripts of Paul the Deacon's *History of the Lombards*, see *MGH Scriptores rerum Langobardorum et italicarum saec. VI–IX* (Hannover: Hahn, 1878), 28–42.

2. On the number of historical autographs, see Garand, "Auteurs latins et autographes," 94–95; for the reasons, see ibid., 80.

3. For these later universal chronicles, see von den Brincken, *Lateinischen Weltchronistik*, 149–210.

However, not all thinkers accepted that history revealed God's plans and intentions clearly or even at all. If one believed, as writers in apocalyptic traditions did, that the time of redemption would come suddenly and unsignaled by secular events, secular history could not be interpreted and was, therefore, meaningless. St. Augustine belonged to this tradition, and thus his work, to the degree that he was influential in this matter, was an impediment to justifying a clerical interest in secular history.[4] For Augustine, the events of secular history stubbornly resisted the imputation of meaning. In the *City of God*, Augustine addressed why good things sometimes happened to the wicked, but he quickly went on to say that a more important question was how people might use whatever happened to them for their spiritual advancement. Good people could not be spiritually harmed by the catastrophes that befell them, and so those catastrophes were, theologically speaking, irrelevant.[5]

Only scriptural history had an unambiguous meaning to Augustine, and that was because it was revealed. Scripture could not provide any sort of paradigm for understanding the history of the earthly city; in fact, when Augustine in the eighteenth book of the *City of God* related the history of the earthly city, he did it for the purposes of comparison so that readers could see the difference between the comprehensibility of the one and the inscrutability of the other. Augustine opposed the kind of crude equation Robert of Torigni made between certain kinds of omens and certain kinds of events. Augustine explicitly forbade his readers to conclude from scripture or experience either that the Church would face more persecutions or that it would not.[6] All that could be known in the future was what had been already revealed in Scripture, and therefore, when Scripture stopped, Augustine stopped too. Augustine rejected the *Seven Books against the Pagans* of Orosius as theologically inadequate precisely because it crudely claimed to set forth the meaning of secular history.[7]

4. Funkenstein, *Heilsplan und natürliche Entwicklung*, ii, 18.
5. Augustine, *City of God*, 1:8, 10.
6. Ibid., 18:52.
7. On the implications of Augustine's thought for history, see Funkenstein,

Despite the unhelpful character of Augustine's ideas about history, the *City of God* was widely available and some historians from time to time tried to write Augustinian history. However, they were generally forced to compromise Augustine's ideas and to manipulate their facts as Orosius had. Otto of Freising, for example, was inspired by the *City of God* to write his own universal history, *The Two Cities,* but Otto simplified Augustine's thought and identified the heavenly city, which in Augustine's writing is the assembly of the saved, with the Church, which to Augustine contained both the saved and the damned. In so doing, Otto substituted a human institution for what had been in Augustine's mind an invisible community, and not only that, a human institution with which Otto was, in support of his nephew Frederick Barbarossa, frequently in conflict. Theology was thus reduced to politics.[8]

Other historians adhered closely to the typology of sacred history and were forced to manipulate their material to make it fit the model. Bede, who in the past was held up as the model of historical sobriety and accuracy, now under greater scrutiny has been found to have played gently with his material in order to make the story come out right.[9] Dudo of Saint-Quentin, who came closest of all the Norman historians to seeing a theological purpose in the past, "discovered" material to do the same thing, a practice which both his successor William of Jumièges and most twelfth-century his-

---

Heilsplan und natürliche Entwicklung, 36–50. See also Henri Irénée Marrou, "Saint Augustin, Orose, et l'Augustinisme historique," in *La Storiografia medievale,* Settimane di Studio del Centro italiano di studi sull'alto medioevo, 17 (Spoleto: Centro italiano di studi sull'alto medioevo, 1970), 1:83–84.

8. Marrou, "Saint Augustin," argues that in Otto of Freising's work, what presents itself as Augustinian is really Orosian. Otto was also influenced by Hugh of Saint-Victor, "*Alter Augustinus;*" see van den Brincken, *Lateinischen Weltchronistik,* 197–99. On Otto's ideas more generally, see also Funkenstein, *Heilsplan und natürliche Entwicklung,* 94ff.

9. See Jones, *Saints' Lives and Chronicles,* 79–93. Jones has given the clearest explanation of Bede's historical work in terms of his concerns as an exegete and explains Bede's use of the term "the true law of history" as meaning that Bede was seeking a higher truth which did not necessarily correspond to physical truth (83). See also Walter Goffart, "The *Historia Ecclesiastica*: Bede's Agenda and Ours," *The Haskins Society Journal* 2 (1990): 29–45.

torians, although notably not Geoffrey of Monmouth, found un-
acceptable.

Augustine did not offer the only theological treatment of history in the Middle Ages and indeed the *City of God* had a smaller
impact on the writing of history than its potential readership
would suggest.[10] From at least the third century, there was a competing non-Augustinian, evolutionary theology of human history.
This view of history was only fully articulated in the twelfth century, most clearly by Hugh of Saint-Victor.[11] This view, no doubt
fostered by Europe's increased prosperity and the decreased violence of European life, saw humanity as progressing gradually
toward improvement through natural means rather than supernatural interventions, and he saw human history as indicative of
the state of human progress and therefore intelligible. Even Hugh,
however, could not argue that history was particularly important.

In the chapter on history in the *Didascalicon*, Hugh posits an
imaginary interlocutor who asks why one should study history,
since so much of it seemed pointless. Hugh responds:

Some things are to be known in themselves; others, although they do not
seem to be worth our labor for their own sake, ought by no means to be
negligently omitted, since without them the former sorts of things could
not be clearly known. Learn everything; you will see that nothing is su-
perfluous. A narrow knowledge is no pleasure.[12]

In other words, history offered primarily collateral benefits, that
is, it prepared one for other studies. It was not a useful form of
knowledge in its own right. Hugh likened history to the elemen-
tary drawings of geometry, the letters of the alphabet, the knowledge of the night sky. "These things," he remarks, "are childish,
but not useless, nor is knowing them much of a weight on my

10. Marrou, "Saint Augustin," 63.
11. See R. W. Southern, "Aspects of the European Tradition of Historical Writing: 3. History as Prophecy," *Transactions of the Royal Historical Society*, 5th ser. 22
(1972), esp. 162–66; also Southern, "Hugh of St Victor and the Idea of Historical
Development," esp. 165–170; also Funkenstein, *Heilsplan und natürliche Entwicklung*, 52, 55.
12. Hugh of Saint-Victor, *Didascalicon*, 115.

stomach."[13] It is not surprising that when so generous a scholar and committed a historian as Hugh could not offer much of a reason for studying history, others less concerned with theories of knowledge and education would not hold history in high regard.

The confusion about history's meaningfulness was exacerbated by the strategy employed by many historians to avoid the dilemma posed by the failure of events to conform to uplifting patterns. Many historians, like Robert of Torigni, asserted that God controlled history but offered no divine interpretation of their evidence.[14] To refuse to interpret, however, was to weaken the claim that history provided theological lessons, and if Hugh of Saint-Victor was correct, there was by the twelfth century already a group of people who felt strongly that history was theologically useless. A stopgap was to draw out the moralities of the individual stories, as Orderic did, but in the process much material was incidentally left unexplained, and Orderic himself retreated into silence at the end of his history in the face of the catastrophes of his time. Thus, although the theological meaning of history was often asserted, history was difficult to use in that way. Historical criticism was used by theologians, but history was used only sparingly, apart from biblical history which escaped from the uncertainties of more modern history.

When the clergy produced history for its own use, it often did so for less elevated and more political ends. For example, ecclesiastical histories addressed local crises and identities. I have already described the connection between the composition of the *Acts of*

13. Ibid., 116. For the equation of learning and digestion implied by Hugh's use of the word stomach where we might use mind, see Carruthers, *Book of Memory*, 165.

14. For example, Robert says, in response to the imagined hostile question as to why history was worth knowing about, "Prodigies, however, and earlier portents, which signify famine or epidemic or some other whip of divine punishment for the merits of the sons of men, as they seem, are by the same means commended to memory through letters, so that when similar things happen, they may remember the fact that they incurred the wrath of God in some sin and may hasten soon to the remedies of penance and confession to placate God though these" (Rob. of Tor., 1:92). Robert does not, however, comment on prodigies and portents when they happen. Any such interpretation is left to the reader.

the Archbishops of Rouen and the attempts by the archbishops of the later eleventh century to establish their authority over the monasteries and suffragan dioceses of the ecclesiastical province. The progenitor of this form of ecclesiastical history, the *Liber Pontificalis* was begun in the context of a similar struggle over authority, when the bishops of Rome were challenged by the Emperor Justinian. Likewise, the eleventh-century *Deeds of the Bishops of Cambrai* was written at a time secular authorities threatened to undermine the authority of the bishop.[15] Thus for the clergy, history was one of the means of defending authority.

Clerics also used history as an instrument of institutional identity. One manuscript compiled in the thirteenth century at Saint-Wandrille, for example, uses history to define the monastery. It contains a genealogy of the Carolingians from the time of Arnulf of Metz (d. c. 640) to 885 (the minor chronicle of Fontenelle), a life of St. Wandrille, a list of the bishops who had come from Saint-Wandrille, a list of the Merovingian and Carolingian kings of France, the *Discovery and Miracles of St. Wulfran,* and the acts of Abbot Mainer.[16] Through this collection of texts, most of which concern the early history of Saint-Wandrille, the compiler expressed pride in his monastery. The authority of his institution and its identity lay partially in the past, in its Merovingian origins and its close association with the Carolingian rulers.[17] It depended in contemporary times on its spiritual aura, the measures of which were the saints whose relics it possessed and the miracles worked by them, and its stature in the ecclesiastical world, as demonstrated

15. On the *Liber Pontificalis,* see L. Duchesne, ed., *Le Liber Pontificalis,* 3 vols. (Paris: E. de Boccard, 1955–57), xxxv f. The first version was composed by a contemporary of John II (533–35), Agapitus (535–6), and Silverius (536–7) and in fact ends in the middle of the Silverius life, which puts it squarely in the midst of the Justinianic wars and the controversy over Theodora's embrace of Monophysitism. For the *Inventio sancti Uulfranni,* see p. 199. For the *Gesta episcoporum Cameracensium,* see Georges Duby, *The Three Orders: Feudal Society Imagined,* trans. Arthur Goldhammer (Chicago: Chicago University Press, 1980), 19, 21–22.

16. Rouen, *Bibliothèque municipale,* Y. 237. A description of the manuscript is available in *CG,* 1:303, #1211.

17. Rosamund McKitterick, *The Frankish Kingdoms under the Carolingians* (London: Longman, 1983), 236.

by the bishops chosen from among its monks. This small, relatively plain book, however, seems neither designed for public reading nor for grand theological purposes but for the private contemplation of a reader interested in the identity of the monastery. At least one reader of the genealogy of the Carolingian rulers wanted more precise dates than the text gave, and he inserted these in the margins.[18]

That the Saint-Wandrille manuscript was probably read privately points to another feature of clerical consumption of most historical writing. It was not institutionally controlled by commentaries or a directed program of reading the way that texts which formed part of the curriculum were.[19] The texts that formed the curriculum were read with commentaries. Biblical exegesis taught the accepted readings of the Bible, as commentaries on Martianus Capella and Virgil showed readers how they were to understand these texts.[20] Hagiographies were also read institutionally, consumed as part of the liturgy and as part of the day's round of *lectio*. The meaning of the texts in part would be derived from the setting of the reading and in part through discussions of the text that would take place as part of supervised monastic reading of the text.[21]

One of the few histories other than hagiographies that *was* institutionally read was Peter Comestor's *Scholastic History*, which nearly alone among histories became part of the curriculum of the schools. Like other school texts, the readings of the *Scholastic History* were partially controlled by glossing. Many of the Norman monasteries had copies of this text, complete with glosses; some had more than one copy, suggesting that this text was as important

18. See, for example, Rouen, *Bibliothèque municipale,* Y. 237, 7r, 8r, and 9r.

19. On institutionalized reading, see Karlheinz Stierle, "Studium: Perspectives on Institutionalized Modes of Reading," *New Literary History* 21 (1990): 116.

20. On commentary, see Stierle, "Studium," 116–17.

21. See, for example, Detlef Illmer, *Formen der Erziehung und Wissensvermittlung in frühen Mittelalter,* Münchener Beiträge zur mediävistik und Renaissance-Forschung 7 (Munich: Arbeo-Gesellschaft, 1971), 36–40, on *lectio* not simply as reading but also as oral rumination on reading, *confabulatio* between older and younger monks.

in monastic education as in the school curriculum.[22] Another important text of this type was Vincent of Beauvais's massive *Mirror of History [Speculum historiale]* (c. 1244–60), which acquired indices in the early fourteenth century, probably to facilitate its use by mendicant preachers.[23]

The texts read as part of monastic public reading were distinctive in their form. They were divided into capitula so that the text could be read bit by bit as time allowed. Most histories were not divided in this way, although the *Authority of Fécamp* was. The distinction is very clear when we consider the texts contained in the "Black Book" of Saint-Ouen, which contained both the *Acts of the Archbishops* and a number of hagiographies. The hagiographies were divided into numbered *lectiones*; the other works were not.[24] Orderic may have intended his work for this kind of institutionalized reading, but he did not divide his text accordingly.[25] Most histories, then, were read only if an individual felt like doing so; there was no institutional pressure to read history.

It is also important to note that the one kind of history for which there was institutional pressure to read, hagiography, was different from other types of histories, and not only in its physical form. Hagiographies were embedded not in the linear time of history

22. I have looked at Rouen, *Bibliothèque municipale*, A. 136, A. 243, and A. 476, all of which contain glosses and all of which belonged at some time to Jumièges, although only only A. 136 has an *ex libris* (fol. 305r). Other copies of the text from the Norman archives are Rouen, *Bibliothèque municipale*, A. 167 (Notre-Dame of Eu); Rouen, *Bibliothèque municipale*, A. 100, (which belonged at various times to Noe, Le Normant, and the Cathedral of Rouen); Rouen, *Bibliothèque municipale*, A. 403 (Saint-Ouen); Eu, *Bibliothèque municipale*, ms. 2 (the canons of Eu); Louviers, *Bibliothèque municipale*, ms. 4, (Bonport); Alençon, *Bibliothèque municipale*, mss. 98 and 99 (Saint-Evroul); Cherbourg, *Bibliothèque municipale*, ms. 4 (no provenance). Lyre lists two copies in its catalog (*CG*, 2:382) and Fécamp has one as well (Ibid., 1:xxvi).

23. Monique Paulmier-Foucart, "L'Atelier Vincent de Beauvais: Recherches sur l'état des connaissances au Moyen Age d'après une encyclopédie du XIIIᵉ siècle," *Le Moyen age*, ser. 4, 34 (1979): 97–98; on the medicants and the *Mirror of History*, see Anna-Dorothee van den Brincken, "Geschichtsbetrachtung bei Vincenz von Beauvais," *Deutsches Archiv* 34 (1978): 438–43.

24. Rouen, *Bibliothèque municipale*, Y. 41.

25. Ray, "Orderic Vitalis and His Readers," 32.

but in the cyclical time of the liturgy. Even though hagiographies might be deeply rooted in a particular time, place, and sequence of events, often they lacked such grounding. For example, the biography of Peter of Avranches, a monk from Savigny, mentions that Peter as an adolescent loved playing musical instruments, particularly the vielle, and this specificity of information strongly calls up a historical individual.[26] In contrast, the life of St. Wulfran, as presented in the *Discovery of St. Wulfran,* was typological and timeless.

Generally, hagiographies written after the eleventh century about contemporary or near contemporary saints contained more specific historical details, probably because monks kept an eye out for those in their community who might be later venerated, a practice that encouraged much monastic biography.[27] However, even when a hagiography was full of historical details—the life of St. Vitalis records several attempts on the saint's life, which accords with our sense of the lawlessness of Robert Curthose's reign—the historical details were not the point. The point of hagiography was the participation of the individual in the life of the saints and the celebration of an individual's relationship with God.[28] The life was both a form of commemoration of the individual and a paradigm for action for the monks.[29] Secular histories, however, did not contain many such paradigms for action. If, for example, monks chose to read William of Poitiers's biography of William the Conqueror,

26. E. P. Sauvage, ed., *Vita b. Petri Abrincensis et b. Hamonis. Analecta Bollandiana* 2 (1883): 479.

27. Chibnall, *World of Orderic Vitalis,* 110.

28. See Marc van Uytfanghe, "L'hagiographie: un 'genre' chrétien ou antique tardif ?" *Analecta Bollandiana* III (1993): 148.

29. One example of the way this might work is demonstrated by Victor Turner, "Religious Paradigms and Political Action: Thomas Becket at the Council of Northampton," in *Dramas, Fields, and Metaphors* (Ithaca, N.Y.: Cornell University Press, 1974): 60–97. Turner argues that the paradigms of sanctity suggested a course of action to Becket in resolving a social drama—the paradigm led him to act out martyrdom. This seems to be what Stock means also in many places in *Listening for the Text* (but see esp. 29f.) when he talks about the way texts create actions. van Uytfanghe also points to a performative rather than informative quality of the hagiography intended to incite veneration or imitation.

it was most likely out of a continued interest in the world outside the monastery, to which monks continued to be tied by patronage, family, and spiritual friendship. It was certainly not to inspire either veneration (in a religious sense) or imitation, although admiration was a possibility.[30]

While monastic communities did create histories, particularly during times of crisis, and while some monks did read histories and write them, the monastery had powerful means at its disposal both to carry out the mediatory and commemorative tasks of history and to create identity and a sense of continuity with the past. It had the cult of its saints, which might regulate conduct as well as providing a focus for devotion. The continuity of the monastery with its past had a physical form of expression in the buildings of the monastery, its lands, and in the training of the bodies of new monks into conformity with the life of the house. It also had an incorporeal presence in the traditions the monks handed down orally. Thus, the monks had powerful alternatives to writing history for many of the needs that history could serve.

When an abbot who wanted a history written assigned it to a socially insignificant writer in his scriptorium, he was tacitly accepting that history, useful though it might be, was too humble a project for someone more important. When a monastery kept annals for a while, then stopped (as happened at Lyre), or when readers eschewed histories for other kinds of reading, as historians continually complained that they did, these readers too were commenting tacitly on the significance of history. As historians complained over and over again, readers saw history as marginal. The work of the Norman historians bears this out: the writing and reading of history were contingent activities.

If history had a limited place in monastic life, it had even less of a place in the cathedral schools and universities of medieval Europe. It was not one of the arts itself, and Hugh of Saint-Victor

30. See Chibnall's comments ("The Place of the Monasteries in Society," *World of Orderic Vitalis,* 45–57) on the connection between the monastic world and the outside world. It is easy to forget that through monastic patronage, monasteries were tied to secular families and relationships.

probably spoke for most schoolmen when he argued that if one were studying the arts, it was better to study treatises directly about the arts than to study the arts through literature (the appendages of the arts).[31] Although historical criticism was developed in the schools, it was applied to topics such as law and theology, which offered their practitioners a sure route to career advancement. Otto of Freising was one of the few educated in the schools who wrote history, and he was not dependent on his historical writing for his livelihood.[32] The history required in the schools was biblical—that need was met by the *Scholastic History* of Peter Comestor.

Despite the private character of most historical reading, however, many of history's functions were public in character. Histories reflected political relationships of various kinds, including relationships between institutions, between institutions and their communities, and between rulers and their subjects. As Karl Morrison has suggested, histories were about power.[33] However, communication about power, about the nature of the world, implies an audience and presumably the public consumption of history. For history to do its work of mediation, of creation of identity, for it to be effective as a monument or even to support a legal case, it had to be widely read and publicly available. Because the histories I have been discussing were written in Latin and seem to have resided primarily in monastic libraries, they were unavailable to perform these operations directly.

The impulse to broaden history beyond these boundaries is clear from the number of histories dedicated to members of the lay elite, to the dukes of Normandy, members of their families, or other important laymen and women. In dedicating their works to women, writers may, in fact, have been trying to give their texts to people who could read them, because laywomen may have been more commonly literate in Latin than men.[34] By dedicating their

---

31. Hugh of Saint-Victor, *Didascalicon*, 54.

32. On Otto's education, see *Chronica sive Historia de duabus civitatibus*, ed. and trans. Adolf Hofmister and Walter Lammers (Berlin: Rütten & Loening, 1960), xxv–xxvi.

33. Morrison, *History as a Visual Art*, 20.

34. On female literacy and patronage, see Herbert Grundmann, "Litteratus–

histories to members of the lay elite, historians brought them to the attention of the court, which was, if not always the locus of historical writing, often the implied audience for historical writing. This was true in the Carolingian period, when the authors, often themselves laymen, such as Nithard and Thegan, wrote for a mixed court audience of clerics and laity. This tradition was reborn in the German imperial court, for which Widukind, Hrosvita, and Wipo wrote. The Norman histories emerged in the Norman court shortly thereafter.

History consequently had a quasi-public place in court culture, where it could be read by only a few, and a private place in ecclesiastical culture, where it was more readily accessible but where it was apparently not much more commonly read. For history to become more important, therefore, it had to find a forum in which it might be read, it had to acquire a function compelling enough for important people to resort to reading and writing it, and it had to become accessible to its potential audience. Once it had done so, it could begin to acquire disciplinary coherence. History began to change in all of these ways simultaneously in the twelfth century, although it was not until the fourteenth century that these changes were fully evident. While these changes are clearly interrelated and simultaneous, it is helpful to consider them separately.

One of the factors which hindered the development of history as a communal project was the absence, as I have suggested above, of access to an audience other than monks. History was generally composed and read in the monastery, which in many cases limited the audience for history to the monks of one community. Even when histories circulated beyond the communities in which they

---

Illitteratus," 10; also, "Die Frauen und die Literatur im Mittelalter: Ein Beitrag zur Frage nach der Entstehung des Schriftums in der Volkssprache" *Ausgewählte Aufsätze,* 3:67–95, (Stuttgart: Anton Hiersmann, 1978). Patrick Geary, *Phantoms of Remembrance,* 5ff., has argued that women were also the primary repositories of the memories of their families, and, therefore, the gift of a history would be particularly appropriate.

were created, their circulation was erratic. Only a few works, those promoted by a patron or those which came to be considered classics, enjoyed very wide circulation. The very structure of the monastery limited its ability to support the study of the complex disciplines; its monks were limited in their mobility and in the time they might devote to study, hence the decline of monasteries as schools in the eleventh century. At the same time, it was difficult to write history anywhere but a monastery. As corporations, monasteries had great longevity and continuity. Thus, they were accretion points for books, documents, traditions, objects, inscriptions, and other historical material. Hence, it made sense for the kings of France to patronize Saint-Denis as their history workshop but also for other writers to use Saint-Denis as archives for their own research. The author of *Girart de Vienne* makes references to the books available at Saint-Denis.[35]

The result of this situation is that most histories continued to be written in monasteries, as they were in Normandy in the twelfth century. The real difference was probably the degree to which the court came to take an interest in and sometimes control the contents of the histories written at one or more monastic centers and to commission historical writing outside of the monastic precinct.

There were really two sorts of historical patronage. One form was predominant among the Norman patrons of history, a personal link between an individual historian, who might be either a monk or a member of the court circle, and an individual ruler. Henry II's historians included the monks Robert of Torigni and John of Marmoutier, who dedicated an abbreviated history of the counts of Anjou to Henry around 1170, the itinerant justice, Roger of Hoveden, and Wace, a secular cleric with a position at Caen.[36] In similar fashion, Henry III (1216–72) assisted Matthew Paris (d. 1259) in keeping the chronicle of St. Alban's, by making sure in-

35. Guenée, *Histoire et culture historique,* 118; Bloch, "Genealogy as a Medieval Mental Structure," 148.

36. Rob. of Tor., 1:334. See Bezzola, *Formation de la littérature courtoise,* pt. 3, vol. 1, 105ff. This volume is entirely devoted to literature at the English court in the second half of the twelfth century.

formation came his way. So that Matthew could see better and record the events more accurately, the king invited the historian up to the royal dais during the offering of a vase of Jesus's blood at Westminster.[37]

A second kind of patronage was more institutionalized. Here a monastic center produced history on an on-going basis for a series of rulers. This did not happen in Normandy (although Marmoutier showed signs of playing this role for the counts of Anjou), but it clearly occurred at Saint-Denis.[38] Abbot Suger of Saint-Denis (d. 1151) produced a biography of Louis VI the Fat (1108–37) and began a biography of his son Louis VII. It may have been on Suger's orders that Odo of Deuil created the set of notes which became his history of the Second Crusade.[39] By the end of the century, the link between the monastery and the king was firmly forged. Rigord, the first historian to be officially titled a royal historiographer and the first to use the term "Augustus" to describe the king, composed his *Deeds of Philip Augustus* (c. 1196) at that monastery.[40]

However, this link between the monastery and the monarchy did not mean that Saint-Denis completely monopolized French royal historiography. Philip II also patronized historical writing by members of his court. Helinand of Froidmont (d. 1215), before his conversion and retirement to Froidmont, was a jongleur at Philip's court, while William Brito, royal chaplain and tutor to Philip's children, continued Rigord's work and wrote a poetic treatment of the history as well. Similarly, Louis IX patronized a historian from his court circle, Vincent of Beauvais, who was both the king's *lector* and, according to Bernard Guy, a familiar of the queen's house-

37. Matthew Paris, *Chronica Majora*, 7 vols., ed. Henry Richard Luard (reprint, Wiesbaden: Kraus reprint, 1964). 4:644–45.

38. On the historical tradition at Saint-Denis, including the genesis of the *Grandes chroniques de France,* see Gabrielle Spiegel, "Studies in the Chronicle Tradition of Saint-Denis," (Ph.D diss., Johns Hopkins University, 1974).

39. On these texts, see Bezzola, *Formation de la littérature courtoise*, pt. 3, vol. 2, 354–55.

40. On Rigord as royal historiographer, see Guenée, *Histoire et culture historique*, 340.

hold. The king received a presentation copy of Vincent's massive *Historical Mirror*.[41] While the title of royal historiographer lapsed for some time after Rigord, the kings of France maintained a great interest in the histories written about them through the fourteenth century. The title was revived in the fifteenth century, when Jean Chartier and Jean Castel (the grandson of the court writer and historian Christine de Pisan) were both official historians.[42] Thus the court, if not the primary place where history was written, became more and more an important factor in its production and a potential audience for historical writing.

Lesser courts also became sites for historical production. Giselbert of Mons wrote his *Chronicle of Hainault* for Baldwin V (d. 1195), whose chancellor he was. Lambert of Ardres wrote his history of the counts of Guines, hoping to regain Count Arnold's favor after an unfortunate misunderstanding.[43] Gaston IV of Foix in the fifteenth century followed that blazed trail by having the keeper of his records, Michael of Vernes, write a history of Foix.[44]

Around the same time that the court began to exercise more control over some historical writing, the city emerged as a new and increasingly important venue for history as well. Most of the extant vernacular civic histories date from the fourteenth century, when they were not uncommon, but their Latin prototypes (for example, the chronicle of Landulf Senior of Milan) appeared as early as the eleventh century. Although the Italian civic chronicles, like those of Dino Compagni, the Villanis, and of Guicciardini are the most famous, civic chronicles were not confined to Italy. Jean d'Outremeuse was the author of a *Deeds of Liège,* and Montpellier had its

41. Auguste Molinier, *Les Sources de l'histoire de France, des origines aux guerres d'Italie,* 6 vols. (Paris: A. Picard, 1901–6), 3:93. See also Paulmier-Foucart, "L'Atelier Vincent de Beauvais."

42. Guenée, *Histoire et culture historique,* 340–42.

43. Lambert of Ardres, *Historia comitum Ghisnensium,* 638.

44. Giselbert of Mons, *Chronicon Hanoniensis* in *MGH SS,* 21:481–601; on Lambert of Ardres, see Bezzola, *Formation de la littérature courtoise,* vol. 3, pt. 2, 431; Michel de Bernis, *Chronique des comtes de Foix et senhors de Bearn* in *Choix de chroniques et mémoires relatifs a l'histoire de France,* Jean Buchon, ed., vol. 1 (Paris: Desrez, 1836).

own civic chronicle, the *Little Treasury (Petit Thalamus)*, begun in the thirteenth century and continued into the fifteenth. Many German cities also produced such chronicles.[45]

𝕼

History was embraced in cities and courts because it was here that people found compelling uses for it. One use was clearly ideological. The Franco-Flemish nobility used history in a pointed way to bolster its authority. This was so compelling that it invoked a royalist historical rejoinder.[46] Obviously the elite of the early thirteenth century did not invent this ideological use of history. It was commonplace among the Roman historians and also among the Carolingians. Charles Martel and his descendents had used history with great finesse.[47] But such uses of history require not only a certain level of literacy but a certain dependence on the written word as well. Both conditions existed to a degree in the Carolingian period, but it was not until the eleventh century that these conditions again began to reproduce themselves.

Increasing numbers of legal disputes also assisted in the process. Debates over rights that might have been settled in the earlier Middle Ages by force were increasingly likely to be adjudicated in in-

45. On the *Petit Thalamus,* see Molinier, *Les Sources,* 4:38. It has been partially edited in *Thalamus parvus. Le Petit Thalamus de Montpellier* (Montpellier: J. Martel, 1840). For Jean d'Outremeuse's *Geste de Liège,* see *Ly myreur des histors, chronique de Jean des Preis, dit d'Outremeuse,* 7 vols. (Brussels: M. Hayez, 1864–87), vol. 5. Many of the German urban chronicles have been published: see *Chroniken der deutschen Städte vom 14. bis in's 16 Jahrhundert,* 36 vols. (Leipzig: S. Hirzel (places and publishers vary), 1862–1931). See also H. Hofmann, "Stadtgeschichte," in "Articulationsformen historischen Wissens in der lateinischen Historiographie des hohen und späten Mittelalters," in *La littérature historiographique,* 2:464–74.

46. Spiegel, "Social Change," 129–30; *Romancing the Past,* 296ff.

47. On the role of Charles Martel's brother, Childebrand, in the continuation of the chronicle of Fredegar, see *The Fourth Book of the Chronicle of Fredegar,* trans. J. M. Wallace-Hadrill (London: Thomas Nelson & Sons, 1960), xxv–xxvii; on the *Royal Frankish Annals,* Nithard, and Angilbert, see Bernard Scholz, *Carolingian Chronicles: Royal Frankish Annals and Nithard's Histories* (Ann Arbor: University of Michigan Press, 1970), 4, 22–23. Angilbert was the author of a history of his monastery, Saint-Riquier, and the *Carmen de Carolo magno* is sometimes attributed to him.

formal or formal courts (although violence never lost its appeal). The treatise on the liberty of Fécamp grew out of one such rather local dispute. More famous cases involve Louis IX's historical inquiry into the relationship between the kings of France and the pope, and Edward III's similar inquiries into his rights in Scotland and France. Froissart described the latter inquiry.[48]

Historians wrote copiously during the great conflicts of the fourteenth and fifteenth centuries. William Guiart wrote his poetic history of the descendents of Philip II, the *Branch of Royal Lineages [Branche des royal lignages]* (c. 1304–6), as a defence of French attempts to conquer Flanders. The *Annals of Ghent [Annales Gandenses]* (to 1308–1310) took the corresponding pro-Flemish perspective.[49] The French royal struggle with the dukes of Burgundy, which lasted for most of the fifteenth century, also spawned abundant history. Thomas Basin (d. 1491) and Enguerran de Monstrelet (d. 1453) wrote on the Burgundian side. The dukes of Burgundy eventually followed French royal practice and appointed Georges Chastellain (d. 1475) and Jean Molinet (d. 1507) as official court historiographers.[50] In addition to the official historians of France,

48. Guenée, *Histoire et culture historique,* 349. Froissart, *Oeuvres de Froissart,* 25 vols., ed. Kervyn de Lettenhove and Joseph Marie Bruno (Brussels: Devaux/Closson, 1867–77), 2:325ff. The third redaction makes reference to an English clerk, "licensed in rights and laws and very learned in three languages, Latin, French, and English," who carried out the argument before Edward III (326). A further discussion of Edward's rights (from the first redaction) is found further along in the text, where one of Edward's party makes reference to claims he enjoys by his familial proximity to the throne. The French king counters by claiming election by the twelve peers and the prelates of the realm (366f.).

49. *Branche des royal lignages, chronique métrique de Guillaume Guiart,* 2 vols., ed. J. A. Buchon (Paris: Verdière, 1828); *Annales Gandenses,* ed. and trans. Hilda Johnstone (New York: Oxford University Press, 1951); also Molinier, *Les Sources,* 3:190–91; 201.

50. Thomas Basin, *Histoire de Charles VII,* 2 vols., ed. and trans. Charles Samaran (Paris: Société "Les Belles Lettres," 1933–44) and *Histoire de Louis XI,* 3 vols., ed. and trans. Charles Samaran (Paris: Société d'édition "Les Belles Lettres," 1963–72); Enguerran de Monstrelet, *Chroniques,* 6 vols., ed. Douët d'Arcq (Paris: Société d'histoire, 1857–62); Georges Chastellain, *Chronique des ducs de Bourgogne,* 2 vols, ed. J. A. Buchon (Paris: Verdière, 1827); Jean Molinet, *Chroniques de Jean Molinet,* 3 vols., ed. Georges Doutrepont and Omer Jodogne (Brussels: Palais des académies,

Matthew d'Escouchy (d. 1482) and Philippe de Commynes (d. 1511) wrote for France.[51] Thus, histories became expressions of the policies of a particular court. They served as indoctrination of the elite into a particular view of things, but they also created the groundwork for resolving political conflicts otherwise than through violence, a tendency which was not fully apparent until the sixteenth century.

In cities, history also served as an accompaniment and sometimes an alternative to factional warfare. Cities were complicated entities, where large numbers of people of diverse classes, occupations, affiliations, and interests were thrown together and forced to coexist. In contrast to the monastic world, where differences between the monks could be reconciled by common rituals, cities exacerbated competition. Like courts, cities were also environments in which the authorities strongly desired the suppression of violence.[52] Authorities were generally unsuccessful in completely suppressing violence, which continued to be a factor in urban life. However, increasingly there were new forms of competition between urban dwellers which did not partake of violence. Because courts and cities were places where significant numbers of educated men and women were concentrated, and because they were environments in which texts might easily be borrowed, copied, or otherwise circulate, competition sometimes took a literary form. Instead of attacking a rival physically, one might instead demonstrate one's intellectual superiority to that individual. Similarly, one

---

1935–37). On the official title granted Chastellain and Molinet, see Guenée, *Histoire et culture historique,* 342–43. On these writers, see Molinier, *Les Sources,* 4:197–98, 245–48, 256–57; 5:47–49.

51. Mathieu d'Escouchy, *Chronique de Mathieu d'Escouchy,* 3 vols., ed. G. Du Fresne de Beaucourt (Paris: J. Renouard, 1863–64); Philippe de Commynes, *The Memoirs of Philippe de Commynes,* 2 vols., ed. Samuel Kinser, trans. Isabelle Cazeaux (Columbia, S.C.: University of South Carolina Press, 1969–73); Kinser warns that the only French edition, *Mémoires de Philippe de Commynes,* ed. Joseph Calmette (Paris: H. Champion, 1924–25), is not adequate.

52. I have been influenced here by Norbert Elias, *The Civilizing Process,* trans. Edmund Jephcott (New York: Urizen Books, 1978) and by Stephen Jaeger's use of Elias's ideas in *The Origins of Courtliness.*

might refute the claims of others by advancing one's own claims in written form. Thus, not only were histories important because they advanced ideological positions, but the writing and reading of history was another form the competition took, for it was a demonstration of the individual's cultivation in a world in which cultivation was increasingly a form of personal capital.

History's exemplary function also became more important as political life became more complex and as readers became more interested in reading about politics. One fourteenth-century vernacular manuscript from Normandy demonstrates that the association between political life and history was clear to the individual who compiled it.[53] The first text is a French history of Normandy, which blended both the Latin historical tradition and the French romance tradition of Norman history, for it included stories about Robert the Devil.[54] This is followed by a poem on governance copied and inserted in the text by a seventeenth-century owner of the manuscript.[55] The chronicle was originally followed by a French mirror of princes, written primarily in prose, and then by Honoré Bonet's *Tree of Battles,* a treatise on the laws of war, although because Bonet's purpose was to subordinate the military nobility to the command and control of the king, it can be said to be about governance as well.[56] In contrast to the plainness of most earlier historical manuscripts, this one contains many illuminations touched with gold, twenty-one in the historical portion of the manuscript alone, suggesting both that the individual who commissioned the work was well-to-do and that he considered the contents important. The fifth folio features a receipt from one mer-

---

53. Rouen, *Bibliothèque municipale,* Y. 26. For a description, see *CG,* 1:309.

54. Robert the Devil has been linked to both Robert the Magnificent and Robert Curthose. On the various versions, see Édouard Frère, *Manuel de bibliographe normand ou dictionnaire bibliographique et historique,* 2 vols. (reprint, New York: Burt Franklin, n.d.) 2:475–77.

55. Fol. 162v, "Fait de la main de Jean Cheminel"; Cheminel's name is written on 163r with the date 1616.

56. On Bonet, see N. A. R. Wright, "The *Tree of Battles* of Honoré Bouvet and the Laws of War," in *War, Literature, and Politics in the late Middle Ages,* C. T. Allmand, ed. (Liverpool: University of Liverpool Press, 1976), 12–31.

chant to another for the purchase of some sheep, which also suggests that the bourgeoisie were now part of the audience for history.

☙

The ability of history to speak to a wider audience was, of course, greatly enhanced by the emergence of vernacular history. Into the twelfth century, the dominance of Latin as the medium of history was unchallenged and clerics encouraged the laity to learn Latin on the assumption that Latin would continue to be the main language of learning. Adémar of Chabannes praised Duke William V of Aquitaine (d. 1030) in the eleventh century for his literacy.[57] Philip of Harvengt (d. 1183) wrote several letters encouraging laymen to acquire Latin letters and become readers. Philip commented in a letter to Henry the Liberal of Champagne that those who learned only the vernacular and not Latin were seized by asinine laziness.[58]

In Philip's lifetime, however, an increasing variety and number of texts were available in the French vernacular. A late-twelfth-century French reader could find moral instruction, saints' lives, lapidaries and bestiaries, books of manners, epics, romances, lyrics, and many histories. The earliest French history, Gaimar's *History of the English,* appeared around 1135, to be followed by other vernacular histories, including the Norman histories of Wace and Benoît of Sainte-Maure. Nobles who might have hesitated to commission a Latin history, commissioned vernacular ones, such as Baudouin d'Avesnes who supervised the compilation of a French chronicle around 1281.[59] Laymen who would never have been able to write a Latin history wrote vernacular ones, like the vernacular prose histories of the Fourth Crusade of Geoffrey of Villehardouin

57. For a discussion of this passage, see Karl Leyser, *The Ascent of Latin Europe* (Oxford: Oxford University Press, 1986), 8–9.

58. On Philip of Harvengt, see James Thompson, *Literacy of the Laity,* 139–41, 143–44; for the text of the letter, see 162f., no. 157.

59. See Molinier, *Les Sources,* 3:175–76. There is no full edition of this long and problematic work, extant in two main versions.

(after 1207) and Robert of Clari (c. 1206–16), and Jean de Joinville's biography of Louis IX.[60] Vernacular history was preferred when the audience for a history was likely to include large numbers of lay people. William of Saint-Paer, in his verse *History of Mont Saint-Michel* (c. 1184), employed the vernacular for that reason; it was designed to inform pilgrims.[61] A century later, William de Nangis, who was the keeper of charters at Saint-Denis and producer of many Latin works, translated his own Latin chronicle to inform visitors to the monastery.[62] By the time William de Nangis produced his work, vernacular history was commonplace.

Vernacular history offered the laity not only access to written history but also the possibility of controlling the contents of history more directly than before. William the Marshall's son commissioned a French biography of his father (c. 1219). In the fourteenth century and fifteenth century, biographies of such paragons became highly popular, enhancing the exemplary functions of history among the laity. Among the men so commemorated were Bertran du Guesclin (d. 1371), the Black Prince (d. 1376), and Jean le Meingre (Marshal Boucicault) (d. 1421). A late but related development was the rise of memoirs in the fifteenth century, such as those of Pierre le Fruitier (c. 1409), Jacques du Clerq (composed between 1448 and 1467), and Philippe de Commynes (c. 1498).[63]

60. Geoffroi de Villehardouin, *La Conquête de Constantinople*, ed. Edmond Faral (Paris: Société d'édition "Les Belles Lêttres, 1938–39); Robert de Clari, *La Conquête de Constantinople*, 2 vols., ed. Philippe Lauer (Paris: E. Champion, 1924).

61. See Paul Redlich, *Roman du Mont Saint-Michel,* 1:

Many pilgrims who come to the Mount often ask, and well they may, how the church was first founded and built. Those who tell them the story that they want to know do not have it well in their memories, thus they go stumbling and making errors in many places. To make it openly heard for those who know nothing of literacy *(clergie),* a young man, a monk of the Mount—God grant him a place in his realm!—recently translated it from Latin and in secret set laid it out in the true vernacular for his monastery.

62. On William de Nangis, see Molinier, *Les Sources,* 3:102–4. There is no edition of the French *Chronique des rois de France,* but there is an edition of the Latin chronicle, *Chronique latine de Guillaume de Nangis,* ed. H. Géraud (Paris: Renouard, 1843).

63. For William the Marshall, see David Crouch, *William Marshall: Court, Ca-*

As the vernacular was increasingly used as a literary language, important Latin works were translated into the vernacular to serve both practical and abstract needs. William of Briane (fl. 1215) translated the pseudo-Turpin chronicle, the Latin history which contained the story of Roland, one of fifteen vernacular versions.[64] Baudry of Bourgueil's *History of the First Crusade* was translated around 1200, as was William of Tyre's *History of Outremer.*[65] Jacques de Vitry's *History of the East* (c. 1240) was translated into French later in the thirteenth century.[66] The great scholastic histories were also translated. The *Scholastic History* of Peter Comestor was translated between 1291 and 1295 by Guiart des Moulins, while Vincent of Beauvais's *Mirror of History* was translated in the fourteenth century by Jean de Vignay.[67] Many vernacular versions of classical histories were also circulating by the early thirteenth century.[68] Around 1260, Alphonse of Poitiers translated the great Latin chronicle kept at Saint-Denis (his version ends in the year 1214), while around 1274, Primat, a monk at Saint-Denis, translated the latest version of the chronicle and created the first part of the *Grandes chroniques de France,* which became official. Thus by the end of the thirteenth century, a critical mass of histories were available to the vernacular audience, not only original works of history but also translations of important Latin works, creating the con-

---

reer and Chivalry in the Angevin Empire 1147–1219 (London: Longman, 1990), 1–2; also P. Meyer, ed., *Histoire de Guillaume le Maréchal,* 3 vols. (Paris: Société de l'histoire, 1891–1901); Cuvelier, *La Chanson de Bertrand du Guesclin,* ed. Jean-Claude Faucon (Toulouse: Éditions universitaires du sud, 1990); Chandos Herald, *La Vie du Prince Noir,* ed. Diana B. Tyson (Tubingen: M. Niemeyer, 1975); *Le Livre des fais du bon messire Jehan le Maingre: dit Bouciquaut, mareschal de France et governeur de Jennes,* ed. Denis Lalande (Geneva: Droz, 1985); Jacques Duclercq, *Mémoires de Jacques Du Clerq,* ed. Frederick Baron de Reiffenbert, 2d ed. (Brussels: Lacrosse, 1835–36).

64. See Spiegel, "Social Change," 131, nn. 4–6.

65. Paul Zumthor, *Histoire littéraire de la France médiévale* (Paris: Presses universitaires de France, 1954), 204–5.

66. Jacques de Vitry, *La Traduction de l'"Historia orientalis" de Jacques de Vitry,* ed. Claude Buridant (Paris: Klincksieck, 1986), 15–19.

67. Zumthor, *Histoire Littéraire,* 185; Molinier, *Les sources,* 3:93–94, 295.

68. See Spiegel, "Social Change," 132–33.

ditions for the intertextual dialogues of the fourteenth and fifteenth centuries that I have already described.

The rise of the vernacular in historical writing did not mean that Latin histories disappeared, but these works were produced for a different audience with different needs and demands. Because it was the language that could transcend the regionalism of the vernaculars, Latin continued in ecclesiastical circles to be the primary language of record until at least the fourteenth century. Most monastic histories continued to be written in Latin, such as the *Chronicle of Fécamp (Chronicon Fiscamnense)* which ended in the mid-thirteenth century.[69] Although some of the biographies of Louis IX, such as those of Joinville and William of St. Pathus (d. 1303), were in the vernacular, many others, such as the Saint-Denis biography (c. 1297) and Gilon of Reims's biography, and the works produced for Louis's canonization dossier, in particular the biographies by Geoffrey of Beaulieu (c. 1274) and William of Chartres (d. 1282), were in Latin.[70] Bernard Guy, the inquisitor and historian (d. 1331), wrote all of his historical works in Latin originally, although his *Flowers of the Chronicles* (1306–31) and *Chronicle of the Kings of France* (1312–20) were translated for Charles V of France in the second half of the fourteenth century by Jean Golein.[71]

Works originally composed in the vernacular might be translated into Latin for the clerical or international audience. Richard, abbot of the Trinity in London, had Ambrose of Evreux's *History of the Holy War* (1190–92) translated from French into Latin around 1222, and Francesco Pipino (mid-fourteenth century) translated the *Book of Eracles* (early to mid-thirteenth century), itself a vernacular translation of William of Tyre's *History of Jerusalem* (c. 1173–84), back into Latin for his universal chronicle.[72] A Latin chronicle

---

69. *Chronicon Fiscamnense,* in *PL,* 147:479–84.

70. The works of William of St. Pathus, the Saint-Denis biographer, Geoffrey of Beaulieu, and William of Chartres have been printed in *Recueil des historiens des Gaules et de la France,* vol. 20 (Paris: Imprimerie royale, 1840); on Gilon of Reims, whose work is now lost, see Molinier, *Les Sources,* 3:116.

71. There are no complete editions of Bernard Guy's Latin historical works; for Bernard Guy and Jean Golein, see Molinier, *Les Sources,* 3:184–87; 4:67–68.

72. Ambrose of Évreux, *L'Estoire de la guerre sainte,* ed. M. G. Paris (Paris:

of the kings of France was kept at Saint-Denis to the end of the Middle Ages, side by side with the *Grandes chroniques*. Not all of the Latin chronicle has survived, however, in contrast to the many manuscripts of the French chronicle.

♔

The vernacular made it possible for lay people to write history for themselves, at least the history of their own times, and these lay writers were joined by increasing numbers of secular clerics; as the audience for history grew outside of the monastery, so did the frequency with which history was composed outside the monastery. However, while from the twelfth century history was increasingly viewed as having important ideological uses and was being more widely read in secular venues such as the court and city, history took a long time to develop the kind of disciplinary cohesion enjoyed by subjects like law, theology, and medicine which were entrenched in the universities. Charles Radding and William Clarke have argued that as these studies attracted increasing numbers of students in the eleventh century, the masters and students engaged in an intense intellectual conversation, both oral and intertextual, that led, by the end of the twelfth century, to the creation of a body of disciplinary material all were expected to master and to the development of common analytic methods.[73] By the thirteenth century, these disciplines had textbooks, and those scholars who wrote in each discipline used common methods of citation and argument which permitted them to critique each others's work.

In the practice of history, however, this kind of intense conversation was absent for most of the Middle Ages. While philosophical and theological ideas were subjected to the close scrutiny of

Imprimerie nationale, 1897); the translation: *Das "Itinerarium peregrinorum,"* ed. H. E. Meyer (Stuttgart: A. Hiersemann, 1962); *Chronique d'Ernoul et de Bernard le Trésorier,* ed. Louis de Mas-Latrie (Paris: Renouard, 1871); Franciscus Pippinus, *Chronicon* in *Rerum italicarum scriptores,* vol. 9, ed. Ludovico Muratori (Milan: Palatina, 1726), 587–752.

73. Radding and Clarke, *Medieval Architecture, Medieval Learning,* 4–5.

debate and public disputation, history was not required to prove its truth in any public forum. This does not mean that there was no intertextual dialogue in the writing of history. The work of the Norman historians shows abundant evidence that such a dialogue existed. Dudo of Saint-Quentin's history of the Norman dukes, after all, was the text with which all later historians of Normandy had to come to terms, and all of the Norman historians were shaped by the histories and other sorts of writing that defined their horizons of expectations.

Despite this dialogue, however, among historians through the twelfth century, there was little of the intense and personal interchange that characterized scholasticism from its inception, and little sophisticated criticism of the work of others. The interest in scholastic ideas called forth immediate reactions from readers to which scholars had to respond. When Anselm published his *Proslogion,* his proof of the existence of God was immediately challenged by Ganilo; Anselm not only modified his argument to take into account Ganilo's objections, but also circulated these comments with his response to them along with his text. For the scholastics, learning was a communal project.[74]

The closest medieval historians came to such a critique of each others' work was the criticism leveled at Geoffrey of Monmouth's work in the last quarter of the twelfth century by William of Newburgh and Gerald of Wales.[75] William of Newburgh's response was interesting, for he compared Geoffrey's work to other histories of the period, and he rejected it because of its disagreement with them. He was thus groping for critical criteria for condemning Geoffrey's work. Gerald of Wales, however, relied on invective. Despite these differences of approach, tellingly neither type of criticism diminished the enthusiasm of other historians for the *History of the Kings of Britain.* Thus, what dialogue there was about history

---

74. On these issues, see Carruthers, *Book of Memory,* 111–12.

75. For William of Newburgh, see above, pp. 124–25; Gerald of Wales, *Girardi Cambrensis Opera,* vol. 6 (Rolls Series, 21), ed. J. S. Brewer (London: Longman, 1862), 58–59, 179.

was carried on in a muted and private way, and did not affect historical writing as a whole.

Because history had not yet developed a body of practice by the fourteenth century, historians like William Guiart and Jean le Bel (d. c. 1370) were still relying on invective to attack works with which they disagreed.[76] There were many possible notions of historical truth, and historians could not agree on these; often they were unable to articulate the criteria by which they rejected one work in favor of another. Historians did not even necessarily strive for internal consistency in their own works. Vincent of Beauvais was content to report in one part of his *Mirror of History* that the Holy Lance was sent by Harun Ar-Rashid to Charlemagne as a gift and in another place that it was found during the siege of Antioch. The inconsistency apparently did not concern him.[77]

These kinds of inconsistencies could only be resolved when history became fully an object of study. There are some indications of movement in that direction by the thirteenth century in Dominican and minorite circles. Vincent of Beauvais originally conceived of his *Great Mirror,* his comprehensive encyclopaedia, as comprising two parts, the *Mirror of History* and the *Mirror of Nature.* Although he later added a third part, the *Mirror of Doctrine* to the other two, by devoting such efforts to history, Vincent indicated his esteem for its study.[78] Other members of the order also devoted much effort to the writing of history. Vincent's contemporary, Gerard de Frachet, wrote a history of the order at the com-

---

76. Guiart, *Branche des royal lignages,* 5–9, lambastes trouvères for filling their histories with lies: "Let God give me the power to finish what I have begun truthfully, because in this book I do not want to follow the trouvères, who to be more pleasing fill their romances with fables and great open lies" (8); Jean le Bel, *Chronique de Jean le Bel,* 2 vols, ed. Jules Viard and Eugène Déprez (Paris: Renouard/Laurens, 1904–5), 1–2, also inveighs against trouvères, although he explicitly relates their lying to their need to make things rhyme. Guiart was writing in verse and the vehemence of his comments may reflect the growing contemporary view that verse was inadequate to the writing of history. On this issue see Spiegel, "Social Change." On Jean le Bel, see also Diana Tyson, "Jean le Bel: Portrait of a Chronicler," *Journal of Medieval History* 12 (1986): 315–32.

77. Paulmier-Foucard, "Ecrire l'histoire au XIII^c siècle," 67–69.

78. Paulmier-Foucard, "L'Atelier Vincent de Beauvais," 88–89.

mand of the general.[79] Geoffrey de Beaulieu and William of Chartres, the biographers of St. Louis, were both Dominicans as well. Franciscan missionaries like William of Ruysbroek contributed accounts of their travels and the histories of the places they went.[80] The next generation of historians included the Dominican inquisitor, Bernard Guy. It is tempting to see the Dominican and Franciscan involvement with the writing of history as arising from their various intellectual roles: as teachers and scholastics trained in the forms of historical inquiry used in the studies of theology and law; as missionaries among strikingly different cultures; and as inquisitors, driven to sift through competing narratives for the one acceptable narrative which would permit the restoration of religious order. More generally, however, history was a mine of *exempla* for orders whose primary function was preaching.

The humanists too granted a greater measure of importance to history, although this was only fully articulated by Bruni. Humanist training revived the habit of framing questions and answers about society historically. I suspect there is a connection between the humanists' overwhelmingly urban origins, the growing importance of historical writing in urban settings, and this new valuation of history. For fifteenth-century humanists, history was a tool in the formation of citizens, and history reappeared in the curriculum for the first time since the study of history had been advocated by Quintilian and Cicero as a matter of some interest for the orator.[81]

The rise of interest in history in the later Middle Ages is also

79. On Gerard de Frachet, see Molinier, *Les Sources*, 3:79–80. There is no modern edition, although there is a translation, *Lives of the Brethren of the Order of Preachers*, trans. Placid Conway (Benziger, 1924).

80. Albert t' Serstevens, ed. and trans., *Les précurseurs de Marco Polo* (Paris: Arthaud, 1959).

81. Quintilian, *Institutiones oratoriae*, X:1:31–34; Cicero, *De oratore*, 2:12;51–63. On the humanist rediscovery of history, see L. F. Green, *Chronicle into History: An Essay on the Interpretations of History in Florentine Fourteenth-Century Chronicles* (Cambridge: Cambridge University Press, 1972); also see Eric Cochrane, *Historians and Historiography in the Italian Renaissance* (Chicago: University of Chicago Press, 1981), 3–9, on Bruni's notions of history.

implied by the pattern of manuscript survivals of histories from the central Middle Ages. While there are seven extant manuscripts of the *Deeds of the Dukes* of Robert of Torigni from the twelfth and thirteenth centuries (and one lost manuscript that we know of), there are fifteen manuscripts from the fourteenth century and afterward. Clearly the *Deeds* was no longer current, but it was nonetheless attracting a new readership.[82] A similar pattern prevailed for the *Two Cities* of Otto of Freising, which was attracting a broader audience in the fifteenth century than it had in the twelfth, judging by manuscript survivals.[83]

History thus found a place and became an object of study before its methods came to be explicitly explored. Giovanni Annio da Viterbo (c. 1432–1502) was the first writer to discuss rules for writing history since the classical period.[84] By then, however, history already occupied a more significant position in the constellation of knowledge than it had enjoyed for most of the Middle Ages.

---

82. On these manuscripts, see van Houts, *GND*, 229–59.

83. Otto of Freising, *Chronicon*, in *MGH SS*, 20:100–114. Roger Wilmans identified more than forty manuscripts of which five date to the twelfth century, two to the late twelfth or early thirteenth century, nine to the thirteenth century, none to the fourteenth century, and twenty to the fifteenth and sixteenth centuries (there is no date given for eight manuscripts).

84. See Cochrane, *Historians and Historiography in the Italian Renaissance*, 432–35. Interestingly enough, Nanni's comments were in the context of a forgery. On this subject and the relationship between forgery and historical criticism, see Anthony Grafton, *Forgers and Critics* (Princeton, N.J.: Princeton University Press, 1990), esp. 38, 49.

ℚ Appendix 1: History and Hagiography

The question of history's relationship with hagiography was first raised in a modern context by Baudouin de Gaiffier.[1] De Gaiffier argued that the hagiographer approached the task of writing a biography of a saint differently from the way a historian approached the same task. The saint's life was the fruit of a cult that demanded new literary forms. Texts were continually "rejuvenated" over time and depended on the Bible for their vocabulary of words and stories.

More recent scholars have since modified some of de Gaiffier's positions in a number of ways. While Martin Heinzel-

1. See Baudouin de Gaiffier, "L'Hagiographe et son public au XIᵉ siècle," in *Miscellanea historica in honorem Leonis van der Essen* (Paris and Brussels: Éditions universitaires, 1947), 135–66; "Mentalité de l'hagiographe médiéval d'après quelques travaux récents," *Analecta Bollandiana* 86 (1968): 391–99; "Hagiographie et historiographie: Quelques aspects du problème," in *La storiografia altomedievale*, vol. 1 (Spoleto: Centro italiano di studi sull'alto medioevo), 139–66 and discussion 179–196; and the essays published in his three collections, *Études critiques d'hagiographie et d'iconologie* (Brussels: Société des Bollandistes, 1967); *Recherches d'hagiographie latine* (Brussels: Société des Bollandistes, 1971), and *Recueil d'hagiographie* (Brussels: Société des Bollandistes, 1977).

mann in his work on translation narratives has accepted de Gaiffier's distinction, he sees translation texts as being more historical than other kinds of hagiographic writing.[2] However, not all scholars have seen a rift between hagiography and history. Thomas Heffernan prefers the term sacred biography to hagiography precisely because he sees lives of the saints as not fundamentally different from the lives of those less holy.[3] Felice Lifshitz advances a similar position, arguing that the failure to treat hagiographies as histories is a relic of positivism and a response to the miraculous content of such biographies, and that the modern discussion of genre arises from genre as currently understood, not as medieval writers would have thought of it.[4] Marc van Uytfanghe has suggested that hagiography be considered a discourse, comprising many genres, most of which did not emerge until well after late antiquity, although he seems to argue for the existence of distinctly hagiographic genres after that time.[5]

These issues are complex, however. For instance, because medieval people often did not make generic distinctions of the type we make, it does not necessarily follow that they made no distinctions. Medieval writers, for instance, did distinguish between texts they thought were true and those that were not, even if once again, their criteria for truth were different from ours. Nor did medieval people always accept miracles as true without question. Marc van Uytfanghe charts the ebb and flow of the acceptance of the miraculous, and particularly the thaumaturgical aspects of the miraculous, in late antiquity and the early Middle Ages.[6] Not only might some people be suspicious of the miraculous but different writers had different conceptions of the miraculous, and these changed over time. André Vauchez has shown that the taste for the miraculous ebbed in the thirteenth century only to surge back in the fifteenth; changing notions of what was necessary for sanctity were reflected in canonization testimony.[7] Indeed, depending on audience, one writer might express a dif-

2. Martin Heinzelmann, *Translationsberichete und andere Quellen des Reliquienkultes* (Turnhout: Brepols, 1979).

3. Thomas Heffernan, *Sacred Biography: Saints and Their Biographers in the Middle Ages* (Oxford: Oxford University Press, 1988), esp. 38–71.

4. Felice Lifshitz, "Beyond Positivism and Genre: 'Hagiographical' Texts as Historical Narrative," *Viator* 25 (1994): 95–113.

5. van Uytfanghe, "L'Hagiographie," 148–49.

6. Marc van Uytfanghe, "La Controverse biblique et patristique autour du miracle, et ses répercussions sur l'hagiographie dans l'Antiquité tardive et le haut Moyen Age latin," in *Hagiographie, cultures et sociétés* (Paris: Études Augustiniennes, 1981), 205–31, esp. 216–19.

7. De Gaiffier, "Hagiographie et historiographie," 147; Marc van Uytfanghe, "L'Hagiographe et son public à l'époque mérovingienne," *Studia Patristica* 16 (1985), 55.

ferent stance toward the miraculous in different works. For example, Stephen of Fougères anticipates the incredulity of his audience in his *Life of St. Vitalis* but makes no reference to incredulity in his *Life of William Firmat*.

Methodological distinctions are probably not helpful in resolving the question of how history is related to hagiography. Some historians were also hagiographers, such as William of Malmesbury, Bede, and Wace, and presumably used similar methods in both sorts of works. Furthermore, the absence of common historical methods meant that historians were free to authenticate their work in the same ways hagiographers employed, and history, like hagiography, sometimes had a performative aspect, calling the reader to emulate the actions of heroes.

However, I am not so ready to throw out the notion of genre as a way of distinguishing between texts, although the notion of genre would have to be refined. In fact, such a description of medieval genre is available, Jauss's idea of the "horizon of expectations."[8] The "horizon of expectations" is the body of texts which influence both how an author shapes a text and how the reader interprets it. The notion of the horizon of expectations recognizes that medieval writers did not invent new forms every time they wrote, but they conceived ideas about how to write their works based on the texts of that kind that they had read. Writers could violate the norms of their "genres" as modern writers can and do, but working within some of the restraints of convention ensured that an audience understood a work.

Genre is one way to differentiate texts from each other; another way to approach the problem is to look at the functions of different kinds of texts, and here there is a significant divergence between history and hagiography. De Gaiffier pointed out early on that much hagiography was used in the liturgy in the eleventh century, and van Uytfanghe raises the possibility that, during the Merovingian period, saints' lives were publicly read.[9] This means that some hagiographies reached a wide audience and did so through publicly institutionalized reading of a kind other sorts of histories did not receive. There is no question but that there was an overlap between hagiographies and histories; however, this overlap did not prevent readers from making practical distinctions between them, based on the special content of hagiographies which emphasized the relationship between the holy man or woman and God, a feature not common in secular biography.[10]

8. See Jauss, *Toward an Aesthetic of Reception*, 22, 28, and *passim*.
9. De Gaiffier, "Hagiographie et historiographie," 147; van Uytfanghe, "L'Hagiographie et son public à l'époque mérovingienne," 55.
10. van Uytfanghe, "L'Hagiographie: un 'genre' chrétien?" 148.

Of course, not all sacred biographies were publicly read. Heinzelmann distinguishes two sorts of hagiographies, those written for public functions and those for private literary reading.[11] Some texts were clearly for slow private or schoolroom consumption, the *Vita sancti Germanus* of Heiric of Auxerre, for example, which was so difficult that the author himself provided *scholia* to assist the reader. Histories, in contrast, show few signs of being designed for public performance, and I know of no case after late antiquity when a Latin history was publicly read in the way a hagiography might be. Vernacular histories do seem to have been read aloud, as Froissart mentions reading his work aloud in the court of Gaston Phoebus of Foix, but whereas a saint's life might also have been read aloud in the context of the court, it is unlikely that histories were ever performed in church.

There are reasons for this, I think. While both histories and hagiographies were intended to instruct,[12] the kinds of instruction possible would depend on the contents of each work. Moral instruction was the main focus of the hagiography, but history was open to other sorts of instruction and indeed might seem dangerously unedifying. While hagiography seems always to have been used in formal instruction, only classical histories tended to be used so.

In consequence, I suspect that the degree to which hagiographers and historians felt themselves to be doing the same thing (or historians felt themselves to be doing the same thing when they wrote history as when they wrote hagiography) varied. History and hagiography, through their narrative accounts of the past, were linked and changes in hagiography were probably related to changes in the larger field of history. Historians in the twelfth century were gradually changing their notions of authentication of their work; hagiographers in the thirteenth, with the arrival of the canonization process with its inquest, seem to have shifted their thinking as well.

Beyond this generalization, however, it is hard to go. When historians themselves did not agree on methods, it is difficult to argue that hagiographers used the same methods as historians. The question of the relationship between hagiography and history can probably only be resolved on the level of individual texts.

---

11. Martin Heinzelmann, "Neue Aspekte der biographischen und hagiographischen Literatur in der lateinischen Welt," *Francia* 1 (1973): 27–44.

12. See Heffernan, *Sacred Biography,* 19f.

🦋 Appendix 2: Notes on the "Acts of the Archbishops of Rouen"

The *Acts of the Archbishops of Rouen* has been preserved in two roughly contemporary manuscripts, one from the cathedral of Rouen and the other from the monastery of Saint-Ouen in Rouen, which was quite nearby. The cathedral version is contained in the *Livre d'ivoire* (Rouen, *Bibliothèque municipale*, Y. 27) along with a metrical catalogue of the archbishops and the lives and deeds of other archbishops. The Saint-Ouen version is in the *Livre noir* of Saint-Ouen (Rouen, *Bibliothèque municipale*, Y. 41), which also contains the metrical catalogue but has some additional saints' lives. The Saint-Ouen version is the longer. In addition to the material recorded at Rouen, it contains an anecdote concerning Archbishop John of Avranches who was miraculously defeated after trying to assert his authority over the monks. This story, the author hastens to assure the reader, is written "not derogatorily, nor to insult but as an example [consultorie]."[1]

While it has generally been assumed that the *Acts* was composed at the cathedral and then copied at Saint-Ouen, where the anecdote about John was added, Felice Lifshitz has argued that the *Acts* was probably written after the verse catalog and

1. Rouen, *Bibliothèque municipale*, Y. 41, 8r.

at Saint-Ouen rather than the cathedral.[2] Her ordering of the pertinent texts is thus: the metrical catalog of the archbishops, which in both the cathedral and Saint-Ouen manuscripts follow the text of the *Acts,* was written first at Rouen, then the *Acts* was written at Saint-Ouen, and finally the text was copied and abbreviated at Rouen, eliminating the embarrassing stories told in the Saint-Ouen version.

Her argument is based on the fact that the diocesan version ends in mid-sentence, that in the diocesan manuscript the two works are written in different hands (and thus were probably not copied at once), that the text contains references to saints important to the monastery but not the cathedral, that the diocesan copy of the *Acts* follows the text of the life of St. Ouen as it appears in the monastic copy of text (which differs from the diocesan copy of the same source), and that the *Acts* devotes a long passage to Remigius, whose relics came to Saint-Ouen in 1090. This latter argument would put the composition of the *Acts,* if written at Saint-Ouen, after 1090.

What this does not explain, however, is why the author of the *Acts* did not then go on to write about William Bonne-Ame, beyond mentioning his election, despite the two blank pages which intervene between the *Acts* and the metrical catalog in the Saint-Ouen version. Nor does it explain the most puzzling issue (something that Lifshitz herself points to as odd), that there is no other instance where an institution produced a history of the rulers of another institution as a way of strengthening its own authority.[3]

In short, Lifshitz has assembled a body of evidence whose interpretation depends on the assumptions one makes about priority. If, however, one assumes that the *Acts* were written at the cathedral, other explanations are possible. It is not clear to me, for example, that the entire text of the *Acts* written at Saint-Ouen *is* in one hand. The hand, for example, gets smaller and more angular on fol. 7v, where the text not common to the two manuscripts begins, and the abbreviations vary. Samarin and Marichal describe the manuscript as being composed in "plusieurs mains recherchant unité."[4] Similarly, the argument of a special interest in certain saints at Saint-Ouen ignores the possibility that co-option could work both ways. If Saint-Ouen only acquired relics of Remigius in 1090, perhaps this was a way of outmaneuvering the cathedral. Furthermore, since the *Livre d'ivoire* was, as Lifshitz points out, bound together in the thirteenth cen-

---

2. Felice Lifshitz, "The *Acta archiepiscoporum Rotomagensium:* A Monastery or Cathedral Product?" *Analecta Bollandiana* 108 (1990): 337–47.

3. Ibid., 343.

4. *Manuscrits datés,* 329.

tury, the author of the *Acts* would not necessarily have been working with the copy of the life of St. Ouen that was bound into that manuscript. Was this copy necessarily the only copy of the text available at the cathedral?

There are other troublesome questions about the origins of the *Acts*. Why did the cathedral version stop with Maurilius if the actual text was written later? Why would the copyist at the cathedral not have substituted something more laudatory about John of Avranches, rather than simply failing to copy the material about John? John, if a difficult man, was in many ways a successful archbishop. If the *Acts* were indeed written at Saint-Ouen, one could also ask why the entry on Ouen himself is so meager and why the monks at Saint-Ouen did not write the *Acts* of their own abbots or a history of their own monastery, proving its independence of the archbishops. Fécamp, for example, wrote its own history in response to archiepiscopal encroachments. Saint-Ouen would seem to be the only institution in the Middle Ages to defend its prerogatives by writing an original history of a rival. Saint-Ouen shows little other evidence of being an active center for historical writing, while annals, as well as the metrical catalog of the archbishops, were composed at the cathedral. If the metrical catalog was the source of the *Acts*, why was it copied after the *Acts* in both manuscripts? (In the *Livre d'ivoire*, the metrical catalog continues on the same page as the end of the *Acts*, so the texts had to have been copied in that order.)

We are left, then, with two institutions less than a mile away from each other, with comparable resources that were clearly traded back and forth, each seeking the materials to ensure its own position. In the absence of a less circumstantial case, the rule of simplicity suggests that the *Acts* was written at the cathedral. Archbishop Maurilius actively encouraged the writing of history, which might explain why the text originally ended with his biography. The cathedral's interest in historical writing is clearly linked in the other cases (and probably in this one as well) with the extension of the archbishops' prerogatives. The anecdote about John, undoubtedly written at Saint-Ouen, may have been intended to warn the archbishops against too aggressive behavior or to inspire the monks, but it also functioned to tame the cathedral's potentially dangerous narrative.

ℬ Bibliography

Manuscripts

Note: I have listed here only the manuscripts I have personally consulted. Descriptions of other manuscripts discussed in the text can be found in *CG* and *Manuscrits datés*.

Rouen, Bibliothèque municipale, A. 136 (catalogue #177). Peter Comestor *Scholastic History.*

Rouen, Bibliothèque municipale, A. 243 (catalogue #179). Peter Comestor *Scholastic History.*

Rouen, Bibliothèque municipale, A. 476 (catalogue #180). Peter Comestor *Scholastic History.*

Rouen, Bibliothèque municipale, Y. 11 (catalogue #1173). Various histories, including Dudo of Saint-Quentin *Customs of the Dukes.*

Rouen, Bibliothèque municipale, Y. 14 (catalogue #1174). Various texts, including Orderic's copy of the *GND.*

Rouen, Bibliothèque municipale, Y. 15 (catalogue #1132). Various histories, including *De monasterii Gemmeticensis fundatione, excidio et reparatione.*

Rouen, Bibliothèque municipale, Y. 26 (catalogue #1233). French chronicles and Honoré Bonet *Tree of Battles.*

Rouen, Bibliothèque municipale, Y. 27 (catalogue #1405). (*Livre d'Ivoire* of Rouen).

Rouen, Bibliothèque municipale, Y. 41 (catalogue #1406). (*Livre noire* of Saint-Ouen).

Rouen, Bibliothèque municipale, Y. 237 (catalogue #1211).

Evreux, Bibliothèque municipale, ms. 60.

Primary Sources

Abrahams, P. *Les Oeuvres poétiques de Baudri de Bourgueil.* Paris: Honoré Champion, 1926.

Acta sanctorum quotquot toto orbe coluntur. Paris: Victor Palmé, 1863.

Ambrose of Évreux. *L'Estoire de la guerre sainte.* Edited by M. G. Paris. Paris: Imprimerie nationale, 1897.

————. *Das "Itinerarium peregrinorum."* Edited by H. E. Meyer. Stuttgart: A. Hiersemann, 1962.

Annales Gandenses. Edited and translated by Hilda Johnstone. New York: Oxford University Press, 1951.

Annals of Bec, see Delisle, Léopold.

Annals of Jumièges, see Laporte, Jean.

Anselm of Bec. *Proslogion. PL* 158:223–48.

Augustine. *City of God.* Turnholt: Brepols, 1955.

Baluze, Étienne. *Stepheni Baluzii miscellaneorum, hoc est, collectio veterum monumentorum quae hactenus latuerant in variis codicibus ac bibliothecis.* Paris: F. Muguet, 1678–1715.

Barlow, Frank, ed. and trans. *The Life of King Edward Who Rests at Westminster.* 2d ed. Oxford: Oxford University Press, 1992.

Basin, Thomas. *Histoire de Charles VII.* Edited and translated by Charles Samaran. 2 vols. Paris: Société d'édition "Les Belles Lêttres," 1933–44.

————. *Histoire de Louis XI.* Edited and translated by Charles Samaran. 3 vols. Paris: Société d'édition "Les Belles Lêttres," 1963–72.

Baudry of Bourgueil. *Carmina.* Edited by K. Hilbert. Heidelberg: Carl Winter Universitätsverlag, 1979. See also Abrahams.

Bede. *Bede's Ecclesiastical History of the English People.* Edited by Bertram Colgrave and R. A. B. Mynors. Oxford: Oxford University Press, 1969.

Behrelnds, F., ed. and trans. *The Letters and Poems of Fulbert of Chartres.* Oxford: Oxford University Press, 1976.

The Carmen de Hastingae proelio of Guy, Bishop of Amiens. Edited by Catherine Morton and Hope Muntz. Oxford: Oxford University Press, 1972.

Chandos Herald. *La Vie du Prince Noir.* Edited by Diana B. Tyson. Tubingen: M. Niemeyer, 1975.

Chastellain, Georges. *Chronique des ducs de Bourgogne*. Edited by J. A. Buchon. 2 vols. Paris: Verdière, 1827.

Chronicon Beccense. In *PL* 150:639–90. See also Porée.

Chronicon Fiscamnense. In *PL* 147:479–84.

Chronicon Novaliciense. *MGH SS*, 7:73–133.

Chroniken der deutschen Städte vom 14. bis in's 16 Jahrhundert. 36 vols. Places and publishers vary, 1862–1931.

Clari, Robert de. *La Conquête de Constantinople*. Edited by Philippe Lauer. 2 vols. Paris: E. Champion, 1924.

Commynes, Philippe de. *Mémoires de Philippe de Commynes*. Edited by Joseph Calmette. 3 vols. Paris: H. Champion, 1924–25.

Coutumiers de Normandie, textes critiques. 3 vols. Rouen: E. Cagniard, 1881–1903.

Cuvelier. *La Chanson de Bertrand du Guesclin*. Edited by Jean-Claude Faucon. Toulouse: Éditions universitaires du sud, 1990.

Dehaisnes, C., ed. *Les Annales de Saint-Bertin et de Saint-Vaast*. Paris: Jules Renouard, 1871.

De libertate Beccensis monasterii. In J. Mabillon, *Annales ordinis sancti Benedicti*, vol. 5, 601–5. Paris: Leonardo Venturini, 1740.

Delisle, Léopold, ed. "Les Courtes annales du Bec." In *Notices et documents publiés pour la Société de l'Histoire de France à l'occasion du cinquantième anniversaire de sa fondation*, 93–99. Paris: Renouard, 1884.

d'Escouchy, Mathieu. *Chronique de Mathieu d'Escouchy*. Edited by G. Du Fresne de Beaucourt. 3 vols. Paris: J. Renouard, 1863–64.

Duchesne, L., ed. *Le Liber Pontificalis*. 3 vols. Paris: E. de Boccard, 1955–57.

Duclerq, Jacques. *Mémoires de Jacques Du Clerq*. Edited by Frederick Baron de Reiffenbert. 2d ed. Brussels: Lacrosse, 1835–36.

Dudo of Saint-Quentin. *De moribus et actis primorum Normanniae ducum*. Edited by J. Lair. Caen: F. Le Blanc-Hardel, 1865.

Egbert of Liège. *Egberts von Lüttich Fecunda ratis*. Edited by E. Voigt. Halle am Saale: Verlag von Max Niemeyer, 1889.

Faral, Edmond. *La Légende Arthurienne, études et documents, première partie: Les Plus anciens texts*. 3 vols. Paris: Honoré Champion, 1929.

Fauroux, Marie. *Recueil des actes des ducs de Normandie de 911 à 1066*. Caen: Société d'impressions Caron et C^{ie,} 1961.

Flodoard of Reims. *Les Annales de Flodoard*. Edited by Philippe Lauer. Paris: A. Picard, 1905.

Fortunatus. *Carmina*. In *MGH, Auctores Antiquissimi*, 4:1–292.

Fredegar. *Chronicarum quae dicuntur Fredegari scholastici libri quattuor*. In *MGH, Scriptores rerum Merovingicarum*, 2:1–214. Edited by B. Krusch. Hannover: Hahn, 1888.

Froissart, Jean. *Oeuvres de Froissart.* Edited by Kervyn de Lettenhove and Joseph Marie Bruno Constantin. 28 vols. Brussels: V. Devaux & M. Closson, 1867–77.

Fulbert of Chartres. See Behrends.

Gaimar, Geoffrey. *L'Estoire des Engleis.* Edited by A. Bell. Oxford: Blackwells, 1960.

Gallia christiana, in provincias ecclesiasticas distributa. 16 vols. 2d ed. Paris: Victor Palmé, 1739–1880.

Geoffrey de Beaulieu. *Vita sancti Ludovici.* In *Recueil des historiens des Gaules et de la France,* 20:3–36. Paris: Imprimerie royale, 1840.

Gerald of Wales. *Girardi Cambrensis Opera* (Rolls Series, 21). Edited by J. S. Brewer. 6 vols. London: Longman, 1862–28.

Giselbert of Mons. *Chronicon Hanoniensis.* In *MGH SS,* 21:481–601.

Grat, Felix, Jeanne Vielliard, and Suzanne Clémencet, eds. *Les Annales de Saint-Bertin.* Paris: Klincksieck, 1964.

Gregory of Tours, *Vita Patrum.* In *Les Livres des miracles et autres opuscules de Georges Florent Grégoire,* 3:132–399. Paris: Renouard, 1862.

Guiart, Guillaume. *Branche des royal lignages, chronique métrique de Guillaume Guiart.* Edited by J. A. Buchon. 2 vols. Paris: Verdière, 1828.

Guibert of Nogent. *Autobiographie.* Edited and translated by Edmond-René Labande. Paris: Société d'édition "Les Belles Lêttres," 1981.

Halphen, Louis. *Chroniques des comtes d'Anjou et des seigneurs d'Amboise.* Paris: Picard, 1913.

———. *Recueil d'annales angevines et vendomoises.* Paris: Picard, 1903.

Heiric of Auxerre. *Vita sancti Germani, MGH Poetae latini aevi Carolini,* 3:421–517. Hannover: Hahn, 1886.

Hellman, H. *Sedulius Scotus.* Munich: C. H. Beck'sche Verlagsbuchhandlung, 1908.

Henry of Huntingdon. *Henrici archidiaconi Huntendunensis historia Anglorum.* Edited by Thomas Arnold. Reprint, Wiesbaden: Kraus reprint, 1965.

Heriger of Lobbes and Anselm of Liège. *Gesta episcoporum Tungrensium, Traiectensium, et Leodiensium.* Edited by Rudolf Koepke. In *MGH SS* 7:134–234.

Historia Francorum Senonensis. In *MGH Scriptores* 9:364–69.

Hugh of Saint-Victor. *Hugonis de Sancto Victore Didascalicon de studio legendi.* Edited by Charles Henry Buttimer. Washington, D.C.: The Catholic University of America Press, 1939.

Isidore of Seville. *Isidori Hispalensis episcopi Etymologiarum sive originum libri xx.* Edited by W. M. Lindsay. Oxford: Oxford University Press, 1911.

Jean d'Outremeuse. *Geste de Liège.* In *Ly Myreur des histors, chronique de*

Jean des Preis, dit d'Outremeuse. 7 vols. 1:587–638, 2:527–766, 3:411–520, 4:601–738, 5:581–694, 6:639–710. Brussels: M. Hayez, 1864–87.

Jocelin of Brakelond. *The Chronicle of Jocelin of Brakelond*. Edited and translated by H. E. Butler. New York: Oxford University Press, 1949.

Joinville, Jean de. *La Vie de Saint Louis: Le Temoinage de Jehan, seigneur de Joinville*. Edited by Neil Corbett. Sherbrooke, PQ: Naaman, 1977.

Jonas of Orléans. *Jonas d'Orléans et son "De institutione regia": Étude et texte critique*. Edited by J. Reviron. Paris: Librairie philosophique J. Vrin, 1930.

Lalande, Denis. *Le Livre des fais du bon messire Jehan le Maingre, dit Bouciquaut, Mareschal de France et governeur de Jennes*. Geneva: Droz, 1985.

Lambert of Ardre. *Historia comitum Ghisnensium*. Edited by Johannes Heller. In *MGH SS* 26:550–627.

Langlois, Ernest, ed. *Le Coronnement de Louis, chanson de geste du XIIᵉ siècle*. Vol. 22, *Les Classiques français du Moyen Age*. 2d ed. Paris: Honoré Champion, 1925.

Laporte, Jean, ed. *Les Annales de l'abbaye de Saint-Pierre de Jumièges*. Rouen: Lecerf, 1954.

———. *Inventio et miracula sancti Vulfranni*. Mélanges de la Société de l'histoire de Normandie, 14th ser. Rouen: A. Lestringant, 1938.

le Bel, Jean. *Chronique de Jean le Bel*. Edited by Jules Viard and Eugène Déprez. 2 vols. Paris: Renouard/Laurens, 1904–5.

Libellus de revelatione, edificatione et auctoritate Fiscanensis monasterii. In *PL* 151:699–724.

Liber Pontificalis, see Duchesne.

Mabillon, J., ed. *De libertate Beccensis monasterii*. In *Annales ordinis sancti Benedicti*, 5:601–5. Paris: Leonardo Venturini, 1740.

Mansi, Giovanni. *Sacrorum conciliorum nova et amplissima collectio*. 53 vols. Reprint, Graz: Akademische Druck- u. Verlagsanstalt, 1960.

Map, Walter. *De Nugis curialium*. Edited by Montague Rhodes James. Oxford: Oxford University Press, 1914.

Mas-Latrie, Louis de, ed. *Chronique d'Ernoul et de Bernard le Trésorier*. Paris: Renouard, 1871.

Matthew Paris. *Chronica Majora*. Edited by Henry Richard Luard. 7 vols. Reprint, Wiesbaden: Kraus reprint, 1964.

Meyer, P., ed. *Histoire de Guillaume le Maréchal*. 3 vols. Paris: Société de l'histoire, 1891–1901.

Michel de Bernis. *Chronique des comtes de Foix et senhors de Bearn*. Vol. 1, *Choix de chroniques et mémoires relatifs a l'histoire de France*. Edited by Jean Buchon. Paris: Desrez, 1836.

Miles Crispin. *Vita Bosonis*. In *PL*, 150:723–34.

———. *Vita Willelmi*. In *PL*, 150:713–24.

[Miles Crispin?]. *Vita Lanfranci*. In *PL*, 150:19–58.

Mirbt, C. *Quellen zur Geschichte des Papsttums*. 5th ed. Tubingen: J. C. B. Mohr (Paul Siebeck), 1934.

Molinet, Jean. *Chroniques de Jean Molinet*. Edited by Georges Doutrepont and Omer Jodogne. 3 vols. Brussels: Palais des académies, 1935–37.

Monstrelet, Enguerran de. *Chroniques*. Edited by Douët d'Arcq. 6 vols. Paris: Société d'histoire, 1857–62.

Niermeyer, J. F. *Mediae latinitatis lexicon minus*. Leiden: Brill, 1984.

Odo of Cluny. *Vita sancti Geraldi*. *PL*, 133:639–704.

Orderic Vitalis. *The Ecclesiastical History of Orderic Vitalis*. Edited and translated by Marjorie Chibnall. 6 vols. Oxford: Oxford University Press, 1969–80.

Otto of Freising. *Chronica sive Historia de duabus civitatibus*. Edited and translated by Adolf Hofmister and Walter Lammers. Berlin: Rütten & Loening, 1960. See also *Chronicon*, in *MGH SS*, 20:83–301.

Paul the Deacon. *Gesta episcoporum Mettensium*. Edited by G. H. Pertz. In *MGH SS* 2:260–68.

———. *Historia Langobardorum*. In *MGH Scriptores rerum Langobardorum et italicarum saec. VI–IX*. Hannover: Hahn, 1878.

Peter of Dives. *Gesta abbatum Beccensium*. In *PL*, 180:1709–18.

Pippino, Francesco. *Chronicon*. In *Rerum italicarum scriptores*, 9:587–752. Edited by Ludovico Muratori. Milan: Palatina, 1726.

L'Abbé Porée. *Chronique du Bec et Chronique de François Carré*. Rouen: Métérie, 1883.

Recueil des historiens des Gaules et de la France. 19 vols. Rev. ed. Paris: Victor Palmé, 1869–80.

P. Redlich. *Der Roman du Mont Saint Michel von Guillaume de Saint-Paier*. Marberg: N. G. Elwert, 1894.

Regesta regum Anglo-Normannorum. Edited by H. W. C. Davis, C. Johnson, H. A. Cronne, and R. H. C. Davis. 3 vols. Oxford: Oxford University Press, 1912–68.

Richer of Reims. *Histoire de France*. Edited by Robert Latouche. 2 vols. Paris: Société d'édition "Les Belles Lêttres," 1964.

Robert of Torigni. *The Chronicle of Robert of Torigni*. *Chronicles of the Reigns of Stephen, Henry II, and Richard I*. Vol. 4. Edited by Richard Howlett. London: Eyre & Spottiswoode, 1889.

———. *Chronique de Robert de Torigni, abbé du Mont Saint-Michel*. Edited by L. Delisle. 2 vols. Rouen: C. Métérie, 1872–73.

Samaran, Charles, and Robert Marichal. *Catalogue des manuscrits en écriture latine portant des indications de date, de lieu ou de copiste*. Vol. 7. *Ouest de la France et Pays de Loire*. Paris: CNRS, 1984.

Sauvage, E. P., ed. *Vitae b. Petri Abricensis et b. Hamonis. Analecta Bollandiana* 2 (1883): 475–560.

———. *Vitae Vitalis et Gaufridi. Analecta Bollandiana* 1 (1882): 355–410.

Sedulius Scotus. See Hellman.

Sigebert of Gembloux. *Catalogus Sigeberti Gemblacensis monachi de viris illustribus: Kritische Ausgabe.* Edited by Robert Witte. Bern: Herbert Lang, 1974.

Stenton, Frank. *The Bayeux Tapestry.* 2d ed. London: Phaidon Press, 1965.

Stephen of Fougères. *Vita sancti Vitalis.* See Sauvage.

———. *Vita de sancto Guilielmo Firmato.* In *AA SS,* April, 3: 336–43.

Stephen of Rouen. *Draco Normannicus.* In *Chronicles of the Reigns of Stephen, Henry II, and Richard I,* 2:589–781. Edited by Richard Howlett. Rolls Series 82. London: Longman and Co., 1885.

———. *Le Dragon Normand.* Edited by Henri Omont. Rouen: C. Métérie, 1884.

Thalamus parvus. Le Petit Thalamus de Montpellier. Montpellier: J. Martel, 1840.

Tractatus de libertate monasterii Beccensis. In *Annales ordinis sancti Benedicti,* 5:601–5. Edited by J. Mabillon. Reprint. Paris: Leonard Venturini, 1940.

van Houts, Elisabeth M. C., ed. and trans. *The* Gesta Normannorum ducum *of William of Jumièges, Orderic Vitalis, and Robert of Torigni.* 2 vols. Oxford: Oxford University Press, 1992–95. See also William of Jumièges.

Vernier, J. *Les chartes de l'abbaye de Jumièges.* Rouen: A. Lestringant, 1916.

Villehardouin, Geoffroi de. *La Conquête de Constantinople.* Edited by Edmond Faral. 2 vols. in 1 bk. Paris: Société d'édition "Les Belles Lêttres," 1938–39.

Vitry, Jacques de. *La Traduction de l' "Historia orientalis" de Jacques de Vitry.* Edited by Claude Buridant. Paris: Klincksieck, 1986.

Wace. *Maistre Wace's Roman de Rou et des ducs de Normandie.* Edited by Hugo Andreson. 2 vols. Heilbronn: Verlag von Gebr. Henninger, 1877–79.

Widukind of Corvey. *Widukindi rerum gestarum Saxonicarum.* Edited by G. Waitz. Hannover: Hahn, 1882.

William of Chartres. *Vita sancti Ludovici.* In *Recueil des historiens des Gaules et de la France,* 20:28–41. Paris: Imprimerie royale, 1840.

William of Jumièges. *Gesta Normannorum ducum.* Edited by Jean Marx. Rouen: A. Lestringant, 1914. See also van Houts.

William of Malmesbury. *Gesta regum Anglorum atque Historia Novella.* Edited by T. D. Hardy. 2 vols. London: Sumptibus Societatis, 1840.

William de Nangis. *Chronique latine de Guillaume de Nangis.* Edited by H. Géraud. Paris: Renouard, 1843.

William of Newburgh. *Historia rerum Anglicarum.* In *Chronicles of the Reigns of Stephen, Henry II, and Richard I.* Edited by Richard Howlett. Vol. 1. London: Her Majesty's Stationers, 1884.

William of Poitiers. *Histoire de Guillaume le Conquérant.* Edited and translated by Raymonde Foreville. Paris: Société d'édition "Les Belles Lêttres," 1952.

William of Saint-Pathus. *Vita sancti Ludovici.* In *Recueil des historiens des Gaules et de la France,* 20:121–89. Paris: Imprimerie royale, 1840.

William of Saint-Paer. See Redlich.

Primary Sources in Translation

Benton, John F. *Self and Society in Medieval France: The Memoires of Abbot Guibert of Nogent.* Reprint, Toronto: University of Toronto Press and the Medieval Academy of America, 1984.

Commynes, Philippe de. *The Memoirs of Philippe de Commynes.* Edited by Samuel Kinser. Translated by Isabelle Cazeaux. 2 vols. Columbia: University of South Carolina Press, 1969–73.

Eusebius Pamphili. *Ecclesiastical History.* Translated by Roy J. Deferrari. New York: The Fathers of the Church, 1953.

Frachet, Gerard de. *Lives of the Brethren of the Order of Preachers.* Translated by Placid Conway. Benziger, 1924.

Fredegar. *The Fourth Book of the Chronicle of Fredegar.* Translated by J. M. Wallace-Hadrill. London: Thomas Nelson & Sons, 1960.

Joinville, Jean de. *The Life of St. Louis.* In *Chronicles of the Crusades,* translated by M. R. B. Shaw, 165–353. Harmondsworth, Sussex: Penguin, 1963.

Livy. *The Early History of Rome.* Translated by Aubrey de Selincourt. Harmondsworth, Middlesex: Penguin, 1960.

Scholz, Bernard. *Carolingian Chronicles: Royal Frankish Annals and Nithard's Histories.* Ann Arbor: University of Michigan Press, 1970.

t' Serstevens, Albert, ed. and trans. *Les Précurseurs de Marco Polo.* Paris: Arthaud, 1959.

Tacitus. *The Complete Works of Tacitus.* Translated by A. J. Church and W. J. Brodribb. New York: Modern Library, 1942.

Vaugh, Sally N. *The Abbey of Bec and the Anglo-Norman State, 1034–1136.* Woodbridge, Suffolk: Boydell, 1981.

Secondary Sources

Adams, Jeremy duQuesnay. "The *Regnum Francie* of Suger of Saint-Denis: An Expansive Ile-de France." *Historical Reflections* 19 (1993): 167–88.

Adigard des Gautries, Jean. "Les Noms de personnes d'origine scandinave dans les obituaires de Jumièges." In *Jumièges: Congrès scientifique du XIIIe centenaire*, 1:57–67. Rouen: Lecerf, 1955.

Albu-Hannawalt, Emily. "Dudo of Saint-Quentin: The Heroic Past Imagined." *The Haskins Society Journal* 6 (1994): 111–18.

Arnoux, Mathieu. "La Fortune du *Libellus de revelatione, edificatione et auctoritate Fiscannensis monasterii:* Note sur la Production historiographique d'une abbaye Bénédictine normande." *Revue d'histoire des textes*, 21 (1991): 135–58.

Auerbach, Erich. *Literary Language and Its Public in Late Latin Antiquity and in the Middle Ages.* Translated by Ralph Mannheim. Princeton, N.J.: Princeton University Press, 1965.

——. *Scenes from the Drama of European Literature.* New York: Meridian, 1959.

Bachrach, Bernard. *Fulk Nerra, the Neo-Roman Consul, 987–1040: A Political Biography of the Angevin Count.* Berkeley and Los Angeles: University of California Press, 1993.

Batany, Jean. "Les 'Moniages' et la satire des moines aux XIe et XIIe siècles." In *Les Chansons de geste du cycle de Guillaume d'Orange*, vol. 3, *Les Moniages, Guiborc*, edited by P. Menard and J.-Ch. Payen, 209–23. Paris: Société d'Édition d'Enseignement Supérieur, 1983.

Bates, David. "Normandy and England after 1066." *English Historical Review* 104 (1989): 851–80.

——. *Normandy before 1066.* London: Longman, 1982.

——. "The Rise and Fall of Normandy, c. 911–1204." In *England and Normandy in the Middle Ages*, edited by David Bates and Anne Curry, 19–35. London: Hambledon, 1994.

Bäuml, Franz. "Varieties and Consequences of Medieval Literacy and Illiteracy." *Speculum* 55 (1980): 237–65.

Bedos-Rezak, Brigitte. "French Medieval Regions: A Concept in History." *Historical Reflections* 19 (1993): 151–66.

Beer, Jeannette M. A. *Narrative Conventions of Truth in the Middle Ages.* Geneva: Droz S. A., 1981.

Benton, John. "The Court of Champagne as a Literary Center," *Speculum* 36 (1961): 551–91.

Bertaud, Emile. "Moines de Jumièges, évêques et abbés." In *Jumièges, congrès scientifique du XIIIe centenaire*, 1:317–26. Rouen: Lecerf, 1955.

Bezzola, René Reto. *Les Origines et la formation de la littérature courtoise en occident (500–1200).* 3 pts. in 4 vols. Paris: Honoré Champion, 1944–63.

Bienvenu, Jean-Marc. "De l'A-sociabilité à la sociabilité: De l'Érémitisme au cénobitisme dans la France de l'ouest aux XIe et XIIe siècles." In

Sociabilité, pouvoirs et société, 525–31. Rouen: Université de Rouen, 1987.

Blair, Carole, Julie R. Brown, and Leslie A. Baxter. "Disciplining the Feminine." *Quarterly Journal of Speech* 80 (1994): 383–409.

Blatt, Franz, ed. *Novum glossarium mediae latinitatis.* Hafniae: Ejnar Munksgaard, 1967.

Bloch, R. Howard. "Genealogy as a Medieval Mental Structure and Textual Form." In *La Littérature historiographique des origines à 1500 (Grundriss der Romanischen Literaturen des Mittelalters,* vol. 11, pt. 1), 135–56. Heidelberg: Carl Winter Universitätsverlag, 1987.

Bonnaud-Delamare, M. R. "Les Institutions de Paix dans la province ecclesiastique de Reims au XIᵉ siècle." *Bulletin philologique et historique du comité des travaux historiques et scientifiques* (1955–56): 143–200.

Bordieu, Pierre. *The Logic of Practice.* Translated by Richard Nice. Stanford, Calif.: Stanford University Press, 1990.

Borst, Arno. "Das Bild der Geschichte in der Enzyklopädie Isidors von Sevilla." *Deutsches Archiv für Erforschung des Mittelalters* 22 (1966): 1–62.

Boüard, Michel de. "Notes et hypothèses sur Maurille, moine de Fécamp, et son election au siège metropolitain de Rouen." In *L'Abbaye bénédictine de Fécamp: Ouvrage scientifique du XIIIᵉ centenaire,* 1:81–92. Fécamp: Durand et Fils, l959.

———. "Sur les origines de la trêve de Dieu en Normandie." *Annales de Normandie* 9 (1959): 169–89.

Bouet, Pierre. "La 'Felicitas' de Guillaume le Conquérant dans les 'Gesta Guillelmi' de Guillaume de Poitiers." *Anglo-Norman Studies* 4 (1982): 37–52.

Boutruche, R. *Seigneurie et féodalité.* 2d ed. Paris: Aubier, 1968.

Brooks, N. P., and H. E. Walker. "The Authority and Interpretation of the Bayeux Tapestry." *Anglo-Norman Studies* 1 (1979): 9–18.

Brown, Donald E. *Hierarchy, History, and Human Nature: The Social Origins of Historical Consciousness.* Tucson: University of Arizona Press, 1988.

Bur, Michel. *La Formation du Comté de Champagne, v. 950–v. 1150.* Nancy: University of Nancy, 1977.

Carruthers, Mary. *The Book of Memory: A Study of Memory in Medieval Culture.* Cambridge: Cambridge University Press, 1990.

Catalogue des manuscrits en écriture latine portant de indications de date, de lieu ou de copiste. Vol. 7, *Ouest de la France et pays de Loire.* Edited by Monique-Cécile Garand, Geneviève Grand, and Denis Muzerelle. Paris: CNRS, 1984.

Catalogue général des manuscrits des bibliothèques publiques de France: Départements. 43 vols. Paris: Imprimerie Plon, 1885–1904.

Cheyette, Frederic L. "Suum cuique tribuere." *French Historical Studies* 6 (1969): 287–99.

Chibnall, Marjorie. "The Empress Matilda and Bec-Hellouin." *Anglo-Norman Studies,* 10 (1988): 35–48.

———. "Orderic Vital et Robert de Torigni." In *Millénaire monastique du Mont Saint-Michel,* 2:133–39. Paris: Bibliothèque d'histoire et d'archéologie chrétiennes, 1967.

———. *The World of Orderic Vitalis.* Cambridge: Cambridge University Press, 1984.

Clanchy, Michael. *From Memory to Written Record: England, 1066–1307.* Cambridge: Harvard University Press, 1979.

Cochrane, Eric. *Historians and Historiography in the Italian Renaissance.* Chicago: University of Chicago Press, 1981.

Crick, Julia C. *The* Historia regum Britanniae *of Geoffrey of Monmouth: IV. Dissemination and Reception in the Later Middle Ages.* Cambridge: D. S. Brewer, 1991.

Crouch, David. "Normans and Anglo-Normans: A Divided Aristocracy?" In *England and Normandy in the Middle Ages,* edited by David Bates and Anne Curry, 51–67. London: Hambledon Press, 1994.

———. *William Marshall: Court, Career and Chivalry in the Angevin Empire 1147–1219.* London: Longman, 1990.

Curtius, E. R. *European Literature and the Latin Middle Ages.* Translated by Willard R. Trask. New York: Harper, 1963.

David, C. W. *Robert Curthose.* Cambridge: Harvard University Press, 1920.

Davis, R. H. C. "The *Carmen de Hastingae proelio.*" *English Historical Review* 93 (1978): 241–61.

———. *The Normans and Their Myth.* London: Thames and Hudson, 1976.

———. "William of Jumièges, Robert Curthose and the Norman Succession." *English Historical Review* 95 (1980): 597–606.

———. "William of Poitiers and His History of William the Conqueror." In *The Writing of History in the Middle Ages: Essays Presented to Richard William Southern,* edited by R. H. C. Davis and J. Wallace-Hadrill, 71–100. Oxford: Oxford University Press, 1981.

Dean, James. "The World Grown Old and Genesis in Middle English Historical Writings." *Speculum* 57 (1982): 548–68.

de Certeau, Michel. *The Writing of History.* Translated by Tom Conley. New York: Columbia University Press, 1988.

Delisle, Léopold. "Les Courtes annales du Bec." In *Notices et documents publiés pour la Société de l'Histoire de France a l'occasion du cinquantième anniversaire de sa fondation.* Paris: Renouard, 1884).

———. *Rouleaux des Morts du IXe au XVe siècle.* Paris: Renouard, 1866.

Devailly, Guy. *Le Berry du Xe siècle au milieu du XIIIe*. Paris: Mouton & Co, 1973.

Dhondt, Jean. *Études sur la naissance des principautés territoriales en France (IXe–Xe siècle)*. Bruges: De Tempel, 1948.

Douglas, David C. "The Norman Episcopate before the Norman Conquest." *Cambridge Historical Journal* 13 (1957): 101–15.

———. *William the Conqueror*. Los Angeles and Berkeley: University of California Press, 1964.

Duby, Georges. *The Chivalrous Society*. Translated by Cynthia Postan. Berkeley and Los Angeles: University of California Press, 1977.

———. *The Three Orders: Feudal Society Imagined*. Translated by Arthur Goldhammer. Chicago: Chicago University Press, 1980.

Du Cange, Charles. *Glossarium mediae et infimae latinitatis*. Paris: Librairie des sciences et des arts, 1938.

Dufief, A. "La Vie monastique au Mont Saint-Michel pendant le XIIe siècle (1085–1186)." In *Millénaire monastique du Mont Saint-Michel*, 1:81–126. Paris: Bibliothèque d'histoire et d'archéologie chrétiennes, 1967.

Dumville, David. "An Early Text of Geoffrey of Monmouth's *Historia regum Britanniae* and the Circulation of Some Latin Histories in Twelfth-Century Normandy." In *Arthurian Literature*, 4:1–36. Woodbridge, Suffolk: Boydell and Brewer, 1985.

Ebenbauer, Alfred. *Carmen Historicum: Untersuchungen zur historischen Dichtung im karolingischen Europa*. Vienna: Wilhelm Braumüller, 1978.

Edbury, Peter and John Rowe. *William of Tyre*. Cambridge: Cambridge University Press, 1988.

Eisenstadt, S. N. "Some Observations on the Dynamics of Traditions." *Comparative Studies in Society and History* 11 (1969): 451–75.

Elias, Norbert. *The Civilizing Process*. Translated by Edmund Jephcott. New York: Urizen Books, 1978.

Engels, L. J. "Once More: The *Carmen de Hastingae proelio*." *Anglo-Norman Studies* 2 (1980): 3–14.

Eyton, R. W. *Court, Household, and Itinerary of King Henry II*. London: Taylor & Co., 1878.

Favreau, R. "Les Écoles et la culture de Saint-Hilaire-le-Grand de Poitiers des origines au début du XIIe siècle." *Cahiers de civilisation médiévale* 3 (1960): 473–78.

Fentress, James and Chris Wickham. *Social Memory*. Oxford: Blackwell, 1992.

Fleischmann, Suzanne. "On the Representation of History and Fiction in the Middle Ages." *History and Theory* 22 (1983): 278–310.

Foreville, Raymonde. "Aux Origines de la renaissance juridique: Concepts juridiques et influences romanisantes chez Guillaume de Poitiers, biographe du Conquérant." *Moyen Age* 58 (1952): 43–83.

————. "Guillaume de Jumièges et Guillaume de Poitiers." In *Jumièges: Congrès scientifique du XIIIᵉ centenaire,* 2:643–54. Rouen: Librairie Lecerf, 1955.

Fournée, Jean. "Le Culte populaire des saints fondateurs d'abbayes pré-Normandes." In *Abbayes de Normandie,* 59–78. Rouen: Société libre d'emulation de la Seine-Maritime, 1979.

Frère, Édouard. *Manuel de bibliographe Normand ou dictionnaire bibliographique et historique.* 2 vols. 1858–60. Reprint, New York: Burt Franklin, n.d.

Funkenstein, Amos. "Collective Memory and Historical Consciousness." *History and Memory* 1 (1989): 5–26.

————. *Heilsplan und natürliche Entwicklung: Formen der Gegenwartsbestimmung im Geschichtsdenken des hohen Mittelalters.* Munich: Nymphenburger Verlagshandlung, 1965.

Gaiffier, Baudouin de. *Études critiques d'hagiographie et d'iconologie.* Brussels: Société des Bollandistes, 1967.

————. "L'Hagiographe et son public au XIᵉ siècle." In *Miscellanea historica in honorem Leonis van der Essen,* 135–66. Paris and Brussels: Éditions universitaires, 1947.

————. "Hagiographie et historiographie: Quelques aspects du problème." In *La storiografia altomedievale,* 139–196. Settimane di Studio del Centro italiano di studi sull'alto medioevo, 17. Spoleto: Centro italiano di studi sull'alto medioevo, 1970.

————. "Mentalité de l'hagiographe médiéval d'après quelques travaux récents." *Analecta Bollandiana* 86 (1968): 391–99.

————. *Recherches d'hagiographie latine.* Brussels: Société des Bollandistes, 1971.

————. *Recueil d'hagiographie.* Brussels: Société des Bollandistes, 1977.

Gallia christiana, in provincias ecclesiasticas distributa. 16 vols. 2d ed. Paris: Victor Palmé, 1739–1880.

Garand, Monique-Cécile. "Auteurs latins et autographes des XIᵉ et XIIᵉ siècles." *Scrittura e civiltà* 5 (1981): 77–104.

Garaud, M. "Les Écoles et l'enseignement à Poitiers du IVᵉ à la fin du XIIᵉ siècle." *Bulletin de la Société des antiquaires de l'ouest,* 3rd. ser., 14 (1946–48): 82–98.

Geary, Patrick. *Phantoms of Remembrance: Memory and Oblivion at the End of the First Millennium.* Princeton: Princeton University Press, 1994.

Geertz, Clifford. "Thick Description: Toward an Interpretive Theory of Culture." In *The Interpretation of Cultures,* 3–30. New York: Basic Books, 1973.

Genet, Jean-Philippe. "Cartulaires, registres et histoire: L'Exemple anglais." In *Le Métier d'historien au moyen age: Études sur l'histoiographie médiévale,* edited by Bernard Guenée, 95–129. Paris: Publications de la Sorbonne, 1977.

Gibson, Margaret T. *Lanfranc of Bec.* Oxford: Oxford University Press, 1978.

Goetz, Hans-Werner. "La Paix de Dieu en France autour de l'an mil: Fondements et objectifs, diffusion et participants." In *Le Roi de France et son royaume autour de l'an mil,* edited by Michel Parisse et Xavier Barral i Altet, 131–43. Paris: Picard, 1992.

Goffart, Walter. "The *Historia Ecclesiastica:* Bede's Agenda and Ours." *The Haskins Society Journal* 2 (1990): 29–45.

———. *The Narrators of Barbarian History (A.D. 550–800): Jordanes, Gregory of Tours, Bede and Paul the Deacon.* Princeton: Princeton University Press, 1988.

Goody, Jack. *The Interface between the Oral and the Written.* Cambridge: Cambridge University Press, 1987.

———. *The Logic of Writing and the Organization of Society.* Cambridge: Cambridge University Press, 1986.

Grafton, Anthony. *Forgers and Critics.* Princeton, N.J.: Princeton University Press, 1990.

Grammont, Paul. "Jumièges et le Bec." In *Jumièges: Congrès scientifique du XIIIᵉ centenaire,* 1: 209–16. Rouen: Lecerf, 1955.

Grant, Lindy. "Architectural Relations between England and Normandy, 1100–1204." In *Normandy and England in the Middle Ages,* edited by David Bates and Anne Curry, 117–29. London: Hambledon Press, 1994.

Green, Judith. "King Henry I and the Aristocracy of Normandy." In *La "France anglaise" au moyen age* (Actes du IIIᵉ congrès national des sociétés savantes, vol. 1), 161–73. Paris: CTHS, 1988.

———. "Lords of the Norman Vexin." In *War and Government in the Middle Ages,* edited by John Gillingham and J. C. Holt, 47–61. Woodbridge, Suffolk: Boydell, 1984.

Green, L. F. *Chronicle into History: An Essay on the Interpretations of History in Florentine Fourteenth-Century Chronicles.* Cambridge: Cambridge University Press, 1972.

Grundmann, Herbert. "Die Frauen und die Literatur im Mittelalter: Ein Beitrag zur Frage nach der Entstehung des Schrifttums in der Volkssprache." In *Ausgewählte Aufsätze,* 3:67–95. Stuttgart: Anton Hiersemann, 1978.

———. *Geschichtsschreibung im Mittelalter.* Reprint, Göttingen: Vandenhoeck & Ruprecht, 1965.

———. "Literatus–Illiteratus: Der Wandel einer Bildungsnorm vom Altertum zum Mittelalter." In *Ausgewälte Aufsätze*, 3:1–66. Stuttgart: Anton Hiersemann, 1978.

Guenée, Bernard. *Histoire et culture historique dans l'occident médiéval.* Paris: Aubier-Montaigne, 1980.

———. "Histoire, mémoire, écriture. Contribution à une étude des lieux communs." *Académie des Inscriptions et Belles-Lêttres, Comptes rendus* (1983): 441–56.

Guillemain, Bernard. "Les Origines des évêques en France aux XIᵉ et XIIᵉ siècles." In *Le istituzioni ecclesiastiche della "societas christiana" dei secoli XI–XII* (Miscellanea del centro di studi medioevali, VII), 374–402. Milan: Vita e Pensiero, 1974.

Guillot, Olivier. *Le Comte d'Anjou et son entourage au XIᵉ siècle.* 2 vols. Paris: A. & J. Picard, 1972.

———. "La Conversion des Normands peu après 911." *Cahiers de civilisation médiévales* 14 (1981): 101–16, 181–219.

Halbwachs, Maurice. *The Collective Memory.* Translated by Francis J. Ditter and Vida Yazdi Ditter. New York: Harper, 1980.

Hallam, Elizabeth. *Capetian France, 987–1328.* London: Longman, 1980.

Haskell, Thomas L., ed. *The Authority of Experts: Studies in History and Theory.* Bloomington: Indiana University Press, 1984.

———. "Objectivity Is Not Neutrality: Rhetoric vs. Practice in Peter Novick's *That Noble Dream.*" *History and Theory* 29 (1990): 129–57.

Haskins, Charles Homer. *Norman Institutions.* Cambridge: Harvard University Press, 1918.

Heffernan, Thomas. *Sacred Biography: Saints and Their Biographers in the Middle Ages.* Oxford: Oxford University Press, 1988.

Heinzelmann, Martin. "Neue Aspekte der biographischen und hagiographischen Literatur in der lateinischen Welt." *Francia* 1 (1973): 27–44.

———. *Translationsberichete und andere Quellen des Reliquienkultes.* Typologie des sources du moyen âge occidental, no. 33. Turnhout: Brepols, 1979.

Hofmann, H. "Articulationsformen historischen Wissens in der lateinischen Historiographie des hohen und späten Mittelalters." In *La Littérature historiographique des origines à 1500* (Grundriss der Romanischen Literaturen des Mittelalters, vol. 11), vol. 2. Heidelberg: Carl Winter Universitätsverlag, 1987.

Hourlier, Jacques. "Le Mont Saint-Michel avant 966." In *Millénaire monastique du Mont Saint-Michel*, 1:13–28. Paris: P. Lethielleux, 1966.

Howlett, D. R., ed. *Dictionary of Medieval Latin from British Sources.* Oxford: Oxford University Press, 1989.

Howorth, H. H. "A Criticism of the Life of Rollo as Told by Dudo of Saint-Quentin." *Archaeologia* 45 (1880): 235–50.

Huisman, Gerda. "Notes on the Manuscript Tradition of Dudo of St Quentin's *Gesta Normannorum.*" *Anglo-Norman Studies* 6 (1984): 122–35.

Illmer, Detlef. *Formen der Erziehung und Wissensvermittlung in frühen Mittelalter* (Münchener Beiträge zur mediävistik und Renaissance-Forschung 7). Munich: Arbeo-Gesellschaft, 1971.

Iser, Wolfgang. *The Act of Reading.* Baltimore, Md.: Johns Hopkins University Press, 1978.

Jaeger, C. Stephen. *The Origins of Courtliness.* Philadephia: University of Pennsylvania Press, 1985.

Jakobson, Roman. "Closing Statement: Linguistics and Poetics." In *Style in Language,* edited by Thomas A. Sebeok, 350–77. Cambridge: M.I.T. Press, 1960.

Jauss, Hans Robert. *Toward an Aesthetic of Reception.* Translated by Timothy Bahti. Minneapolis: University of Minnesota Press, 1982.

Jeauneau, Edouard. "Heiric d'Auxerre, disciple de Jean Scot." In *L'École carolingienne d'Auxerre de Murethach à Remi, 830–908,* 353–70. Paris: Beauchesne, 1991.

Jones, C. W. *Saints' Lives and Chronicles in Early England.* Ithaca, N.Y.: Cornell University Press, 1947.

Jumièges: Congrès scientifique du XIIIe centenaire. 2 vols. Rouen: Lecerf, 1955.

Kelley, Donald. "Clio and the Lawyers: Forms of Historical Consciousness in Medieval Jurisprudence." *Medievalia et Humanistica,* n.s., 5 (1974): 25–49.

Laporte, Jean. "L'Abbaye du Mont Saint-Michel aux Xe et XIe siècles." In *Millénaire monastique de Mont Saint-Michel,* 1:53–80. Paris: Bibliothèque d'histoire et d'archéologie chrétiennes, 1967.

———. "Jumièges et Saint-Wandrille." In *Jumièges: Congrès scientifique du XIIIe centenaire,* 1:191–98. Rouen: Lecerf, 1955.

Latouche, Robert. "Un Imitateur de Salluste au Xe siècle: l'historien Richer." *Annales de l'université de Grenoble,* n.s. *Lettres-droit* 6 (1929): 289–305.

Lawrence, Anne. "Anglo-Norman Book Production." In *Normandy and England in the Middle Ages,* edited by David Bates and Anne Curry, 79–93. London: Hambledon Press, 1994.

LeBlond, Bernard. *L'Accession des Normands de Neustrie à la culture occidentale.* Paris: A. G. Nizet, 1966.

Lemarignier, J.-F. "Paix et réforme monastique en Flandre et en Normandie autour de l'année 1023: Quelques observations." In *Droit privé et institutions régionales. Études historiques offertes à Jean Yver,* 443–68. Paris: Presses Universitaires de France, 1976.

Le Patourel, John. "Normandy and England, 1066–1144." In *Feudal Empires Norman and Plantagenet*, article VII. London: Hambledon Press, 1984.

Lesne, Emile. *Histoire de la propriété ecclésiastique en France*. In *Les Écoles de la fin du VIIIᵉ siècle à la fin du XIIᵉ*, vol. 5. Lille: Facultés Catholiques, 1940.

Leyser, Karl. *The Ascent of Latin Europe*. Oxford: Oxford University Press, 1986.

Lifshitz, Felice. "The *Acta archiepiscoporum Rotomagensium:* A Monastery or Cathedral Product?" *Analecta Bollandiana* 108 (1990): 337–47.

———. "Beyond Positivism and Genre: 'Hagiographical' Texts as Historical Narrative." *Viator* 25 (1994): 95–113.

Lot, Ferdinand. *Études critiques sur l'abbaye de Saint-Wandrille*. Paris: Librarie ancienne Honoré Champion, 1913.

Loud, G. A. "The *Gens Normannorum*—Myth or Reality?" *Anglo-Norman Studies* 4 (1982): 104–16.

Marenbon, John. *From the Circle of Alcuin to the School of Auxerre: Logic, Theology and Philosophy in the Early Middle Ages*. Cambridge: Cambridge University Press, 1981.

Marrou, Henri-Irenée. "Saint Augustin, Orose et l'Augustinisme historique." In *La Storiografia medievale*, 1:59–87. Settimane di Studio del Centro italiano di studi sull'alto medioevo, 17. Spoleto: Centro italiano di studi sull'alto medioevo, 1970.

Martindale, Jane. "Succession and Politics in the Romance-Speaking World, c. 1000–1140." In *England and Her Neighbours, 1066–1453*, edited by Michael Jones and Malcolm Vale, 19–41. London: Hambledon, 1989.

Matthew, Donald. *The Norman Monasteries and Their English Possessions*. Oxford: Oxford University Press, 1962.

McKitterick, Rosamund. *The Carolingians and the Written Word*. Cambridge: Cambridge University Press, 1989.

———. *Frankish Kingdoms under the Carolingians*. London: Longman, 1983.

Merrilees, Brian. "Anglo-Norman Literature." In *The Dictionary of the Middle Ages*, 1:259–72. New York: Charles Scribners' Sons, 1982.

Meyer, Hans Eberhard. "Staufische Weltherrschaft? Zum Brief Heinrichs II von England an Friedrich Barbarossa von 1157." In *Friedrich Barbarossa*, edited by Gunther Wolf, 184–207. Darmstadt: Wissenschaftliche Buchgesellschaft, 1975.

Meyer, P. "Les Premières compilations françaises d'histoire ancienne." *Romania* 14 (1885): 1–81.

Millénaire monastique du Mont Saint-Michel. 2 vols. Paris: Bibliothèque d'histoire et d'archéologie chrétiennes, 1967.

302   *Bibliography*

Mink, Louis O. "Everyman His or Her Own Annalist." *Critical Inquiry* 7 (1980–81): 777–83.

———. "History and Fiction as Modes of Comprehension." *New Literary History* 1 (1970): 541–58.

Mittelalter-Rezeption: Ein Symposion. Edited by Peter Wapnewski. Stuttgart: J. B. Metzlersche Verlagsbuchhandlung, 1986.

Molinier, Auguste. *Les Sources de l'histoire de France, des origines aux guerres d'Italie.* 6 vols. Paris: A. Picard, 1901–6.

Moore, R. I. *The Formation of a Persecuting Society.* Oxford: Blackwells, 1987.

Morgan, M. *The English Lands of the Abbey of Bec.* London: Oxford University Press, 1946.

Morlais, M. *De vita et scriptis Roberti de Torinneio abbatis sancti Michaelis.* Paris: E. Thorin, 1881.

Morrison, Karl. *History as a Visual Art.* Princeton: Princeton University Press, 1990.

Munz, Peter. *Frederick Barbarossa: A Study in Medieval Politics.* London: Eyre and Spottiswood, 1961.

Murray, Alexander. *Reason and Society in the Middle Ages.* Corrected edition, Oxford: Oxford University Press, 1985.

Musset, Lucien. "Les Abbayes normandes au moyen-age: Position de quelques problèmes." In *Les abbayes de Normandie,* 13–26. Rouen: Société d'emulation de la Seine-Maritime, 1979.

———. "Ce qu'enseigne l'histoire d'un patrimoine monastique: Saint-Ouen de Rouen du IX^c au XI^c siècle." In *Aspects de la Société et de l'économie dans la Normandie médiévale (X^c–XIII^c siècles),* edited by Lucien Musset, Jean-Michel Bouvris, and Véronique Gazeau, 115–129. Caen: Centre d'Études Normandes, 1988.

———. "Chapelles et chapelains du duc de Normandie au XI^c siècle." *Revue historique de droit français et étranger,* 4th ser., 23 (1975): 171–72.

———. "Les Destins de la propriété monastique durant les invasions Normandes (IX^c–XI^c s.): L'Exemple de Jumièges." In *Jumièges: Congrès scientifique du XIII^c centenaire,* 1:49–55. Rouen: Lecerf, 1955.

———. "La Formation d'un milieu social original: Les Chapelains normands du duc-roi au XI^c et au début du XII^c siècle." In *Aspects de la société et de l'économie dans la Normandie médiévale (X^c–XIII^c siècles),* 91–114. Caen: Centre d'études Normandes de l'Université de Caen, 1988.

———. "Le Mécénat des princes normands au XI^c siècle." In *Artistes, artisans et production artistique au moyen age,* vol. 2, edited by Xavier Barral I Altet, 120–33. Paris: Picard, 1987.

———. "Monachisme d'époque franque et monachisme d'époque ducale en Normandie: Le problème de la continuité." In *Aspects du monachisme en Normandie (IVe–XVIIIe siècles)*, 55–74. Paris: J. Vrin, 1982.

———. "Le Satiriste Garnier de Rouen et son milieu." *Revue du moyen âge latin* 10 (1954): 237–66.

Nichols, Stephen G. *Romanesque Signs: Early Medieval Narrative and Iconography*. New Haven: Yale University Press, 1983.

Nora, Pierre. "Entre mémoire et histoire: La Problematique des lieux." In *Les Lieux de mémoire*, vol. 1, edited by Pierre Nora, xv–xlii. Paris: Editions Gallimard, 1984.

Nortier, G. *Les Bibliothèques médiévales des abbayes bénédictines de Normandie*. Paris: Bibliothèque d'histoire de d'archéologie chrétiennes, 1971.

Novick, Peter. *That Noble Dream: The Objectivity Question and the American Historical Profession*. Cambridge: Cambridge University Press, 1988.

Partner, Nancy. "Making up Lost Time: Writing on the Writing of History." *Speculum* 61 (1986): 90–117.

———. "The New Cornificius: Medieval History and the Artifice of Words." In *Classical Rhetoric & Medieval History*, edited by Ernst Breisach, 5–59. Kalamazoo, Mich.: The Medieval Institute, 1985.

———. *Serious Entertainments: The Writing of History in Twelfth-Century England*. Chicago: University of Chicago Press, 1977.

Paulmier-Foucart, Monique. "L'Atelier Vincent de Beauvais: Recherches sur l'état des connaissances au Moyen Age d'après une encyclopédie du XIIIe siècle." *Le Moyen age*, ser. 4, 34 (1979): 87–99.

———. "Ecrire l'histoire au XIIIe siècle: Vincent de Beauvais et Helinand de Froidmont." *Annales de l'Est*, ser. 5, 33 (1981): 49–70.

Potts, Cassandra. "Normandy or Brittany? A Conflict of Interests at Mont Saint-Michel (966–1035)." *Anglo-Norman Studies* 12 (1989): 135–56.

Prentout, Henri. *Étude critique sur Dudon de Saint-Quentin et son histoire des premiers ducs Normands*. Paris: A. Picard, 1916.

Radding, Charles M. and William W. Clark. *Medieval Architecture, Medieval Learning: Buildings and Masters in the Age of Romanesque and Gothic*. New Haven: Yale University Press, 1992.

Rankin, Susan. "Carolingian Music." In *Carolingian Culture: Emulation and Innovation*. Edited by Rosamund McKitterick. Cambridge: Cambridge University Press, 1994.

Ray, Roger. "Medieval Historiography through the Twelfth Century: Problems and Progress of Research." *Viator* 5 (1974): 33–59.

———. "Orderic Vitalis and His Readers." *Studia Monastica* 14 (1972): 15–34.

Renoux, Annie. "Palais capétiens et normands à la fin du Xe siècle et au début du XIe siècle." In *Le Roi de France et son Royaume autour de l'an mil,* edited by Michel Parisse and Xavier Barral i Altet, 179–91. Paris: Picard, 1992.

Reynolds, Susan. *Kingdoms and Communities in Western Europe, 900–1300.* Oxford: Oxford University Press, 1984.

———. "Law and Communities in Western Christendom, c. 900–1140." *American Journal of Legal History* 25 (1981): 205–24.

Richard, Charles. *Notice sur l'ancienne bibliothèque des échevins de la ville de Rouen.* Rouen: Alfred Peron, 1845.

Riché, Pierre. *Écoles et enseignement dans le Haut Moyen Age.* Paris: Picard, 1989.

Richter, Michael. "Kommunikationsprobleme im lateinischen Mittelalter." *Historische Zeitschrift* 222 (1976): 43–80.

———. "A Socio-Linguistic Approach to the Latin Middle Ages." In *The Materials Sources and Methods of Ecclesiastical History,* edited by Derek Baker, 69–82. Oxford: Blackwell for the Ecclesiastical History Society, 1975.

Sanford, Eva M. "The Study of Ancient History in the Middle Ages." *Journal of the History of Ideas* 5 (1944): 21–43.

Schmale, Franz-Joseph. *Funktion und Formen mittelalterlicher Geschichtsschreibung: Mit einem Beitrag von Hans-Werner Goetz.* Darmstadt: Wissenschaftliche Buchgesellschaft, 1985.

Searle, Eleanor. "Fact and Pattern in Heroic History: Dudo of Saint-Quentin." *Viator* 15 (1984): 119–37.

———. *Predatory Kinship and the Creation of Norman Power, 840–1066.* Berkeley and Los Angeles: University of California Press, 1988.

Shopkow, Leah. "The Carolingian World of Dudo of Saint-Quentin." *Journal of Medieval History* 15 (1989): 19–37.

———. "Norman Historical Writing in the Eleventh and Twelfth Centuries." Ph.D. diss., University of Toronto, 1984.

Smalley, Beryl. *The Study of the Bible in the Middle Ages.* 3d ed. Oxford: Blackwell, 1983.

Sot, Michel. *Gesta episcoporum, gesta abbatum.* Turnhout: Brepols, 1981.

———. "Historiographie épiscopale et modèle familial en occident au IXᵉ siècle." *Annales: E. S. C.* 33 (1978): 433–49.

———. "Organisation de l'espace et historiographie épiscopale dans quelques cités de la Gaule carolingienne." In *Le Métier d'historien au moyen age: Études sur l'historiographie médiévale,* edited by Bernard Guenée, 31–43. Paris: University of Paris, 1977.

Southern, Richard W. "Aspects of the European Tradition of Historical Writing: 1. The Classical Tradition from Einhard to Geoffrey of Monmouth." *Transactions of the Royal Historical Society,* 5th ser., 20 (1970): 173–96.

————. "Aspects of the European Tradition of Historical Writing: 2. Hugh of St Victor and the Idea of Historical Development." *Transactions of the Royal Historical Society*, 5th ser., 21 (1971): 159–79.

————. "Aspects of the European Tradition of Historical Writing: 3. History as Prophecy," *Transactions of the Royal Historical Society*, 5th ser., 22 (1972): 159–80.

————. "Aspects of the European Tradition of Historical Writing: 4. The Sense of the Past." *Transactions of the Royal Historical Society*, 5th ser., 23 (1973): 245–56.

————. *The Making of the Middle Ages*. New Haven: Yale University Press, 1953.

Spiegel, Gabrielle M. "Genealogy: Form and Function in Medieval Historical Narrative." *History and Theory* 22 (1983): 43–53.

————. "History, Historicism, and the Social Logic of the Text in the Middle Ages." *Speculum* 65 (1990): 59–86.

————. *Romancing the Past: The Rise of Vernacular Prose Historiography in Thirteenth-Century France*. Berkeley and Los Angeles: University of California Press, 1993.

————. "Social Change and Literary Language: The Textualization of the Past in Thirteenth-Century Old French Historiography." *Journal of Medieval and Renaissance Studies* 17 (1987): 129–48.

————. "Studies in the Chronicle Tradition of Saint-Denis." Ph.D. dissertation: Johns Hopkins University, 1974.

Stierle, Karlheinz. "Studium: Perspectives on Institutionalized Modes of Reading." *New Literary History* 21 (1990): 115–27.

Stock, Brian. *The Implications of Literacy*. Princeton: Princeton University Press, 1983.

————. *Listening for the Text*. Baltimore, Md.: Johns Hopkins University Press, 1990.

Streuver, Nancy. "The Study of Language and the Study of History." *Journal of Interdisciplinary History* 4 (1974): 401–15.

Swietek, Francis R. "King Henry II and Savigny." *Cîteaux* 38 (1987): 14–23.

Tabuteau, Emily Zack. *Transfers of Property in Eleventh-Century Norman Law*. Chapel Hill: University of North Carolina Press, 1988.

Temple, Elzbieta. *Anglo-Saxon Manuscripts, 900–1066*. London: Harvey Miller, 1976.

Thompson, A. Hamilton. "Diocesan Organization in the Middle Ages: Archdeacons and Rural Deans." *Proceedings of the British Academy* 29 (1943): 153–94.

Thompson, James Westfall. *The Literacy of the Laity in the Middle Ages*. New York: Burt Franklin, 1960.

Thompson, K. "William Talvas, Count of Ponthieu and the Politics of the Anglo-Norman Realm." In *England and Normandy in the Middle Ages,* edited by David Bates and Anne Curry, 169–84. London: Hambledon Press, 1994.

Turner, Ralph. "The *Miles Literatus* in Twelfth- and Thirteenth-Century England: How Rare a Phenomenon?" *American Historical Review* 83 (1978): 928–45.

Turner, Victor. "Religious Paradigms and Political Action: Thomas Becket at the Council of Northhampton." In *Dramas, Fields, and Metaphors,* 60–97. Ithaca: Cornell University Press, 1974.

———. "Social Dramas and Stories about Them." *Critical Inquiry* 7 (1980): 141–67.

Tyson, Diana. "Jean le Bel: Portrait of a Chronicler." *Journal of Medieval History* 12 (1986): 315–32.

Valin, L. *Le Duc de Normandie et sa cour.* Paris: L. Larose & L. Tenin, 1916.

van den Brincken, Anna-Dorothee. "Geschichtsbetrachtung bei Vincenz von Beauvais." *Deutsches Archiv* 34 (1978): 410–99.

———. *Studien zur lateinischen Weltchronistik bis in das Zeitalter Ottos von Freising.* Dusseldorf: Michael Triltsch Verlag, 1957.

van Houts, Elisabeth M. C. *Gesta Normannorum ducum.* Ph.D. Dissertation, University of Gröningen, 1982.

———. "The *Gesta Normannorum ducum:* A History without an End." *Anglo-Norman Studies* 3 (1981): 106–18, 215–20.

———. "Historiography and Hagiography at Saint-Wandrille: the 'Inventio et miracula sancti Vulfranni.'" *Anglo-Norman Studies* 12 (1990): 233–51.

———. "Latin Poetry and the Anglo-Norman Court 1066–1135: The *Carmen de Hastingae proelio.*" *Journal of Medieval History* 14 (1989): 39–62.

———. "Quelques remarques sur les interpolations attribuées à Orderic Vital dans les *Gesta Normannorum ducum* de Guillaume de Jumièges," *Revue d'Histoire des Textes* 8 (1978): 213–22.

———. "Scandinavian Influence in Norman Literature of the Eleventh Century." *Anglo-Norman Studies* 6 (1984): 107–21.

van Uytfanghe, Marc. "La Controverse biblique et patristique autour du miracle, et ses répercussions sur l'hagiographie dans l'Antiquité tardive et le haut Moyen Age latin." In *Hagiographie, cultures et sociétés,* 205–31. Paris: Études Augustiniennes, 1981.

———. "L'hagiographe et son public à l'époque mérovingienne." *Studia Patristica* 16 (1985): 54–62.

———. "L'hagiographie: un 'genre' chrétien ou antique tardif ?" *Analecta Bollandiana* 111 (1993): 135–88.

Vauchez, André. "L'Influence des modèles hagiographiques sur les représentations de la sainteté, dans les procès de canonisation (XIIIᶜ–XVᶜ)." In *Hagiographie, cultures et sociétés*, 585–96. Paris: Etudes Augustiniennes, 1981.

———. *La sainteté en Occident aux derniers siècles du Moyen Age*. Rome: École française de Rome, 1981.

Veyne, Paul. *Did the Greeks Believe in Their Myths?* Translated by Paula Wissing. Chicago: University of Chicago Press, 1988.

Vopelius, Barbara. *Studien zu Dudo von Saint-Quentin, dem ersten Geschichtsschreiber der Normandie (987–1015)*. Ph.D. dissertation, University of Göttingen, 1967.

Ward, John. "Gothic Architecture, Universities and the Decline of the Humanities in Twelfth-Century Europe." In *Principalities Powers and Estates: Studies in Medieval and Early Modern Government and Society*, edited by L. O. Frappel, 65–75. Adelaide: Adelaide University Union Press, 1979.

Werner, Karl Ferdinand. "Quelques observations au sujet des débuts du 'duché' de Normandie," In *Droit privé et institutions régionales. Études historiques offertes à Jean Yver*, 691–709. Paris: 1976. Reprinted in *Structures politiques du monde franc (VIᶜ–XIIᶜ siècles)*. London: Variorum, 1979.

———. "Untersuchungen zur Frühzeit des französischen Fürstentums (9.–10. Jahrhundert)." *Die Welt als Geschichte* 18 (1958): 256–89; 19 (1959) 146–93; 20 (1960): 87–119.

White, Hayden. *Metahistory: The Historical Imagination in Nineteenth-Century Europe*. Baltimore: Johns Hopkins University Press, 1973.

———. "The Value of Narrativity in the Representation of Reality." *Critical Inquiry* 7 (1980–81): 5–27.

White, Stephen. *Kinship, Customs and Gifts to the Saints: The Laudatio Parentum in Western France*. Chapel Hill: University of North Carolina Press, 1992.

Wolter, Hans. "Jumièges et Saint-Evroul." In *Jumièges: Congrès scientifique du XIIIᶜ centenaire*, 1:223–32. Rouen: Lecerf, 1955.

———. *Orderic Vitalis*. Wiesbaden: Franz Steiner Verlag, 1955.

Wright, N. A. R. "The *Tree of Battles* of Honoré Bouvet and the Laws of War." In *War, Literature, and Politics in the Late Middle Ages*, edited by C. T. Allmand, 12–31. Liverpool: University of Liverpool Press, 1976.

Yerushalmi, Y. H. *Zakhor: Jewish History and Jewish Memory*. Seattle: University of Washington Press, 1982.

Yver, Jean. "Les Premières institutions du duché de Normandie." In *I Normanni e la loro espansione in Europa nell'alto medioevo*, 1:299–366.

Spoleto: Centro di studi sull'alto medioevo, 1969.

Ziolkowski, Jan. *Jezebel: A Norman Latin Poem of the Early Eleventh Century*. New York: Peter Lang, 1989.

Zumthor, Paul. *Histoire littéraire de la France médiévale*. Paris: Presses universitaires de France, 1954.

✑ Index

History and Community: Norman Historical Writing in the Eleventh and Twelfth Centuries was composed in Galliard by Brevis Press, Bethany, Connecticut with Cataneo display type by Kachergis Book Design, Pittsboro, North Carolina; printed on 60-pound Natural Smooth and bound by Braun-Brumfield, Inc., Ann Arbor, Michigan; and designed and produced by Kachergis Book Design.